'The publication of Arnold Rachman's *Psychoanalysis and Society's Neglect of the Sexual Abuse of Children, Youth and Adults: Re-addressing Freud's Original Theory of Sexual Abuse and Trauma* is a long overdue and necessary step toward correcting the record on psychoanalysis' neglect of childhood sexual trauma, its sequelae, and clinical treatment. Rachman identifies the taboo surrounding a discussion of Freud's analysis of his daughter Anna Freud. His focus on the inherent emotional seduction in that analysis, as Freud satisfied his own narcissistic needs, is ground-breaking. He courageously draws our attention to topics psychoanalysis has turned away from, calling out the field's "death by silence" attack on dissenters and the damage explicitly done to the reputation of Sándor Ferenczi. The latter confirmed the reality of sexual abuse among children after Freud had abandoned his original hypothesis. Rachman also brings to light the 1906 trial of Ernest Jones for the sexual abuse of children. Up till now, we knew Jones as a critic of Ferenczi, who joined Freud to discredit him. Dr. Rachman calls for an apology from the international psychoanalytic community for silencing Sándor Ferenczi's work, and for keeping his pioneering contributions to both theory and clinical method from the analytic community to the detriment of the general welfare of society. This is a landmark book.'

– **Ann D'Ercole, PhD, ABPP,** NYU Postdoctoral Program Psychotherapy, Psychoanalysis, Distinguished Visiting Faculty, William Alanson White Institute, author of *Clara Thompson: The Life and Work of an American Psychoanalyst*, at Routledge Press, forthcoming

'For over three decades Arnold Rachman has been an important figure in the revival of interest in Sándor Ferenczi and the Budapest School of Psychoanalysis. His research into Ferenczi's iconic case and treatment with Elizabeth Severn is an important milestone in this revival. A central theme of Arnold's work is to uncover and break a "Todschweigen", a conspiracy of silence, an effort intended to conceal and cover up.

In his latest volume *Psychoanalysis and Society's Neglect of the Sexual Abuse of Children, Youth and Adults: Re-addressing Freud's Original Theory of Sexual Abuse and Trauma,* he fearlessly and methodically makes the case for an apology owed to the Ferenczi community from the International Psychoanalytical Association.

This book will be of interest to scholars of the history of psychoanalysis and contemporary directions that the field of psychoanalysis may take.'

– **Fergal Brady** is President of the Irish Psycho-Analytical Association and a psychoanalytic psychotherapist based in Dundalk, Ireland

Psychoanalysis and Society's Neglect of the Sexual Abuse of Children, Youth and Adults

This book takes a comprehensive look at the understanding and treatment of child sexual abuse in psychoanalytic theory and practice, and in society as a whole.

This book demonstrates how prophetic Ferenczi's ideas about sexual abuse and trauma were, and how relevant they are for contemporary psychoanalysis and society. Sexual abuse, its traumatic effect, and the harm caused to children, youth, and adults will be described in the neglect of confronting sexual abuse by psychoanalysis and society. This neglect will be discussed in chapters about the abuse of children by religious leaders, students by teachers, youth in sports by coaches, and aspiring actors by authorities in the entertainment industry. It covers key topics such as why there has been silence about abuse in psychoanalysis, psychoanalytic theories, and practices that can be counterproductive or even harmful, case studies of abuse in the wider community, and how psychoanalysis as a profession can do better in its understanding and treatment of child sexual abuse both in psychoanalytic treatment and in its interaction with other parts of society.

This book appeals to all psychoanalysts and psychoanalytic psychotherapists, as well as scholars interested in the history of psychoanalysis.

Arnold Wm. Rachman, PhD, FAGPA, is a trained individual and group psychoanalyst who is a clinician, traumatologist, and psychohistorian. He is the author of 125 scholarly articles, 13 books, and 250 professional presentations given in the United States, Europe, and South America. He is a member of the International Sándor Ferenczi Network Community, Honorary Member of the Sándor Ferenczi Society, Budapest, Hungary, and donor of the Elizabeth Severn Papers to the Library of Congress, Washington, DC, USA.

Psychoanalytic Inquiry Book Series

Series Editor
Joseph D. Lichtenberg

Like its counterpart, *Psychoanalytic Inquiry: A Topical Journal for Mental Health Professionals*, the Psychoanalytic Inquiry Book Series presents a diversity of subjects within a diversity of approaches to those subjects. Under the editorship of Joseph Lichtenberg, in collaboration with Melvin Bornstein and the editorial board of *Psychoanalytic Inquiry*, the volumes in this series strike a balance between research, theory, and clinical application. We are honored to have published the works of various innovators in psychoanalysis, including Frank Lachmann, James Fosshage, Robert Stolorow, Donna Orange, Louis Sander, Léon Wurmser, James Grotstein, Joseph Jones, Doris Brothers, Fredric Busch, and Joseph Lichtenberg, among others.

The series includes books and monographs on mainline psychoanalytic topics, such as sexuality, narcissism, trauma, homosexuality, jealousy, envy, and varied aspects of analytic process and technique. In our efforts to broaden the field of analytic interest, the series has incorporated and embraced innovative discoveries in infant research, self psychology, intersubjectivity, motivational systems, affects as process, responses to cancer, borderline states, contextualism, postmodernism, attachment research and theory, medication, and mentalization. As further investigations in psychoanalysis come to fruition, we seek to present them in readable, easily comprehensible writing.

After more than 25 years, the core vision of this series remains the investigation, analysis, and discussion of developments on the cutting edge of the psychoanalytic field, inspired by a boundless spirit of inquiry. A full list of all the titles available in the *Psychoanalytic Inquiry* Book Series is available at https://www.routledge.com/Psychoanalytic-Inquiry-Book-Series/book-series/LEAPIBS.

Psychoanalysis and Society's Neglect of the Sexual Abuse of Children, Youth and Adults

Re-addressing Freud's Original Theory of Sexual Abuse and Trauma

Arnold Wm. Rachman

LONDON AND NEW YORK

First published 2022
by Routledge
2 Park Square, Milton Park, Abingdon, Oxon OX14 4RN

and by Routledge
605 Third Avenue, New York, NY 10158

Routledge is an imprint of the Taylor & Francis Group, an informa business

© 2022 Arnold Wm. Rachman

The right of Arnold Wm. Rachman to be identified as author of this work has been asserted by him in accordance with sections 77 and 78 of the Copyright, Designs and Patents Act 1988.

All rights reserved. No part of this book may be reprinted or reproduced or utilised in any form or by any electronic, mechanical, or other means, now known or hereafter invented, including photocopying and recording, or in any information storage or retrieval system, without permission in writing from the publishers.

Trademark notice: Product or corporate names may be trademarks or registered trademarks, and are used only for identification and explanation without intent to infringe.

British Library Cataloguing-in-Publication Data
A catalogue record for this book is available from the British Library

Library of Congress Cataloging-in-Publication Data
Names: Rachman, Arnold W., author.
Title: Psychoanalysis and society's neglect of the sexual abuse of children, youth and adults : re-addressing Freud's original theory of sexual abuse and trauma / Arnold Wm. Rachman.
Description: Abingdon, Oxon ; New York, NY : Routledge, 2022. | Series: Psychoanalytic inquiry series | Includes bibliographical references and index.
Identifiers: LCCN 2021026365 (print) | LCCN 2021026366 (ebook) | ISBN 9780367278731 (hardcover) | ISBN 9780367278748 (paperback) | ISBN 9780429298431 (ebook)
Subjects: LCSH: Sexually abused children. | Sexual abuse victims. | Psychic trauma in children. | Psychic trauma. | Psychoanalysis. | Freud, Sigmund, 1856–1939.
Classification: LCC RJ507.S49 R33 2022 (print) | LCC RJ507.S49 (ebook) | DDC 618.92/85836--dc23
LC record available at https://lccn.loc.gov/2021026365
LC ebook record available at https://lccn.loc.gov/2021026366

ISBN: 978-0-367-27873-1 (hbk)
ISBN: 978-0-367-27874-8 (pbk)
ISBN: 978-0-429-29843-1 (ebk)

DOI: 10.4324/9780429298431

Typeset in Times New Roman
by MPS Limited, Dehradun

Dedication

To Elizabeth Severn, Sándor Ferenczi's analysis, and co-creator of "The Confusion of Tongues" paradigm and Trauma Analysis: "I will speak...of the importance of trauma...in the production of all neuroses. I wish here to emphasize the difference between the accepted psycho-analytic mode of treatment, which is purely dissecting in nature and which places its reliance chiefly on the mental grasp or reconstruction the patient can gain of his past; and a method which having found the trauma of specific cause of the illness, not does not scorn to play mother or be Good Samaritan to the injured one, and which encourages the full reproduction of the emotions and feeling – tone of the traumatic period of events under different and better circumstances. It takes more time, it takes more patience, and it takes above all an emotional capacity or 'gift' on the part of the analyst, who unless he can do this, is not a true 'physician of the soul.'" (Mrs. Elizabeth Severn, 1933 – The Discovery of the Self: A Study in Psychological Cure, p. 95).

Contents

Dedication	vii
List of Figures	xii
Acknowledgment	xiii
Foreword	xv

1 "A new motto: what has been done to you, poor child?" (Sigmund Freud, December 22, 1897) 1

2 The origin of psychoanalysis in the discovery of the sexual abuse of children by their parents 4

3 Freud's neglect of his childhood sexual trauma 22

4 Freud's analysis of his daughter Anna: his emotional blindness to sexual trauma 30

5 Sándor Ferenczi's Confusion of Tongues paradigm: introduction of trauma theory and trauma analysis 40

6 Sándor Ferenczi's iconic case of Elizabeth Severn: development of the study and analysis of trauma 51

7 A pedophile among us?: Ernest Jones's trial for the sexual abuse of mentally defective girls 65

8 Todschweigen, Death by Silence (Rachman and Menaker): traditional psychoanalysis's punishment of dissidents 95

x Contents

9 Sexual abuse of children within the family: the case of
Lisa Steinberg   98

10 A mother invites her daughter to incest: parental
neglect of childhood abuse   106

11 The "sensuous psychiatrist": the case of Julie Roy vs.
Renatus Hartogs, MD, PhD: landmark case of sexual
abuse by a therapist   119

12 A group analyst's neglect of childhood sexual abuse   122

13 The Catholic Church sexual abuse scandal   128

14 A Catholic priest's audacious proposal: "the church
should ordain women to be priests to reduce child
abuse"   142

15 The conspiracy within the Orthodox Jewish
Community to protect sexual abusers   159

16 Sexual abuse in the Catholic Church in Australia   167

17 The Eleventh Commandment: thou shall not lie down
with children   169

18 The child sexual abuse scandal at Pennsylvania State
University: Coach Joe Paterno, from idolatry to shame 178

19 The worst example of sexual abuse in sports history:
the case of Lawrence G. Nassar, MD   192

20 Two sports champions and emotional heroes:
R.A. Dickey and Kayla Harrison, find their voices
about their sexual abuse   196

21 Sexual abuse of children in our schools: St. George's,
Elite Boarding School in Rhode Island   203

Contents xi

22 Untying the Confusion of Tongues in Hollywood: the advent of the #MeToo movement, sexual survivors find their voice 213

23 "The Casting Couch": Harry Cohn, the godfather of sexual abuse of female actors 222

24 Harvey Weinstein: the heir apparent to Harry Cohn, Hollywood's sexual predator 224

25 Psychodynamics of sexual abuse in Hollywood: Uma Thurman and Mira Sorvino 231

26 Celebrity privilege and sexual abuse: the case of Roman Polanski 237

27 Celebrities and sexual assault: Woody Allen, Bill Cosby, and Matt Lauer 244

28 The Confusion of Tongues explanation for psychoanalysis' neglect of childhood sexual abuse 256

29 My attempts to confront the Todschweigen, Death by Silence campaign against Sándor Ferenczi, Elizabeth Severn and the Budapest School of Psychoanalysis 264

30 Contemporary activities which contribute to an appreciation of Ferenczi and the Budapest School of Psychoanalysis 296

31 Truth and reconciliation: traditional psychoanalysis owes Ferenczi an apology for their Todschweigen campaign against him 311

References 319

Index 341

Figures

0.1	Drawing by W. of Arnold, December 15, 1993	xvi
0.2	Mother and Child painting by W. December 2018	xxiii
0.3	Sigmund Freud's analysis of his daughter, Anna. Collage by Arnold Wm. Rachman. April 1, 2012.	33
0.4	Ferenczi's Confusion of Tongues Presentation, September 4, 1932	41
0.5	Mrs. Elizabeth Severn photography during the time she was in analysis with Sándor Ferenczi	53
0.6	Dr. Sándor Ferenczi. Photograph, Budapest, Hungary, August 1926	54
0.7	Lashon Hara: the consequence of hate speech. Public displays of prohibition against speaking evil about someone. Signs displayed in Israel	164
0.8	Eleventh Commandment: Thou Shalt Not Lie Down With a Child	176
0.9	Freud's Confusion of Tongues: book cover collage	297
0.10	Announcement. Irish Psych-Analytical Association Conference. May 11, 2019	299

Acknowledgment

In anticipation of writing this book on the significance of sexual abuse for psychoanalysis and society, I had been collecting publications for about 10 years, which I had intended to use as material for this book. Some of this material became useful. But, something unforeseen happened, which made it necessary to also integrate new material in this publication. In October 2017, while I was beginning to write this book, an explosion of data occurred when the Harvey Weinstein sex scandal became part of the dialogue. It is important to recognize the contributions made by the reporting of *The New York Times*, especially by the courageous team of Jodi Kantor and Megan Twohey. In addition, Ronan Farrow, investigative reporter with *The New Yorker* magazine, published a separate article. This trio had evidence that Harvey Weinstein had for more than 20 years, sexually abused young girls and women. For the first time, the deafening silence that engulfed Hollywood was shattered as Kantor, Twohey, and Farrow exposed Weinstein as a serial sexual predator through the voices of the women he abused. These reporting and the women's poignant voices helped bring the #MeToo movement into prominence. Kantor, Twohey, and Farrow received Pulitzer Prizes for their groundbreaking investigations and reporting. *The New York Times* must also be acknowledged for their significant reporting on the child sexual scandal among the Catholic clergy, which also dominated the news for the past several years. The data provided from these important articles have been integrated into this publication.

Harold Kooden, PhD, one of my dearest friends, co-author, and colleague, was invaluable in helping me go over the manuscript and add meaningful changes. Herb Westphalen contributed his creative and artistic talent to preparing the images that appear in this book. Katherine Fallon was able to translate my handwritten pages into a professional manuscript, for which I am very grateful. Nancy Rachman graciously contributed her technical expertise to produce the images. I am always grateful to Kate Hawes, Publisher, Routledge Press, and manuscript corrections for her guidance and expertise.

Foreword

"The Evolution of Darkness" by Mr W.; November 2018

I have had the privilege of co-creating a Trauma Analysis with the incest survivor and outsider artist I have labeled, W. In a previous book devoted to the theory and analysis of the Incest Trauma, a chapter was devoted to his remarkable history of abuse and, in his 70s, self-motivated capacity to analyze and recover from trauma (Rachman & Klett, 2015, pp. 189–230). As I have noted in ending this chapter, I discussed a drawing he made of me during the first 6 months of our analysis on December 15, 1993, which included his positive response to our relationship (see Figure 0.1). I was very emotionally moved by his understanding of the nature of "a curative relationship" and ended the chapter with saying:

> Working with W. has helped me become a better analyst and person. (Rachman & Klett, p. 229, see Image No. 2, W.'s drawing of Arnold).

When thinking about writing this book, I believed it would be of enormous importance to educate psychoanalysts as well as the lay public the nature of sexual trauma and the damage done to the individual when a parent (or parental surrogate) intrudes sex into their relationship with a child. My plan was to write a chapter that clearly illustrated the sexual abuse, as described by the incest survivor, as well as the damage the abuse inflicted on his/her personality development. Then I thought, it would be more important to present this description in the first-person account of the individual. Finally, one day Mr W., who was continuing his analysis,

Figure 0.1 Drawing by W. of Arnold, December 15, 1993.

told me about a poem he was writing about his childhood traumas. I asked him if he could lend me a copy of this narrative when finished, which he did. After reading this poem, "The Evolution of Darkness," by Mr W., November 2018, I felt this poem was an emotional gut-wrenching description of his childhood trauma with both of his parents. It illustrated the horrific experience of abuse, the damaging effect it had on his psyche, and the feeling of death, inability to feel, think, hear, touch, and speak. The abuse split him in half. He felt he was owned by his abusers. In Mr. W.'s use of words and images, we hear the scatological infiltration of his mind and soul. His body image is damaged. The damage, in his poetic free-associations, seems, at times, to describe "a broken person," pre-occupied with having been through an emotional holocaust, which, I now recall, he did use to describe his childhood.

His life is described as, "The Heart of Darkness," in which Satan, guilt, sex, anger, and women are prominent themes. Mr W.'s capacity to recover from such darkness can be viewed in his drawings, other poems, and his narratives of his inner and outer selves (Rachman &. Klett, 2015).

Shortly after he sent me the poem, he wanted me to have a painting he had done, entitled, *Mother and Child*, December 2018. During his analysis, he worked on and through the emotional disturbance of his sexual experience with his mother, which allowed him in his 70s to form a meaningful relationship with a woman and marry her. Continuing on with his exploration of his feelings about his mother, he said the following about his painting:

> I have worked to paint the reality of a female. It is the mother and child in an unusual way. I am recovering the mother, as if she has always been there. I am trying to incorporate everything about the female. I didn't know what a need I had for her. I have to forgive my enemy. You know what they did to me. (W. Commentary on his painting, *Mother and Child*, December 2018).

"The Evolution of Darkness," 21 March 2019.

1.

Who plundered our beds
Late at night,
Ladling their kisses of death
Across our thighs,
Were lesbians.

In that obsession I've always had
Of always having known two women first
And never wondering why, I died.

I am a novitiate, living outside
Of time and place, working on a
Work in progress.
Unable to feel. Unable to think.
Unable to see. Unable to hear.
Unable to touch. Unable to speak.
Unable to steal. Unable to be.

When thoughts first arose,
Without our permission, I froze,
Instantly knowing,
Without knowing why,
That thoughts would have to be suppressed
At all costs.
Instead of remaining docile and timid,
I became reckless and fearful,
Splitting myself in two,
My body and mind.

2.

I am reluctantly agreeing to give
Myself permission to write about
My father's excesses, a catalogue
Of retribution which owned us completely.
He who thrived deep inside the depth
Of utter darkness owned the
Very air I breathed.
He owned my stool.
He owned my flesh.
He owned my body.
He owned my mind.
He owned my brides.
He owned my breasts.
He owned my slaves.

He owned my sex.
He owned my morning star.
In the context of nonexisting
And the absences of flesh,
I became the prodigal son;
My naked women in bed with God,
And they in bed with me.

3.

In the altogether
Becoming a Christian nevertheless
Vowing to work for the IRS;
They to be forgiven
And we to be condemned,
Appealed to me.

4.

I brought strangers together.
I brought cowards together.
I brought mothers together.
I brought women together.
My God I was original sin!

5.

In the best and the worst of
All but impossible bathrooms
Which I detest, something was amiss,
Somehow wildly funny.
Something about my Bris.
Something about my silence,
Which should have triggered a response,
But never did and it cost me.

Recently I was astonished
To see myself having sex,
Without casting a shadow.

6.

I urinated all parts of speech.
Then flushed them down the toilet
To keep myself alive.
I could not will the words of God,
I had to kill my father first.
I etched my mother's face
On leather plates then wrote
About them in reverse.
My mother's voice became a curse
A ceaseless stream of ugly chatter
That met us on the road to Mecca,
And the sounds of their deaf inflections
Became accursed;
An unseen wind, stopping the first
And second letters of every verse
That felt like flesh.

7.

Because I could not stop for men
That could not stop for me.
Leather bound for innocence.
Leather bound for skin.
Leather bound for excrement.
Gurgling for vomit.
Gurgling for spit.
Gurgling for evidence.
I am a terrestrial
Looking for signs of life hidden
Throughout the vestibules
Of inner freedom.
I had hoped to discover the northern lights
That would have helped me to atone for the fingerprints
I left inside their hearses
A sacrilege witnessed by their tit.

8.

Because I could not die
Without them, I continued
To lie about them;
My mother's pounds of flesh.
They were weapons of mass destruction,
Forbidden to be touched and
When they were, I became the golem
And she became the pope.

We sallied forth throughout
The Heart of Darkness,
To and from Golgotha,
Without a trace of innocence.
Outside of time and place
Without a taste of forgiveness,
I lost my way.
Having already lost my shadow
Inside the furnaces of dread that followed us
Becoming more and more like a faggot
And less and less like a child,
My mother's nipples tasting like me.

9.

Needing to know more about hate
And less about love.
More about Adam and less about Eve.
More about Satan and less about blame.
More about freedom and less about guilt.
More about sex and less about boredom.
More about anger and less about sin.
More about women and less about mothers.
More about Absolem and less about Trump.

10.

In the beginning
Were the words of God,

And the words of God
Were people; people who stood,
People who sat, people who talked.
And they seized the day,
Holding it hostage for the light.
A ransom that was never paid.
And my obituary was lost
And so were naked women.

Asking was taken for rebellion.
Thinking was taken for sin.
Nonsense was taken for purpose.
Chaos was taken for granted.
And similar things
As simple as silence,
Were taken to be omniscient.

11.

Given the universe,
Where women were thin
And apples were poor,
A poetry of motion
Was born, bestriding
The phallic horses
Of my father's religion,
Galloping out of doors
Into the unforbidden light
Of night and day,
So that Delilah's breasts
Can be seen and heard,
As islands of the Lord.

The poem, *The Evolution of Darkness*, expresses the range of intensity of W.'s feelings about his childhood trauma, which cast a shadow of darkness over his life. He struggled to confront the darkness, which caused an emotional holocaust in his life. Both his mother and father harmed him to the extent he lost a sense of himself. His narrative poetry is, at times, difficult to comprehend because his mind was altered by his trauma during recent time due to aging. He speaks from a wounded place where words cannot convey the hurt in a rational manner. Turning to the spiritual he searches for a loving God, betrayed by his parents, who should have protected him from harm. When parents are the agents of the devil, the individual can become unhinged. They lose the safety and anchor of a loving family. W. struggled all of his life to shed the anger that his mother and father's abuse bestowed on him. In the ninth decade of his life, he is able to entertain loving feelings toward his mother, realizing his need for her.

The painting, *Mother and Child* (see Figure 0.2), by Mr W., was explained in the following way:

> I have worked to paint the reality of a female. It is the mother and the child in an unusual way. Recovering the mother, as if, she has always been there. I am trying to incorporate everything about the

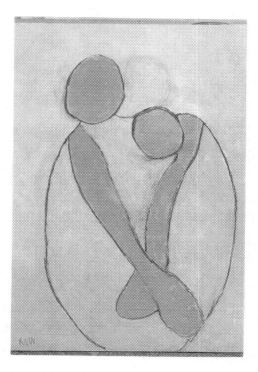

Figure 0.2 Mother and child. Painting by W. December, 2018.

female. Incredible reality, I didn't know what a need I had for her. I have to forgive my enemy. You know what they did to me. I have to forgive. I should take full responsibility for original sin, which allows the Son of Man, comes forward. Christ, I believe the Messiah has already come. Jews have a long way to go. Resurrection, the killing of the God head, …I suffered enough. Until the Jews take on responsibility for being a fucked-up people.

Post Script

Mr. W. died at the age of 92 in December 2019. He was a courageous individual who at the dawn of his life confronted and recovered from childhood traumas. I admired the man and the analysand for his willingness and capacity to accomplish this difficult task.

Chapter I

"A new motto: what has been done to you, poor child?" (Sigmund Freud, December 22, 1897)

At the turn of the 19th century, Vienna became one of the centers of intellectual inquiry, as Freud struggled to understand the origin of psychological disorder. In his letters to Wilhelm Fliess, his friend and muse, he outlined his exciting intellectual journey as he noted, a step-by-step unfolding of the sexual traumas children suffer at the hands of their parents (Masson, 1984). The period of discovery occurred from 1887 to 1904 in consort with Wilhelm Fliess, an otolaryngologist (surgical and medical management of head and neck), who for a time became Freud's best friend. The two met at the suggestion of Josef Breuer. Fliess attended several conferences with Freud beginning in 1887 in Vienna. The two soon formed a close friendship. Freud said Fliess left a deep impression on him. Freud's interchanges with Fliess became an important stepping stone in his attempt to sort out the role of sexuality in the origin of neurosis. Freud's original attempt to sort out this issue, in collaboration with Breuer, was not successful because Breuer did not agree with Freud's emphasis on the role of sexual impulse in the causation of hysteria (Breuer & Freud, 1895; Stafford-Clark, 1965). Through their extensive correspondence and personal meetings, Fliess came to play an important part in the development of psychoanalysis. The Fliess/Freud friendship grew through their frequent letters and regular meetings in Vienna and Berlin. They arranged 2- or 3-day trips away from home (they called these special meetings "congresses"). They not only exchanged their unorthodox scientific ideas, but also Freud provided intimate details of his own life (which he withheld from his wife). In fact, it has been claimed that Freud used these letters as "self-analysis" (Wilson, 1997, p. 49).

DOI: 10.4324/9780429298431-1

2 "What has been done to you, poor child?"

The authenticity of sexual trauma: letter from Freud to Fliess, December 22, 1897

In this letter sent to Fliess, 10 years into their relationship and correspondence, Freud sends an important letter to his friend and intellectual muse, describing a clinical case of infantile sexual trauma, which he feels provides the clinical evidence to believe in the authenticity of actual sexual trauma as a significant psychodynamic in the origin of psychological disorder. In particular, Freud described a female patient who was sexually abused by her father as a 2-year-old child. He inflicted her with gonorrhea, and she became ill by the loss of blood and vaginitis. In the session that Freud described, the patient recalls an incident when she was 3-year old, where she goes into a dark room where she sees her mother in a strange and very disturbing activity. Her mother is yelling (supposedly at her father), telling him he is a *rotten criminal* and she will not do what he requests of her. The mother becomes distraught and hysterical and tears her clothes from her body with one hand, and with her other hand she presses her clothes against it (Freud does not specify what "it" is. Presumably, it is a part of the mother's body that the father wants to invade, which the mother considers *a criminal invasion*). The mother's emotional reaction reaches a crescendo, much like a psychotic experience. Her face is contorted with rage, she covers her genitals with one hand and pushes something with the other. The mother's agony continues, shouting and cursing, she bends over and falls backward onto the floor. The scene ends with the mother in pain and utter despair.

Freud interprets the patient's description of the father's criminal assault on the mother with what is identified as anal rape. There were two other incidents when the patient saw her father-inflicted incidents of bleeding on the mother. The recall of the mother being emotionally torn apart by the father's psychopathic brutality, signaled the father turning toward his daughter for his brutal sexual needs.

Freud's description of this disturbing case of sexual abuse is presented in such a compelling narrative that one can feel both the sexual assault of the child and mother as well as the destruction to the individual psyche. Did the sexual brutality and the psychological damage described by his patient so move Freud that he noted at the end of this letter, first, his desire to turn away from this horror – "Enough of my smut"? (Masson, 1984, p. 289). What is more, Freud was so moved about hearing these firsthand reports of sexual abuse he realized that adults were mistreating children, and psychoanalysis had to inform the profession and the public about this. Hence, he declared psychoanalysis would raise our consciousness with:

> A new motto: What has been done to you, poor child? (Masson, 1984, p. 289)

This book will explore how psychoanalysis and society has not paid sufficient attention to Freud's original concern about the sexual abuse of children.

Chapter 2

The origin of psychoanalysis in the discovery of the sexual abuse of children by their parents

Between 1897 and 1902, Sigmund Freud carried on a lively, exciting, and intellectually adventuresome exchange of letters with Wilhelm Fliess. They both shared a mutual interest in the sexual aspects of human behavior. Freud presented his Seduction Hypothesis to Fliess in these letters as it evolved from an embryonic idea to a definitive conclusion. A glimpse into this fascinating material is contained in a description of the moment of discovery. In a letter to Fliess on April 28, 1897, Freud described the interaction he had with a patient when she reached an obstacle in their clinical interaction. As is often the case in the exploration of childhood sexual trauma, the patient is reluctant to continue on with the exploration. The interaction is described as follows:

Pt: You must allow me to mention no names.
Freud: Names don't matter. What you mean is your relationships with the people concerned. We can't draw a veil over that.
Pt: What I mean is that earlier the treatment would have been easier for me than now. Earlier I suspect it, but now the criminal nature of certain things has become clear to me, and I can't make up my mind to talk about them. On the contrary, I should say that a mature woman becomes more tolerant in sexual matters.
Freud: Yes, you're right. When I consider that the most excellent and high-principled men are guilty of these things, I'm compelled to think it's an illness, a kind of madness, and I have to exclude them. Then let us speak plainly. In my

DOI: 10.4324/9780429298431-2

analysis, I find it's the closest relatives, fathers or brothers, who are the guilty men.

Pt: It has nothing to do with my brother.

Freud: So it was your father, then (Freud, 1954, p. 195 – Letter from Sigmund Freud to Wilhelm Fliess, April 28, 1897).

This clinical interchange clearly shows Freud's remarkable capacity to understand and empathize with the childhood sexual seduction of his female patient. It is perhaps, the first formal analytic clinical interchange focused on understanding actual trauma, and specifically, emotional carnage that sexually abusing a child can produce.

Although Freud was known as "the father of interpretation" as the methodological golden road to analyzing the Oedipal Conflict, in his early years, as this cited clinical interchange illustrates, he illustrates a capacity for empathy and activity. These clinical capacities receded into the background as he became wedded to his Oedipal Theory of neurosis, and encouraged his favorite pupil, Sándor Ferenczi, to formally introduce activity and empathy into clinical psychoanalysis (Rachman, 1997a). His capacity to attune to the subjective experience of a patient struggling emotionally and connecting to her dissociated childhood sexual abuse by her father allowed for a breakthrough, as she began to bring her trauma into consciousness. Freud reports this process of uncovering:

And it then turned out that her supposedly otherwise noble and respectable father regularly took her to bed when she was from eight to twelve years old and misused her without penetrating ("made her evet", nocturnal visits). She felt anxiety even at the time a sister, six years her senior, with whom she talked thing over many years later, confessed to her that she had had the same experience with the father. (Freud, 1954, p. 196)

It is generally believed that psychoanalysis emerged from the continued clinical experience by Freud, with what we would now call "incest survivors." The letters to Fliess conveyed his clinical experiences and his emerging thoughts about his, Seduction Hypothesis, making his friend a witness to history:

6   Origin of psychoanalysis

> Not that among other things, I suspect the following; that hysteria is conditioned by a primary sexual experience (before puberty) accompanied by revulsion and fright; and that obsessional neurosis is conditioned by the same accompanied pleasure. (Freud, 1954; Letter Freud to Fliess, October 15, 1895, p. 126)

> Have I revealed the great clinical secret to you either in writing or by word of mouth? Hysteria is the consequence of a presexual sexual shock... "Presexual" means before puberty. (p. 126)

> I am practically sure I have solved the riddle of hysteria...with the formulation of infantile sexual shock...I am just as sure that... neuroses are radically curable now – not just the individual symptoms but the neurotic disposition itself. (Freud, 1954; Letter Freud to Fliess, October 16, 1895, p. 128)

Freud was thrilled with this discovery of the origin of neurosis in the sexual seduction of a child by a parent conveying his enthusiasm to Fliess, as if he had solved one of the great intellectual mysteries of human life, and, of course this is what he had done.

Freud presented a paper in 1896 entitled, "The aetiology of hysteria" (Freud, 1896) before the Society for Psychiatry and Neurology in Vienna, which became the first formal statement of the Seduction Hypothesis. The source of internal psychic pain lay in an actual act inflicted on the child. Family members were the seducers of children. Freud's theory was very negatively received by the Viennese Medical Society and he was crushed by the rejection (Masson, 1984). What is more, the medical journals did not publish the Seduction Hypothesis. Apparently, Freud did not present his evidence for the Seduction Hypothesis, which came from the actual data of his clinical cases and his method to retrieve these data, the psychoanalytic method. He felt the medical community would not respond positively to actual reports of fathers sexually abusing their daughters. The social climate them, in the 1890s, was not receptive to such a dramatic and disturbing statement about family relations. Are we any more receptive now to the same clinical observation that sexual abuse of a child by a parent can be the locus of psychological disorder? One cannot underestimate what a significant event Freud's original formulation for neurosis was for psychoanalysis and society. He brought together, for the first time, the finding that actual sexual molestation by a parent of a child was connected to adult psychological disorder. Freud was not only contributing to the understanding of a societal issue, but also suggesting an important new treatment, psychoanalysis. However, Freud's enthusiasm waned.

In a letter to Fliess, dated September 21, 1897, Freud started to express his doubts about the Seduction Hypothesis. First, he referred to his inability to "bring a single analysis to a real conclusion" and the absence of "complete success," which he had hoped to accomplish (Freud, 1954, p. 215). Second, he indicated his "surprise that in all cases, the father, not excluding my own, had to be accused of being perverse." He began to question the "realization of the unexpected frequency of hysteria...whereas surely such widespread perversions against children are not very probable" (Freud, 1954, pp. 215–216). Third, Freud argued that in an unconscious state, it is difficult to distinguish the fact from the fiction. In the unconscious state, there is no sign of reality, so one cannot differentiate between the truth and the fiction invested with feeling. Fourth, Freud wrote of his belief that in deep-reaching psychosis, unconscious memories do break through to the conscious, "so the secret of childhood experience is not disclosed even in the most confused delirium" (Freud, 1954, p. 216). In the same letter, Freud wrote that his loss of faith in his theory would remain known only to himself and Fliess, a fact he did not reveal in his own writings until 1914 (Freud, 1914). The shift in emphasis led to Freud's new theory of infantile sexuality. The impulses, fantasies, and conflicts that Freud claimed to have uncovered beneath the neurotic symptoms of his patients derived not from external contamination, he now believed, but from the mind of the child itself (Rachman, 2012).

At the time Freud was conveying his ideas to Fliess about the origin of neuroses in the incest trauma, he was involved in another historically significant experience. He was involved in his self-analysis. This self-analysis was cited in these same Freud/Fliess letters (Freud, 1954) and his first published book, *The Interpretation of Dreams* (Freud, 1900). One can conclude that the development of his Seduction Hypothesis is emotionally linked to his self-analysis. The important question is: Did Freud use his personal data to inform his theories and, if so, in what way? There has been a great deal of debate in psychoanalysis and psychotherapy about Freud's behavior in changing psychoanalysis' focus from the Seduction Hypothesis to the Oedipal Complex. Ernest Jones, Freud's official biographer, felt the change to the Oedipal theory was in intellectual tour-de-force for Freud (Jones, 1957). In fact, Jones was incredulous that Freud could ever entertain the Seduction Theory. Jones reflected the official response of orthodox or traditional psychoanalysis. Speaking for her father's desires, Anna Freud told Jeffrey M. Masson, a psychohistorian of psychoanalysis, that Freud believed in, and wanted to maintain, the Oedipal theory as the cornerstone of psychoanalysis (Masson, 1984). To the far left of Jones, Masson put forth the idea that Freud had a loss of courage in abandoning the Seduction Theory. The very negative reception Freud and Breuer faced when they introduced the concept of "infantile sexuality" before the Viennese Medical Society, Masson concluded, had a severe emotional impact on Freud because he badly wanted and needed acceptance and then from his Viennese peers, Freud abandoned his Seduction Theory (Masson, 1984). Masson's assertion, of course, angered both traditional and nontraditional analysts. When Masson was Secretary of the Freud Archives, it was an outrageous intellectual and emotional charge to make about Freud. When the dust settled, however, it was possible to examine Masson's assertions in a rational way. There is some credible argument for suggesting negative motivation by Freud for abandoning the Seduction Hypothesis. For example, when Freud studied with Charcot in Paris, he had firsthand experiences of child abuse through autopsies he witnessed on sexually abused children as well as Charcot and other French physicians' interest in trauma history (Masson, 1984, pp. 14–54). Masson found evidence of Freud's attempt to silence Ferenczi's Confusion of Tongues idea, which would have returned the theory to actual sexual trauma. More of this important issue later on in our discussion. Although I do not join Masson in accusing Freud of a loss of courage, I believe Masson's work along with Paul Roazen's writing (Roazen, 1975) and my own research (Rachman, 1997a, 1997b, 1999a), indicate that Freud, Jones, Ettingon, and others did attempt to silence Ferenczi and his work on the Incest Trauma. I want to trace Freud's change from the Seduction to the Oedipal Theory, which presents a trajectory of interest in the Incest Trauma in the history of psychoanalysis, from enthusiasm to neglect. Psychoanalysis lost interest in the Incest Trauma because of a series of dramatic changes associated with Freud's intellectual development and personal life. There are two historical moments of great importance, which are related to the assertion I will make about the Incest Trauma. Intellectually, Freud's development of the Oedipal Complex to explain neurosis and its prominence as the cornerstone of psychoanalysis is of great importance for the loss of interest in the Incest Trauma. And, second, Freud's self-analysis and the discovery of his own childhood sexual seduction are also of great importance. I will offer a series of hypotheses that both of these historically important issues affected Freud's theory building, and dramatic reaction to Ferenczi's attempt to return psychoanalysis to the study and treatment of the Incest Trauma.

Freud's introduction of the Oedipal Complex: focus on fantasy and the unconscious

It was a significant moment in psychoanalytic history when Freud turned his attention toward the introduction of the Oedipal Complex and away from the Seduction Hypothesis. Freud did not abandon his original idea that childhood experiences are at the heart of the development of psychological disorder, but, a monumental shift in emphasis took place. That theoretical shift defines the cornerstone of psychoanalyses until another paradigm shift takes place when Ferenczi attempts to introduce the role of trauma as another dimension in the development of psychological disorder. The original outline of the Oedipal Complex comes from Freud's book, *The Interpretation of Dreams*:

> According to my already extensive experience, parents play a leading part in the infantile psychology of all persons who subsequently become psychoneurotic.

> Falling in love with one parent and hating the other forms part of the permanent stock of the material of the subsequent neurosis. (Freud, 1900)

We can see from the beginning sentence of the Oedipal Complex formulation that Freud is beginning to conceptualize the origin of neurosis in *a sexual drama between child and parent, which originates in the child's imagination.* Remember, the Seduction Hypothesis had said *the actual sexual interaction between a parent and child was the source of the development of hysteria.* Freud goes on to make an important distinction between psychoneurotic and so-called "normal," suggesting that the child's internal experience of love and hate are universal in human behavior:

> But I do not believe that psychoneurotics are to be sharply distinguished in this respect from other persons who remain normal – that is, I do not believe that they are capable of creating something absolutely new and peculiar to themselves. It is far more probable – and this is confirmed by incidental observations of normal children – that in their amorous or hostile attitude toward their parents, psychoneurotics do no more than reveal to us, by magnification, something that occurs less markedly and intensively in the mind of the majority of children. (Freud, 1900)

Freud does not mention the nature of the extensive observations on adult psychoneurotic or normal children to which he used as data for these formulations. We know his observances and experiences with victims of child molestation. Is his observation of normal children based on his self-analysis, his own children, children of colleagues, and friends of the family? It was a bold assertion that Freud put forth about the universality of the child/parent rivalry. And this rivalry focused on the male child's rivalry with his father.

It seems as if Freud's greatest evidence he cited for the validity of the Oedipal Complex is the Greek playwright Sophocles and the legend of King Oedipus and Oedipus Rex, which Freud summarized as follows:

> Oedipus, who is the son of Laius, King of Thebes and Jocasta is exposed as a suckling, because an oracle had informed the father that his son, who was still unborn, would be his murderer. The child Oedipus is rescued, and grown up as a king's son at foreign court, until, being uncertain of his origins, he, too, consults the

oracle, and is warned to avoid his native place, for he is destined to become the murderer of his father and the husband of his mother. On the road leading away from his supposed home he meets King Laius, and a sudden quarrel strikes him dead. He comes to Thebes, where he solves the riddle of the Sphinx, who is baring the way to the city, whereon he is elected king by the grateful Thebans, and is rewarded with the hand of Jocasta.

A plague breaks out which causes the Thebans to consult the oracle... the messenger brings the reply that the plague will stop as soon as the murderer of Laius is driven from the country.

Oedipus himself is the murderer of Laius, and the he is the son of the murdered man and Jocasta. Shocked by the abominable in ignorance of the crime, which he as unwittingly committed, Oedipus blinds himself, and departs from his native city. The prophecies of the oracle have been fulfilled. (Freud, 1900)

Freud apparently was so moved by the Oedipal tragedy that he used it to form the basis of his new theory of psychoanalysis. He believed that Oedipal legend strikes the chord in every man's psyche:

We are all destined to direct our first sexual impulses toward our mother, and our first impulses of hatred and violence toward our fathers...it is nothing more or less than a wish fulfillment...of our childhood....Like Oedipus, we live in the desires that offend morality, the desires that nature has forced upon us, and after their unveiling, we may well prefer to avert our gaze from the scenes of our childhood. (Freud, 1900)

Freud using his self-analysis found the Oedipal myth in his own psyche:

I have found love of the mother and jealousy of the father in my own case, too, and now believe it to be a general phenomenon of early childhood, even if it does not always occur so early as in children who have been made hysterics.

Every member of the audience was once a budding Oedipus in phantasy, and the dream-fulfillment played out in reality causes everyone to recoil in horror, with the full measure of repression which separates his infantile from his present state. (Freud, 1954, Letter Freud to Fliess, October 15, 1897, pp. 223–224).

Freud generalized from these personal insights to introduce the Oedipal Complex, which was the nucleus of the neurosis because a decisive shift or change takes place in the mind of the child during this period. The shift takes place universally. Whether the parent(s) is seductive or not, the male child develops incestuous desires for the mother and hate for the father; this causes intense conflict. The mother is also hated because she is having sex with the father, which the child experiences as rejection. It is also a natural tendency to identify and be like the father. For female children, the Oedipal conflict is resolved through modification of values. She must accept her lack of a penis, and her wish to have her own aids her in giving up her desire for the father.

The Oedipal assumptions changed psychoanalysis's explanation for psychological disorder and the view of treatment:

1. Actual sexual seduction was diminished in importance for an understanding and analysis of psychological disorder.
2. Fantasy, unconscious wishes of sexual feelings became predominant.
3. If the fantasy of seduction is universal, there is no need to search out the actual behavior of a seducer.
4. The recognition of real seduction and its negative consequences is not a concern.
5. Any focus on real seduction, the actual interpersonal experience of seduction, and need to recover from seduction would be a resistance to uncovering the unconscious Oedipal wishes that is the cause of neurosis. (Rachman, 1997a, p. 326)

In traditional psychoanalysis, it has been an institutionalized idea that "Freud's correction" that sexual fantasy replaced actual sexual experience was an intellectual triumph that established psycho-analysis as the science of the unconscious. Freud seemed determined to replace the seductions of children with the notion that one had to account not only for the parent's aggression toward their children, but also with the children's feelings towards their parents. This was a remarkable change in Freud's thinking, as far as I am concerned. But traditionalists seem to think that the change was an indication of greater intellectual sophistication, where symbolism is more meaningful than actual experience. This idea was best expressed by Anna Freud. When Masson wrote to her that her father was wrong in abandoning the Seduction Hypothesis, she replied:

> Keeping up with seduction theory would mean to abandon the Oedipus complex, and with it the whole importance of phantasy life, conscious or unconscious phantasy. In fact, I think there would have been no psychoanalysis afterwards. (Masson, 1984, p. 113)

Masson's research indicated that Freud had doubts about abandoning the Seduction Hypothesis. In an unpublished letter, which Anna Freud and Ernst Kris, the editors of the Freud/Fliess Letters, deliberately omitted from their official 1954 edition, Freud said:

> My confidence in the father-etiology has risen greatly. (Masson, 1984, Letter Freud to Fliess, December 12, 1897, p. 114)

What is more, in another letter to Fliess later in the same month, which was also expunged from publication, Freud described in a dramatic, open and moving way of a case history that illuminates sexual seduction. Freud said:

> The following little scene which the patient claims to have observed as a three-year-old speaks for the intrinsic genuineness of infantile trauma. (Masson, 1984, Letter Freud to Fliess, December 22, 1897, p. 116)

Freud described the violent rape of a child and mother by the father. At the end of the case history, Freud adds:

> A new motto: what have they done to you, poor child? But now,

enough of my filthy stories. (Masson, 1984, Letter Freud to Fliess, December 22, 1897, p. 116)

As Masson so eloquently described, Freud was empathically attuned to the incest trauma after he changes his mind about it. The motto, "What have they done to you, poor child?" was Freud's way of showing how moved he was by the case history and suggested that the motto, which is a line from a poem by Goethe, should become the motto of psychoanalysis from then on. This sentiment, case history, and motto were removed from psychoanalysis (Masson, 1984, pp. 117–119). Today, I would like to revive this Freudian motto, and make it the theme of my book:

What have they done to you, poor child?

Masson's book *Assault on Truth* (Masson, 1984), for all its criticism of Freud, also had an important message, which I would like to quote:

> *Studies on Hysteria* and *The Interpretation of Dreams* are revolutionary books in ways that no subsequent book written by Freud would be. True, he enabled people to speak about their sexual lives in ways that were impossible before his writings. But by shifting the emphasis from an actual world of sadness, misery, and cruelty to an internal stage on which actors performed invented dramas for an invisible audience of their own creation. Freud began a trend away from the real world that, it seems to me, is at the root of the present-day sterility of psychoanalysis and psychiatry throughout the world. (Masson, 1984, p. 144)

Freud's Confusion of Tongues with Dora: trauma by interpretation

Professor Paul Mattick and I are working on a book entitled, *Freud's Confusion of Tongues with Dora: A relational perspective* (Rachman & Mattick, 2019). Freud's case of Dora (Freud, 1905) has been written about more than any other of his cases. You may ask us then, why contribute to the already existing voluminous literature? We were so struck by Freud's thinking and clinical behavior in this case, we could not resist writing about it. What we found so interesting was Freud's formulations as to Dora's psychological disorder stemming from an Oedipus Complex and his clinical behavior as forcefully imposing Oedipal interpretations on Dora. Dora, a pseudonym for Ida Bauer, was a teenager when she was sent to Freud. Her father became concerned when he found a suicide note she had left. On examination by Freud, she had other psychological symptoms, such as dyspnea (difficulty in breathing and hysterical choking); depression; avoidance of social contact; fainting spells; and aphonia (loss of voice). This array of symptoms was taken to conclude that Dora suffered from a neurosis.

Dora came from a typical middle-class Viennese Jewish family, similar to Freud's. she was about 17 years old when the therapy began. The analysis seems to have consisted of three sessions of 2 hours, conducted around 1900, the times when Freud was writing *The Interpretation of Dreams* in which he introduced the Oedipus Complex. After a break of about 15 months, there was one further session in March 1902. The case study was published in 1905 and has been recognized as:

> "...the first of Freud's great case histories" and which has taken its place as "one of the classic reports in the psychiatric literature." (Loewenberg, 1985, p. 188; Marcus, 1986)

Freud focused on Dora's hysteria as being a function of an unresolved Oedipus Complex with her father. Paul Mattick and I believed that Dora was suffering from an actual sexual trauma due to her experience with Herr K, a family friend, as well as emotional trauma due to her experiences with her mother and father. Dora was enmeshed in a complicated set of emotional relationships with her family and their friends, which were more significant to her emotional functioning than any Oedipal issues. Dora's mother was diagnosed as suffering from what Freud derisively called "housewife psychosis" because she confined her interests to the household and was obsessed with cleanliness. The father had venereal disease, which could be used to explain the mother's concern for cleanliness. Freud did describe a fundamental emotional disturbance in the mother/daughter relationship:

The relations between the girl and her mother had been unfriendly for years. The daughter looked down on the mother and used to criticize her mercilessly, and had withdrawn from her influence. (Freud, 1905, p. 20)

There was a complex and traumatic connection between Dora's family and a friend of her father, Herr K. This relationship is the source of a sexual trauma. Dora and Herr K's families often went on holidays together. Dora looked after the K's young children. She was particularly friendly with Frau K. Herr K, who was in his 40s, and was sexually interested in Dora. Herr K had been pursuing Dora since she was 14 years old, reaching a crescendo during a joint family vacation at Herr K's residence on a lake. When Dora was 16 years old, Herr K pulled Dora to him while they were walking and forcibly kissed her. This event, which Dora told Freud, is a screen memory for another related event that happened when Dora was 14. The earlier sexual seduction involved Herr K arranging to meet Dora at his office, telling his wife not to come, and sent all his office staff home so he could be alone with Dora. He then kissed her passionately. Dora had also discerned that her father was having an affair with Frau K. Freud mentioned all these sexual events as if they were secondary. Freud thought that the Oedipus Complex was at work here, when Dora reported that the office kiss imposed on her by Herr K "disgusted her":

I should *without question* consider a person hysterical in whom an occasion for sexual excitement elicited feelings that were preponderantly or exclusively unpleasurable. (Freud, 1905, p. 28)

To Freud's credit, he believed Dora's account of her father's affair with Frau K and her description of Herr K's sexual advances. But, he interpreted these events in terms of Dora's Oedipal feelings. Freud acknowledged that "the forced kissing episode" was a sexual trauma. But, *the trauma in his thinking was that Dora reacted neurotically to sexual pleasure.* Freud does not conceive of this episode as one of sexual seduction harassment, intrusiveness, aggression, or frightening. He does not conceptualize Dora as being angry, scared, or confused. His emphasis is on how Dora displaced the sexual episode. It is not an interpersonal experience, but a biologically driven intrapersonal one. It is not a two-person but a one-person experience. We can say that Freud had a Confusion of Tongues with Dora, because of his *insistence on defining her reality as sexual*. By doing so, *Freud sexualized their relationship*, filling their interaction with sexual innuendos through his aggressive Oedipal Complex interpretations. He attempted to convince Dora that she had an unresolved love relationship with her father, which the sexual experience with Herr K triggered off.

Paul Mattick and I believe that Dora left the treatment because an intense erotic transference developed. She experienced Freud as a "sexual abuser," who was making sexual verbal advances to her via his Oedipal/sexual interpretations about her and her father. Freud, at that point in his theory building, had not yet identified the countertransference reaction, which was to come about 10 years later (Freud, 1910, 1912). As Hanna Decker has pointed out in her important book on Dora (Decker, 1991), Freud contributed to the erotic transference by his own positive feelings for Dora of which he was, apparently, not aware. Dora may have prematurely terminated because she wanted to escape from Freud's "sexual advances" in his verbal contamination of their therapeutic relationship with incestuous sexual content.

We need a word about Dora's aforementioned maternal trauma. Freud, as we have mentioned, quoted Dora as having had an emotionally and interpersonally distant relationship with her mother. But, nowhere in the case study does he link Dora's depression, suicidal ideation, or psychosomatic symptoms with the disturbed relationship with her mother. We believe that Dora came to therapy wanting tenderness, affection, and empathy, the qualities of a human relationship that were missing in her relationship with her mother and father. The father showed a lack of understanding that his own disturbed behavior with his daughter and his lack of empathy for the sexual behavior toward his daughter by his friend, Herr K.

When Dora decided to end treatment with Freud, he had a moment of reflection on their relationship and his part of the premature termination. He sensed she needed tenderness and warmth, but could not, or would not give that to her:

> No one who, like me, conjures up the most evil of those half-tamed demons that inhabit the human breast and seeks to wrestle with

them, can expect to come through the struggle unscathed. Might I perhaps have kept the girl under my treatment if I myself had acted a part, if I had exaggerated the importance to me of her staying on, and had shown personal interest in her – a course which, even after allowing for my position as her physician, would have been tantamount to providing her with a substitute for the affection she longed for, I do not know. (Freud, 1905, p. 109)

Jeffrey M. Masson and the seduction hypothesis

I know that if I intellectually embrace some of Jeffrey M. Masson's ideas about Freud's abandonment of his seduction hypothesis that I will be aligning myself with someone who has discarded psychoanalysis, and someone who psychoanalysis has discarded. In the past several years when I referred to him as someone I wanted to include in a paper or book, I received a variety of negative reactions:

1. When I wanted to include Masson's thoughts about Ferenczi's Confusion of Tongues paper, an European analyst told me: "I don't think you should use him; he has been discredited."
2. I consulted with an analyst/academic about Masson's citation in his *Assault on Truth* book (Masson, 1984), where he cites that Muriel Gardner had told him, Ruth Mack Brunswick had written a paper on The Wolf Man, that was not published or conveyed to Freud, the response I immediately received was: "I would not go on Masson's word alone. You should get verification about the Brunswick paper from another source."
3. In the past, I had entertained the idea of asking Masson to write a foreword to a book, to which a colleague responded: "Don't do that! It will be bad for your career."

First, I want to make it clear I do not agree with Masson's idea that Freud abandoned the Seduction Hypothesis because of "a failure of courage" (Masson, 1984, p. 29). It should be clarified that Masson said this, "with the greatest reluctance" (Ibid, p. 29). I was attracted to Masson's other ideas because he was for me, a courageous analytic scholar and psychohistorian. Masson made several important contributions to psychoanalysis:

1. He unearthed material about the Seduction Hypothesis that was deliberately omitted by Anna Freud, Ernst Kris, and Marie Bonaparte, the editors of the 1954, Freud/Fliess Letters published as *The Origins of Psychoanalysis* (Freud, 1954).
2. He brought back Ferenczi's neglected and suppressed paper, Confusion of Tongues (Ferenczi 1933), into psychoanalytic study (Masson, 1984), for contemporary psychoanalysis. There were three previous attempts to return the Confusion of Tongues to a place of prominence, namely, Balint (1949), Fromm (1954), and Roazen (1975).
3. Masson provided evidence in the form of Freud's letters to Ferenczi that were hidden in a desk in Freud's office because it was felt that Ferenczi's Confusion of Tongues idea would threaten the Oedipal Complex theory (Masson, 1984).
4. In his interaction with Anna Freud, Masson reported that she disclosed she found these letters painful and asked him not to publish them. Other analysts told Masson to turn away from the Confusion of Tongues paradigm and Ferenczi's extension of the Seduction Hypothesis (Masson, 1984).
5. I share Masson's assumption:

Freud was the first psychiatrist who believed his patients were telling the truth. These women were sick, not because they came from "tainted" families, but because something terrible and secret had been done to them as children. (Masson, 1984, p. 28)

6. Masson reported that Muriel Gardner, MD, had told him that Ruth Mach Brunswick, MD, the second analyst of the Wolf Man/Sergei Pankejeff, was told by her analysand that he was anally raped by a family member as a child (Masson, 1984). Freud did not know this. I researched this possibility at the Library of Congress and found an unpublished paper by Brunswick, which indicated that Pankejeff did tell her he was anally raped by a family nursemaid (Rachman, 2019a).

My idea has always been that Freud got it right the first time when he described the actual sexual abuse of a child as the origin of a psychological disorder. Freud, I believe, made frantic attempts to prove his Oedipal Theory in the Cases of Dora (Rachman & Mattick, 2009) and the Wolf Man (Rachman, 2018). A cottage industry developed around interpreting Freud's abandonment of the Seduction Hypothesis from Masson's (1984) claiming Freud lacked the courage to maintain his theory in response to his Viennese medical critics, to Krüll's (1984) dissertation that Freud was obeying his father's taboo not to investigate family sexual secrets, to a host of critics who believed that Freud physically and verbally pressured his patients to produce ideas and images of sexual scenes, which he reconstructed (Borch-Jacobsen, 1991; Cioffi, 1999; Esterson, 1998; Schimek, 1987). The pressuring patients to produce fragmentary sexual "memories" seems similar to the False Memory Syndrome, where therapists "implant" the idea of childhood sexual abuse in their patients. I shared Masson's experience:

> It had never seemed right to me, even as a student, that Freud would not believe his patients. I did not agree that the seduction scenes represented as memories were only fantasies or memories of fantasies. (Masson, 1984, p. 28)

Masson (1984) believed that the letters and papers he uncovered in the Freud House in Maresfield Gardens indicated that the actual sexual trauma of children was an idea that remained with Freud. The implication being that he never fully abandoned the theory, may have continued to believe, at some level, his original formulation as to the origin of psychological disorder had merit. I believe there was also a psychodynamic component in Freud's neglecting the incest trauma, which I will discuss in detail in the chapters to come, but, for now, I will mention them: Freud's childhood sexual trauma; Freud's analysis of his daughter, Anna; Ferenczi's analysis of Elizabeth Severn; the development of the Confusion of Tongues paradigm and Trauma Analysis, and Freud and his orthodox followers' development of Todschweigen, Death by Silence, the traditional method of removing dissident voices from the mainstream.

Masson was a voice for the importance of childhood sexual abuse as an issue in psychoanalysis and society, as I believe the early Sigmund Freud, Sándor Ferenczi, Eric Fromm, and Paul Roazen were. Also, Masson, Fromm, and Roazen made an important contribution to the Ferenczi Renaissance, helping the psychoanalytic community to rediscover the importance of Ferenczi as a pioneering and neglected figure of revolutionary importance to psychoanalysis. When analysts decided his accusation that Freud had a loss of courage in abandoning the Seduction Hypothesis, he was seen as being disrespectable to the most revered figure of psychoanalysis. Critics of Masson "killed the messenger with his message." He became disheartened, his discoveries were ridiculed, and he was considered a fraud. He left psychoanalysis and became one of its greatest critics. We lost an important scholar and psychohistorian. Can we reconsider Masson's attempt to open up the discussion of the Todschweigen experience in psychoanalysis as an attempt to identify in Freud's personal and political behavior that influenced the continued neglect of the sexual abuse issue in psychoanalytic theory and treatment?

Chapter 3

Freud's neglect of his childhood sexual trauma

Since psychoanalysis' fundamental mission is built on a psychodynamic explanation for human behavior, society deserves a psychodynamic explanation for the neglect of the incest trauma. Freud, Jones, and the orthodox circle that surrounded Freud, did not hesitate to use psychodynamic explanation to understand and to criticize dissidents (Rachman, 1999). I believe, one of the most taboo areas of scholarship has been any meaningful discussion of Freud's personal functioning. There are two such areas of personal functioning, Freud's childhood sexual trauma and his analysis of his daughter, Anna, that are relevant to the present topic of psychoanalysis' neglect of sexual trauma as a significant issue in society and in our profession.

It has been particularly puzzling to me, why psychoanalysis has instituted a silence regarding Freud's own childhood sexual seduction since he clearly outlined it in his own words, in his letters to Wilhelm Fliess (Freud, 1954). This discovery demonstrated the importance of childhood sexual abuse within the family of origin for the development of psychological disorder (see Chapter 1). Why then, did Freud so question this discovery that he lost interest in the Seduction Hypothesis and turned his attention to developing the completely new idea of the Oedipal Conflict? Understanding this mystery of neglecting actual sexual trauma as the etiology of psychological disorder and concentrating all attention on unconscious, symbolic manifestations of behavior was a way of protecting the Oedipal theory.

DOI: 10.4324/9780429298431-3

Freud's childhood sexual trauma

Freud's childhood sexual trauma with an adult abuser was chronicled in the Freud/Fliess Letters (Freud, 1954). To Freud's credit, he openly discussed this with Fliess in their correspondence. These self-disclosures, as well as the ones in Freud's Interpretation of Dreams, were the result of Freud's self-analysis. It is a remarkable accomplishment of great emotional courage and therapeutic skill that Freud was able to retrieve his childhood sexual abuse when, those of us who work with incest survivors know how difficult it is for them to accomplish this feat. In fact, years into analysis, some analysands cannot own that they have been sexually abused. Freud's exploration of his sexual abuse has implications for his idea about "child sexuality." More specifically, for the implication of Freud's personal experience with child sexual abuse for the abandonment of the Seduction Hypothesis and the development of the Oedipal Complex. From the Freud/Fliess correspondence, which is considered the origins of psychoanalysis, the following sequence was reconstructed to elaborate Freud's childhood sexual trauma:

1. In Freud's attempt to uncover the mystery of whether his parents were involved in the development of his neurosis he said this about his father:

   I can only say that in my case, my father played no active role, though I certainly projected on to him an analogy from myself. (Freud, 1954, p. 219 – Letter, Freud to Fliess, October 3, 1897)

   My "primary originator," was an ugly, elderly but clever woman; (between the ages of two and two-and-a-half) libido towards *matrem* [mother] was aroused; the occasion must have been the journey with her from Leipzig to Vienna, during which we spent a night together and I must have had the opportunity of seeing her *nudom* [naked]. (You have long since drawn the conclusions from this for your own son, as remark of yours revealed). (Freud, 1954, p. 219 – Letter, Freud to Fliess, October 3, 1897)

   Last night's dream produced the following under the most remarkable disguises:

> She was my instructioness in sexual matters, and chided me for being clumsy and not being able to do anything...Also, she washed me in reddish water which she had previously washed herself (not difficult to interpret; I find it nothing of the kind in my chain of memories; and so I take it for a genuine rediscovery); ... (Freud, 1954, p. 220 – Letter, Freud to Fliess, October 4, 1897)

> Freud's nursemaid,...played a role of extraordinary importance during his early life in Freiberg. Since R. Glicklhorn's and J. Sajner's researches on her identity, most biographers, including myself, had assumed she was Monika Zajic, a member of the family in whose house the Freuds lived. However, J. Sajner and I have recently discovered an entry in the list of visitors taking the cure at Roznau (see Table 13) [Table 12 – Facsimile of entry in Roznau Register of Spa visitors for 5 June 1857: 108, Amalie Freud wool merchant's wife with child Sigmund and maid Resi Witteck from Freiberg, No. 180 (photograph by J. Sajner and P. Swales] "which makes it most likely that she was in fact Resi Wittek." (Krüll, 1986, p. 119)

2. But, on a note of optimism, Freud said that 4 days of self-analysis he had been making progress in identifying the origins of his neurosis. At this point, he was still trying to verify his Seduction Hypothesis, looking from incidence of sexual seduction in his own childhood. In a remarkable moment in psychoanalytic history, Freud recovered his childhood sexual seduction and self-disclosed it to Fliess as if he had solved "the riddle of the Sphinx." Freud named his nursemaid as the primary source of sexual seduction.

3. Freud continued his self-analysis about his sexual seduction through the reporting and analysis of a dream he reported to Fliess on the following day, after his first self-disclosure.

4. Freud was not able to name his "instructioness: in sexual matters." Research by a German sociologist, Marianne Krüll, who investigated his family and childhood, identified Freud's nursemaid.

Krüll goes on to elucidate Resi Wittek as a person:

> She was a Czech and a Catholic,...and it is possible that she was solely responsible for little Sigmund at the time of Julius's death [Freud's brother] and Amalie's new pregnancy followed by the birth of Anna, from April to December 1858 [Amalie Freud born Amalie Nathanson was his father's second or third wife and Freud's mother]. It is not known if Resi Wittek was married and had children of her own, but she had obviously taken little Sigmund to her heart, and he supposed later that he must have loved her in turn. (Freud 1900 [1898-99] The *Interpretation of Dreams Standard Edition IV – V*) (Krüll, 1986, p. 120)

Both Freud and Krüll indicate that Resi Wittek took little Sigmund to church. He would come home and lecture his parents about God and Hell. His parents did not seem to realize how emotionally attached were little Sigmund and Resi Wittek.

> I have succeeded in finding a number of real points of reference. I asked my mother whether she remembered my nurse. "of course," she said, "an elderly woman, very shrewd indeed. She was always taking you to church when you came home you used to preach, and tell us all about God conducted his affairs." (Freud, 1954, p. 222 – Letter, Freud to Fliess, October 15, 1897)

> All the shiny Kreuzers and Zehnrs and toys that had been given you were found among her things. Your brother Philipp went himself to fetch the policeman, and she got ten months. (Freud, 1954, pp. 221–222 – Letter, Freud to Fliess, October 15, 1897)

5. Freud also disclosed his emotional struggles to establish whether his recovered memories of childhood sexual abuse with Resi Wittek were real or imagined, as we now know, is a fundamental issue with which all incest survivors struggle (Rachman, 2000, 2003a, 2013). Freud asked his mother if his retrieved memories were real.

6. Freud's early childhood experience with Resi Wittek also produced an "abandonment trauma." His mother told him that his nursemaid was a thief and was sent to jail.

Freud was able to verify that his nurse was taken away from him. Freud admitted that a "screen memory of the cupboard haunted him.":

> A scene occurred to me which for the last twenty-nine years has been turning up from time to time in my conscious memory without any understanding. (Freud, 1954, p. 222 – Letter, Freud to Fliess, October 15, 1897)

He went on to describe the emotional remnants of the missing nursemaid, Resi Wittek, when she disappeared after she was sent to jail for 10 months and never returned to the Freud family:

> I was crying my heart out, because my mother was nowhere to be found. My brother Philipp...opened a cupboard...and when I found that she was not there either I cried still more until she came through the door, looking slim and beautiful. What can that mean?...I feared she must have vanished, like my nurse not long before. I must have heard that the old woman had been locked, or rather "boxed"...up...The fact that I turned to him [Freud's brother Philipp] shows that I was well aware of his part in my nurse's disappearance. (Freud, 1954, p. 223 – Letter, Freud to Fliess, October 15, 1897). [The screen memory of the cupboard was used in Freud's *The psychopathology of everyday life*.]

The data from Freud's disclosures from his self-analysis in his letters to his closest colleague at the time, clearly indicated that Freud admitted he was the victim of childhood sexual abuse by his nursemaid, Resi Wittek. Freud and Resi Wittek had an emotionally and interpersonally close relationship. It is likely they shared loving feelings and physical closeness. Freud's parents may not have realized how important his nursemaid was in his life. They did not seem to know about their sexual relationship. What is more, they did not know about her being a thief. When Resi Wittek was sent to prison and never returned it clearly created an "abandonment trauma."

Freud indicated that as an adult, he was preoccupied with the feeling of emotional abandonment in his "screen memory of the cupboard." Freud was not allowed to mourn when Resi Wittek disappeared.

Krüll (1986) had translated her investigation in Freud's childhood and family into her idea that Freud turned away from the Seduction Hypothesis because of his unconscious fear of violating taboos against betraying secrets about the family. Krüll also had speculations about Freud's childhood trauma.

7. To Freud's self-disclosure regarding the sexual experiences with his nursemaid, Resi Wittek, we can also add Krüll's interesting formulations – Krüll speculates about Wittek's additional sexual behavior of manipulating Freud's genitals:

> Now why did she [Resi Wittek] think Freud clumsy and incompetent? Perhaps it was because of his toilet training, his inability to urinate without wetting the floor? ...Did Resi perhaps manipulate his penis, not simply when teaching him to urinate but on other occasions, too? Freud wrote: It is well known that unscrupulous nurses put crying children to sleep by stroking their genitals. [Freud (1905) three essays on the theory of sexuality Standard Edition 7:125] p. 180 f. cf and (1931) Female Sexuality. Standard Edition 22:223] "Did his nursemaid also send little Sigmund to sleep in this way?" (Krüll, 1986, p. 121)

> Sigmund aged two and a half, probably did not understand why Resi disappeared so suddenly...She was simply gone, and he missed her very much. The picture of a screaming child who asked Phillip to open the box because he was afraid that his mother had been "boxed up" like the nursemaid who had just disappeared...clearly reflects this feeling, that the episode was traumatic is also borne out by the fact that he kept recalling it year after year without really understanding what had happened. (Krüll, 1986, p. 122)

8. Resi Wittek's disappearances from Freud's life was also an issue of speculation by Krüll.

28 Freud's neglect of his trauma

Integrating the data, from Freud and Krüll about Freud's childhood sexual seduction and abandonment trauma experiences, I suggest that:

1. Freud's childhood sexual and abandonment experiences became a Confusion of Tongues Trauma (Rachman, 1994, 1997a, 2003a, 2013). As a child, Freud was seduced and abandoned by an adult.
2. His parents had no idea of the nature of the relationship between their son and their nursemaid. What is more, Resi Wittek's sudden disappearance was a further shock that was perpetuated on him by his family. His parents were unaware of the "sexual matters" between their son and his nursemaid. They took the nursemaid away from their son, with no idea of the emotional trauma it might cause or that he needed comfort to deal with the trauma.
3. Little Sigmund could not turn to them for solace or help with his trauma. The family felt they were doing the proper thing in getting rid of a thief in their midst and protecting their child from a negative influence. Ironically, they were unknowingly helping him to break a sexual seduction experience.
4. Freud could also not speak of his trauma because he was told by his father to maintain the family prohibition on not revealing "family secrets" (Krüll, 1986).
5. Freud repressed his childhood traumas. He became "tongue-tied," another element of the Confusion of Tongues trauma. The child's inability to speak of his/her trauma, can be characterized as "elective mutism." The child is alone in their trauma, fearing that the abuser will further injure them, if they give voice to the trauma (Ferenczi, 1933).
6. We know from the contemporary study and treatment of the incest trauma (Rachman, 2000, 2003a, 2013) that the split off portions of the personality can produce disturbed feelings, thoughts, and behavior unavailable to consciousness and rationality. I believe this is what happened to Freud. His childhood traumas were unavailable to him because he would not confront them in his self-analysis and would not allow anyone else to analyze him. He became disassociated. He turned down Jung and Ferenczi who had at different times

offered him help with his neurotic issues. Freud would not relinquish his role as head of the psychoanalytic movement (Rachman, 1997a).

7. His repressed sexual trauma emerged as moral outrage toward Ferenczi for focusing so dramatically on the role of childhood sexual trauma in the development of personality and psychological disorder (Rachman, 1997b).

8. Freud and the orthodox analytic community were successful in suppressing Ferenczi's idea about the incest trauma. At least, four generations of analysts and mental health professionals were unaware of the significance of the incest trauma in the development of psychological disorder. It was not until the 1980s when Ferenczi's *Clinical Diary* was finally published in French and English that a renaissance developed in psychoanalysis about the importance of childhood sexual abuse as significant in the development of personality disorder.

9. The women's movement and incest survivors have led the way toward helping to lift the veil of denial regarding the prevalence of incest trauma.

10. Psychoanalysis needs to contribute to the awakening of our profession and the general public to the necessity to maintain the study and treatment of children, youth, and adults who have been sexually molested.

Chapter 4

Freud's analysis of his daughter Anna: his emotional blindness to sexual trauma

Unraveling the mystery of who analyzed Anna Freud

We owe a great deal of debt to the political scientist and historian of psychoanalysis, Paul Roazen, PhD, for unraveling the mystery of who analyzed Anna Freud. Roazen undertook a major research project in the 1960s to interview all living people who had contact with Freud as a way to write a more personal history of psycho-analysis (Roazen, 1975). His book, *Freud and his Followers*, was the result of this investigation, which turned out to be a revisionist history of psychoanalysis, when compared to Ernest Jones traditional version of psychoanalytic history. Roazen's book did not meet the approval of the orthodox analytic community. As Roazen noted, Young-Bruehl (1988) made no mention of him in her discussion of Anna Freud's analysis, although he was the first one to identify her father as her analyst in print (Roazen, 1969). The opportunity to conduct personal interviews with colleagues, family members, and analysands of Freud produced a series of revelations, which are relevant to Anna's analysis.

It is possible to reconstruct the secrecy surrounding the issue of Anna's analysis by using the data from Roazen's interviews and other published sources. In an interview with the Viennese analyst, Robert Jokl, in December 1965, Jokl reported that Anna denied her father had analyzed her in the 1920s. Jokl met Anna one night walking in old Vienna looking depressed. Jokl suggested that she undertake an analysis. Anna seemed to indicate she had done that. But, when Jokl asked her if the analysis was with her father, she said no. In the summer of 1965, Roazen also

DOI: 10.4324/9780429298431-4

interviewed Kata Levy, a Hungarian analyst, analyzed by Freud. Levy reported that Freud, who was grateful for the financial support by Kata Levy's brother, volunteered in 1918, while he was in Hungary for the famous Budapest Congress, to analyze Kata Levy. When she seemed surprised by the offer, Freud said, "he had begun to analyze Anna, and that he would just as soon have both of them at the same time" (Roazen, 1993, p. 110). In an interview with Sandor Rado, he was incredulous that Roazen was aware that Freud analyzed his daughter Anna. In contrast, when Helene Deutsch was asked about the subject, she stared into the distance and remained silent "as if she had not heard what I had been saying" (Roazen, 1993, p. 117). This was another example of Todschweigen, which seem to verify Menaker's experience in Deutsch's seminar, when Ferenczi's death was given the silent treatment.

The late Kurt Eissler, the former archivist of the Freud Archives and a traditionalist who was one of the "keepers of the keys" in American psychoanalysis, offered his thoughts about the analysis. As a response to Roazen's revelation about Anna's analysis he said it was: "'well-known', although he could not cite a single published reference on the subject" (Roazen, 1993, p. 110). Eissler was practicing the traditional method of psychoanalysis, Todschweigen, Death by Silence (Rachman, 1999), silencing any issue connected to Freud that is considered taboo.

In actuality, the mystery of Anna's analyst continued until Roazen had the courage to print the following information:

> Perhaps the most extraordinary illustration of Freud's allowing himself privileges he might have condemned in any other analyst was his analyzing his youngest child, Anna. In letters Freud was quite open about this analysis, and it became a public secret to a small group of his inner circle. (Roazen, 1965, p. 100)

Roazen went on to specify his findings: In footnote No. 8, in his statement of Anna's analysis, he noted:

> Mrs. Edward Hitchmann, Dr. Anny Katan, Dr. Edith Jackson, Dr. Herman Nunberg, Dr. Inmarita Putnam, and Dr. Sandor Rado have all confirmed that Freud did indeed analyze Anna. (Roazen, 1965, p. 215)

This revelation about Freud being Anna's analyst made Roazen a pariah. Rather than welcoming the news, which would have lifted the veil of denial and allow a scholarly discussion of the subject matter, Roazen, the messenger, was attacked for having the intellectual and emotional daring to speak the truth to authority.

The next segment of this issue involved Roazen's interview in April 1965 with the Italian analyst, Edoardo Weiss, MD. In this interview, Weiss revealed that Freud had said he was Anna's analyst in a letter he had written to Weiss (Roazen, 1975, p. 439). Weiss had sought Freud's advice on the advisability of analyzing this son. The letter said the following:

> Concerning the analysis of your hopeful son, that is certainly a ticklish business. With a younger, promising brother it might be done more easily. With one's own daughter I succeeded well. There are special difficulties and doubts with a son. Not that I really warn you against a danger; obviously everything depends upon the two people and their relationship to each other. You know the difficulties. It would not surprise me if you were successful in spite of them. It is difficult for an outsider to decide. I would not advise you to do it and have no right to forbid it. (Letter from Sigmund Freud to Edoardo Weiss, 1935 – Weiss, 1970, p. 81)

Freud's analysis of his daughter Anna

One of the most taboo subjects in psychoanalytic history has been Freud's analysis of his younger daughter, Anna (see Figure 0.3). The analysis is dated from the fall of 1918 until 1924 (Young-Bruehl, 1988). During the period, there was no analytic prohibition on dual relationships, crossing boundaries of family and friendship to analyze someone. Not only was it Freud's idea to analyze his daughter, but also he felt he had done a good job. In analyzing his daughter, Freud was myopic to the emotional seduction involved in such a complicated enterprise. By virtue of his dedication to his Oedipal theory, he had a mandate to analyze his daughter's Anna's Oedipal Complex. It is reasonable to assume that she would discuss her sexual feelings and fantasies about him, both past and present. Such interaction in their analytic sessions would constitute a form of overstimulation, "emotional seduction," if

Figure 0.3 Sigmund Freud's Analysis of His Daughter, Anna. Collage by Arnold Wm. Rachman. April 1, 2012.

you will. This behavior also violated the maintenance of unconscious boundaries between a parent and child. A child needs the psychological space to entertain Oedipal feelings without the intrusion of a parent. Oedipal feelings and fantasies are sacrosanct (Rachman, 1997a). Freud's blindness to the possibility of the "emotional seduction" of his daughter is particularly puzzling since he condemned Ferenczi for what he falsely interpreted as sexual acting with analysands. *Freud confused sexuality for tenderness* in Ferenczi's behavior. If Freud could not acknowledge his emotional seduction issues, his daughter could. In a letter to Lou Andreas-Salomé, Anna wrote that she acknowledged:

> The absence of the third person, the one onto whom the one acts out and finishes off the conflicts…the analyst who was supposed to be a neutral party, "blank screen" was, in the nature of the case, missing.

And, further, Anna understood clearly that what she called her "extra-analytic closeness" to her father produced "difficulties and temptations to untruthfulness in the analysis." (Quoted in Young-Bruehl, 1988, p. 123 – Letter from Anna Freud to Lou Andreas-Salomé, May 24, 1924)

A father's misguided love

I believe a scholarly examination of Freud's unusual clinical behavior with his daughter, Anna, is long overdue and will help to lift the taboo that has existed in our field ever since the analysis occurred in the early 1920s. Such an examination is in the tradition of dissidence that Esther Menaker pioneered in her questioning of Freudian tradition (Menaker, 1995). The desire to enter into an extra-parental relationship with one's child has occurred in science, before and after, Freud's analysis of his daughter, Anna:

> There has also been the innovators investigations of their own children_cf. Darwin's studies of his first son; Piaget's observations of his children's cognitive development. It is possible that Roentgen conducted experiments on his children, etc." (M. Tolpin, 1992, p. 11 f4)

I, therefore, make a distinction between Freud's desire to analyze his daughter Anna, and his actually performing the analysis. It can be an act of love to entertain the fantasy to help your child by offering them your expertise. This is especially true if the parent is the world's expert in psychoanalysis, a field he founded. Without comparing myself to Freud, I have had the fantasy of analyzing my children. My rationale goes something like this: "I have spent so much emotional, intellectual, and interpersonal energy analyzing other people's children, shouldn't I offer these same services to my children? The desire became particularly intense at periods when my children were having significant difficulty in their lives. But, I never did analyze them. I encouraged them to seek out help, recommending analysts who I thought would take special care of my children." Even when they saw therapists who were not helpful, I never assumed the analysis myself. At these difficult moments, I discussed with them changing analysts. I would encourage them to change and help them, once again, find someone new, and hopefully better. It was emotionally difficult to suffer through their bad analysis, when I knew I could do better. But, the analysis needed to be performed by someone other than their father. It is not an act of love to actually analyze one's child, no matter how well intentioned is the desire. It is likely to be an expression of some neurotic issue. I believe Freud's analysis of his daughter, although well intentioned, was born of a desire to fulfill narcissistic needs.

Freud and childhood seduction

There are many issues to examine in the analytic experience between Sigmund and Anna Freud. The one that has fascinated my attention is the debate about the abandonment of the seduction theory, more specifically, was Freud's willingness to analyze his daughter, an indication of an emotional blindness to the issue of sexual seduction in theory and method? Was Freud's vehement and mean-spirited objections to Ferenczi's courageous attempts to re-formulate the seduction theory, especially in his Confusion of Tongues paper (Ferenczi, 1933) and *Clinical Diary* (Ferenczi, 1988), also partially fueled by his emotional blindness to the issue of seduction? In fact, was Freud's campaign to suppress and censor Ferenczi's Confusion of Tongues paper, one of psychoanalysis' dirty little secrets (as was the secret of Anna's analysis)? In a series of letters and telegrams, it is clear that Freud, along with Jones, Eitingon, Revère, and others prevented Ferenczi's Confusion of Tongues paper from being published (Rachman, 1997a, 1997b), through the practice of Todschweigen (Rachman, 1999).

Freud, in an amazing statement, suggested the analyst cannot traumatize, corrupt, or seduce a child by introducing sexual material into their discussion (Rachman & Mattick, 2009). Consequently, he freely introduced sexual interpretations into the analysis of Dora (Freud, 1905) because the presence of her "hysterical" symptom *meant Dora had sexual thoughts*. Freud believed the symptom is the expression of a sexual wish. An hysteric is like a repressed pervert, they have sexual feelings and ideas they do not sublimate but, they repress and turn the desire into symptoms. Freud therefore, felt fully justified to say sexual things to Dora, like she had the fantasy of wanting to have oral sex with her father, when there is no evidence to support this (Rachman & Mattick, 2012) or he could analyze his own daughter, without concern of emotionally seducing her. Freud's statement about seduction in the analytic situation, as he stated in the Case of Dora, was as follows:

> There is never any danger of corrupting an inexperienced girl. For where there is no knowledge of sexual processes even in the unconscious, no hysterical symptom will arise; and where hysteria is found there can no longer be any question of "innocence of mind" in the sense in which parents and educators use the phrase. With children of ten, or twelve, or of fourteen, with boys and girls alike, I have satisfied myself that the truth of this statement can invariably be relied upon. (Freud, 1905, p. 42)

Esther Menaker: Anna Freud's analysand reflects on her analysis

I was privileged to have as a colleague and friend, Esther Menaker, PhD, whose first analyst was Anna Freud (Menaker, 1989, 1991, 1996). Esther was introduced to me by two colleagues, Robert Prince, PhD, and Joyce Nathan PhD, who while we were working together told me that I should become a friend of Esther since we were similar in temperament and perspective. I am very grateful to them as I enjoyed a professional and personal relationship with Esther for about a 20-year period. She generously welcomed me into her life, inviting me on a regular basis to have dinner with her at her home, across the street from the Museum of Natural History on Manhattan's West Side. I was a younger colleague to this diminutive icon of psychoanalysis and could not believe of my good fortune to be breaking bread with someone who studied with the Freuds at the Vienna Psychoanalytic Institute. Actually, Esther was a better dinner companion than was my mother, who never showed any interest in my intellect. What is more, Esther was warm, friendly, and affectionate, much like my Jewish grandmother (Rachman, 2018). Besides dinners during the week, we would meet Sunday mornings, at a time before she would have regularly scheduled telephone conversations with her son and his family.

At the time of our first meeting, I felt like a loner in the psychoanalytic landscape. I was not part of an established alternative perspective, like Self Psychology or Interpersonal Psychoanalysis. I had discovered the work and ideas of Sándor Ferenczi and The Budapest School of Psychoanalysis (Rachman, 1997a, 2016) and I was looking for a psychoanalytic home. I remember a supervisor telling me that a colleague had referred to me as, a maverick, despairingly suggesting I was a rebel without an established, legitimate perspective. My conversations with Esther, where she was personally open and shared her own difficult journey from Freudian Psychology (Menaker, 1989) to an appreciation of Otto Rank, to embracing the self psychology perspective (Menaker, 1982b) helped me feel my difficult journey to become a psychoanalyst (Rachman, 2018) was a legitimate struggle for someone who was trying to integrate their own sense of self into an established frame of reference. Esther encouraged me to write my first book on Ferenczi (Rachman, 1997a). We collaborated on several projects: A course on the history of psychoanalysis, emphasizing the contributions of Sándor Ferenczi and Otto Rank; A symposium on "Freud's analysis of his daughter Anna: Implications for the theory and technique of psychoanalysis," which also included the psycho-historian, Paul Roazen, PhD. At New York University Psychoanalytic Society in 1996; Developed the concept of "Todschweigen, Death by Silence," published in (Rachman, 1999). We felt this was a much needed defense of the dissident voices in psychoanalysis for our field to maintain its evolution.

Esther Menaker was willing to be self-disclosing about her analysis with Anna Freud. I have mentioned that I have felt that Eric Fromm, Jeffrey M. Masson, and Paul Roazen have been courageous figures for me in the history of psychoanalysis. I also want to unequivocally add Esther Menaker to this list. I so admire Esther's courageous statement about her analyst's functioning:

> In the early weeks of my analysis in 1930 when I was a passionate young idealist in my early 20s, and Anna Freud was...35...[I said to her]...there are so many splinter movements – Jung, Adler, Rank. If you are all searching for the truth about human personality, why can't you work together? Her reply..."Nothing is as important...as the psychoanalytic movement...to keep [psychoanalysis] free of contamination"...her answer offended me. Would she sacrifice the "truth" for the movement? I think her life demonstrates that she would. (Menaker, 1991, p. 607)

Esther's analysis of her analysis with Anna Freud is another example of her personal courage and the independence and pioneering thinking as an analyst. Anna Freud, she wrote, was her father's daughter, having never separated and individuated from him and became devoted to him and the field which he created, namely psychoanalysis (Menaker, 1989). Esther felt Anna Freud gave up her own personal and erotic life for her father. Esther felt this was difficult for her as an analysand because:

> [as] a recently married young woman...who needed to feel in her analyst an understanding of erotic feelings and the adjustments that are required in the context of sexual interactions. Anna provided almost none of this. Instead she came across as an ascetic, virtuous, and conscientious schoolgirl..., but asexual. I had to project onto her person fantasies of a sex life in which I could scarcely believe. (Menaker, 1991, pp. 608–609)

What is more, Esther reported their analytic relationship:

> [was] not about feelings, not about human relationships, but [about] the mechanics, of a traditional analytic process...Anna Freud did not help me to mature as a person; she did not help to make human relationships easier and more joyful for me. (Menaker, 1991, p. 610)

Esther Menaker was a witness to the Sigmund and Anna Freud analysis. Her analysis by Anna Freud demonstrated the flaws in a parent analyzing the child. According to Esther, Sigmund Freud's assessment of his analysis of his daughter: "I succeeded well" (Weiss, 1970, p. 81) was flawed. His daughter lacked the capacity to provide Esther Menaker the emotional and relationship capacities she needed to work through childhood neurosis. Their analysis had a barrenness that, I believe, reflected Freud's analysis of his daughter. Sigmund was unaware that his daughter, Anna, needed to analyze her unconscious and real feelings to him in the area of dependency, sexuality, individuation/separation, and seduction.

Esther's powerful assessment of the shortcomings in her analysis by Anna Freud and her insightful analysis of Sigmund Freud's "emotional blindness" to the difficulties he caused his daughter in taking her on as an analysand have helped me to formulate my own assessment of its importance for understanding the neglect of actual sexual trauma in theoretical and clinical psychoanalysis.

Why Freud did not send his daughter, Anna, to Ferenczi for an analysis?

The most puzzling issue in the analysis of Anna Freud, is why Freud did not send her for an analysis to his favorite pupil, Sándor Ferenczi? Freud analyzed Anna in the years of 1921–1924. During this period, Freud and Ferenczi were at the height of the positive experience in their relationship. There was no dissidence in Ferenczi's theoretical or clinical behavior. Anna Freud liked Ferenczi, and he had positive feelings about her. A father interested in their child's emotional/interpersonal welfare, could naturally send their daughter to an esteemed colleague, who had an international reputation for being an outstanding clinician.

Traveling to Budapest from its sister city Vienna was commonplace for travelers. Therefore, Anna Freud could easily go from Vienna to see Ferenczi in Budapest. Ferenczi would have been a good choice as an analyst for Anna. His focus on empathic understanding, his warmth and tenderness, and his understanding of Freud would have been helpful to analyzing Anna. The fact that Freud did not seem to consider referring Anna to another analyst suggests he felt he wanted to be her analyst. Did he feel he was the only one who could properly analyze her? Or, did he not want anyone else to influence her? Ferenczi, for example, established very meaningful relationships with analysands.

Chapter 5

Sándor Ferenczi's Confusion of Tongues paradigm: introduction of trauma theory and trauma analysis

The Confusion of Tongues theory of childhood seduction

The issue of child seduction returned to psychoanalytic attention in the form of Ferenczi's "Confusion of Tongues" paper, delivered in 1932, at the 12th International Psychoanalytic Congress at Wiesbaden (Ferenczi, 1933) (see Figure 0.4). The Confusion of Tongues paper could have ushered in a new era in psychoanalysis. But, it caused such an enormous controversy that the message it conveyed was lost in the battle to deliver and publish it. In actuality, the controversy surrounding the Confusion of Tongues paper constitutes one of the darkest moments in the history of psychoanalysis. But, more of this controversy after we hear what frightened and so angered Freud that he refused to shake Ferenczi's hand and turned his back on his on his one "favorite son," at their last meeting (Fromm, 1959).

Ironically, Ferenczi presented new evidence that encouraged him to reconsider Freud's original seduction hypothesis:

> I obtained above all new corroborative evidence for my supposition that the trauma, especially the sexual trauma, as the pathogenic factor cannot be valued highly enough. Even children of very respectable, sincerely puritanical families fall victim to real violence or rape much more often than one had dared to suppose. Either, it is the parents who try to find a substitute gratification in this pathological way for their frustration, or it is people thought to be trustworthy such as relatives (uncles, aunts, grandparents, governesses or servants), who misuse the ignorance and the innocence of the child. (Ferenczi, 1933, p. 161)

DOI: 10.4324/9780429298431-5

Ferenczi's Confusion of Tongues   41

Figure 0.4 Ferenczi's Confusion of Tongues Presentation, September 4, 1932. Collage by Arnold Wm. Rachman.

What is more, Ferenczi challenged the traditional notion, found both in Freudian psychoanalysis and in the lay public that the report of sexual abuse is the fantasy of the child, and therefore, is unreliable:

> The immediate explanation that these are only sexual fantasies of the child, a kind of hysterical lying – is unfortunately made invalid by the number of such confessions, e.g., of assaults upon children, committed by parents actually in analysis. (Ferenczi, 1933, p. 161)

The Confusion of Tongues Theory is my expansion of Ferenczi's Confusion of Tongues paradigm into a theory of a relational-based trauma. It is an elaboration of the interpersonal/ relational dimension of the family drama, based on the real experiences between parents and children, not solely on the child's intrapsychic developmentally driven fantasy life. As such it was an alternative to the Oedipal Tragedy. This relational version encourages the clinician to examine the nature of the object relations between family members, acknowledge the actual trauma, help individuals to differentiate their pathologies from the caretakers, and develop strategies to recover from the interpersonal damage of abusive relationships (Rachman, 1994, 2000, 2003, 2014, 2015, 2016, 2018; Rachman & Mattick, 2012). By referring to the parent/child experience where seduction and trauma predominate, one can outline this theoretical framework.

The parent, usually the father, misinterprets the natural need for affection and relatedness by his child, usually the daughter, as lust, which is his own projection onto the child. This does not mean the child does not have sexual feelings. There is a phase appropriate element of sexuality and sensuality embedded within the overall, total parent/child interaction. But the overtly sexual interaction must be kept at the level of fantasy. When the parent, under the pressure of his/her own unhealthy narcissistic and inappropriate needs, distorts the total motivation of the child, reducing it to a predominately sexual, erotic one, the stage is set for pathological incestuous, acting out with the child.

The parent confuses the natural phase appropriate longing for tenderness, sensuality, affection, and attachment-oriented play by the child for erotic sexuality, thereby, reducing the complexity of normal attachment striving for merely one of its components. In object relations terms, the parent initiates a part-object relationship, and uses the child as a discharge object rather than as a whole object, in which the capacity for sublimation and concern predominates.

The child's sense of reality can be seriously altered in such an interaction with an adult, where the adult exercises status, power, and control over the child. Ferenczi first emphasized the sexual seduction of the child and mentioned the parental unresponsiveness to the child's needs (Ferenczi, 1933). Balint extended Ferenczi's ideas of trauma elaborating the nature of trauma in nonsexual experiences (Balint, 1968). What is more, the parent is emotionally unavailable to help the child understand what has happened to him/her. This is especially true when the adult denies the reality of the seduction experience or the unresponsiveness, attempting to convince the child that a different experience has taken place. In the case of sexual seduction, the parent attempts to convince the child that a loving experience has occurred. In the case of emotional unresponsiveness, neglect or abuse, the child also feels abandoned and at the mercy of his/her own feelings, without parental acknowledgement that a disturbing experience has occurred. The parental seducer can seriously influence the child's sense of reality, because the child's reality testing is still in the process of developing. A child's sense of reality can easily be destabilized when trauma and associated reactive fantasies intrude. Fantasies that occur as a reaction to real trauma are distinguished from the traditional (Freudian) notion that there are innate sexual fantasies caused by innate drives. The child is developmentally inclined to believe the parent's presentation of reality because acceptance of parental authority is associated with love, protection, and object attachment. Seduction fosters a profound sense of betrayal, not in just the perception of the parent, but in the capacity to perceive reality accurately. This, then engenders a serious difficulty in trusting one's perceptions and feelings.

The child becomes confused about the reality of his/her experience. What is more, a child can actually deny his/her subjective experience while adapting to the parent's distorted reality. The child is then left in a confused state, which, once dissociated, remains essentially the same. Because the sexual experience is traumatic the child splits off the traumatic experience, including the image of him/herself at the time as a victimized, helpless, overwhelmed, frightened, angry, and confused individual (Bollas, 1987; Modell, 1990; Searles, 1986). Once repressed, this dissociated state fails to change (it remains unconsciously timeless), becomes semi-autonomous, and continues to influence the adult personality, unconsciously. It thereby exerts an ego-weakening, disruptive effect on healthy adult functioning, especially in the area of mature object relations.

Beside the alteration of reality, parental authority also prevents the child from talking about his/her sense of confusion. The child is confused, realizing at some level that his/her experience is derived from the parent's, but they cannot give voice to this difference, since it is associated with the danger of loss of parental love, retaliation, and abandonment. In essence, *the child becomes tongue-tied*, but literally and figuratively. This further compounded by the fact that the child actually needs the parent's help to understand and verbalize what has happened to her or him. This requires truthful explanations given in the context of emotional support, something which the abusive parent is quite unable to do (Ferenczi, 1928, 1933; Rachman, 1991, 1993, 2000, 2003). Emotional support cannot come from a parent who is narcissistically intruding his/her needs onto a child and is hence insensitive to the child's needs. Because the child is not helped to understand and verbalize the effects of the seduction, a pathological split-off nucleus (of traumatic affect, self-image, relationship interaction) develops and becomes the basis for later psychopathology by arresting and distorting moral development. This effects all subsequent developmental stages and tasks, including the ego function of drive regulation, reality testing, self and affect regulation, and object relations during each stage.

The major defenses that Ferenczi described that enable the child to cope with the actual sexual seduction are: splitting, dissociation, denial, detachment, blunted affect, confusion and identification with aggressor (Ferenczi, 1933). Identification with the aggressor (IWA), a mechanism first mentioned by Ferenczi in 1933 in his Confusion of Tongues paper (p. 162), is ironically interwoven with Anna Freud's life, both professionally and personally. This defense mechanism has been attributed to Anna Freud having supposedly been introduced in her book *The Ego and The Mechanisms of Defense* (A. Freud, 1936). Masson (1984), was first to point out that Ferenczi's mention of this defense mechanism at The Wiesbaden Conference in 1932, predates Anna Freud's mention of it, 4 years later in 1936. What is more, Anna Freud was the secretary of the IPA during that conference and was therefore, obligated to take some form of notes to report on the proceedings, which she did in the *International* in 1933 (A. Freud, 1933). Anna Freud, therefore, heard Ferenczi speaking about identification with the aggressor and probably took notes on his Confusion of Tongues. In presenting this paper, was Ferenczi trying to send a message to Freud and Freud's daughter about the relationship between parental/child seduction? Was Ferenczi trying to communicate to Anna about the Confusion of Tongues experience in her relationship with her father? What is very interesting about Ferenczi's message to the analytic community that day, was that Anna presumably heard, retained and integrated a particular portion of the Confusion of Tongues Theory. Anna, without acknowledging it directly, was captivated by the notion of identification with the aggressor. She unconsciously adapted this concept, making it an integral part of her theory of ego functioning and the manner of dealing with anxiety. So one could speculate, that Ferenczi was successful in reaching the daughter, in a way he could not influence the father.

For those of us, who work with the incest trauma, identification with the aggressor has particular significance. It is a complicated mechanism that can help explain the masochistic bond that develops in an abusive situation:

> The child, instead of "rebelling" or rejecting the hated and abusive object, psychologically attaches itself to the parental seducer. It is a desperate but effective way to gain, or continue, an "affectionate" tie with the parent, maintaining the fiction (delusion, if you wish), that the seduction is an act of tenderness. By introjecting the bad object, the child attempts to master the trauma by becoming the oppressor. (Rachman, 1994, p. 243)

The attempt to suppress and censor the Confusion of Tongues

Freud's intensely negative and judgmental reaction to the Confusion of Tongues paper bears examination. The reaction to the Wiesbaden presentation was uniformly negative by Freud and the traditional analytic community for some other very important reasons as well: (1) Ferenczi suggested that members of the middle and upper class families were guilty of incest; (2) he verified that parents in respectable families were regularly molesting their children; (3) by implication, the audience who heard Ferenczi's paper, who were upper middle class males were akin to those fathers in his clinical studies who molested their daughters; (4) Ferenczi's clinical findings on sexual trauma could also be applied to the few women analysts who attended the Confusion of Tongues presentation. By implication, were these the daughters who were molested by their fathers?; (5) Ferenczi's notion of retraumatization in the psychoanalytic situation due to coldness, detachment, unresponsiveness, and clinical hypocrisy must have been perceived as an attack on Freud and the classical method, rather than as a step toward the evolution of a two-person psychology and empathic method; (6) did Anna and the audience of male analysts hear Ferenczi indict not only themselves, but also what was worse, Sigmund Freud?; and (7) Did Ferenczi's frank and compassionate plea for the understanding of the dilemma of the molested child stimulate an unconscious chord in the analytic gathering? Did they reject his ideas, so that they could protect their denial system regarding their professional and personal issues regarding seduction?

Freud's decision to suppress Ferenczi's theory was a complicated and overdetermined reaction. Among the plausible explanations for censorship are: (1) Freud's desire to protect his Oedipal explanation of neurosis as the cornerstone for psychoanalytic theory (Masson, 1984); (2) Freud's *mistaken conclusion* that Ferenczi's Trauma Analysis and Confusion of Tongues paradigm were born of regressive thinking psychopathology rather than creativity (Rachman, 2018); (3) Freud's anxiety that Ferenczi's dissidence signaled his desire to reject him and leave mainstream psychoanalysis as Jung and Rank had done (Gay, 1988); (4) Freud's denial that sexual seduction was a relevant clinical variable in his own life (Rachman, 2016); (see Chapter 3); (5) Freud's disdain for the more disturbed patients who needed empathic rather than interpretive interaction (Ferenczi, 1933); (6) Freud's clinical practice and philosophy of therapy sufficiently differed from Ferenczi (Roazen, 1975). Freud, during the period of the Confusion of Tongues paper, was involved in many training analyses of individuals who wanted to become psychoanalysts while Ferenczi was analyzing incest survivors. Freud, although he was more clinically flexible than is generally known (Roazen, 1975), did believe in psychoanalysis as a treatment for neurosis. Ferenczi, on the other hand was extending the boundaries of clinical psychoanalysis to include pregenital disorders (narcissistic, borderline, and psychotic disorders).

Freud's abandonment of the seduction theory and the development of the Oedipal theory served some very important functions: (1) it shifted the focus of a sexual act to a sexual wish or fantasy. (2) It described the sexual experience as an intrapsychic event, not an interpersonal occurrence. (3) At issue was the child's sexuality, not the parent's sexuality. (4) It removed any idea that the sexuality was occurring in a disturbed object relationship where parents were mistreating (abusing) their children. This not only served a theoretical function, but also, perhaps, a personal one. Freud could maintain the continued denial that childhood seduction had not played a role in his own life (Rachman, 2016a). (5) The issue of parental/child sexuality became a developmentally appropriate phase in personality development. There was no need to search for parental responsibility.

Implications for the abandonment of the seduction theory

The Freudian dynamic of child abuse was very different from the Ferenczian Confusion of Tongues dynamic. There have been attempts to examine the Zeitgeist in Europe, and in Vienna in particular, which can shed light on the issue of childhood abuse during Freud's training as a physician and during his formative years of clinical practice. Masson has chronicled the incidence of child abuse and child murder to which Freud was exposed during his period of training with Charcot (Masson, 1984). In fact, Freud participated in autopsies of child abuse victims. Recent meticulous research in German archives has shown that Freud was a pediatrician for a 10 year period, from 1886 to 1896, where he was responsible for the department for nervous diseases at the "Public Institute for Children's Diseases" in Vienna, directed by Max Kassowitz (Bonomi, 1994). For this 10-year period, he worked with hysterical children 3 days a week. As Bonomi has stated:

> There are very few studies on the beginnings of psychoanalysis which mention it [Freud's pediatric activity], and no study which includes Freud's specific training on infantile nervous disturbances as a relevant part of his general training. This attitude is closely related to Freud's tendency to cancel the traces of his first medical involvement with hysterical children from his autobiography. (Bonomi, 1994, p. 56)

In a fascinating study, a historian has researched the incidence of reported child abuse, at the Fin-de-Siècle in Freud's Vienna (Wolff, 1988). Child abuse was very prevalent in Freud's Vienna, and chronicled in the daily newspaper. There were four sensational cases of child battering and murder at the turn of the century in Vienna, which dominated the newspapers and caused dramatics in the courtroom trains about it. These child abuse sensations of 1899 were not commented on by Freud, whose great intellectual spirit, dominated the landscape of Fin-de-Siècle Vienna.

Of particular importance, in my opinion, was that the child abuse cases of 1899 did not seem to have any influence on his first case study, the analysis of Dora, undertaken about 1902, three years later (Freud, 1905). In Dora, we have an adolescent, the victim of an attempted molestation by Herr K., an adult old enough to be her father. In a letter to Wilhelm Fleiss dated October 14, 1900, Freud announced he had found the ideal case (The Dora Case) to demonstrate the efficacy of his Oedipal theory:

> I have a new patient, girl of eighteen; the case has opened smoothly to my collection of picklocks. (Freud, 1954, p. 325)

Paul Mattick and I have re-analyzed the Dora case from the vantage point of the Confusion of Tongues Theory (Rachman and Mattick, 2002). We have found several passages that indicated that material relevant to child molestation was overlooked, deemed irrelevant, or interpreted as Oedipal data:

1. Dora's relationship with her mother was very disturbed, but no analysis of the significant object relationship was included, or was any investigation made of possible parental abuse.
2. The negative feelings for the mother was treated as Oedipal jealousy, and no thought was given to any real trauma in their object relationship.
3. Freud's presentation of the case was used to demonstrate the efficacy of the Oedipal Complex. Clinically, it ignored an attempt at molestation by Herr K. In fact, this incident is used to demonstrate Dora's sexual difficulty. Freud was incredulous that Dora was repelled by Herr K's attempt to kiss and embrace her?
4. In a classic example of a Confusion of Tongues dilemma, Freud interpreted Dora's negative reaction to Herr K's attempt at seduction as her aversion to her Oedipal longings for her

father. Eventually, Freud interpreted Dora's symptomatology as manifestation of her unresolved Oedipal wishes for her father, Herr K, and her analyst.

5. At no point, in the Dora essay is any investigation or comment made about the imprudent assault by Herr K, as being an example of sexual seduction or abuse. Freud actually thought Dora should have been grateful that Herr K was interested in her.

6. Ten years after analyzing Dora, Freud's Schreber Case was another dramatic example of ignoring or denying child abuse as a causal factor in psychological disorder. Schreber's father was a so-called pedagogue, who developed child-rearing devices that were tantamount to child abuse (Lothane, 1992). Freud was only interested in the case as a matter of paranoid delusion.

7. The Oedipal theory then has children seducing their parents, into some form of abuse, physical or sexual, but not parents actually seducing children.

Freud coined the term, affectionate abuse, which indicated at the very least his ambivalence about actual abuse. In the case of the Wolf Man he said:

> My patient's father had the characteristics, shown by so many people in relation to their children, of indulging in "affectionate abuse"; and it is possible that during the patient's earlier years his father (though he grew severe later on) he may, more than once, as he caressed the little boy or played with him, have threatened in fun to "gobble him up." (Wolff, 1988, p. 212)

As I have described in a recent evaluation of the Wolf Man/Sergei Pankejeff, I have suggested he was an incest survivor (Rachman, 2018). What is more, there is some evidence which details he was anally raped by a nursemaid (Rachman, 2019a).

Freud's abandonment of the seduction theory has had a profound effect on the evolution of psychoanalysis (Rachman, 1991, 1997b). The suppression of Ferenczi's work, and his ideas and technical innovations was so successful, that the study of his work was virtually stopped for over 50 years. In particular, the absence of Ferenczi's work also meant that the study of the incest trauma virtually disappeared from psychoanalysis. There are critics who called Masson's attempt to re-introduce the seduction theory in valuing Ferenczi's Confusion of Tongues perspective as an outmoded and inadequate formulation. But, Ferenczi's reformulation of the Seduction Theory was more than adequate, it was prophetic. He originated the development of a new field of study, Trauma Disorder, and a new form of treatment, Trauma Analysis (Rachman, 2018). In a recent survey of my clinical practice, I found more than 40% of analysands had a history of childhood sexual abuse. What is more, recent research and clinical findings indicate a growing body of sexual abuse data (Alpert, 1995; Frawley & Davies, 1994; Shengold, 1989; Van der Kolk, McFarlane & Weisaeth, 1996). Analysts coming to terms with the issue of sexual abuse involves its appearances and disappearances within this history of psychoanalysis.

Chapter 6

Sándor Ferenczi's iconic case of Elizabeth Severn: development of the study and analysis of trauma

Case studies and the evolution of psychoanalysis

Changes in theory and techniques in the history of psychoanalysis can be viewed from the perspective of Great Case Studies. Freud's Great Case Studies are always used to illustrate his contributions. The Case of Anna O (Berta Pappenheim) began the talking cure for neurosis (Breuer & Freud, 1895), the Case of Dora (Freud, 1905) was used to demonstrate the Oedipal explanations for neurosis, and the Case of the Wolf Man (Freud, 1919 [1918]) has been used to illustrate the study of depression and illuminating the psychosexual stages of development. Carl Gustav Jung, the Swiss psychiatrist, who was an original partner of Freud and later found his own form of psycho-analysis called analytic psychology, reported on a case, which is famous and infamous at the same time. Sabina Spielrein, Jung's first analysand, has been used as an illustration of the analytic treatment of severe emotional disturbance as well as an example of the pitfalls of intimate relationship between analyst and analysand (Bettleheim, 1990; Kerr, 1994). D.W. Winnicott, the British analyst who is one of the founders of British Object Relations and a leading figure in the Independent Group at the British Psychoanalytic Society, had a series of important case studies, one of which was the analysis of Margaret Little, herself an analyst (Little, 1990). There have been other Great Cases in the history of Pscyhoanalysis and Psychotherapy which have defined an era. The Case of Ellen West (Binswanger, 1958) is considered the iconic case of existential analysis and one of the most famous cases in modern psychiatry (May, Angel

DOI: 10.4324/9780429298431-6

& Ellenberger, 1958). Heinz Kohut reported on the Case of Miss F. (Kohut, 1971), which is considered to be the paradigm case of self-psychology.

Ferenczi's iconic case study

Ferenczi's Case of R.N. was first outlined in his *Clinical Diary*, first published in English in 1988, although it was written in the year of 1932–1933 (Rachman, 1997a). This delay contributed to psychoanalysis neglecting sexual trauma, since there was a 55-year silence about the case and its importance for introducing Trauma Analysis into psychoanalysis. Masson (1984) identified R. N. as Elizabeth Severn. Her life was first researched by Christopher Fortune (1993, 1996).

In the recent years, I have been able to obtain *The Elizabeth Papers*, which are her professional and personal items that she left to her daughter, Margaret (Rachman, 2016b). In discussing these materials I want to convey to you the relationship between an emotionally disturbed American psychotherapist and a Hungarian psychoanalysis who had the emotional courage to accept her for treatment and to sustain an analysis with, "the most difficult of all difficult *cases.*" In the last years of Ferenczi's clinical career, he agreed to accept for psychoanalysis, Mrs. Elizabeth Severn, a psychotherapist from the United States (see Figure 0.5). From the fall of 1925 until February 1933, shortly before Ferenczi's death from pernicious anemia in May 1933, Severn and Ferenczi collaborated on an analytic enterprise that was to change the face of psychoanalysis. The Ferenczi/Severn analysis is a historical example of the struggles to help an individual with severe emotional, physical, and sexual traumas (Rachman, 2018). What was so important about the analysis was that it contained significant pioneering advances for psychoanalysis: (1) it was the first attempt to conduct a formal analysis of a Trauma Disorder; (2) it was the first collaborative effort in an analysis, where analyst and analysand contributed their ideas and clinical suggestions to enhance the analytic encounter; (3) it was an analysis that expanded the boundaries of analytic technique by relying on noninterpretative measures to conduct the clinical encounter; (4) it formulated a new clinical concept, Clinical Empathy and Trauma Analysis; and (5) it set the stage for the origins of a Relational Perspective in psychoanalysis.

Ferenczi's iconic case of Elizabeth Severn 53

Photograph - "Mrs. Elizabeth Severn During the Time She was in Analysis with Sándor Ferenczi"

Figure 0.5 Mrs. Elizabeth Severn photography during the time she was in analysis with Sándor Ferenczi © from the Estate of Elizabeth. Arnold Wm. Rachman, Ph.D. Literary Executor.

The first formal analysis of the incest trauma and trauma disorder

Elizabeth Severn was a seriously disturbed individual who had a history of severe and multiple childhood traumas (Ferenczi, 1988). In contemporary terms, she would be diagnosed as a severe borderline or

Photograph - "Dr. Sándor Ferenczi, Budapest, Hungary, August, 1926

Figure 0.6 Dr. Sandore Ferenczi. Photograph, Budapest, Hungary, August 1926 © from The Estate of Elizabeth Severn, Arnold Wm. Rachman, PhD, Literary Executor.

psychotic-like disorder. Ferenczi used a variation on the term, schizophrenia, to refer to her condition. Prior to seeking out Ferenczi, she had been in therapy for most of her adult life, with little success. After a consultation with Otto Rank, a collaborator of Ferenczi's and author of the birth trauma (Ferenczi & Rank, 1925), Severn was convinced that Ferenczi was her only hope for change, when she moved to Budapest to begin an 8-year analysis with him (see Figure 0.6, p. 54).

Ferenczi knew, from the beginning of the clinical interaction, that this was to be *the most difficult of his difficult cases*. What were these difficulties? Ferenczi had an initial negative reaction to Severn. He though she had masculine qualities, was aggressive, very self-assured, and told him how to treat her. He admitted he had difficulty empathizing with her when they began (Rachman, 2018). Severn's childhood traumas were severe: she was incested by her father; he tried to poison her; he threw her out of the house; and he emotionally and physically abused her. All her life, she suffered from severe depression, suicidal thoughts, and was hospitalized on several occasions. As serious as her disturbance was, Severn had many positive attributes: she was intelligent; she had privately studied different forms of counseling and therapy and became a successful therapist; and she developed positive parts of her personality, which Ferenczi recognized and affirmed. As disturbed as Severn may have been, she had enough positive resources to make a contribution to their analysis.

Their analysis was focused on retrieving and analyzing Severn's traumas. Ferenczi called this "Trauma-Analysis" (Ferenczi, 1988). The idea was that trauma was a real occurrence in an interpersonal relationship within a family and between individuals and needed to be analyzed. Trauma was the origin of a psychological disorder and could be analyzed. Besides the traditional means of analytic interaction such as analysis of resistance, dreams, fantasies, and transference, Severn and Ferenczi introduced new clinical interactions. For example, Severn would enter into a "trance-like state" during their sessions. Her intention was to deliberately alter her consciousness, so that she could retrieve the memory of her childhood trauma (Severn, 1916). Balint would later term this idea, therapeutic regression (Balint, 1968). Neither Ferenczi, nor any other analyst of his time had seen such behavior from an analysand. He became frightened and frantically began to make interpretations to force Severn to come out of her trance-like state. What happened next was amazing and, I believe, demonstrated the unique qualities of Severn, and the special relationship she formed with Ferenczi, which produced a new form of therapy. Severn became annoyed at Ferenczi for interfering with her idea of how to deal with her trauma. As he continued to interpret her silence, she actually told Ferenczi to, "shut up." At first, Ferenczi was shocked. To his credit, he analyzed his reaction. After a period of reflection, he was able to integrate Severn's new methodology into their analysis. In essence, he stopped interpreting, listened to her, and became an empathic presence (Rachman, 2018).

Another unusual and remarkable set of interactions centered on the enactment of Severn's trauma within the psychoanalytic situation. This set of interactions is now considered to be examples of countertransference analysis and co-created mutual analytic interactions. Toward the later part of their analysis, Severn accused Ferenczi of hating women, and what is more, she said his hatred for her was interfering with their analysis. Ferenczi had created an empathic atmosphere where an analysand could express her clinical assessment of her analyst. With trepidation, Ferenczi entertained Severn's diagnosis of hating women. What is more, Ferenczi adopted some ideas from Severn. During a series of sessions, when Severn became the analyst and *Ferenczi, the analysand, he went back into his childhood and retrieved a childhood memory of his own sexual abuse.* First, he used Severn's method (Severn, 1916) by concentrating on his childhood experiences. He retrieved a childhood sexual abuse by a nursemaid through a dream sequence. He remembered that as a young boy, the nursemaid rubbed him into her genital area. Ferenczi had the emotional courage and the desire to help Severn that he was willing to let Severn analyze him, until he found the genetic source of his hatred toward women. He was able to trace the origin of his negative feelings to his mother. The collaborative analytic method with Severn produced positive results. The untraceable resistance in the Ferenczi/Severn was lessened, so that the analysis could return to the focus on Severn's trauma.

Although Ferenczi's collaboration with Severn has come under criticism by the members of the original analytic community, such as, Freud, Jones, Ettingon, Joan Riviere (Masson, 1984), as well as a contemporary analyst (Maroda, 1992). In addition, there are contemporary analysts who believe mutuality is the forerunner for a two-person psychology for psychoanalysis and broadens the scope of countertransference analysis (Aron & Harris, 1993; Rachman, 2018).

The fact that Ferenczi was able to retrieve his own childhood sexual trauma and was able to trace its genetic origin indicates how meaningful a therapeutic encounter Ferenczi and Severn could develop. I believe, that Ferenczi was able to develop the Confusion of

Tongues paradigm for understanding the incest trauma because he could confront and integrate his own incest trauma. This separated Ferenczi from Freud, who was not able to integrate his childhood trauma and never allowed anyone to help him although Jung and Ferenczi offered to do so (Rachman, 1997a).

When Severn left Budapest she went to London to live with her daughter, Margaret. Her daughter was a famous American modern dancer. With the help of her daughter, and her expressed need to separate from Ferenczi (Eissler, 1954), Severn began her recovery. She lived with her daughter for about 3 years. Severn resumed her clinical practice, but, this time she began calling herself a psychoanalyst. After all, Ferenczi referred to her as his colleague and "Dr. Severn" (Rachman, 2018). What is more, in those pioneering days of psychoanalysis, having analysis with a senior analyst, and discussing ideas and techniques, which Ferenczi and Severn did on a regular basis, was the informal way analytic training began. Freud's daughter, Anna, was a prime example of this early approach. As discussed, Anna did not have any degrees and her analytic training consisted of her clandestine analysis with her father (see Chapter 3). Severn was a therapist before she began her analysis with Ferenczi, using her own brand of American pragmatism, spirituality, and Christian Science to develop a therapeutic approach, which she chronicled in three books (Severn, 1914, 1920, 1933). Her analysis with Ferenczi therefore had a profound effect on her, both personally and professionally. Her last book written about a year after her analysis, integrated the psychoanalytic ideas that she and Ferenczi had shared (Severn, 1922). In fact, Severn's last book can be viewed as a joint collaboration. If we combine Ferenczi's *Clinical Diary* with Severn's *Discovery of the Self* we have the first analytic view of the importance of trauma from the analyst and analysand's perspective.

After London, Severn settled in New York City and conducted a successful practice at Park Avenue and 87th Street until her death in 1959 (Rachman, 2018). On Sunday afternoons, Severn would entertain colleagues and friends for afternoon tea. An eyewitness to this Sunday afternoon teas, Maria Lysova, told me, the mother/daughter relationship was characterized as being "too close...the mother being dominant" (Lysova, in Rachman, 2016). Other evidence as to the closeness of mother/daughter are the letters exchanged between the two over a period of 17 years (Rachman, 2018). Margaret Severn wrote her mother letters during that time period, sometimes every day, while she was on tour as a modern dancer. The Severns seemed to share every thought, feeling, and behavior experienced. Their continued love-bond was also an indication that her analytic relationship with Ferenczi aided her emotionally.

Signs that Severn was able to reduce the deleterious effects of her childhood incest traumas as well as the retraumatization with Ferenczi due to the premature termination of the analysis, was indicated in her return to work as a therapist, publishing of a significant book on trauma analysis, and enjoying affectionate relationships with her daughter, colleagues, and friends. I would like to add two additional indicators. As far as can be determined, Elizabeth Severn never again suffered from the same kind of severe psychopathology that she showed before the analysis with Ferenczi. In addition, she was never hospitalized for emotional disorder again.

I have reviewed an interview which the late Kurt Eissler, MD, conducted with Elizabeth Severn (Eissler, 1954). At first, the interview was sequestered at the Library of Congress. After several attempts, I was able to convince the former Secretary of the Freud Archives to lift the ban on reproducing this interview. I found this document to be remarkable. My impression of this interview was that Severn showed herself to be a well-functioning, perfectly rational, thoughtful analyst. She was Eissler's equal in their interaction. She had very positive feelings about Ferenczi:

1. Severn was intelligent, articulate, and emotionally engaged during the entire interview.
2. She expressed positive feelings about Freud and Ferenczi.
3. She visited Freud on two occasions for a consultation. She found Freud to be rigid in his ideas and clinical behavior. She felt his ideas were too conservative for dealing with trauma. When she shared her feelings about her analysis with Ferenczi, Freud had only praise for his "most cherished" student. She visited Freud during the middle phase of the analysis, roughly 1928–1930. This would be before the more intense last phase characterized by the therapeutic regression and the reliving of the childhood traumas. Once Freud knew more about the analysis and was negatively influenced by Clara

Thompson's spreading a rumor that she had erotic contact with Ferenczi, he became condemning (Rachman, 2018).

4. Severn bore no ill will toward Ferenczi. She did not feel the experience with Ferenczi was a failed analysis.

5. Severn was the intellectual, emotional, and interpersonal equal to Eissler. It was clear to me, that his questioning of her was aimed at flushing out any improprieties between Ferenczi and Severn in their clinical interaction. Severn answered his questions without defensiveness, indicating there was no sexual acting out, and no behavior that was a violation of personal or professional ethics. Severn was not intimidated by, or felt subservient to Eissler.

6. Overall, my impression of Severn's functioning was very positive. I was not surprised to see an emotionally disturbed individual being interviewed by the formidable Kurt Eissler, the keeper of the keys of psychoanalytic tradition. Severn came across to me as a well-functioning psychoanalyst who was very thoughtful about psychoanalytic theory and technique. Severn was very open about her analysis. She agreed that she needed to emotionally separate from Ferenczi. Apparently, their trauma–analysis interactions, especially, the collaborative interactions when they were analyzing each other was difficult. Although Severn insisted on Ferenczi analyzing his negative feelings toward her and he reluctantly agreed to do so, it took its toll. It suggests that although collaborative efforts between analyst and analysand can be helpful, the emotional space between the therapeutic duo must be appropriately maintained to protect the vulnerability of the analysand.

The new data of *The Elizabeth Severn Papers* (Rachman, 2016) and the Severn/Eissler interview (Eissler, 1954) was not available 20 years ago, when the Ferenczi/Severn analysis was first published in English in 1988 (Ferenczi, 1988). In introducing these new data, I am trying to add in the reassessment of the Ferenczi/Severn analysis. We need to challenge the established idea that the Ferenczi/Severn was a failure and violated clinical boundaries. It remains an unappreciated iconic case of psychoanalysis:

1. I agree with Balin's assessment, which he made in 1968, that Severn improved but was not cured (Balint, 1968). But, what is cure in the

analysis of a severely traumatized individual? Or, better yet, should we talk about cure in psychoanalysis? I do not believe I was cured in my analysis, which I consider very successful. I do believe that I was helped. In the same way, I believe Severn was helped by her analysis with Ferenczi. I however, do not believe Ferenczi was cured in his analysis by Freud. The analysis was a "partial analysis," not only because of the limited period of the analysis, but also, more importantly, Ferenczi's childhood sexual trauma was unanalyzed.

2. Severn was able to retrieve and confront her childhood traumas. What is more, in collaboration with Ferenczi, she helped develop pioneering ideas and methods to deal with trauma, including an important book, *The Discovery of the Self* (Severn, 1933), which in combination with Ferenczi's *Clinical Diary* (Ferenczi, 1988), constitutes the first psychoanalytic perspective on trauma.

3. Severn recovered from the malignant regression she suffered when Ferenczi could not finish the analysis due to his ill health and subsequent death. Her recovery was due to a combination of the positive effects of the analysis and her own positive resources and her relationship with her daughter, Margaret.

4. Severn's life after Ferenczi, from 1933 until 1958, was a period of productivity and positive mental health. For that 25-year period, she practiced psychoanalysis, gave lectures, and wrote articles and books. Her papers contain testimonials to her practice and her writings from individuals who benefitted from her functioning (Rachman, 2016).

5. Severn appeared to enjoy meaningful relationships with her analysands, her daughter, colleagues, and friends. She initiated contact with Freud to better understand her analysis and the theory of psychoanalysis. Each week, during the years she practiced in New York City, she would invite colleagues and friends to her apartment for social interaction. The evidence suggests that Severn led a life of work and love (Rachman, 2018).

Changes in the structure and function of the analytic encounter

By the 1920s, Freud's theoretical and clinical contributions established the standard psychoanalytic technique. With the establishment of the Oedipal Complex Theory of neurosis, the analytic encounter was defined by several dimensions.

> The analysand is asked to assume, "the analytic position". The analyst primary structural dimension is the "analytic couch", which was originally defined by Freud's couch and his chair positioned to the side of the couch. The analytic couch was a Victorian-era chaise lounge or Fainting Couch (Hunt, 2016). These pieces of furniture have one end of the couch raised used as a head rest. These couches were used by women in the nineteenth century because of two speculative reasons: (1) Women wore such tight corsets, which restricted blood and oxygen flow, that caused dizziness or fainting. The couches were easily available for lying down and resting during a fainting spell; (2) These couches were used in the home to treat female "hysteria" through manual pelvic massage by home doctors and midwives (Maines, 1999). As the type of message could be a long procedure, a casual, comfortable couch would be most suitable for this purpose.

Female hysteria was a common diagnosis during Freud's time, but the diagnosis was dropped by the American Psychiatric Association in 1952. Originally, this medical diagnosis of women involved the following symptoms: anxiety, shortness of breath, fainting, nervousness, sexual desire, insomnia, fluid retention, heaviness in the abdomen, irritability, loss of appetite for food or sex, sexually forward behavior, and difficulty in relations with others (Maines, 1999). Freud's important contribution to the issue of female "hysteria," of course, was that it was not a physical disorder, but was an emotional one caused by previous trauma that lead to not enjoying sex in the normal way (Gilman, King, Porter, Rousseau & Showalter, 1993). Freud's choice of the analytic couch emerged out of his desire to create a relaxed and comfortable emotional and physical atmosphere so that his hysterical patient could concentrate on his/her disturbed emotionality.

The analyst's chair was positioned to the side of the couch, so Freud could be easily heard, but could not be seen. Freud could see his beloved antiques, which were lined up on his desk, which was in his direct view. The analysand's closest view was of an oriental rug that was hung on the wall above the couch. The analytic ambience that was created involved a funneling of the analysand's attention to his/her inner psychological space. Interestingly, Freud's office was filled with objects, books, pictures, furniture. One could experience this as a busy scene, not necessarily an atmosphere to calm one's emotions. But, I think what his couch and office conveys is a warm, comfortable, "homey" atmosphere. After all, Freud did not choose a separate office physically separate from his family's apartment. Whether this choice may have had convenience and financial considerations, the choice enhanced a homey, emotionally friendly experience. I believe Freud had the patient's well-being in mind. It is also true that Freud arranged his office to please himself, to create an analytic ambience, as well as to provide himself with the capacity to feel comfortable in his own surroundings. It has been said, he also did not feel comfortable with patients staring at him all day long.

Toward the third decade of psychoanalysis, it became clear the analytic encounter was created to produce an exercise in silent withholding, tension, emotional distance, and minimal and controlled interaction. As psychoanalysis crossed the Atlantic Ocean, it became the province of physicians where conservative medical attitudes overturned the humanistic attitude of the European Zeitgeist of the Fin-de-Siècle (Rachman, 1997a).

The Balints (Balint & Balint, 1939) had questioned whether the analytic conditions in the structure and functioning in the analyst's consultation room and in his/her behavior really presented a blank screen transference. They suggested that the analyst's personality, manner, and style of relating, the way he/she dressed, and the structure of the office convey a personal image to the analysand, not a blank screen. Consequently, there is no such phenomenon as a blank screen or an emotionally free environment.

American physicians who created a stranglehold on psychoanalysis in the New World, championed the golden-age of silence and interpretation. The analyst's elected silence was intended to produce a nonverbal vacuum, which was filled by forcing the analysand to invert, to fall back on his/her own inner resources. What ardent Freudians did not understand that prolonged silences and lacking an empathic presence produces an experience of coldness and distance (Rachman, 2018). After Ferenczi's attempt to educate psychoanalysis with his formal introduction of clinical empathy into psychoanalysis (Rachman, 1988), Kohut built the Self Psychology perspective on the necessity of empathy in the analytic encounter (Kohut, 1984). First Ferenczi, then Kohut, were convinced that in an analytic relationship, which after all, is a human relationship, it is unnatural and detrimental to create emotional coldness and such interpersonal distance by being "analytic." We now know that in the necessary development of the nourishing relationship between parent and child, prolonged silence and emotional distance is traumatogenic (Beebe, 2005).

It has always fascinated me that traditional psychoanalysis has chosen to maintain silence and interpretation as primary and empathy and responsiveness as secondary interventions. My own training and clinical experience, combined with the previous research cited, leads me in the direction of Ferenczi and Kohut (although Kohut never credited Ferenczi as his progenitor (Rachman, 1989). As I was told in a science class at City College of New York as an undergraduate:

> Do not believe traditions because they are old and handed down through many generations...do not believe...because presumption is in its favor...do not believe anything on the mere authority of teachers... *whatever according to their own experience and after thorough investigation agrees with thy reason and is conducive to their own will and to that of all other living things, that accept as the truth and live so accordingly.* (Gautama Siddhartha Buddha – Rachman, 1997a)

A dramatic professional experience highlighted Buddha's caution regarded orthodoxy in thinking and functioning. A clinical example providing a lasting education on the meaning of silence, emotional distance, and lack of empathy between a mother and child. An adult woman in her 40s presented severe symptoms of disturbed relationships with authority, so that she could not maintain a positive work relationship with any authority. She was frequently fired or left her employment because of heated and contentious interchanges. Only when she founded her own business was she able to become a regular wage earner. In addition, she had difficulty in maintaining positive relationships with men. Inevitably, she would feel abused or expressed intense anger in any discussion of relationship difficulty. She also had severe bouts of depression and loneliness.

The most dramatic expression of psychopathology was evident in her relationship with her mother. Whether in person or on the telephone, most conversations would become opportunities to berate her mother with torrents of anger, criticism, rejection. Hearing her describe the childhood derivations of her anger, hurt, frustration, and loneliness clearly exposed a childhood traumatic mother/child relationship generated by silence and interpersonal distance. In the analysis of this woman's hurt and rage, she recounted a prototypical emotional trauma sequence:

> Her controlling, domineering and obsessive mother would make a demand on her, for example, to go to bed at a certain time. The child, who had a lively natural spirit, could not comply with the early curfew. Subsequently, the mother would first, become angry, then if her daughter continued to disobey by not fulfilling the order to sleep, she would impose serious emotional consequences. The mother's frequent emotional punishment was, *stone cold silence*. The next day, after the night of so-called disobedience, her mother would begin a campaign of silence, which emotionally broke down her daughter's resistance. The mother would emotionally and physically turn away from her daughter. She would not say a word to her, for as long as a week at a time, until her daughter would apologize or tell her mother she would do what she asked of her. The mother would enlist the father in this horrific emotional deprivation by telling him to speak to her daughter on her behalf.

There is no adequate way to convey the disintegration of this woman's spirit and soul by the deliberate withholding of speech and touch by her disturbed mother. As Ferenczi so adequately described, the parent's narcissism took precedent over an empathic understanding of a child's need to be affirmed and appreciated for their differences.

Chapter 7

A pedophile among us?: Ernest Jones's trial for the sexual abuse of mentally defective girls

Psychoanalytical community's view of Jones.

A wise analyst; Sándor Lorand, an analysand and student of Ferenczi, raised an interesting issue that arises in psychoanalytical work. He wrote:

> My friend Betram Lewis many years ago drew my attention to what he considered a major divisive element within the psycho-analytical movement. Inevitably, he felt, dissension and discord arise among those who work with unconscious material for any length of time. (Lorand, 1975–1976, p. 706)

In considering Jones's personal and professional functioning, we need to go beyond an occupational hazard to understand his behavior, especially in relationships with Sándor Ferenczi as well as in the history of psychoanalysis (Lorand, 1975–1976).

We need to thoroughly examine Jones's clinical functioning, in addition to his character and personality to understand his 1906 trial for the sexual abuse of two mentally defective girls.

Carl Jung said the following about Jones:

> Jones is an enigma to me. He is so incomprehensible that it's quite uncanny.. an intellectual liar…Too much adulation on one side, too much opportunism on the other? (McGuire, 1974- Letters from Carl Jung to Sigmund Freud, July 12, 1908)

Jones, the outstanding critic of Ferenczi, and, with Freud one of the founders of the Todschweigen campaign developed against Ferenczi and

DOI: 10.4324/9780429298431-7

Severn, has not received the examination of his functioning, especially, since he has been the leader in attempting to destroy an analytic colleague, his analyst, and a pioneering contributor to psychoanalysis.

Lorand also had interesting things to say about Jones:

> In 1923, for example, my old friend Ernest Jones would find it, "monstrous that personal factors should be pushed into scientific movements like ours". Yet, Jones himself proved to be extremely jealous about his position in English psychoanalysis and kept competitors at a distance. When Reik wanted to move to England, he prevented it, and he also effectively kept Eidelberg from settling in London, urging him to settle in Oxford instead. It was Jones also who ruled that no qualified analyst could give lectures on psychoanalysis in London without his approval. (Lorand, 1975–1976, p. 706)

Jones also had such personal issues with Ferenczi. Jones, as he sat in the waiting room while his girlfriend Loe Kahn was being analyzed by Freud, fantasized also about being so analyzed by the Master. He also may have fantasized that he would replace Jung as Freud's *Gentile Prince if Psycho-analysis* to make the *Jewish Science of Psychoanalysis* more acceptable to the Gentile world.

Neither having Freud as his analyst nor becoming the Gentile Prince came to fruition. Freud turned down Jones for an analysis, but more of this in a later section. What is more, Freud never turned to Jones as he did to Ferenczi to become his Paladin and Grand Vizier (Rachman, 1997a). There are two recently published materials which give us a new opportunity to re-assess Jones. The psychoanalytic community has neglected the examination of Jones professionally and personally. The publication of the Ferenczi/Jones correspondence (Eros et al., 2013) allows us now to re-assess Jones's character and personality as stated by Freud, Ferenczi and other analysts. A second source of new information is an entire issue of a journal, *Studies in Gender and Sexuality,* entitled, "Ernest Jones Revisited: A Symposium," Volume 3, Number 4. The major essay is by Phillip Kuhn, entitled, "Romancing with a Wealth of Detail": Narratives of Ernest Jones's 1906 Trial for Indecent Assault." There are discussions by Elizabeth Young-Breuhl, Glenn O. Gabbard,

M.D., George J. Markari, M.D., and John Kerr, M.D. This monograph addresses the area of sexual abuse of children, a long neglected issue in the psychoanalytic community.

Ferenczi's relationship with Jones

The relationship between Jones and Ferenczi began well but ended badly. Ferenczi and Jones first met in 1908 at the Salzburg Congress. After the Congress, Jones visited Budapest. At Clark University, in Worcester, Massachusetts, in 1909, at the famous lecture where Freud introduced psychoanalysis to the United States, once again, they met. Their correspondence began in 1911.

The issue of plagiarism by Jones of Ferenczi's ideas was a source of discontent between them (Sklar, 2016). Ferenczi felt part of his paper on suggestion (Ferenczi, 1909), as well as the issues of introjection and transference was plagiarized by Jones (Jones, 1911). Furthermore, Ferenczi felt his ideas were not properly credited in another article (Jones, 1923). There was also serious disagreement between Ferenczi and Jones about Dr. Franklin, and English analysand for membership in the British Psychoanalytic Society against Jones's wishes. Ferenczi wrote to Jones after their analysis:

Dear Ernest,

Your complaint against me in the case of Dr. Franklin is not justified but she was evidently too modest to take it to you; believing that, after being invited to work at the Institute, it was unnecessary.

Personally I can only report that she really deserves the recommendation which I gave you. Of course she still has some personal difficulties in her character but her capacities and scientific knowledge are so valuable that we that we must be lenient, all the more since she is constantly improving. And who of us is quite free of character difficulties? Of course, she needs the friendly support of her colleagues. Please influence them in this direction without divulging these rather personal details. (Ferenczi Letter to Ernest Jones, December 13, 1926 – Eros et al., 2013, p. 127)

Jones appears to be judgmental in his approach to an analytic candidate. Ferenczi on the other hand clearly illustrates his empathetic approach to analysands, as well as supervises in contrast (Rachman,1988, 1997a, 2003) to Jones's reputation as a disciplinarian (Roazen, 1975).

Jones and Ferenczi also were divided on fundamental dimensions of theory. Jones theoretically supported Melanie Klein in the British Group, where Ferenczi supported Anna Freud. Despite Jones's pressure, Ferenczi declined to openly take sides. Ferenczi had complained to Freud about Jones's preferring Klein to Anna Freud:

> ...the prominent influence that Frau Melanie Klein has had on Jones and almost the entire group. Jones's is adopting not only Frau Klein's method, but also er more personal relations to the Berlin group etc., - Aside from the scientific value of his work, I find in this a point directed toward Vrenna. Jones wanted to press me to take sides in this question as well; but I refused, and said that was a scientific and not a partisan matter. (Letter from Ferenczi-Freud-Falzeder, Brabont & Giampieri-Deutsch, 2000, p. 313)

In contrast to Jones's orthodox analytic approach, as in his non-relational death instinct at the beginning of psychic life, Ferenczi was developing the more complex idea of the significance of the maternal-child relationship. These very different analytic directions, which began to solidify in the so-called Controversial Discussions held between 1942 and 1944 when the British Society, chaired by Jones, divided into three groups: Anna Freud group; the Kleinians; and the Middle or Independent Group, sharing power in the Educational Committee (Sklar, 2013).

Ferenczi/Jones on lay analysis

Ferenczi and Jones had an issue on the problem of lay analysis. While Jones was the president of the British Psychoanalytic Society there were lay analysts who were members of the group. He was however against Freud's positive position on lay analysis. At the same period he sided with the American's position of opposition to lay analysis (Sklar, 2013). Ferenczi wrote to Jones about this:

Your ambiguous behavior with regard to the question of lay analysis (!) had contributed a great deal in the increase in negativity on my part[2] Even though you yourself are president of a group with lay members, you have acted not infrequently in a manner designed to encourage the opponents of lay [analysts], e.g. at the Innsbruck Congress[3], (Eros et al., 2013, p. 145 – Letter from Sándor Ferenczi to Ernest Jones, January 6, 1930, pp. 145–146)

F2: "Ferenczi supplied the introduction for 'The question of lay analysis in 1926 and was, along with his Hungarian colleagues, committed to lay analysis. Ferenczi had felt for some time that Jones was unpleasantly antipathetic to Rim in relation to lay analysis. Freud wrote to Jones on 6, July 1927, (Ferenczi…expressed to me… regretting only that he did not obtain more far reaching agreement with you on the lay-question. You know that he fully shares my viewpoint, I know that you do not. (Freud, 1926, pp. 620–621)

F3: The Tenth Psychoanalytic Congress took place in Innsbruck from 1 to 2 September 1927. It was dominated by the topics of lay analysis… Eitingon was elected President. He described the impressions of Jones and Ferenczi to Freud:

> *Jones was horrid, intent on causing annoyance, on needling one,* while creating the impression that he has more in stock, which he is keeping back to spare us…*A lust for evil is unmistakable,* whether more or less clear intentions are involved too is difficult to say. *I had to punish him for it,* but did so most reluctantly, *because he – Jones – deserved it.* I saw a lot of Ferenczi…he was as accessible, kind, enthusiastic and understanding as ever…Altogether, Ferenczi was a pleasure. (Eros et al., 2013, p. 148, *Letter from Eitingon to Freud*)

We now have the data from Ferenczi, Freud, and Eitingon's negative impressions regarding Jones's character and functioning with colleagues.

Jones character and personality

Both Freud and Ferenczi questioned Jones's character and personality. Freud thought Jones had defects in his character, as he exclaimed:

[Jones had] real defects in character and behavior with which one can't confront him quite honestly and which he must conceal by means of some arrangement or other. (Brabant, Falzeder, & Giampieri-Deutsch, 1933, p. 313)

Freud also recognized Jones's tendency toward sexual acting out:

I pity it very much that you should not master such dangerous cravings well aware at the same time of the source from which all these evils spring, *taking away from you nearly all the blame but nothing of the dangers.* (*Paskouskas, 199.3, Letter from Sigmund Freud to Ernest Jones – January 14, 1912, p. 124*)

Gabbard, one of the discussants of the Kuhn's paper about Jones's trial described Jones's reputation, "as a rather seedy practitioner," which he described:

It was rumored that he was recommending masturbation to patients, sharing obscene postcards with his patients to arouse sexual feelings and prescribing visits to prostitutes as part of therapy for young male patients (Hale, 1971). One of his former analysands threatened to complain that he sexually exploited her, so Jones slipped her $500 on hush money to avoid a public scandal. (Gabbard, 2002, p. 380)

What is more, in a letter of January 13, 1911, to James Jackson Putnam (Hale, 1971), Jones described the potential complainantas a hysterical lesbian who was emotionally unstable. This is reminiscent of Renatus Hartog who was accused of sexual abuse and was put on trial. He never admitted the abuse, calling the complainant a lesbian (see Chapter 11).

Jones admitted to Freud that he was:

always been conscious of sexual attractions to patients, my wife was a patient of mine. (Paskauskas, 1993, p. 380)

Ferenczi's psychoanalysis with Jones

Ferenczi, of course, had a special perspective to observe and experience Jones's character and personality, being his analyst. Jones's was in analysis with Ferenczi, on a twice daily basis in June and July 1913. This occurred before Ferenczi's analysis with Freud, which lasted for 3 weeks in October 1914 and for another 3 weeks (with two sessions daily) in June 1916 (Freud, 1933).

Jones's referral to Ferenczi for an analysis by Freud has psychological implications for understanding Jones's functioning. Jones sat in Freud's waiting room, as Freud analyzed his girlfriend Loe Kahn, fantasizing having an analysis with Freud. But, when Jones turned to Freud for analysis, Freud turned him down. Freud sent Jones to Ferenczi. This analysis could not have gone well as there were negative feelings by both analyst and analysand toward each other. In discussions of their analysis, Ferenczi reveals his negative feelings toward Jones:

> excessive kindness works as a hindrance in the analysis; *his dreams are full of mockery and scorn towards one.* (Falzeder, Brabant, & Giampieri-Deutsch, 2000, – Letter from Sándor Ferenczi to Sigmund Freud, p. 493)

When Jones openly makes an anti-semetic remark about Otto Rank, calling him, "a swindling Jew," which Jones did not deny (Sklar, 2016), Ferenczi writes Jones a letter about returning to analysis:

> [I] am firmly of the opinion that you are in need if analysis, not only because of your, as I believe, unconsciously motivated actions, but also because I must consider you previous analysis incomplete just on the grounds of my technique having been far less perfected at the time. (Eros et al., 2013, Letters from Sándor Ferenczi to Ernest Jones, October 7, 1923, p. 91)

Ten months after Ferenczi offers to re-analyze Jones, a reply is forthcoming:

> I still have a strong desire to continue the analysis, chiefly because the most perfect attainable is the ideal we should all aim at in connection with psychoanalysis. On the other hand, the continuing expenses of my life and arrangements here make it absolutely impossible to be away from my work for more than

the shortest time, which would obviously not be satisfactory. I can only console myself with the thought that anyone who is so happy in his love-life as I am and able to work so satisfactorily cannot be in urgent need of further analysis and I am sure you would agree with this criterion. (Eros et al., Letters from Ernest Jones to Sándor Ferenczi, August 7, 1924, pp. 103–104)

Sklar (2016) believed that Jones's reply, which turned down Ferenczi's offer to re-analyze him, and the delay in the response, showed superficiality, mockery, and scorn. Sklar used John Rickinan, another Ferenczi analysand as a comparison. He left his clinical practice and political work with the British Psychoanalytic Society, and went to Budapest to be in analysis with Ferenczi because he was motivated to continue his personal analysis. Reading and analyzing the letters that Jones wrote to Ferenczi lead a contemporary psychoanalyst, Sklar, to feel Jones had personality issues.

The technical issue which Ferenczi felt needed greater development was the handling of the transference. It can be said, that Ferenczi did not sufficiently analyze Jones's negative transference to him. Roazen (1975) hypothesized an interesting idea about the anger Jones had toward Ferenczi. Their relationship ended in a tragic event, as Jones was the lead critic in the Todschweigen campaign to defame his analyst and remove Ferenczi's pioneering contributions from psychoanalytic history. The explanation Roazen (1975) offered for Jones's fierce desire to destroy his analyst resided in the idea that Jones's inability to forgive Ferenczi for being his analyst. I believe Roazen's hypothesis is plausible. My analysis of his interpretation is from a Relational Analytic Perspective focused on Trauma Analysis (Rachman, 2018):

1. Jones had unconscious rage toward Freud from the intense feelings of rejection when Freud did not take him for personal analysis.
2. Jones could not express anger toward Freud. He did not want to run the risk of losing Freud's support and love. Jones was needy for Freud's affirmation of him.
3. He split-off his anger from Freud and projected it onto Ferenczi, who was not the object of his need for support and love. Jones may have sensed Freud's unconscious anger toward Ferenczi.

4. Jones expressed his anger onto Ferenczi by joining Freud in the Toschweigen campaign which was an intense expression of anger toward Ferenczi.
5. Jones's rage toward Freud for his rejection of him was translated into activities which caused Ferenczi harm, intellectually, emotionally, and interpersonally.
6. Freud's approval of Jones's anger and rejection of Ferenczi allowed Jones to receive the affirmation and love he so desperately needed from Freud.
7. Freud expressed his anger toward Ferenczi for the feeling his "favorite son" was trying to kill him off by developing an alternate theory and technique. This Oedipal concern by Freud was likely his own fantasy. In reality, Ferenczi's purpose was to report his own clinical observations and theoretical understanding of his work with trauma disorders (Rachman, 2018; Rachman & Klett, 2015). Ferenczi was not trying to symbolically "kill off the father" as Freud may have believed. As has been stated, over and over again, *Ferenczi's purpose in offering the Confusion of Tongues paradigm and the development of Trauma Analysis was to expand the boundaries of psychoanalysis to understand and treat trauma disorders* (Rachman, 2018).
8. Freud did not want Ferenczi to be a rival and have the analytic community respond to Ferenczi's alternate ideas of psychoanalysis and lessen their allegiance to Freud's Oedipal Complex Theory. Freud considered the Oedipal theory as the cornerstone of traditional psychoanalysis. Freud was not able to share the theoretical and clinical stage with Ferenczi. He could not let his "favorite son" become a peer of his. Ferenczi had to remain under Freud, the father, authority and control (Fromm, 1959). But Ferenczi wanted to be a son who could find his own voice and move from an obedient son to a cherished colleague. This development was the natural process of human growth which allows a son to become a man with his own sense of identity (Erikson, 1950).
9. Jones was the prototype of a company man, someone who was intensely emotionally connected to Freud, the authority, as well as being intensely connected to the analytic community.

74 A pedophile among us?

Consequently, Jones's activity involved being Freud's servant and the political operator in the Todschweigen campaign.

Jones's "political assassination" of Ferenczi: Ferenczi's so called "madness"/psychosis

It is important that I clarify my position on Jones, because I admit having very intense negative feelings about him as being, along with Freud, one of the leaders of the Todschweigen campaign deliberately developed to harm Ferenczi's personal and professional reputation. Jones, with Freud's approval, instituted a series of events which lead to Ferenczi being "damned by diagnosis." Psychiatrically, he was diagnosed by Jones as being "mad," psychotic (Jones, 1957). Over a period of time, he commented about Ferenczi's behavior, focusing on what he considered a serious indication of personal psychopathology. At the 1910 International Psycho-Analytic Congress, Jones (1955) asserted that Ferenczi's "dictatorial side" encouraged "a great storm of protest" (p. 69). Jones agreed with Freud that Ferenczi had an exaggerated need for love:

> For several years Hungary did not seem favorable soil for psychoanalysis, but later on relieved Frenczi from his loneliness by providing a number of excellent analysts. (Jones, 1955, p. 74)

Jones in his Freud biography, described what he considered the "emerging madness" of Ferenczi. He described what he considered Ferenczi's pathology when he refused to be Freud's secretary when he thought he was invited to be his co-author on writing the Schreiber case on their Sicily trip in 1911:

> But behind those manifestations lay *severe trouble in the depths of his personality…he was haunted by a quite inordinate and insatiable longing for his father's love.* It was the dominating passion of his life and was indirectly the source of the unfortunate changes he introduced into his psychoanalytic technique twenty years later, which had the effect of estranging him from Freud (though not Freud from him). (Jones, 1955, p. 82)

Jones demonstrated his mean-spiritedness in the above quote when he described what was a negative experience for Ferenczi. Freud's need for domination, power, control, and status made him turn Ferenczi into a secretary. Jones turned this into Ferenczi's pathologic need for Freud's approval and love. The purpose of the Sicily vacation, as Freud told Ferenczi, was to collaborate on writing the *Schreiber* case. But when the time came to work on writing the material, Freud began speaking his thoughts on the case and expected Ferenczi to write down his ideas. Ferenczi was angry, objected, and voice his displeasure (Grosskurth, 1991). Freud was not happy with what he considered Ferenczi's immaturity. It was the beginning of Ferenczi's attempt to create a colloquial relationship with Freud, which was never realized, as his mentor could not give himself over to a peer-to-peer relationship as Jung had earlier attempted with him on their trip to America (Rachman, 1997a) because of his need to maintain his authority (Fromm, 1959). Jones could not believe that Freud had the need to always be the authority, not the peer, when he noted Freud did not estrange himself from Ferenczi. It was only Ferenczi that has estranged himself from Freud.

Jones believed it was Ferenczi's psychopathology which caused the relationship between Freud and Ferenczi to be stretched to the breaking point. Jones made significant contributions to the Todschweigen campaign to defame Ferenczi by protecting Freud against Ferenczi, as if, Ferenczi was trying to harm Freud.

> The generosity and tactfulness Freud constantly displayed towards Ferenczi, and his great fondness for him preserved a valuable friendship for many years until, long after the episode, *Ferenczi's own stability began to crumble.* (Jones, 1955, p. 84)

In the third volume of Jones's Freud biography, he mentioned his confabulated psychosis of Ferenczi several times:

> Adherence to what psychoanalysis had revealed signifies the same as retaining one's insight into the workings of the unconscious, and the ability to do so presupposes a high degree of mental stability. My hope…was the the six of us [Society of Rings] were suitably endowed for that purpose. It turned out, alas, that only

76 A pedophile among us?

four of us were. Two of the members, Rank and Ferenczi, were not able to hold out at the end....*Ferenczi more gradually toward the end of his life, developed psychotic manifestations that revealed themselves in, among other ways, a turning away from Freud and his doctrines. The seeds of a destructive psychosis, invisible for so long, at last germinated.* (Jones, 1957, p. 45)

Jones turned his personal attack on Ferenczi to attack his functioning as a psychoanalyst. Jones's confabulated, mean-spirited accusation, no, self righteous condemnation of Ferenczi as psychotic was terrible enough, but, he had the mendacity to link his lie to Ferenczi's theoretical and clinical ideas. He linked Ferenczi's pioneering and evolutionary clinical work with Elizabeth Severn, developing an understanding and treatment regime for traumatic disorder, as, "a turning away from Freud and his doctrines." What is more, when Ferenczi was invited to the New School of Social Research in New York City to give a course of lectures in 1926, Jones was against Ferenczi accepting the invitation, feeling he would be spreading his dissident ideas to America. Jones made sure to declare that Ferenczi's triumphant positive responses to his lectures was just another indication of his psychological disintegration:

The outcome was to justify my foreboding. Ferenczi was never the same a again after that visit, although *it was another four or five years before his mental deterioration became manifest* to Freud. (Jones, 1957, p. 127)

The period of "four or five years" links Freud's awareness of Ferenczi's so-called "mental deterioration" to the part of Ferenzi's analysis with Severn, which I have suggested was a period of pioneering achievements (Rachman, 2018).

Jones prevents Ferenczi's publication of the Confusion of Tongues

When Ferenczi died of pernicious anemia on May 22, 1933, this sad event appeared to move Jones to create a dramatic moment in the Todschweigen campaign to silence his analyst. Jones's campaign to remove one of Ferenczi's most significant contributions from psychoanalytic history was described in a letter to Freud 1 month after Ferenczi's death:

I hope that Ferenczi himself would not publish it, [Confusion of Tongues paper.] but when I received the proof of the ZEITSCHRIFT I felt he would be offended if it were not translated into English and so asked his permission for this. He seemed gratified, and we not only translated it but put it up in type as the first paper in the July number. *Since his death I have been thinking over the removal of the personal reason for publishing it.* Others also have suggested that it now be withdrawn and *I quote a letter of Mrs. Rivere's with which I quite agree: "Now that Ferenczi has died I wondered whether you will not reconsider publishing his last paper.* It seems to me that it can only be damaging to him and a discredit. While now that he is no longer to be hurt by its not being published, no good purpose could be served by it. His scientific contentions and statements about analytic practice are just a product of delusions, which can only discredit psychoanalysis and give credit to its opponents. It cannot be supposed *that all Journal readers will appreciate the mental condition of the writer,* and in this respect one has to think of posterity too!" (Paskauskas, 1993– Jones letter to Freud, June 3, 1933)

Jones clearly endorsed Rivere's personal and professional condemnation of Ferenczi. They both believed his Confusion of Tongues paper was not a contribution to psychoanalysis. What is more, they, along with Freud, strongly felt it was a danger to psychoanalysis. Consequently, they were convinced that the paper should never have been allowed to be presented to the psychoanalytic community. Once, Ferenczi found the courage to follow his own clinical observations (Rachman, 1997a) and found his voice in being able to overcome Freud's mean-spirited objections (Fromm, 1959; Rachman, 1997b), presenting his paper, Freud, Jones, Rivere, and other orthodox members of Freud's group, escalated the Todschweigen campaign to silence Ferenczi by not allowing his Confusion of Tongues paper to be published in English. Allowing the paper to be only available in German, meant generations of

78 A pedophile among us?

analysts, analytic candidates, psychotherapists, and mental health professionals were prevented from studying Ferenczi's ideas and methods. It was not until the Ferenczi Renaissance was ushered in by the publication of another Ferenczi document, his *Clinical Diary* that was first published in French (Ferenczi, 1985), and then in English in (Ferenczi, 1988). The diary was written in 1932–1933, was also lost to the Todschweigen campaign. Ferenczi's ideas and methods became unknown to the analytic and mental health communities (Rachman, 1999).

Rivere's letter and Jones's approval of her condemnation of Ferenczi helped bring forward the Todschweigen campaign which contributed to the idea that Ferenczi was emotionally unstable and his ideas and methods were a function of his madness, not his genius. Jones's elaboration of the so-called "madness of Ferenczi" has been challenged by psychoanalysts (Bonomi, 1999; Falzeder, 2010; Haynal, 2002; Rachman, 1997a, 1997b). Three of Ferenczi's students and analysands, Michael Balent, Clara Thompson, and Elizabeth Severn, who were eye-witnesses to Ferenczi's last days provided data which should finally erase this outrageous and false claims that Ferenczi suffered from: "delusions"; a "mental condition"; "mental deterioration"; "psychotic manifestation"; "destructive psychoses"; "severe trouble in the depths of his personality"; "haunted by a quite inordinate and insatiable longing for his father's love"; and his "stability began to crumble."

There are, however, first-hand accounts of Ferenczi's emotional functioning with challenge Jones's negative assertions. Michael Balint shared his eyewitness observation of Ferenczi's emotional functioning:

> I want to state that I saw Ferenczi frequently – once or twice almost every week – during the illness, a pernicious anemia which led to a rapidly progressing combined degeneration of the cord. He soon became ataxic [impaired coordination] for the at few weeks, had to stay in bed, and for the last few days had to be fed; the immediate cause of his death was paralysis of the respiratory centre. *Despite his progressive physical weakness, mentally he was always clear ... I saw him on the Sunday before his death; even then – though painfully weak and ataxic – mentally he was quite clear.* (Balint, 1958, p. 68)

Clara Thompson, another Ferenczi analysand and student, was with him from 1932 until his death on May 22, 1933. She also contradicted Jones's unfounded accusations that Ferenczi suffered from psychosis:

> except for the symptoms of his physical illness, there was nothing psychotic which I observed. I visited him regularly, and talked to him, and there was not a single incident, aside from memory difficulties, which would substantiate Jones's picture of Ferenczi's psychosis or homicidal mood. (Fromm, 1963, p. 139)

Elizabeth Severn, Ferenczi's most controversial analysand, who finished her training as an analyst with Ferenczi, was in a relationship with him for 8 years, from 1925 to 1933. I have researched all the papers, notes, and letters she left to her daughter, Margaret (Rachman 2016). In addition to her papers, there are additional important documents, such as her published books (Severn, 1913, 1920, 1933). There is also a very important interview conducted by Kurt Eissler for the Freud Archive, which he founded (Eissler, 1952). It can be said that Severn was one of the individuals who was intimately involved in Ferenczi's personal and professional life.

Severn knew and had regular personal contract with Ferenczi and his wife Giselle. She had accompanied them on a vacation trip to Madrid in 1926 (Rachman, 2018), When in the course of their difficult analysis, when she could not get out of bed, he conducted sessions at her apartment (Ferenczi, 1988). Their analysis was conducted at times, on a daily basis, including more than one session daily. This type of intense contact lasted over an 8-year period. Such intense emotional contact was also described in Eissler's interview of Severn (Eissler, 1952). All these data can indicate that Severn may have had the most interpersonal/emotionally connected relationship with Ferenczi. Keeping this in mind, in all of Severn's papers and documents, *she never mentioned that Ferenczi showed any emotional instability, inappropriate clinical interaction, boundary violations* or *intellectual problems* (Rachman, 2018). Rather, Severn indicated she thought Ferenczi was an excellent psychoanalyst who she felt was intellectually emotionally and interpersonally sound individual. What is more, it was clear that he conducted the best analysis she had out of the four analyses.

80   A pedophile among us?

It is time to allow the eye-witness reports of three significant individuals in the history of psychoanalysis, who seriously contradicted Jones's false and mean-spirited accusations of Ferenczi's emotional disorder and clinical dysfunction to replace Jones's-biased confabulations. The continued silence regarding Freud, Jones, Rivere, and other analysts' Todschweigen campaign to defame Ferenczi and Severn should be acknowledged and stopped. What is more, as I have discussed in this book (see Chapter 31), traditional psychoanalysts should offer an apology to the International Sándor Ferenczi Community for the now, 57th year of their silence condemning Ferenczi and Severn.

In the history of science, the *political and symbolic personal assassination* of a prestigious and pioneering member of scientific community, is a rare phenomenon. But, in psychoanalysis, a precedent was established early in its history when members of the community, like Adler, Ferenczi, Jung, Rank, and Severn were labeled dangerous dissidents, and unacceptable psychoanalysts. To attack an analyst because you disagree with their ideas is a hateful form of Todschweigen, Death by Silence (Rachman, 1999). Personal attacks on the dissident, which assault his functioning as a human being, so that his intellectual and clinical accomplishments are disregarded as a function of his madness are not only unacceptable but also abhorrent. How can analysts like Freud, Jones, and Rivere, whose professional challenge was to provide understanding and concern for individuals with emotional disorders, attempt to *silence and politically assassinate* Ferenczi because he believed that actual traumatic experience that occurred in family interaction were important for psychoanalysis to study and treat? In particular, Ferenczi was calling attention to the issue of sexual abuse in family interaction which he observed as a psychodynamic factor in the analysands he reported on in his *Clinical Diary* Ferenczi, 1988). Ferenczi should have not been considered mad because he verified Freud's pioneering findings on sexual abuse in family interaction (Freud, 1954). Why did Ferenczi's idea of Confusion of Tongues cause such a furore in the orthodox analytic community that moved its founder and leader, Sigmund Freud and his followers, such as Ernest Jones and Joan Rivere to attempt to destroy Sándor Ferenczi, personally and professionally?

Jones's successful suppression of Ferenczi's theory that actual sexual abuse of children were the source of psychological disorder, and his formulation of such theory can be seen as Jones's attempt to protect Freud's Oedipal theory of psychoanalysis. If Ferenczi's idea of actual trauma in the experience of sexual abuse of children by their parents and parental substitutes were to be accepted by the analytic community and then society, this would have been a threat to Freud's stature and influence. Abandoning the Seduction Hypothesis and turning to the Oedipal Complex Theory would mean Freud indulged himself in a "literary, pseudo-psychological fantasy." What is more, it would have protected both Freud from confronting their own personal sexual abuse experiences. As I have discussed elsewhere, Freud was the victim of childhood sexual abuse by a nursemaid, Resi Wittek (Rachman, 2016a).

As we have seen in presenting the new data now available, Jones has been described to have issues with sexuality. In the examination of Jones's 1906 trial for sexual assault of two young girls, we shall be presented with additional data about Jones's sexual functioning. This trial and its meaning for Jones's functioning and psychoanalysis' neglect of childhood sexual abuse will be illuminated.

Kuhn's narrative of Ernest Jones's 1906 trial for pedophilia

Psychoanalysis's Neglect of Jones's Trial

Phillip Kuhn, a poet, historian and a Freudian Scholar, has made a significant contribution to the history of psychoanalysis by meticulously researching the trial reports of a neglected part of analytic history, namely, the trial of Ernest Jones in 1906, for "indecently assaulting two young 'mentally defective' girls at a special school in South East London" (Kuhn, 2002, p. 344). The accusation of Jones being a pedophile has been an hidden part of analytic history, like Freud's analysis of his daughter Anna (Rachman, 2003).

Like the Todschweigen campaign instituted to silence unacceptable dissidents, *secrets in psychoanalysis* are attempts to silence events which also would bring shame or criticism to traditional psychoanalysis. Jones's closeness to Freud, and Freud's embrace of him, would be questionable if Jones's sexual assault of two young girls and a subsequent examination of his character and personality were forthcoming. Hence, Kuhn's pivotal monograph on Jones's 1906 trial and the discussion of his narrative by Glen D. Gabbard, MD, J. Makari, MD, and John Kerr, PhD, finally allow the psychoanalytic community to be fully aware of, confront and discuss this dramatic aspect of neglected psychoanalytic history, namely, the alleged sexual abuse of children by one of psychoanalysis; pioneers.

Kuhn (2002) also points out another important aspect to the neglect of Jones's trial confronting child sexual abuse. The 1906 trial was in the same year *Freud publicly abandoned his Seduction Theory*, which was the original theory of hysteria/neurosis, stating that childhood sexual trauma was the origin of neurosis (Freud, 1896). In 1906, Freud then made a dramatic historic, theoretical correction which was to influence psychoanalysis to this day. He said he overestimated the influence of actual sexual trauma of children, correcting this assumption to believing they were the analysands fantasies of being seduced. These analysands were defending against their own sexual activity, such as masturbation. Freud's so-called "correction" introduced the prominence of the Oedipal Complex Theory as the cornerstone of psychoanalysis. As the chapters in this book have repeatedly stated, the theoretical correction from Seduction to Oedipal Theory seriously contributed to the neglect of actual sexual trauma as a significant psychodynamic in the development of psychological disorder.

There is a personal reaction I would share about Kuhn's narrative description of Jones's trial. It would easier to understand and follow if Kuhn had not buried the experience of the trial in excessive academic language and references. Reading the narrative was, as if, Kuhn was creating a mystery story that needed interpretation and references to others accounts of the event. As will be discussed in my interpretation of Jones's guilt, the mystery element in Kuhn's narrative may have emerged from his antiseptic attempt to remove any judgment from his account of the trial. This being said, both Kuhn and the editors and editorial board of *Gender and Sexuality*, which was published in 2002, are to be highly congratulated for the historically important monograph that has finally brought Jones's questionable behavior into the light of psychoanalytic examination.

The 1906 trial of Jones

Kuhn read all of the existing documents surrounding Jones's description of his trial, and all other texts relating to the trial (Kuhn, 2002). Jones was 27 years old at the time of the trial. Jones described becoming aware of the accusations:

> One morning...in 1906, Dr. Kerr, sent me...[a] summons, to meet at a school for mental defectives..., I was puzzled to know what he wanted, and should have been more perturbed had I known. To my amazement and horror *I was confronted...with a teacher who said that two small children...maintained I had behaved indecently during the speech test...what was worse, she appeared to believe them.* (Jones, 1959, p. 145)

After the two girls, Dorothy Freeman and Fanny Harrigan, 13 years old, made their complaints of Jones's indecent behavior to Mrs. Amelia Hall, head-teacher, of Edward-Street School for Mentally Defective Children, Jones was arrested, arraigned, and remanded on bail. Two other children, Elizabeth Overton, 14 years old, and a boy named Johnson were also complainants. Jones asked Mrs. Hall if anyone in the school had ever been accused of sexual abuse of children, to which she said no. Jones acted, as if, the accusation of his sexual abuse of these children were completely out of the realm of possibility. Was he expressing his being a sociopath, who lacked empathy, who lied, and was dismissive of reality when it suits him? Or, was he suffering from a dissociative disorder, which can be part of a sexual trauma for the abuser as well as the abused (Rachman & Klett, 2015)?

Dr. Kerr, the head of the department, Jones, and Mrs. Hall arranged a meeting to discuss the accusation of sexual abuse. One of the girls, Fanny Harrigan's accusation was that Jones:

> *spoke and acted in a grossly indecent manner...Dorothy Freeman [said] requesting her to act as the girl Harrigan had done. She declined to do so.* (Kuhn, 2002, pp. 354–355)

An interchange between Dr. Kerr and Mrs. Freeman revealed that they thought the alleged incident was "serious, disgraceful, and disgusting" (Kuhn, 2002, p. 355).

In a remarkable moment, Jones responded to the disparaging remarks of Mrs. Freeman by exclaiming:

> My good woman, if I had done such a thing I should deserve to be horsewhipped and placed in an asylum. (Kuhn, 2002, p. 355)

Jones's responded with what appeared to be a deceptive remark that could be analyzed as follows:

> I could not be guilty of such a disgusting and disgraceful act toward children because I would never place myself in a position to be beaten and sent away to an insane asylum.

Once again, Jones does not take any responsibility for the possibility be may be involved in an act of sexual abuse with children. Clearly, Mrs. Freeman does not believe Jones's exclamation of his complete and utter innocence by continuing to confront him:

> *Mrs. Freeman then called [Jones] several names and said he was only fit to be burned.* (Kuhn, 2002, p. 355)

Jones, interestingly enough did not answer Mrs. Freeman's dramatic and rageful remarks. But Dr. Kerr rushes to Jones's defense telling her to be reasonable and follows up with a statement of denial:

> You are labouring under a delusion[9]. These things do not and cannot occur in our schools. (Kuhn, 2002, p. 355)

Imagine, Dr. Kerr tells a mother whose daughter said she was sexually abused by Jones that she was crazy to believe that Jones could have abused her daughter. Mrs. Freeman appeared to be an assertive individual who believed her daughter and did not allow two doctors to intimidate her. She answered him:

> *How do you know I am labouring under a delusion? You were not there and I believe my child is speaking the truth.* (Kuhn, 2002, p. 355)

Amazingly, Dr. Kerr, like Jones, cannot confront sexual abuse in their own experience and, following the tradition in society which turned on the victim, as he said:

> *I am afraid the girls have made this up between themselves*, and I would like to know where it originated. That will be the thing to find out. You go home Mrs. Freeman, and *make your mind easy*, as *I feel sure this has never occurred.* (Kuhn, 2002, p. 355)

Kuhn (2002) injected an important fact which suggested that Dr. Kerr was delusional, not Mrs. Freeman. Two men, a headmaster and a workman in this same school system were dismissed and convicted of sexual assault of school children, during this same period of time.

The continuous exchange between Mrs. Freeman and Dr. Kerr did not let up because she would not let herself be intimidated, nor would her husband remain quiet. She made it clear she would contact the police. Kuhn (2002) believed that Dr. Kerr, as Jones's colleague, could not believe he was guilty. But Kerr was required to follow procedure, thereby, suspending Jones from all his duties:

> extraordinary allegations were made against doctors...after receiving a formal report...were inclined...*to order Dr. Jones's suspension from the school.* (Kuhn, 2002, p. 357)

The formal complaint against Jones did not stop Mr. and Mrs. Freeman from entering a sexual abuse complaint with the police. At this time, one of the girls mentioned a significant piece of evidence. One of the girls, Fanny Harrigan mentioned a *"green baize table cloth,"* which was in the room when Jones conducted his examination of the girls. The green cloth was found to have markings that "were regarded of great importance" (Kuhn, 2002, p. 357). Jones was confronted with this potential evidence of abuse and once again; proclaimed his innocence. Jones was arrested and the school's Education Committee report read:

> *The allegations and additional materials [green table cloth] were placed before the chairman of the council...who gave instruction for the prosecution* which the police had decided to institute. (Kuhn, 2002, p. 359)

The testimony during the trial involved several witnesses. Dorothy Freeman, age 13 years old, first said that:

> Jones asked her questions *"of a rude nature"* and described an *"alleged assault,"*...[where] *"she tried to get away,"* but he would *not let her go"* (Kuhn, 2002, p. 361)

She did not call out when the abuse happened, or tell any of the girls about it. She did, however, tell her mother and Dr. Kerr. As has been mentioned, her mother believed her about the abuse, but, Dr. Kerr did not. Kuhn (2002) points out that it is necessary to interpret the court reports realizing that there were hidden material by the adults in the children's testimony, which added the following:

> The girl [Dorothy] stating *that the doctor interfered with her clothing, asked her an improper question, and subsequently acted in a grossly indecent manner.* The girl told [the] witness, (for the prosecution) that *Dorothy (and Fanny) had alleged that the doctor...indecently exposed himself he "asked" Dorothy to touch his genitals...*The press similarly omitted Dorothy's next statement, which, I suggest was that, when she refused [to touch Jones's genitals], *Jones grabbed hold of her and forced her to touch his genitals.* (Kuhn, 2002, pp. 367–368)

Kuhn (2002) identified the "persecuted portion of Dorothy's narrative" in a "rare verbatim fragment of her evidence to the court: "She tried to get away but he would not let her go" (Kuhn, 2002, p. 368). Kuhn made it clear in the data he was able to uncover in the court records and press statements that the children's statements were not reported verbatim and he believed they were suppressed.

The green baize table cloth cover was the primary piece of evidence in Jones's trial:

> *the table cover was clearly the key to Jones's prosecution.* And yet its narrative, like the girls' testimonies, is also persecuted from the court reports...In an age where it was the practice for the disbelief of the child...*Dr. Burney's evidence made clear that the stains on*

the table cover were consistent with semen stains. It even seems
that the evidence was so compelling. (Kuhn, 2002, p. 370)

The conclusion of the trial seem controversial in terms of contemporary standards. The Magistrate took into consideration that
Dr. Kerr testified to the mental defectiveness of the girls. The prosecution also emphasized their family history which proved their
incompetence. These testimonies was key in reaching the following
conclusion:

> Having heard the evidence and the cross-examination and the
> points which Dr. Kerr had called attention to *medically*, he [Mr.
> Baggallay] did [not] think a jury could possibly convict Jones.
> (Kuhn, 2002, p. 372)

The Magistrate dismissed the case, raising the issue that the girl's
testimony of being sexually abused by Jones and the presence of
semen on the green table cloth were not sufficient evidence to convict
Jones of being the perpetrator. It gives some credence to Kuhn's
thesis that the girl's accusations and testimony were "persecuted
speech." The girl's words were not believed because they were mentally defective, young, and women. What is more, their testimony was
neglected and suppressed. Kuhn (2002) seemed to convey, with his
idea of persecuted speech, that Jones got away with being adjudicated
for pedophilia because of his idea of *persecuted speech* while in the
culture of the time children were silenced by a disturbed society.

Reassessing Ernest Jones, The Jones Trial and Kuhn's Narrative

Kuhn's narrative is a very important contribution to psychoanalysis as
it addresses a neglected issue of the Jones trial for the accusation of
pedophilia. I have a special interest in Jones's personal and professional functioning in the light of his horrific negative accusations about
Sándor Ferenczi (Rachman, 1997a, 1997b, 1999, 2018). Kuhn's scholarly and exhaustive examination of archival data about the trial, as
well as the discussions by Glen Gabbard, MD, George J. Makari, MD,
and John Kerr, PhD, had provided data that is enlightening and

significant to re-assess Jones's functioning as a psychoanalyst and person. I will attempt to use this new material to form a more informed discussion of Jones's contribution to the Todschweigen campaign in which he was one of the key figures in silencing and removing Ferenczi and Severn's ideas and methods from psychoanalysis.

Why Kuhn has not used his scholarly and exhaustive research to demonstrate "Jones's flawed account" of the girl's sexual abuse allegations and the trial? (Kuhn, 2002, p. 400). Could Kuhn reassess and clarify Jones's guilt by demonstrating he had found the truth in the actual data he uncovered? He answered this question in the tone of the philosopher and historian, to which he is so closely identified:

> In my historical researches and writings, I deliberately avoid seeking "the truth", not least because I do not believe "it" to be the Holy Grail of historical inquiry...I would rather, therefore, consider my researches to be a process of inquiry and my historical discourse, "necessarily a process of deliberation" where debate...should not be suppressed by "truth." (Kuhn, 2002, pp. 401–402)

Kuhn's pleas for being completely free of preconceived notions when *searching for a truth, not the absolute truth*, is refreshing and intellectually compelling, especially, when examining the history of the prejudicial claims against Ferenczi in the traditional analytic community, as I have done (Rachman, 1997a, 1997b, 2018, 2021). I wish the writing of Freud, Jones, and others who used their own conjectures to evaluate Ferenczi as an unfit person and psychoanalyst could have used Kuhn's superior moral and intellectual framework with which to evaluate data on an individual's interaction with others.

There is another side, however, to my description of Kuhn's evaluation of Jones in the light of his alleged sexual transgressions with mentally defective girls. I must confess that I am enormously disappointed that Kuhn did not use his long overdue important evaluation of Jones to help overthrow the damage to Ferenczi's reputation. In reading, Kuhn's narrative of Jones's trial for sexual abuse of girls, and Gabbard, Makari and Kerr's own conclusions about the trial and Jones's behavior, character, and personality defects, *I have concluded there is a sound intellectual, emotional and interpersonal data to conclude that Jones was guilty of sexual abuse of the mentally defective girls.* What is more, from the data discussants have presented, they also appear to conclude that Jones was guilty of sexually abusing the girls.

Kuhn insisted his presentation of the Jones trial in the documents he uncovered was an intentional scholarly attempt to leave space for the reader to reach his/her own conclusion. But, why go to the trouble of researching such a neglected and controversial historical and important event in psychoanalytic history to avoid contributing to greater clarity and understanding of Jones's accusations of pedophilia and his negative personal characteristics? Kuhn rightly noted that the psychoanalytic community has neglected the issue of the sexual abuse of children. I greatly commend him for putting this neglect in print. My own attempt to contribute to the re-assessment of this neglect has felt to be a lonely enterprise (Rachman, 2012; Rachman & Klett, 2015). The question still must be asked: Did Kuhn in pursuing an uncontaminated scholarly investigation approach unwittingly contribute to the continued neglect of confronting the issue of sexual abuse in the analytic community. The need to actively rehabilitate what I have called the analytic community's Todschweigen, Death by Silence campaign to remove Sándor Ferenczi and Elizabeth Severn's ideas and work on sexual abuse and trauma (Rachman, 2018) has significantly contributed to its neglect. Kuhn's approach to Jones's pedophile case, unfortunately, contributes to that neglect.

Makari's (2002) discussion of the trial narrative suggested that Kuhn hints at a plausible truth of Jones's guilt of sexual abuse of the children. Why cannot Kuhn who can now be seen as the world's authority on Ernest Jones's trial for pedophilia venture a conclusion about Jones's guilt or innocence? Does not a distinguished historian such as Kuhn usually reach conclusions after such a thorough examination of the documents were made? This historical issue needs illumination, not continued controversy. I would argue that Kuhn owes psychoanalysis greater clarity about Jones's accusations. The psychoanalytic establishment has, since the 1930s, conspired to accuse Sándor Ferenczi of inappropriate clinical behavior and personality disturbance, which removed his theoretical and clinical innovation from mainstream psychoanalysis. What punishment did Jones suffer as a result of his transgressions? Jones was embraced by Freud and traditional psychoanalysis, never facing a Todschweigen campaign aimed at removing him from the analytic community. We need to use Kuhn's ground breaking essay to re-assess Jones as an important and prominent figure in psychoanalysis who has received praise.

We need to integrate Kuhn's narrative and the discussions by Gabbard, Makari and Kerr to help us to re-assess Jones as a very flawed psychoanalyst and individual. I suggest, their assessment of Jones's functioning suggests his guilt as a pedophile, boundary violator of clinical functioning, and a seriously flawed sexual predator.

As Gabbard (2002) has demonstrated, Jones had a proclivity for sexual acting out with patients. Does this give some credence to the incident of the children making accusations that Jones acted out sexually with them which initiated his trial for pedophilia, early in his career? Gabbard seemed to re-assert that on the basis of his research, he believed Jones admitted he had active sexual feelings toward patients, in fact, Gabbard's description of Jones as a "rather seedy practitioner" (Gabbard, 2003, p. 380), indicated that he had participated in a remarkable array of boundary violations. It is especially disturbing to examine this evidence of Jones's sexual acting out in the light of Jones's vicious attacks on Sándor Ferenczi's functioning as a person and psychoanalyst that were sanctioned by Freud and the analytic community. Freud and the analytic community never sanctioned Jones for his sexual abuse, which, on the basis of the new evidence described in this chapter, had a basis of truth.

Jones's ambition to replace Ferenczi as Freud's favorite disciple may have motivated, in part, his political assassination of Ferenczi. In essence, Jones became Freud's assassin of Ferenczi because Freud believed that Ferenczi was sexually acting out with his analysands. In actuality, Ferenczi did not act out sexually with analysands (Rachman, 1993).

Ironically, although Freud and Jones were openly critical and damning of Ferenczi, there has been a silence in the analytic community about Jones's inappropriate clinical behavior and moral lapses, until Phillip Kuhn's research on Jones's 1906 for indecent assault (Kuhn, 2002).

Freud made if clear how concerned he was about Jones's personal and clinical sexual issues:

> I pity it very much that you should not master such dangerous cravings, well aware at the same time of the source from which all these seeds spring, taking away from you nearly all the blame but nothing of the dangers. (Paskauskas, 1993, p. 124 – Letter from Sigmund Freud to Ernest Jones – January 14, 1912)

Interestingly, Freud never wrote such an indictment of sexual impulses to Ferenczi as this letter to Jones contained. Yet, Freud, in consort with Jones, openly accused Ferenczi of sexual transgressions. Why has the traditional psychoanalytic community been silent about Jones's transgressions and shamelessly falsely condemned Ferenczi (Rachman, 2018)? As has been said, I believe the traditional analytic community owes a formal apology to the Ferenczi Community for this devastating mistake (see Chapter 31).

Gabbard (2002) recognized that psychoanalysis has neglected the issue of sexual transgressions among analysts:

> Until recently...sexual transgressions were largely kept sequestered from public view. Institutes and societies assumed that the transgressor simply needed more analysis, so a slap on the wrist and a suggestion to return to the couch was the advice most frequently proffered. The victim of the sexual exploitation was often treated as the perpetrator, and little regard for their welfare was shown. Analysts assumed that the drives could not really be tamed and therefore, "boys would be boys from time to time". The harm done to patients was regarded as "acceptable casualties". However a change has occurred in the institutional responses to unethical behavior. Sexual boundary violations are now viewed as highly damaging behaviors that destroy analysis, and such violations are taken seriously by ethics committees and licensing boards. (p. 382)

Kerr (2002), as do the other discussants, (Gabbard and Makari), believed that Kuhn's narrative informed him of the following:

> *I think Jones did in fact, do what the girls said he did...it did involve ejaculation and some force –* "she tried to get away, but he would not let her go..." *What he did was very bad, and it changed one's opinion of the man.* (p. 412)

Kerr also enumerated Jones's historic contributions to psychoanalysis: his political contributions, his friendship and assistance to Freud, and, mostly, his authorized biography of Freud. But, I find it difficult to endorse Kerr's contributions of Jones. Kerr believed Freud's inclusion of women into psychoanalysis, which was highly commendable, is credited to Jones. If Freud was aware of Jones's sexual transgressions, which Kerr believed he knew and influenced him, why didn't he speak out about them? Freud's silence about Jones's transgressions is not befitting the scholar who founded psychoanalysis or the man who was the leader of a science who changed society. Even more so, why did Freud embrace Jones so closely, for all of the analytic community to view? Freud chose Jones as an important colleague and friend. Of particular concern to me, is why did Freud condemn Ferenczi, his cherished friend, once "favorite son," and psychoanalytic pioneer, for so-called sexual transgressions with analysands, of which he was not guilty (Rachman, 1993)? Yet, Freud remained silent about Jones's sexual transgressions, which several scholars of psychoanalytic history appear to believe did occur. What seems unthinkable to me, is that Freud enlisted Jones in the Todschweigen campaign to discredit Ferenczi's contribution to the evolution of psychoanalysis (Rachman, 1998, 2007; Rachman, 2018; Rachman & Klett, 2015). Was Freud so narcissistically connected to his own invention of the Oedipal Complex at the cornerstone of psychoanalysis, and the only version of psychoanalysis, that he would unite with Jones, his sycophant, to condemn Ferenczi? Jones was the company man who did Freud's bidding (Fromm, 1959). Freud was threatened by Ferenczi's innovations, which were intended to expand and improve psychoanalysis, not to supplant Freud. Ferenczi wanted the Oedipal Complex and the Confusion of Tongues theories to stand side-by-side (Rachman, 1997a).

Jones's Freud biography should be considered to have made a limited contribution to psychoanalytic history. His contribution should be tempered with the consideration that his third volume

(Jones, 1957) was used by him to "politically assassinate" Ferenczi (Rachman, 1997a, 1999, 2018). This was a shameless, mean-spirited use of intellectual literature. I find Jones's attack unforgivable.

Kerr does not mention one of Jones's contributions as being the, Editor, of the *International Journal of Psychoanalysis*. This contribution also has a dark and negative side. Jones, along with Freud, and a group of his orthodox followers, suppressed the publication of what can be considered one of Ferenczi's most important and influential paper, The Confusion of Tongues (Fromm, 1959; Rachman, 2019), into an English translation (Rachman, 1997a, b, 1999). The suppression of this paper broke Jones's pledge to Ferenczi to publish the paper in an English translation. Freud, Jones, and the orthodox analytic followers intended the suppression of Ferenczi's "paradigm shift paper" to be removed permanently from psychoanalytic literature.

Although I have been critical of Kuhn's reluctance to present an opinion of guilt of pedophilia, it is of prime importance to acknowledge his contribution in presenting the trial research to the analytic community to encourage and acknowledge the importance of the issue of sexual abuse of children:

> I suggest…that my paper is of interest to the editor and reader of *Studies in Gender and Sexuality* only because in confronts an important historical conjunction: that Jones is of "significance" to the psychoanalytic community. (Kuhn, 2002, p. 399)

As this book is dedicated to examine the neglect of the psychoanalytic community to the existence of sexual abuse of children (as well as youth and adults), Kuhn must be lauded for his concern about the sexual abuse of children as an issue that must be illuminated and confronted:

> By refusing to question Jones's account [Jones, 1959, account of the trial], the psychoanalytic community could be accused of unwitting collusion in Jones's subsequent attempts to silence the children [persecuted speech]. (Kuhn, 2002, p. 400)

Kuhn's research and narrative about Jones's trial for sexual abuse of children can be considered a significant contribution to help the psychoanalytic community to become more open and willing to discuss the contemporary incidence of sexual abuse of children (see Chapters 9, 10, 13, 15, 16, 17, 19, 21, 26, 27). It can also be seen as a contribution to reversing the Todschweigen campaign developed against Ferenczi and Severn. Their work was an attempt to establish sexual trauma as a significant psychoanalytic issue, which is now illuminated as meaningful by Kuhn's research on Jones's neglected trial for pedophilia.

Chapter 8

Todschweigen, Death by Silence (Rachman and Menaker): traditional psychoanalysis's punishment of dissidents

The silent treatment or "Todschweigen" (Rachman, 1999, 2018, 2019) is a very important mechanism in the analytic community to deal effectively with dissident voices. In essence, it involved totally ignoring the dissident voice, so that its message and potency is diminished or rendered lifeless. The hidden message in the silent treatment is stated as follows: "this analyst, this theory, this technical variation is not worthy of debate; if we ignore it, it will die a natural death (which it deserves)." In essence, Todschweigen, is "death by silence." The practice of Todschweigen was originally developed to silence dissidents, such as Jung (Roazen, 1975), Ferenczi (Rachman, 1997a, 1997b) and Rank (Menaker, 1982). Todschweigen took an interesting turn, when the silent treatment was successfully used to keep secret that Sigmund Freud analyzed his daughter, Anna.

Why were such stringent measures, such as Todschweigen, necessary to deal with theoretical and technical developments that promised to revolutionize psychoanalysis? Freud's analysis of his youngest child, Anna, can be placed in the context of these issues. Freud seemed "blinded" to the possibility that in analyzing his daughter he was involved in a form of emotional seduction, which had decided sexual overtones. This analysis occurred, even though there were other very qualified psychoanalysts who could perform the clinical task.

My opinion is that Freud, Jones, and the orthodox analytic community's attempts to suppress, censor, condemn, and silence Ferenczi were the darkest moments in the history of psychoanalysis (Rachman, 1997b). The process can be outlined in several stages:

DOI: 10.4324/9780429298431-8

96 Todschweigen, Death by Silence

1. Ferenczi decided to withdraw from Freud's influence by concentrating on analyzing the Incest Trauma and develop the Confusion of Tongues paradigm and Trauma Analysis. He separated from Freud and his orthodox followers so that he could be connected to and supported by his Hungarian colleagues, such as Michael Balint and Sándor Lorand. Ferenczi knew Freud would not accept this work. Ferenczi was correct. Freud heard about this work through the psychoanalysis grapevine and was afraid Ferenczi was planning to break away and found his own school, as Rank had done (Gay, 1984). It was at this time of separation and independence, roughly 1929–1933, that Ferenczi wrote his *Clinical Diary* (Ferenczi, 1988), unbeknownst to Freud.

2. Ferenczi, as a sign of respect and to honor Freud as well as to maintain their personal relationship, contacted Freud to give him a private reading of his Confusion of Tongues paper before he gave it at the 12th International Psychoanalytic Congress in 1932. Ferenczi read his paper to Freud, hoping for a positive response, but Freud became angry and dismissive. He actually turned his back on Ferenczi and refused to shake Ferenczi's hand to say goodbye after the paper was read to him (Fromm, 1959). Ferenczi was emotionally shattered by Freud's rejection. It was a trauma for Ferenczi (Rachman, 1997b).

3. At the Wëisbaden Congress, Ferenczi's Confusion of Tongues paper was unanimously condemned (Masson, 1984). A telegram was sent to Freud, who could not attend the Congress because of his struggle with mouth cancer, saying that Ferenczi's paper was "stupid" and "regressive" (Rachman, 1997b). Thus, began a process to formalize the repudiation of Ferenczi as not a psychoanalyst worthy of respect and study.

4. Apparently, Ernest Jones, with Freud's approval, began the process of Todschweigen. First, Jones reneged on a promise to publish the Confusion of Tongues paper, in English, in the official organ of psychoanalysis, *The International Journal of Psychoanalysis*. After Ferenczi's death, Jones did not publish the paper. A generation of analysts were deprived of the Confusion of Tongues paper until Ferenczi's student, Michael Balint, published it in the *International* in 1949 (Balint, 1949). The second dimensions of Jones's campaign to

discredit Ferenczi occurred in his Freud biography (Jones, 1957). In this biography, Jones deliberately and falsely accused Ferenczi of being mad or psychotic. Jones linked Ferenczi's so-called madness to his deviations in theory and technique (Jones, 1957). Jones's logic was that anyone who deviated so far from the Oedipal theory as Ferenczi did, must be mad (Rachman, 1997b). Balint defended Ferenczi saying that he was at his deathbed, was intellectually lucid and emotionally appropriate to the end (Balint, 1958).

5. The final dimension of silencing Ferenczi was developed when his work was removed from study in the approved traditional Psychoanalytic Institutes (Rachman, 1997b). After Ferenczi's death in 1933, his significance disappeared in the United States for about 50 years. It was not until his *Clinical Diary* was published in English in 1988 (Ferenczi, 1988), that his reputation and work began a rehabilitation. The Relational perspective claimed Ferenczi as their originator (Aron & Harris, 1993; Rachman, 1997a, 2003, 2010), as did Interpersonal Psychoanalysis (Wolstein, 1989, 1993), Object Relations (Balint, 1968), and Self-Psychology (Basch, 1984; Bausch, 1986; Rachman, 1989).

6. Jones's animosity toward Ferenczi needs to be examined. It has been assumed that Jones was jealous of Freud's closeness to Ferenczi and Freud's preference for Ferenczi over Jones. It was also hypothesized that Jones was angry that Ferenczi was his analyst, and, not his first choice, Freud. In actuality, Freud sent Jones to Ferenczi, when Jones asked Freud to be his analyst. Roazen (1975), developed an interesting idea about Jones's negative attitude toward Ferenczi, his former analyst. Roazen thought that Jones, in an emotional reversal, was initially angry at Freud for rejecting him for analysis and sending him to a peer rival for Freud's affection and recognition. But, Jones could not openly express his anger at the Master. The anger was suppressed and directed at Ferenczi.

The Todschweigen campaign will further be discussed in Chapter 28, My Attempts to Confront the Todschweigen, Death by Silence Campaign Against Ferenczi, Elizabeth Severn, and the Budapest School of Psychoanalysis.

Chapter 9

Sexual abuse of children within the family: the case of Lisa Steinberg

One of the meaningful findings of Freud's original findings in the Seduction Theory was that he shattered a social myth that located the sexual abuse of children in the hands of sinister strangers who lured unsuspecting children into back alleys to abuse them. What Freud, then Ferenczi presented was their clinical research, which indicated that childhood sexual abuse was prevalent in the cases of the middle- and upper-class patients they both regularly treated. Freud's original discovery that sexual predators were located in our families, not in our alleyways and castaway neighborhoods was stated as follows:

> It turned out that her supposedly otherwise noble and respectable father regularly took her to bed. (Freud, 1954, p. 195)

Freud's patients did not come from the lower classes, but from his own social class. The middle and upper classes of Viennese society were the individuals who first were intellectually and emotionally attracted to psychoanalysis, which was being identified in the European culture at the Fin-de-Siècle of the 20th Century.

If we examine Freud's iconic cases, we can re-evaluate that in the Case of Dora, Ida Bauer was a young girl who had sexual issues with a family friend, came from a middle-class family, whose father was a businessman (Freud, 1905). In the iconic case of the Wolf Man, Sergei Pankejeff, the patient was an upper-class Russian nobleman (Freud, 1919 [1918]).

We can now examine how prophetic Freud and Ferenczi were at the beginning of the 20th century when they informed society and

DOI: 10.4324/9780429298431-9

The case of Lisa Steinberg   99

psychoanalysis that we should look to ourselves to understand the sexual abuse of individuals in our society. In the next chapter, we will turn to one of the most notorious examples of child sexual abuse in a middle-class family in the history of the United States.

The case of Lisa Steinberg: a horrific case of child abuse in a middle-class family

On November 2, 1987, New York City police responded to a 911 call from Hedda Nussbaum, the common law wife of Joel Steinberg. Nussbaum was a former editor of children books at Random House. Steinberg was characterized as a millionaire lawyer. The couple lived in Greenwich Village with two illegally adopted children, Lisa and Mitchell. The family lived a life of squalor, drug abuse, systematic beatings, and paranoia behind a middle-class façade. When police entered the family apartment in Greenwich Village, they found the Steinberg's 6-year-old daughter, Lisa, beaten and unconscious. Joel and Hedda were arrested. Lisa died on November 5, 1987. Prosecutors later dropped any charges against Hedda, realizing she was also an abuse victim of Steinberg. Joel Steinberg was charged with second-degree murder and first-degree manslaughter. Convicted of manslaughter in 1988, in the first televised murder trial in the United States, Steinberg was given a sentence of 8-and-a-third to 25 years and released from prison in 2004. The trial included 7 days of damaging testimony from Nussbaum, which indicated that Steinberg had been a physical, emotional, and sexual abuser of his daughter. What is more, his abusive behavior lead to the child's death (Kantrowitz et al., 1988; King, 2003). At the trial of Joel Steinberg, Hedda Nussbaum testified that a 2-year-old Lisa Steinberg showed clear signs of sexual abuse in 1983, but that she did nothing about it (New York Times, 1988).

Joel Steinberg, the devil parent, and Lisa Steinberg, the murdered child

The night Hedda Nussbaum phoned police, there were a series of bizarre events that led to Lisa's tragic death. Apparently, Steinberg took Lisa into the bathroom, apparently to punish her. Minutes later, Steinberg was holding Lisa in his outstretched arms. The child was limp. When Nussbaum asked for an explanation, he answered in an incoherent way:

What's the difference what happened? This is your child. Hasn't this gone far enough? (Kantrowitz, Wingert, King, Robbins, & Namuth, 1988, p. 57)

In her testimony at his trial, Nussbaum clarified what had happened. Steinberg was angry at Lisa for staring at him. It is likely, his paranoid attitude fueled by substance abuse was active, since he was in a phase of heavy drug abuse. Steinberg admitted this:

I knocked her down and she didn't want to get up again. This staring business had gotten to be too much. (Kantrowitz et al., 1988, p. 58)

When Nussbaum tried to revive the child, Steinberg in an apparently detached and dissociated state told Nussbaum to relax and go with the flow. He left for dinner, telling Nussbaum to let her sleep, and he would take care of it when he returned. While Lisa lay comatose and dying on the bathroom floor, Nussbaum believed Steinberg's healing powers would bring her back to life when he returned 3 hours later. Nussbaum's emotional trauma fueled the belief the child would be healed by Steinberg. Lisa died 3 days later. As in the case of Elizabeth Smart, her sexual abuser, the person who believed he was a healer was really the devil (Rachman, 2016).

Joel Steinberg: the "devil parent"

One of the ways a sexual survivor educated me as an analyst to understand and treat a sexual trauma was to make me emphatically attuned to his repeatedly declarations that his mother was "evil," "she tried to kill me" (Rachman, 1988, 1991; Rachman & Klett, 2015). At first, and now I am referring to about 50 years, when Winston first said these words to me (Rachman & Klett, 2015), I felt they were an exaggeration. There were no data that his mother was a criminal or a psychopath. I did not understand then, that Winston was honestly revealing the interior of the darkest segments of his emotional interior to me. In the spaces of these dark crevices of his mind, he was trying to tell me what had been created by his interactions with his mother, and other members of his family during his childhood and beyond, which lead to him to feel so insecure, frightened, threatened, paranoid, and helpless that he feared for his life. By the time he was 8 years old, he would wake up in the middle of the night, and believe that his mother was out to kill him. In actuality, there were times when he would make up in the middle of the night and his mother was in the room, standing over his bed, staring at him. She believed that she was in the room because she needed to give a loving glance at her cherished son. What she did not understand was that her son was *experiencing her as the devil*, not a loving parent. This is what Winston taught me to understand the phenomenology of the analysand's experience. He insisted, in the same way Elizabeth Severn did with Sándor Ferenczi, when she insisted he listen to her attempts to tell him he had negative feelings with their clinical relationship (Rachman, 2018). As Ferenczi successfully searched his own subjective experience to understand that he was involved in a negative countertransference reaction to Severn. I struggled to understand what Freud and Ferenczi first understood: Middle-, upper-middle and upper-class parents can seriously abuse their children. The abuse Winston withstood was emotional, not the physical/sexual abuse of Joel Steinberg of Lisa Steinberg. But, Winston's narcissistic, and perhaps, borderline mother also created sexual abuse that damaged her child for the rest of his life (Rachman & Klett, 2015). Steinberg's abuse of Lisa was not different in that he chose sexual, physical, and emotional abuse. Winston's mother was perceived as the devil, in the same way Joel Steinberg acted in his horrific abuse of his daughter Lisa.

The designation of a abusive parent as the "devil" was so clearly annunciated by another abused analysand, when during a session he described his father's horrific anal rape of him when he was 9-years old. His description of his father's behavior speaks for itself:

> Your parents are supposed to be God's presence here on earth. They are supposed to protect you, love you, they are not supposed to be the devil, here on earth, and abuse you. It is so hard to accept your father, is the devil. But, he was! (Rachman, 1993)

In 1990, Geraldo Rivera, the investigative reporter, interviewed Joel Steinberg at a prison in upstate New York, when he was serving his eight-and-one-third to 25 years sentence for the manslaughter conviction in the death of his adopted daughter, Lisa. In the interview, Rivera described his personal reaction when he tried to have a meaningful conversation with Steinberg about his version of what happened the night of Lisa's injury and death:

> But I must also tell you Joel Steinberg is one of the most difficult, controlling, paranoid and unpleasant people I have ever interviewed. He made even a monster like Charles Manson seem almost pleasant by comparison. (Rivera, 1990, p. 2)

When I went over this transcript of the interview my impression was that Steinberg was a hostile respondent: He is angry that he is being blamed; he was in a dissociative state, wishing to maintain his position as being totally innocent; he is an *evil predator*, or, all three.

Three decades after the death of his daughter, Lisa, Joel Steinberg had been released early from prison, serving a 17-year term. The early release was based on his being a model prisoner. The now 76-year old lives a marginal life, as an aging loner in the Harlem section of New York City. He has been seen scrounging cigarettes from strangers and hitting up a local vegetable store for rotting fruit and vegetables for fertilizer for his ground floor garden outside his apartment. He ekes out a living as a disbarred lawyer. When he was interviewed in 2017, he did not show any remorse for his horrific child abuse of his daughter, took no responsibility for killing his daughter or the abuse of his common-law wife, Hedda Nussbaum. In fact, he complains that he is the victim in this story, who never gets any concern for the emotional difficulty he has sustained (Fenton, Rosner & Golding, 2017). Steinberg is an interesting example of how both parties in the Confusion of Tongues paradigm (Ferenczi, 1933) become involved in an emotionally damaging experience. As the interview material of Steinberg in 2017 revealed, he seems to be in the same dissociative state he was when in 1988, he left his daughter Lisa lying comatose on the floor, was absent for 3 hours and returned with the delusion that his healing powers would return his daughter to good health. Both Steinberg and Nussbaum became emotional captives in a Confusion of Tongues trauma, sharing the same delusion that he had healing powers. Nussbaum did not call 911 during the 3 hours that Steinberg was away, believing he would heal his daughter when he returned

The case of Lisa Steinberg   103

from dinner. We have rarely paid attention to the emotional disorder that ensues in the abuser as a result of creating a trauma in another.

Although Ferenczi's main focus in the Confusion of Tongues paradigm was on the victimization of the child by the adult, it is clear from his formulation that the adult perpetrator is also emotionally altered by the trauma of abuse. The adult abuser's expression of their narcissistic needs on the child is only a momentary satisfaction that will need continued satisfaction by a less powerful object (Rachman, 1997, p. 233).

Hedda Nussbaum: a study in the Confusion of Tongues trauma

Hedda Nussbaum can be described as a survivor of a Confusion of Tongues trauma (Rachman, 1992). In her relationship with Joel Steinberg, she became confused, dissociated, dysfunctional, and traumatized as a result of her relationship with Steinberg. She became an emotional captive of Steinberg, worshipping him as having special capacities to heal. The Confusion of Tongues trauma was established by Steinberg through his domination, control, and manipulation of her, his physical abuse and threatening behavior, and his encouragement of her to join him in free-basing cocaine. She became a victim of his abuse, as Ferenczi described the child becoming the victim of the parental abuser (Rachman & Klett, 2015). In her words, Nussbaum described this Confusion of Tongues experience:

> I often think about "what if" and I wish I had been able to [protect the children]. But I know why I didn't act – and that's what Joel Steinberg had done with the brainwashing and the control he had over me. He is the one [who] is responsible. (Connor, 2003)

Nussbaum's physical abuse by Steinberg was horrific. According to her, Steinberg first hit her in 1978. Unfortunately, she chose to ignore the violence. Over the years to follow, Steinberg continued his physical abuse of Nussbaum that lead to her sustaining black eyes, broken bones, burns, and beatings that she detailed at Steinberg's murder trial. An examining physician, when he was brought to the hospital, added to the details of the physical trauma, indicating:

she suffered from anemia and was a hunchback due to calcium deficiency. She also had cuts on her lip, broken cheekbones, a broken nose, a large bruise on her right buttock, multiple broken ribs and ulcers on her legs so widespread that they were life threatening. (Gado, 2003)

Dr. Samuel Klagsbrun, the director of Four Winds Hospital in Westchester, New York, a psychiatric hospital, treated Nussbaum gratis. After her release from custody, he called her physical condition:

[the] worst case of a battered woman I have ever seen... [comparing her to a] concentration camp victim coming out of a deep freeze. (Goldberg, 1989, p. 16)

Nussbaum's battered face became the grotesque symbol of abuse in family interaction in America.

As damaging as was Nussbaum's physical abuse by Steinberg, her emotional abuse transformed her from an attractive, high-functioning editor at Random House to an individual who was in an emotional stupor, looked like a punch drunk fighter, who was an emotional prisoner of her partner. Nussbaum testified that in 1983, she began to believe she was involved in a cult that hypnotized others through staring and made her have sex with men (Whitaker, 1989). Steinberg was paranoid, fueled, at least in part, by a cocaine addiction. The cult fantasy of Nussbaum may have also been fueled by Steinberg who regularly stared at her. He struck his daughter, Lisa, which lead to her death, when he felt she was staring at him. Nussbaum was clearly what Ferenczi (1933) called an "automata," a person who becomes a robot due to abuse by an authority. She became an emotional prisoner of Steinberg. Dr. Klagsbrun, the medical doctor at Four Winds Hospital, said the following about their emotional relationship:

She was a slave, totally submissive to this man, with no ability or will to save her own daughter. (Krantrowitz, Wingert, King, & Robbins, 1988, p. 57)

Hedda's own assessment of her relationship with Joel matched her psychiatrist's assessment:

I know that he, like other abusive men, wants power and control. That's their main goal. Whatever excuses they give, that's what they want. And he seemed to thrive from it…He little by little – he just needed the next kick to be higher. (King, 2003, p. 23)

Nussbaum, after a year in Four Winds Hospital, was able to put her life back together.

Chapter 10

A mother invites her daughter to incest: parental neglect of childhood abuse

This is a story of a disturbed and unusual relationship between a mother and daughter in a family of privilege. They had diametrically opposed reactions to dealing with the issue of sexual abuse. The difference in the mother and daughter's way of dealing with their childhood traumas greatly influenced their personal adjustment and interpersonal relationship. Rather than being able to support each other, sharing their traumas and struggles to cope, they became enemies. Their contentious relationship pushed the two to the edge of their existence. This case has great relevance to the issue of confronting and recovering from childhood sexual trauma. Some of the individuals who have been accused of sexual abuse of women, such as Harvey Weinstein (see Chapter 23), have not honestly encountered their behavior or been motivated to change it. In the present example, the mother completely distances herself from her childhood trauma and then, when her daughter became aware of her childhood sexual trauma, the mother, in essence, attacked her daughter, rather than show empathy. The unfolding of this mother/daughter drama can be used to understand the road to recovery from childhood sexual trauma.

A young woman from a privileged family, Soma, in her early 20s sought analysis, referred by her new-age therapist she had seen during her college years. The therapist was very helpful in helping in reducing the daughter's anxiety and depression she had suffered since childhood. Since adolescence, Soma had been experiencing a series of intense physical and psychological symptoms. The physical symptoms were very intrusive and when they began to become dominant

DOI: 10.4324/9780429298431-10

in her adolescence, they interfered with her physical well-being. Soma came from a privileged family. Her father was an international businessman, traveled frequently to various countries, and was financially very successful. He was experienced as a kind person, who provided very well for his family. However, his time and energy were channeled into his work. Her mother's background was modest, coming from a working-class family. She, through her ambitions, parlayed her good looks, intelligence, and her husband's wealth and social status, into elevating herself into upper-class status. Her happiness seemed to be exemplified by enjoying her life of privilege, hobnobbing with socially prominent men and women, living in one of the important addresses in an important city, and having the freedom to shop for whatever pleased her to purchase, for example, clothes, furnishings, entertainment, or food. Her husband was often away on business. She was *one of the ladies who lunched*, as Tom Wolfe had characterized the upper-class women whose main activity during the weekdays would be to meet each other for lunch. Although she was very intelligent and had graduated Magna Cum Laude from an Ivy League college, she used her intellect as a sideline to pursue some areas of interest to her, such as history, literature, and the theater.

The life of privilege did not produce contentment for this family. The father was sexually active with women other than his wife, to which he used an overactive sexual drive as an explanation. His wife was not a woman who was a passive, despondent individual. She decided to free herself as a victim of her husband's sexual activity by developing a network of men who were available, with whom she would have sexual contact. These men were walkers with favors, younger men who enjoyed being a companion to and having sex with older women. Both the father and mother's activities were family undercurrents. But, the daughter's issues were visible and preoccupied the family narrative.

Since early adolescence, the daughter manifested a group of physical symptoms, such as stomach pains, cramping, bloating, gas, and diarrhea. As she entered adolescence proper, her symptoms intensified and there were periods where she was hospitalized because of severe abdominal pains, frequent bathroom trips, inability to metabolize certain foods, weight loss, and a lack of appetite. The family zeroed in on their child's problem as a medical issue. The physicians to whom the family turned for help were the top-rated diagnosticians in their field. The daughter was given tests, her body was scanned, X-rayed, scoped, and fully examined. The physicians agreed on the diagnosis of Irritable Bowel Syndrome (IBS) (Chey, Kurlander, & Eswaran, 2015). Approximately one in five adults in the United States have this disorder. Women are more likely to experience these symptoms which usually begin in late adolescence or early adulthood. There is no known specific cause, but some experts suggest people who suffer from IBS have a colon that is more sensitive and reactive to certain foods and stress. People with IBS frequently suffer from anxiety and depression, which can worsen their symptoms. The colon is in part controlled by the nervous system, which responds to stress. Evidence also suggests that the immune system, also responding to stress, plays a role. IBS can also make you feel more anxious and depressed. What is more, research has found that 50%–90% of individuals have a psychiatric disorder such as an anxiety disorder or depression (Zhang, Ross & Davidson, 2004).

This family searched their memory and questioned extended family members as to whether there was any family history of IBS. There was no history of anyone in the present extended family or in the history of the family in several generations with IBS, or a related medical condition. How or when the daughter developed IBS was a family mystery and preoccupation. Both parents did everything they could to treat their child's medical condition.

There was, however, an ever-present disturbed relationship between the mother and daughter. In fact, one could say, there was an ever-present psychological warfare between the two. The daughter's contribution to the disturbed relationship was treating her mother as a servant. She had the mother on tenderhooks, afraid to say anything to her daughter that would lead to her daughter releasing angry outbursts, or her daughter instituting the silent treatment. The daughter would stop talking to her and only say, "yes" or "no," to the mother's attempts to have a conversation. The mother attributed her daughter's anger to an irritability associated with her IBS. The mother rationalized the daughter's enslavement of her, as her willingness to sacrifice her needs and functioning to please her daughter who was suffering from intense physical and emotional disturbances. The mother suppressed her anger toward her daughter's abuse. In actuality, both for mother and daughter acted out their anger, taking turns being the slave and master. At no time, did any members of the family ask the question: what is the meaning of this disturbance between mother and daughter? The best explanation the father gave was his daughter was going through the normal adolescent difficulties. Neglecting the possibility of any psychological explanation for the mother/daughter difficulties imitated the neglect of considering any psychological factors for the daughter's IBS disorder. The daughter's family, the extended family, and the physicians who consulted with the family, all collaborated in neglecting any thought or possibility that there was psychological factors on the daughter's physical difficulties or her medical disorder.

A turning point in the daughter's and the family's life began when she was sent to boarding school during her early adolescence. On the one hand, boarding school was a family tradition, but, on the other hand, it may have served an unconscious motivation. Sending her to boarding school removed the difficulties from the everyday concern of the mother and father. Interestingly enough, sending the daughter away had an unsuspected effect. Separating from the family of origin for a significant period of time, allows the child to begin to hear and respond to the voice of other authorities and, especially, *the voice of the peer* (Rachman, 1975).

At boarding school, she made friendships easily since she is an intelligent, likeable, sweet, and responsive person. She was sought out by classmates. Slowly, she started sharing her anxieties about her illness. In this way, when she was not available to meet with her friends, they would know she was in bed with cramps, or was spending time on the toilet. Her medical issues did not abate while attending preparatory school or college. Although she was intellectually gifted, her academic success was limited, as there were frequent school absences due to ill health, including hospitalizations.

The daughter was befriended by the school nurse in college, to whom she is frequently sent to deal with her illness. This nurse observed the daughter's anxiety and depression. This was the first adult to understand that she had serious emotional issues. A semi-therapeutic relationship began, where this young emotionally needy young woman began to share her emotional life with the nurse. It did not take long for the nurse to realize her young ward needed ongoing therapy by a mental health professional. The nurse wanted to refer the daughter to a therapist, but Soma was not ready for a formal therapy relationship with an adult. She was not ready to trust an adult with her interior life since she had never had an experience like that until the nurse had reached out to her. The nurse had an interest in psychology and knew about groups that were led by a variety of therapeutic orientations. The nurse referred this young woman to a college-age group with a focus on relationships with parents.

At first, curiosity fueled her attendance at these weekly seminars. Apparently, she was ready to explore her inner world as she became increasingly more comfortable in the group within a month or so. In the same way, she felt comfortable and connected to her school mates, she became attached to her group members. Going to group became as important as going to school. In her quiet, intelligent, and gentle way, she told of her anxiety and depression, which she believed she lived with since grammar school. For the first time, she could share and begin to understand the noise she had heard inside her head since she was a lonely little child. The group leader was a woman in her 30s who was knowledgeable about family dynamics and was empathic and kind in the way she led the group. It was a new and welcome experience, contrasting with the aggressive and know-it-all attitude of her mother.

With the help of the group leader, Soma was being helped to examine what might have happened to her as a child that caused her misery rather than suffer from it. Something was beginning to become clear in her thinking and feeling. She began to allow herself to feel she had serious angry feelings toward her parents. But she was confused about the origin of her anger as well as what to do with these feelings.

Soma was now in the third year of college as she settled in to finishing her degree and going to group regularly. She noticed something about her functioning that was actually hard to believe. She noticed she was not suffering as much with her IBS as she had in the past. That had never happened before. Before she graduated from college, she asked the group leader to recommend an individual therapist for her. The group leader said she would, and then, spent some time with her advising Soma to use her group experience to uncover the origins of her parental anger. She was also told to see an analyst who specialized in early childhood trauma. What happened next in this young woman's life became a tipping point. She became completely absorbed in uncovering and confronting what turned out to be an instance of a childhood sexual experience with her father.

Soma now became intensely involved in a three time a week analysis with a female analyst who was a trauma specialist. It was very instructive to see a young woman from a family who was not psychologically minded become immersed in uncovering and analyzing her childhood incest traumas. I believe what this case can illustrate is the importance of creating an empathic and accepting atmosphere for a trauma survivor, which allows the unfolding of the formerly dissociated split-off trauma experience, while creating a holding environment for *the poison of a relational holocaust caused by being raped by a parent*. The protype sexual abuse experience that came into focus was as follows:

> The father would come into his daughter's bedroom in the middle of the night and molest her. In her younger years, ages 4-6 years, he would play with her genitals as she faked being asleep. As she became a child of 6-8 years, he began to molest her in a more sexually aggressive way. He would wake her up to play with his penis. As this sexually abused child became increasingly terrified as her father escalated the abuse to placing his penis in her mouth, she developed a plan to escape her nights of terror.

Soma, as an eight-year-old child, developed the following plan of escape:

> Soma would go to sleep as usual. Then she would set her alarm clock for 4 am, about one half hour before her father would come into her room. When her alarm clock sounded, she would leave her bedroom, which was on a lower floor of the house. She then would hide in her bathroom, which was next to her bedroom. She locked the bathroom from the inside and stayed there for about one hour or so, trembling on the cold tile floor. When her father went looking for her and kept trying to open the bathroom door, she remained silent. After several such incidents, the father rationalized she locked herself into the bathroom because she

was having flair-ups in her IBS. After a month or two of her disappearances, the father realized his daughter had found a way to escape from his sexual abuse.

The molestation by the father was conducted in total silence, the abuser and the abused never uttering a word between them. What is more, the daughter never spoke to anyone about the abuse. It ended in a dead silence, but the abuse did end.

The mother was not only a *bystander to the sexual abuse* (Miller, 1984), but, as we shall see, she had her own inner silence with which to deal. Their joint inner silences created a dramatic crisis between herself and her daughter. The aftermath of uncovering the childhood sexual abuse by her father changed the daughter and family's life. Once the child sexual abuse trauma was firmly established and being worked through, Soma and her analyst felt it was time to bring the parents into the therapeutic situation. To work through her trauma, Soma wanted to tell her father about her abuse, which he had, all these years, studiously avoided. She wanted to face her abuser with the terrorizing feelings of her childhood, which caused her to develop the physical disorder of IBS and the psychological symptoms of anxiety and depression. She wanted her father to feel what she felt, the "terrorism of suffering," which was the concept that Ferenczi used to describe the phenomenology of a child being sexually abused by a parent (Ferenczi, 1933). Part of this desire was based on her rage for the suffering that her father had inflicted on her when he would molest her during the early mornings, breaking the warmth and safety of her sleep. *He turned a child's private reverie into a terrorist's attack.* He demonstrated that terrorism, as both Freud and Ferenczi first showed us, can reside in the ramparts of the family castle. Soma suffered such terrorism. She also wanted to have some kind of relationship with her father that could be reconstructed on the basis of reconciliation. Afterall, if Israel and world Jewry can have a meaningful relationship with present-day Germany, after the Holocaust, perhaps she could accomplish a reconciliation with her father.

Soma, in breaking through her dissociation, found both her anger and her love for her father. She wanted to work through the terrorism of the trauma and reach an affection for her father. She knew he also wanted that. In this process, an attempt was first made to reduce

Soma's anger before the necessary consultation session with her father. She was encouraged to join a gym to translate her anger into discharge of energy in a creative activity. In this way, a therapeutic zone would be established to talk about the issues, after becoming enamored with the physical and emotional benefits from regularly working out. When she felt her anger was subsiding, she told the analyst she was ready to meet her father.

The father met his daughter at the analyst's office. Soma kissed her father on the cheek before the session. The father noticed she was noticeably nervous. The analyst did his best to make the father comfortable. Soma was ready to begin the session and invited him to respond to information he knew, but never wanted to confront. When his daughter began the session with her father, it became clear they were both ready to be open and caring with each other. She began by simply saying to him:

> Dad, all my work in therapy during the last years says many of the problems I have is due to the fact that you molested me as a child. I know you and Mom do not want to talk about this. *But, we have to!* Ok?

Then her father responded by saying:

> You're right, it is time to talk. I know I wasn't willing to before, but, I am now,

The atmosphere was set to confront the childhood abuse. For the 1½ hour session that was scheduled, daughter and father cried, hugged each other, showed anxiety, and relief. In the midst of the emotions expressed, a remarkable event occurred. Soma made a very important contribution to this event. She did not accuse her father, nor did she vent her anger toward him. Rather, she invited him to join her on working through their horrific trauma. The father responded quickly and positively. He gave a remarkable response to her invitation to talk about her molestation:

> Yes, honey I did do those awful things to you. *I am so sorry, please forgive me.* I was in a sick, bad place. I will do whatever you now need to get better. I can assure you of that.

Soma started to cry after his confession, and, then they both cried and hugged each other. There was a vulnerability that the father showed as if he was liberated by the daughter's confrontation with him.

In the next stage of the reconciliation stage of working through the incest trauma, the experience with the mother was much more difficult than with the father. We will gain an important understanding from analyzing the mother's interaction with her daughter as well as the parent's psychodynamics in working on their issues in the sexual trauma of their child. The mother was not invited to the session with the father because Soma was aware of her mother's intensely negative reaction when she was told about the daughter's childhood molestation by her husband. After Soma felt she was emotionally able to deal with her angry mother, a 1½ hour session was scheduled. However, the day proceeding their session, Soma had a reoccurrence of severe gastrointestinal (GI) symptoms. Ironically, she felt this type of a somatic reaction would have happened before her session with her father. In a sense, the mother's negative reaction was a re-traumatizing experience. As we shall see, the mother could not accept the daughter's account that her father repeatedly molested her. When Soma recovered from the GI attack, the mother agreed to attend a joint session with her daughter's analyst. Once again, the daughter demonstrated great courage. She began the session by repeating the molestation charge against her father. However, this time she could add that her father admitted he molested her. The father's admission to the sexual abuse did not convince the mother of the reality of the abuse. In fact, the mother was adamant that this abuse could not have happened. She would exclaim:

> How could your father have sexually abused you for years and, I did not know about it? That is not possible!

There was a second defense against the abuse allegation. She told her daughter she had done a great deal of research on the topic and she had her own evidence to the contrary.

It is necessary to investigate the mother's psychology to understand the discrepancy between her daughter and her husband's idea about the issue of sexual abuse and her own.

The mother had graduated from one of the most prestigious colleges in the United States. The mother's intellect was a gift, which she used to academically achieve, gain status, and self-esteem. She was proud of her gift and had great confidence in her capacity, "to figure things out." Unfortunately, she could not really "figure out" what her daughter was talking about. The fundamental confrontational statement, the mother would offer over and over again to the issue of her daughter's childhood sexual abuse was:

> Don't you think I would know if my husband had sex with my daughter?

On the surface, her question has some superficial validity. It seems inconceivable that a mother would be totally unaware of a regular sexual experience between her husband and her daughter. Yet, all the clinical research on father/daughter incest indicated from Ferenczi onward, that mothers were fundamentally unaware of the sexual crimes in their own homes.

The mother seemed to be in trauma that her daughter accused her husband with incest. She was being blamed for bringing a pervert into her family. It was inconceivable that this could have happened. A cacophony of emotional chords ran through the mother's brain as if she were going through shock therapy against her will. There was only one way to reduce the emotional shock. She needed to take control of this crisis herself, using her considerable intellect as the major tool.

First, she read the self-help books on incest, and then, she moved on to the professional materials. She was actually creating a tutorial course for herself on the incest trauma. But, this tutorial had a particular focus. Soma's mother was not researching this subject to help her empathically understand her daughter, but rather, to demonstrate she was a hysterical liar. In her research, the mother found and completely embraced the False Memory Syndrome (Whitefield, Selberg & Fink, 2001). It is true, that overly aggressive trauma therapists have been responsible for encouraging certain vulnerable individuals to retrieve questionable childhood memories of sexual abuse. In these instances, the therapist's aggressiveness and narcissism and the individual's vulnerability can produce false memories of childhood sexual abuse.

There is a fascinating psychodynamic in the founding of the False Memory Syndrome Institute that parallels Soma and her mother's conflict over the incest trauma. The founders of the False Memory Syndrome were Peter and Pamela Freyd, the father and mother of Jennifer Freyd. Jennifer Freyd accused her father of incest (Freyd, 1996, 2015). Therefore, the founding of the False Memory Institute was an attempt to discredit the daughter, Jennifer's, accusation of incest. Soma's mother used her research, try as she may, to discredit her own daughter's accusation of incest.

Before mother and daughter met at the analyst's office, Soma needed an individual session prior to the joint session with her mother. The analyst clearly gave her the idea he would help her to talk honestly to her mother. Soma had spoken to him several times to prepare her for her mother's intellectual approach to her emotional trauma. She needed to accept her mother's method of coping with severe emotional issues. Neither the analyst nor Soma were prepared for the mother to enter the joint session with a lawyer's briefcase filled with handwritten note pads, typed papers, reprints of articles, and bound and paper-back books. After a brief exchange of pleasantries, the mother used almost three-quarters of the session defending the False Memory Syndrome, and the impossibility of her not being aware of her husband's molestation of her daughter. The analyst was able to empathize with the crisis the daughter's revelation has caused the mother. The analyst said that she believed the daughter was telling the truth. She came to that conclusion as a result of tracing the origins of Soma's anxieties, fears, and symptoms. There was an internal consistency about her story and her personal functioning. As a specialist in treating trauma survivors, he had heard and treated Soma's kind of story many, many times. What is more, the literature on trauma studies also verifies Soma's experience. Since the mother had a strong intellectual orientation, the analyst would be happy to give her meaningful references on child sexual abuse to be compared to the ones she had already researched. The mother was initially speechless but nodded yes, she would accept the references.

As the time approached for the end of this joint session, it was clear to everyone present, ending the session would be a blessing. Soma graciously thanked her mother for being willing to attending such a difficult meeting. Her mother had tears in her eyes, as her daughter's kind words helped sooth her wounds. The analyst waited until the mother and daughter had their moment together, and then asked the therapeutic duo if they would have another session. Soma deferred, and her mother softly said, "yes."

After about a month, the mother contacted the analyst. He told Soma that the joint session she had was a triumph of her capacity to empathize with her mother's emotional struggle at a time when her own struggle was so uppermost in her mind. The analyst said to her he was very proud of her emotional courage and interpersonal maturity in the way she was relating to her mother. Her mother, the analyst thought, was having a more difficult time with her incest trauma than she was. All these comments seem to help Soma. But, the mother was struggling.

The analyst had expected the mother to have contacted her as soon as she heard the word incest. But, knowing her tendency toward intellectualization, he realized the mother was trying to treat this crisis with her own resources. As is often the case, when defending against confronting sexual abuse, denial, dissociation, and intellectualization can take you so far, and no further. The simple fact was that the mother could not accept emotionally, that her daughter was incested by her husband. The analyst empathized with her struggle and how difficult it was to wrap her head around this tragedy. Soma's mother found the courage to ask him directly:

Please, please tell me honestly, do you think my daughter was incested?

There was only one way to answer the question, so he offered her the following:

There is no way I can really know if Soma was incested. I tend to take her word for it because she has described the experience in the same way I have heard from the incest survivors with whom I have worked for over thirty years. I don't understand why your daughter would make this up.

If you don't want to believe it's true, I can understand this too. Just see Soma's trauma as something that is real to her. Help her come to peace with it by being on her side.

A final word. Don't lose your relationship with your daughter over this issue. Please, this is the emotional test of your life. You have all the emotional, intellectual, social goods, and maternal instincts to pass this test.

She did not fight with the analyst about what was said to her, hoping she would move from the darkness into the light.

When Soma evaluated the results of the joint sessions she had with her parents, she felt she had accomplished a great deal. She found her voice, lost since her childhood trauma. She was able to share her secret of incest with them. Now, the family of origin knew about the psychological derivation of their daughter's illness. Confusion, criticism, improper medical treatment, could give way to empathy, understanding, and recovery from trauma. And most of all, they could observe in their daughter's struggle to uncover her incest trauma, her confronting her demons, and tell her secret to them. She presented herself, not as a sickly, passive, rebellious dropout, but, as a vital, determined, courageous young woman.

Soma's physical health improved. She began to understand the psychosomatic aspects to her IBS. Her intense anxiety and depression was triggered by her father's sexual abuse, which found a somatic outlet in a vulnerable organ site, her GI system. She now had a two-prong treatment for her illness. Medical treatment for her physical symptoms and analysis for her emotional disturbance.

Chapter 11

The "sensuous psychiatrist": the case of Julie Roy vs. Renatus Hartogs, MD, PhD: landmark case of sexual abuse by a therapist

When I was a newly trained analyst in the late 1960s, there was a frequently traveled rumor in psychotherapy and psychoanalytic circles that there was a psychiatrist that was famous for two issues. It was widely known from the firsthand account reports of former patients that Renatus Hartogs, MD, waiting room was usually overflowing with patients. From rumors and former patient reports, Hartogs would see patients for very brief drug consultations, 5 or 10 minutes at a time, for high fees. These reports of his exploitative behavior were amplified by the rumors that Hartogs had sex with his patients. These issues became more of a heightened undercurrent as the encounter movement experimented with physical contact as part of the therapeutic encounter (Back, 1972). Anytime, I heard the gossip about Hartogs sexual behavior with patients, the reaction by analysts was criticism without any negative statement of his activity or willingness to report or investigate the unethical behavior. I had the same reaction, feeling *nothing could be done because the field of psychotherapy/psychoanalysis wanted to maintain silence about exposing the sexual abuse of a psychiatrist*. This was an example of neglecting the issue of sexual abuse. If a neophyte analyst had heard about the sexual abuses of patients by Hartogs, certainly, senior analysts and senior administrative members of the mental health profession knew about his abusive behavior. However, nothing was done to deal with the problem in an effective way. As a result of the neglect of confronting a therapist about the sexual abuse of a patient, the harm to the patient was not only continued, but also lead to,

DOI: 10.4324/9780429298431-11

according to the patient, hospitalization due to deteriorating emotional functioning.

The silence about Hartogs' sexual abuse of patients was broken, not by the profession, but by an abused patient. In 1971, a 31-year-old woman, Julie Roy, filed a legal suit against Hartogs, accusing him of forcing her to have sexual relations with him, trying to convince her that it was a therapeutic method to help her cure her lesbianism.

Renatus Hartogs, MD, PhD, also referred as René, was born in Mainz, Germany, on January 22, 1909. He received a PhD from the University of Frankfurt and a medical degree from the University of Brussels Medical School and practiced as a psychologist. Before he fled the Nazis, he was the editor of a psychological journal. He immigrated to the United States in 1940. To practice medicine in the United States, he had to study medicine again, this time in Montreal, Canada, and psychopathology in New York City. He was the Chief Psychiatrist at Youth House in New York City.

Hartogs became involved in the President Kennedy assassination investigation because he had examined Lee Harvey Oswald at Youth House. He examined Oswald in 1953, when he was 13 years old because of school truancy. Hartogs published a book about this experience (Hartogs, 1976). His testimony about Oswald for the Warren Commission can be found online (Liebeler & Hartogs, 1964).

This biographical statement was found in the archive of the Leo Baeck Institute, which is a depository for German Jews of note (Ritchey, 2011). It is a sanitized version of his noteworthiness, since it does not mention his notorious and landmark sexual abuse case, (Roy vs. Hartogs, 1976). The case is one of the most important legal suits in the area of the alleged sexual abuse by a therapist of a patient. A 31-year-old secretary, Julie Roy, was "treated" by Hartogs, a New York psychiatrist, from March 1969 to September 1970. Ms. Roy accused Hartogs that his treatment method included regular sexual intercourse, which he convinced her was a therapeutic contribution to her therapy. She reported that Hartogs forced her to have sexual relations with him "under the guise" of psychiatric treatment (Chesler, 1972):

> As a result of this improper treatment, counsel alleged that the plaintiff [Julie Roy] was so emotionally and mentally injured that

she was required to seek hospitalization on two occasions during 1971. (Roy vs. Hartogs, 1976)

At the trial (Roy vs. Hartogs, 1976), the fifth causes of action, malpractice, was tried. At the trial, the following was established:

Hartogs under the guise of medical therapy to cure his patient's lesbianism, during a period of 13 months prescribed and personally administered, repetitive doses of *Fornicatus Hartogus*, Hartogs prescribed sexual contact with himself as if it was a medical prescription. Judgment for over $150,000 was entered for the plaintiff against Hartogs who, since this defendant disclaimed coverage, was defended by his own attorney. While the appeal was pending, the defendant insurer, despite its disclaimer to Hartogs, settled with the patient and satisfied a reduced judgment.

In this action, Hartogs seeks to recover his costs and expenses in defending the action in which he was adjudicated as having indulged *Concupiscentia medicus*, which means his own desires were camouflaged as medicinal.

Renatus Hartogs, PhD, MD, went on trial because a sexually abused patient sued him for punitive damages. The case centered on discussing whether the defendant's improper behavior deserved financial compensation. Why the legal issue was not focused on charging the psychiatrist with rape? Why the forceable sexual behavior of the psychiatrist on a female patient was not considered equivalent to rape? Was it that the rape laws were different, at the time of the Roy/Hartogs trial in 1975–1976? As this manuscript has argued psychoanalysis and society need to confront sexual abuse directly and speak the truth, as Ferenczi had done by identifying the abusers and embracing the abused.

Chapter 12

A group analyst's neglect of childhood sexual abuse

It is clear now, that after years of serious neglect of actual childhood sexual trauma, that contemporary psychoanalysis is paying some attention to this issue. The Self-Psychology, Interpersonal, and Relational Analysis perspectives have focused on the theory and treatment of adult survivors of childhood sexual abuse (Davies & Frawley, 1994; Nemiroff, Schindler & Schrieber, 2000; Schwartz, 2000; Street, 2008). We have entered into an era of new perspectives as psychoanalysis was able to re-integrate Freud and Ferenczi's earliest findings of actual sexual trauma in children as a central psychodynamic in development of psychological disorder. However, there are still instances of contemporary psychoanalysts of neglecting childhood sexual abuse.

During a recent session, on May 15, 2018, in the analysis of an incest survivor, the tradition of not only neglect but also discouraging the analysis of actual childhood sexual trauma occurred. The analysand in a regularly scheduled individual session reported an incident that occurred in her group analysis that she had regularly attended as part of her conjoint therapy regime. As the analysand became less dissociated, she was able to confront and analyze her childhood sexual abuse at age of 4 years by an adult male neighbor. She then became interested in sharing and examining her trauma with the group. In the past, there was no regular interaction in group about childhood sexual abuse, even though my analysand had introduced the topic several years ago. The analysand and I had had regular interaction about her using the group to help her work through her sexual abuse issues. I had suggested to her that in her

DOI: 10.4324/9780429298431-12

reports of group interaction I had felt the group interaction neglected exploration of sexual material, which does not contribute to her psychological well-being. In fact, I had felt there was what could be called, "a wall of silence" in regard to sexual issues, both in childhood and adulthood in the group interaction.

In our May 15, 2018 session, the analysand began by voicing her discontent with the group analyst from his interaction with a sub-group of women who had childhood sexual abuse experiences. Interestingly, all the male group members were absent for the session, which may have had an effect on allowing the women to speak more freely about their sexual abuse experiences. My analysand began the group interaction by telling the group how a recently seen movie, which had a sexual abuse theme, had emotionally opened her up to the childhood abuse. She entered the group the day after watching the movie wanting to discuss the emotional ramifications with the two other women in the group who were also sexual abuse survivors. When she began the group, the two other women quickly joined her in talking about their childhood traumas. The group, according to my analysand, was alive with the possibility of fully exploring the members' traumas. What is more, the women were eager to do so.

My analysand and the group members were shocked by the group analyst's comments, half-way through the group, which were reported as:

> You people know enough about your trauma by now, you should move on from this. We don't have to remember and bring sexual abuse to the fore.

My analysand and the other group members were shocked by the group analyst's response. It was the first time the three women wanted to jointly talk about their sexual abuse. My analysand went on to say:

> [her childhood abuser] broke into my childhood. I was having a hard enough time dealing with my family. After the sexual trauma, I pleaded with my family and my father not to ever leave me alone with again. If I was left with him I would become mute and never speak another word. Also, I would not be in this

world. I would go, further and further away. I would have shut down completely.

Realizing she had been thwarted in exploring her reaction to the movie, I engaged her in an exploration of her desire to explore the personal meaning of the film about childhood sexual trauma with a group of peers. One has to understand the important need of a childhood sexual survivor's desire to no longer be alone with the abuse; to no longer suffer alone. The survivor needs confirmation and affirmation because through dissociation, they disown their trauma. That is why the analysand appreciated the space to say the following:

> Yes, it is important. *Being sexually abused holds you back.* I never learned to swim or roller skate – I was scared. If I allow myself to let go, I am going to lose control. When I was sexually abused, I was losing control. When I had sex with a man, it scared me when he had an orgasm. *I have to be in control.*

It was clear that the analysand was happy to release her thoughts to me.

The next individual session the analysand wanted to continue the discussion about the group analyst's shutdown of the discussion of the three women's childhood sexual trauma, but, more importantly, she wanted to continue talking about her childhood sexual trauma. She recalled that in the group session she was ready to reveal an ongoing sexual fantasy. She now said to her group:

> My ongoing fantasy is that I am living with six guys who want to have sex with me.

Then, she reported that the group analyst responded to her self-disclosure by interpreting her fantasy as meaning she was expressing her own desire to have sex with a lot of men. The implication was that she was expressing a positive desire to be fully sexual with no limits introduced. The analysand was annoyed at the group analyst's response. She felt he did not empathically understand her emotional struggle.

We continued on with our individual session with the hope I could create an empathic clinical atmosphere that would help the analysand more fully explore her childhood trauma. It was clear to me that the analysand needed to be free to express her dissatisfaction with the group analyst and have an opportunity to continue her desire to open up about her trauma. The analysand felt that the group analyst was not empathically attuned to her trauma as she said the following:

> When he implied that my fantasy was just a positive, natural desire, *he doesn't acknowledge my childhood sex experience was a trauma.*

She then proceeded to continue to explore her fantasy:

> I was having sex. All these guys were having sex with me. They had a raffle and the winner was going to sleep with me. Then all of a sudden [her childhood abuser]'s head started to make me sick. Then the fantasy ends.

I asked her what is her interpretation of the fantasy. She said the following:

> Wanting sex and not wanting it. I want it, in my own time, in my own way. Don't force it on me.

We continued on with my suggesting she is trying to work through the sexual abuse in the fantasy, to which she agreed. She goes further and explained she was enjoying her sexual fantasy when she evoked her abuser to halt a real childhood sexual experience coming through. Given that she was beginning to free association, I asked her if she was willing to continue on with the exploration of the fantasy to go beyond the evocation of the abuser to stop going further. She said she will try, and then free associates:

> I was enjoying my fantasy, when the memory of comes through. Sex is not horrible, bad; it feels good, it's fun. But, when came into the picture, it became bad. It made it worst for me.

After the abuse, I said to my father – I don't want to stay with him. I'm scared. I was OK when his wife was around.

Our session ended as the analysand expressed her positive feelings for the opportunity to explore her fantasy:

I feel angry about being sexually abused. I want to bring it into myself. I want to own it. I haven't accepted it yet. I was pushing it away before. I acknowledge I haven't owned it. I want to be able to be in a different place. I want to be able to see the world in a different way.

A word about the group analyst's response to the analysand's fantasy. Although all major alternatives to the Freudian perspective, such as the Interpersonal perspective (Nemiroff et al., 2000), the Self-Psychology perspective (Street, 2008) or the Relational perspective (Davies & Frawley, 1994; Schwartz, 2000), acknowledge childhood sexual abuse as an important psychodynamic in the development of psychological disorder. But, the group analyst seemed to consciously discourage the analysis of childhood sexual trauma. When I asked my analysand this question:

Why do you think your group analyst said to discontinue exploring your childhood trauma?

She answered:

Analysts have had sexual abuse in their childhood, which they don't want to touch, so they don't confront it in their patients.

I would also add a note about the group analyst's frame of reference. From his response, I gather he was attempting to address, at least, two issues. First, he may believe that continued attention to a disturbance fixates an individual on exploring negative issues. Such exploration does not allow the analysand to liberate themselves to affirm their capacities to go beyond their trauma. Second, in response to the dream, the group analyst was affirming the positive capacity of the analysand to express her natural desires for sexual expression, rather than interpret the dream as an expression of a pathologic need. The problem with both of these ideas is that they do not empathically address the analysand's need to continue to work through her unresolved anger toward her abuser, which still exists, as well as to confront her sexual abuse as a traumatic experience (Rachman & Klett, 2015).

Chapter 13

The Catholic Church sexual abuse scandal

On Tuesday, August 16, 2018, the Attorney General of the State of Pennsylvania, Josh Shapiro, announced *The Grand Jury Report on Child Sex Abuse in Pennsylvania's Roman Catholic Dioceses* (Staff, 2018). The 40th Statewide Investigating Grand Jury Report into the Roman Catholic Dioceses was the most extensive investigation into clergy child abuse conducted by any state. The grand jury heard the testimony of *dozens of witnesses who reported they were the victims of sexual abuse by priests.* The grand jury also *reviewed a half of a million pages of internal diocesan documents.* These documents, the investigation concluded *contained credible allegations against over 300 predators.* The report *identified over 1,000 child victims. Most of the victims were boys* (but there were some girls, too). The victims were *mostly prepubescent and teenagers.*

  The Pennsylvania dioceses had what was referred to as a "playbook." This was an agreed on plan to *avoid "scandal."* The Federal Bureau of Investigation reviewed the evidence received by the grand jury. *The FBI agents specializing in sexual crime identified a series of practices* that regularly appeared in the church practices, which was like *a playbook for concealing the truth.* There were seven actions in the playbook:

1. Never use real words to describe sexual assault, for example, never say "rape," say "inappropriate contact."
2. Do not conduct professional investigations to investigate accusations.
3. Create an appearance of integrity.

DOI: 10.4324/9780429298431-13

The Catholic Church sexual abuse scandal   129

4. When removing a priest for sexual abuse, do not tell the truth.
5. If a priest is raping children continue to support him financially, even if this supports his activities.
6. If a priest is a predator, do not remove him from the priesthood, transfer him to a new location.
7. Under no circumstances contact the police. Do not treat the sexual abuse as a crime.

An example of the "cover-up playbook" indicated a priest in the Diocese of Allentown admitted that he molested a boy and asked for psychological help. The diocese, however, concluded the sexual abuse was not a significant trauma. The only treatment they recommended was the victim and the family should be given *an opportunity to ventilate*. This remarkable report indicates that there has been a deliberate campaign by the Catholic Church hierarchy to cover-up the sexual abuse scandal epidemic, which has defined the church in contemporary times. We need to now examine and confront the actual issue of Catholic priests sexually abusing children. Rather than hide or neglect this significant issue we will try to shine a light into the darkness of priest pedophilia. The problem is pedophilia not homosexuality among the religious community who sexually abuse children.

While Pope Francis was asking his Irish Catholic flock for forgiveness for the horrific abuse of nuns and priests in Ireland of children in their care, Archbishop Carlo Maria Vigano, the former chief Vatican diplomat in the United States, presented to the conservative Catholic world a 7,000 word letter that called for the resignation of Pope Francis, accusing him of covering up sexual abuse and giving comfort to what he called, "a homosexual current in the Vatican" (Horowitz, 2018). Vigano's letter was distributed to the conservative Catholic Church with no evidence to back up his claim. The journalist, Marco Tosatti, who helped Vigano by editing his letter, was clear that this document was not only an attempt to challenge the Pope, but also to explore a homosexual network within the church. Gay priests are being allowed to destroy the charge by molesting children. Pope Francis, he argues, is protecting these abusers by his liberal social justice policies and being complicit in covering up the sexual abuse of what Vigano considers to be homosexual pedophiles. Apparently, Vigano's letter exposed a

Catholic civil war between the conservative wing of the church and Pope Francis's more socially minded members. The Pope announced his approach soon after his election in 2013, by saying:

> If someone is gay and he searches for the Lord and has good will, who am I to judge?...[the church] cannot be obsessed with issues like abortion, homosexuality and birth control. (Pérez-Peña, 2018, p. A9)

Vigano's explosive accusations against Pope Francis confound a very important issue in the Catholic Church's sexual abuse scandal, that is, the necessary distinction between homosexuality and pedophilia.

In distinguishing homosexuality from pedophilia, there are several meaningful statements that can be made. Homosexuality and pedophilia are two different sexual preferences (and concepts). Homosexuality is a gender preference and pedophilia is an age preference. Homosexuality is no longer considered a psychiatric disorder. Pedophilia is a diagnostic psychiatric disorder. While 2%–4% of men have homosexual preferences, 25%–40% of pedophiles have homosexual preferences (Blanchard et al., 2000). Thus, homosexuality can be said to be overrepresented in the pedophile population. There is also bisexual interest among pedophiles than among men who prefer adults (Freund & Langevin, 1976; Freund & Watson, 1992; Quinsey & Chaplin, 1988).

Gay people, most often, especially, gay men, have routinely been portrayed as a threat to children and have been labeled pedophiles. In recent years, anti-gay activists have routinely said that gay people are child molesters. This accusation has been revisited with the revelations about the sexual abuse of children by priests. The Catholic Church's early response to the Boston Globe's reports of widespread sexual abuse by priests was to declare that gay men should not be ordained. If the church is to implement a decree banning all homosexual men, either from becoming priests or remove such men who are already in the church, they would run the risk of decimating their numbers. Available figures for homosexual priests in the United States range from 15% to 58% (Martin, 2000). These figures were reported by Fr. James Martin, the Jesuit scholar on sexual abuse in the Catholic Church. Elizabeth Stuard, a former convener of the

Catholic Caucus of the Lesbian and Gay Christian movement, believes that 33% of all priests in the Roman Catholic Church in the United States are homosexual (Stuard, 1993).

Homosexuality, pedophilia, and Pope Francis

Pope Francis, apparently, agrees with the psychiatry, psychology, and social work professions, which does not view homosexuality as a disease. Here are some of his thoughts and actions about homosexuality:

1. "...when God looks at a gay person, does he indorse the existence of this person with love, or reject this person? We must always consider the person..." (Hale, 2015).
2. In October 2014, Catholic bishops attended Pope Francis's Synod on the family. The document issued said that the church should create a more inclusive space for LGBT Catholics, saying the LGBT community has "gifts and qualities to offer to the Christian community...are we capable of welcoming these people, guaranteeing to them a fraternal space in our communities?" (Hale, 2015).
3. Early in 2015, Pope Francis had several encounters with LGBT individuals and groups, which included meeting with a transgender man from Spain who was excluded from his parish community, and gave the VIP treatment to a pro-LGBT American Catholic group visiting Rome. After the Supreme Court's ruling in support of same-sex marriage, Blase Cupich, Pope Francis's hand-picked archbishop of Chicago, said the church's respect for LGBT individuals: "must be real, not rhetorical, and ever reflective of the Church's commitment to accompanying all people" (Hale, 2015).
4. Pope Francis said on the flight back to Rome from vising Armenia: "I believe that the church must say it's sorry... to the person that is gay that it has offended..." (McElivee, 2016).

Pedophilia should be discussed as a psychiatric disorder defined in the Diagnostic and Psychiatric Manual – DSM-5, as involving intense and recurrent sexual urges toward and fantasies about pre-pubescent children that have either been acted on or which cause the person with attraction distress or interpersonal difficulty (Berlin,

2014; DSM-5, 2014). A person who is diagnosed with pedophilic disorder must be at least 16 years old, and at least 5 years older than the prepubescent child. The criteria for prepubescent age varies from under the age of 10 or 11 for girls and 11 or 12 for boys (Seto, 2008).

After researching, the recent revelations about the sexual abuse scandal in the Catholic Church, especially referring to the United States Conference of Catholic Bishops report (John Jay Report, 2004), the Boston Globe exposé (Boston Globe Investigative Staff, 2003), and the Pennsylvania Grand Jury Report (Staff, 2018), it is very difficult not to entertain an *evil narrative* to priests, bishops, cardinals, and the papacy. It seems impossible not to have a dark view of the abuse of children within the Catholic Church based on these remarkable reports, which have opened up the Vatican vaults to the church's secrets.

The Catholic Church's sexual scandal should be focussed on confronting the incidence of pedophilic disorder in the Catholic clergy; the establishment of a pedophilic community within the church community; the church's deliberate attempt to protect predatory priests; the sacrifice of Catholic children to fulfill the narcissistic needs of their clergy: the church hierarchy's absolute need to maintain power, control and status over children and women; the *evil plan* by clergy to carry out sexual abuse of children and youth.

After years of ultraconservative rule, the election of Pope Francis signaled a change in the Catholic church's philosophy and activity toward consideration of people over doctrine. Pope Francis has moved in the direction of people, particularly in the area of the poor. As I have tried to indicate, Francis seems to be cordial to the homosexual community. How much this cordiality is changing the basic attitude of the church is open to question. Archbishop Vigano's accusation that Francis has helped create "*a homosexual current in the Vatican*" (Horowitz, 2018), may be the function of an arch-conservatist who is angry over Pope Francis's more humanistic attitude. Clergy like Vigano seem to have forgotten the definition of the concept of Catholic, which is love. Vigano seems more concerned about maintaining the church's dogma toward homosexuality.

There is an issue in the area of sexuality that needs clarification in the church's functioning, namely, the church must focus on the issue of *pedophilic priests*, to deal effectively with the horrific scandal of the

The Catholic Church sexual abuse scandal 133

Catholic clergy sexually abusing children. Various remedies have been offered to stem the sexual abuse of children, such as prevent homosexuals from entering the priesthood, allow priests to marry, allow women to become priests, none of which addresses the issue of priests who suffer from pedophilic disorder. Adults who are driven to have sexual contact with prepubescent children are coping with a mental illness. This illness causes marked distress, interpersonal disturbance, acting on their urges and fantasies. Pedophiles usually come to medical or legal attention by committing an act against a child because most do not find their sexual fantasies distressing or ego-dystonic enough to voluntarily seek treatment (DSM-5, 2013). The Catholic Church has to come to terms with the reality of the existence of *predatory pedophilic priests* in their midst. Pedophiles are no longer "dirty old men," lurching in playgrounds or back alleys. In fact, that myth has never been true. Sexual abusers of children have always lived among us. Freud and Ferenczi pointed the way to this understanding.

Pedophiles usually report that their attraction to children begins around the time of their puberty or adolescence, but this sexual attraction to children can also develop in later life (Freund & Kuban, 1993). The longstanding tradition in the Catholic Church is to encourage young men to go to Catholic schools, which funnel youth and young men into seminaries for the priesthood. As the priest who will be discussed in Chapter 13, he believed he made a serious mistake when he entered the seminary at 17 years old. Looking back at this decision, he felt he was emotionally, interpersonally, and sexually immature. It would have been better, he felt, if he waited to make his final decision to be a priest until he was 21 years old. In a way, he was suggesting that entering the seminary at 17 years was in the vicinity of "child abuse." The church was taking advantage of the youth's emotional devotion to the church, dedication to God, the authority of the church, and the warmth of fellowship in the religious community. In the Pennsylvania Grand Jury Report (Staff, 2018), a group of predatory priests singled out children and youth who were fatherless, realizing they would be responsive to the physical and emotional attention of father figures.

The age of entering the initial stages for studying the priesthood should be raised to the adulthood years, 21 years, the generally accepted period for adulthood in industrialized western society, which can serve as the marker for entering the study for the priesthood. We can also use other indicators beside chronological age. At the age of 22–23, the human brain has developed. Learning can still occur. Adult plasticity exists, but the neural structures are not going to change (Steinberg, 2014). To add to the neuroscience of the emergence of adulthood, we can add the psychosocial aspects in the works of Erik Erikson (Erikson 1950; Erikson & Erikson, 1998; Havinghurst & Neugarten, 1947; Levinson, Darrow, Klein & Levinson, 1978; Levinson & Levinson, 1996). Havinghurst laid the foundation for the concept of developmental tasks. He proposed a bio/psychosocial model wherein the developmental tasks at each stage of life are influenced by an individual's biology, physiological maturation, and genetic makeup, his psychology (personal values and goals), as well as his sociology (specific culture to which the individual belongs). He pointed out the importance of sensitive periods which are ideal teachable moments during which an individual demonstrates maturation at a level that is most conducive to learning and successfully performing the developmental tasks. Psychological factors that emerge from the individual's maturing personality and psyche are embodied in personal values and goals. These values and goals are another source of some developmental tasks such as establishing one's self-concept, developing relationships with peers of both sexes, and adjusting to retirement or to the loss of a spouse. There are other developmental tasks, however, that arise from the unique cultural standards of a given society and as such, may be observed in different form in varying societies. Alternatively, they may be observed in some cultures but not in others. Once such task would be preparing oneself for an occupation. Havinghurst proposed a list of common critical developmental tasks, categorized into six stages of development. The stage that is related to the bio/psychosocial stage of development for the priesthood would roughly be the stage of adolescence. This stage, occurring from 13 to 17 years, involves establishing emotional independence from parents, equipping self with skills needed for productive occupation, achieving gender-based social roles, and establishing mature relationships with peers of both sexes. Havinghurst's formulations were elaborated, brought up to date, and integrated into a psychoanalytic framework by Erik H. Erikson and his wife Joan Erikson (Erikson, 1950; Erikson & Erikson, 1998).

Erikson's stages of psychological development is a comprehensive psychoanalytic theory that identifies a series of eight stages that a healthy developing individual should pass through from infancy to late adulthood. These stages characterize an individual advancing through the eight life stages as a function of negotiating his or her biological and sociocultural forces. Each stage is characterized by a psychosocial crisis of two conflicting forces. If an individual does successfully reconcile these (favoring the first mentioned attribute in the crisis), he/she emerges from the stage with the corresponding virtue. This experience is illustrated in Stage Five: Fidelity, Identity vs. Role Confusion (adolescence, 13–19 years), which is relevant to the years when a Catholic youth is contemplating the priesthood. The existential question that is being contemplated is: "who am I/ and what can I be?" As the transition is being made from childhood to adulthood, youth ponder the roles they will play in the adult world. It is a time when youth experiment with a variety of thoughts, feelings, activities, and roles. This experimentation is very necessary. Youth try on for size, so to speak, the ideas, beliefs, and activities of adult role models, to develop the notion of who they are inside and outside of themselves (Rachman, 1975). It is through this psychosocial process of experimentation that youth find their identity; who they are and where their lives are headed. They must achieve identity to occupation, gender roles, authority, and, in some cultures, religion.

Erikson developed the concept that this fifth stage of development was a turning point in human development, as it marks an *identity crisis*. The youth needs to reconcile the person he/she wants to be from the alternatives one samples from the alternate voices available from which to sample. Some voices provide negative experiences, delay, detour, which attenuates or interferes with identity formation. Role confusion is the inability to develop a sense of identity. It is a reluctance to commit to who you are and where you want to go in life, which can haunt the individual throughout life. What is necessary for an individual to positively resolve the identity crisis period is a *psychosocial moratorium*, where he/she can freely experiment and explore. In an atmosphere of empathy, acceptance, and affirmation, what emerges is a firm sense of identity, an emotional and deep awareness of who he or she is (Erikson, 1950; Erikson & Erikson, 1998; Levinson et al, 1978; Levinson & Levinson, 1996; Rachman, 1975).

Youth who are encouraged to enter the clerical high schools, for example, seminaries and yeshivas, in adolescence, are encouraged to begin the process of becoming part of the clergy before their sense of ego identity has been able to solidify. As has been discussed, a Catholic youngster of 17-years old has not had the intellectual, social, emotional, and sexual development to feel secure in his identity. Rather, such a young male has been placed on a path in his Catholic education and interaction with teachers, clergy, family, and friends to steer a clear path toward becoming a priest. If such a youth has emotional, social, intellectual, or authority problems, the mechanisms for pausing and examining these issues are not built into the youth's journey. In the same way, if the youth were to become a seminarian, these same issues would not be the focus of authorities. As the Catholic priest who is discussed in the next chapter, Chapter 13: A Catholic Priest's Audacious Proposal, if he would have an opportunity to voice his doubts about a clerical vocation, had an opportunity to discuss his concerns with a counselor, or had psychosocial space to mature, he may have not become a priest.

Pedophile priests, "ravenous wolves," and the Wolf Man

Pedophile priests are "ravenous wolves." The historic convening of the Catholic Church's clerical leaders by Pope Francis in February 2019, to openly address the church's sexual abuse of children scandal, has drawn criticism, mostly from sexual abuse survivors. Francis, to his credit, has been the first Pope to openly and clearly address the issue that has threatened the church's meaningfulness in the age of the #MeToo movement. As the landmark Vatican meeting ended, he did condemn the abusers no longer being part of the Catholic Church.

> ...*an all-out battle against the 'abuse of minors' from ravenous wolves.* (Horowitz & Dias, 2019, p. A1, [see Figure 0.3]).

Outing *sexually abusive priests as wolves* is an important change for the church. Francis is condemning sexually abusive priests as predators of children, no longer protecting these priests, as the previous Popes and the church hierarchy had done by not reporting them to civic authority or moving the abusive priests to other dioceses. This moves the church from protecting the abusers to identifying them as pariahs of the church, who need to be removed. Pope Francis has used language of sexual survivors to characterize sexually abusive priests:

> Consecrated persons, chosen by God to guide souls to salvation, let themselves be dominated by their human frailty or sickness and thus become tools of Satan....In abuse, we see the hand of the evil that does not spare even the innocence of children. No explanations suffice for these abuses involving children. (Horowitz & Dias, 2019, p. A10)

Pope Francis's transparency about sexual abuse within the Catholic Church has not, however, satisfied survivors of priest's sexual abuse or critics of the church. In his criticisms, the Pope seemed to appeal to *the better angels of our nature* (Pinker, 2011), that is, to change the hearts and minds of church leaders at the local level throughout the world. Basically, he has hoped to rally his clerics to change their behavior. He appeals to bishops, archbishops, and cardinals to realize the severity of the sexual abuse problem. Pope Francis no longer wanted to protect these *wolves in clerical garments*, rather remove them from abusing children. It is not clear, however, if the Pope wished to have *the wolves of the church* to be turned over to the police for prosecution. The survivors of the priests' sexual abuse have made their criticisms of Pope Francis's behavior most clear. A lay Catholic leader, Anne Barrett Doyle, who monitors incidents of abuse in the church (BishopAccountability.org), said the following:

> Pope Francis' talk today was a stunning letdown, a catastrophic misreading of the grief and outrage of the faithful...As the world's Catholics cry out for concrete changes, the pope instead provides tepid promises, all of which we've heard before. (Horowitz & Dias, 2019, p. A1)

The question must be raised, why has Pope Francis taken a mild, almost tepid stance to deal with a tsunami of a church problem that can bring down the church? We know that the Pope can change church doctrine by issuing an *encyclical*, a papal document, which addresses a significant issue of importance to practicing Catholics.

Why does not Pope Francis issue a Papal Encyclical regarding the evilness of child sexual abuse by priests: the church taking responsibility for the transgression; apologizing to survivors for the sexual abuse; outline the church's activity to helping survivors rehabilitate from their trauma?

Society's perception of wolves as predators

The Pope's selection of the phrase *ravenous wolves* to describe and condemn priests who sexually abuse children continues a tradition in society of equating the wolf with predatory behavior. The obvious attribute of the wolf is in its nature of a predator and therefore, its association with danger and destruction. The wolf is the symbol of an animal who is a primary predator on any area in which it is located. Pedophile priests can be seen as one of the primary predators in society using their power as religious to prey on children. The tale of *Little Red Riding Hood*, first written in 1697 by Charles Perrault, is largely considered to have more influence than any other source of literature in forging the wolf's negative reputation in the western world. The wolf in this story is portrayed as a potential rapist, capable of human speech (Marvin, 2012).

Pedophile priests speak the language of the Confusion of Tongues. They come to children knowing they desire love and tenderness. Priests, as one of the incest survivors I analyzed told me, "are God's angels here on earth." They are here to protect, love, and cherish children. But, predatory sexual abusing "wolf priests" offer children sexuality, disguised as love. These wolves offer sex to satisfy their own needs. The child's need for attachment, love, belief in the protection of God (authority), is shattered. The wolf feeds on its prey for their survival. Prey is destroyed. It is clear from all the descriptions that survivors have given of priest abuse, their lives have been shattered. *They became human prey of the wolf priests-predators.*

The Wolf Man

The symbol of the wolf, connected to sexual abuse, has been an undercurrent in psychoanalysis. Freud's iconic case of The Wolf Man/Sergei Pankejeff was given this title because the analysand reported a dream of wolves, which was interpreted to be the central psychodynamic of the analysis. Sexuality was interpreted by Freud as the central issue. But, his focus was on their child, Sergei, viewing their parents' sexual behavior, which was interpreted to have a profound effect on his sexual development. This case became a way to prove the validity of psychoanalysis by bringing together the unconscious, sexuality, and dream analysis.

Recently, I was inspired to search for an unpublished paper relevant to the Case of Elizabeth Severn the Wolf Man, which I ran across in rereading Jeffrey M. Masson's book, *The Assault on Truth* (Masson, 1984). Masson was a psycho-historian who I admired for his meaningful work in trying to remove the Todschweigen experience from Sándor Ferenczi's work. I have always been most grateful for his research on revealing the attempt to suppress Ferenczi's Confusion of Tongues paper by Freud, Jones, and members of his traditional followers. When I began to research the Wolf Man's case as Freud's most difficult case comparing it to Ferenczi's most difficult case, I began to have my own thoughts about Freud's interpretation of the case. My clinical experiences with incest survivors, my theoretical attempts to understand the effects of childhood sexual abuse on personality development and adult survival (Rachman, 2016a; Rachman & Klett, 2015), led me to develop an alternate interpretation for the Wolf Man's psychodynamics, which involved childhood sexual abuse (Rachman, 2018). I decided to take advantage of an opportunity to see if the traditional psychoanalytic community would welcome a re-evaluation of the Wolf Man Case. Combining previous presentations I had known about by P. Blum, MD, and Eva Papiasvili, PhD, about revising the Wolf Man Case, I made the following panel proposal to the Internal Psychoanalytic Congress, which was to take place in London, England in July 2019:

A Contemporary View of Freud's Case of the Wolf Man: New Ideas from the Object Relations, French Intersubjective and Relational Perspectives

Freud's 1918 case study of the Wolf Man, Sergei Pankejeff, with the famous dream of wolves will be reconsidered from current psychoanalytic perspectives. We will go well beyond the traditional view of the Oedipal Complex to view this iconic case with the understanding of the Object Relations, French Intersubjective and Relational Perspectives. We will examine the mind of the man, which fascinated Freud, but, left the patient with a lifetime of pathology.

Harold P. Blum, MD

The famous Wolf Man will be seen with new eyes, far beyond the symbolism of primal scene trauma. Today, we can understand that the Wolf Man had a severe personality disorder, in which developmental object relations issues highlight the reality perception, identity formation, and the fragile narcissism that promoted psychic arrest and an interminable treatment dilemma.

Eva Papiasvili, PhD, ABPP

Dr. Papiasvili will expand on...psychic conflict, processes of trauma...with consequent alterations to affective-cognitive functioning...pertaining to borderline personality organization...of the Wolf Man.

Arnold Wm. Rachman, PhD., F.A.G.P.A.

The Wolf Man, Sergei Pankejeff...was a survivor of an unanalyzed childhood sexual trauma...the Oedipal and primal scene interpretation of the dream of wolves were not a parsimonious analysis of the case material...a Relational Analysis perspective...of sexual trauma will [focus] on the following:

1. Pankejeff was sexually abused by his older sister...
2. Ruth Mac Brunswick, who also analyzed Pankejeff, [said] he was anally raped by a family member.
3. The dream of wolves is a dream of incest.
4. Pankejeff reported that Freud and Brunswick's Oedipal interpretations did not produce any fundamental changes in his functioning. He was very unhappy with the analysis.
5. It is conceivable that if Pankejeff's childhood sexual trauma had been analyzed, he would have recovered from his trauma.

My proposal for "A Contemporary View of Freud's Case of the Wolf Man" was rejected by IPA, with no explanation. I wrote to the contact person for IPA and asked for an explanation for the symposium's rejection. I never received a response from IPA. In turning to my two symposium participants, I did not get any further explanation. I thought my proposal was rejected because of my proposal to interpret the Wolf Man's psychodynamics as originating in a childhood sexual assault within his family interaction. I have always felt that Freud's psychology, from the time Ferenczi introduced the Confusion of Tongues paper and actual sex abuse as a psychodynamic in the origin of psychological disorder, did not believe conscious psychological data would aid the psychoanalysis of the unconscious. In fact, by the time the Confusion of Tongues paradigm was introduced, Freud had developed the idea that his student *was deliberately developing an alternate theory for psychoanalysis because he wanted to supplant his teacher as the new head of psychoanalysis.* No one in the analytic establishment understood that Ferenczi was not as alienated from Freud as Freud was alienated from Ferenczi. A struggle to find his own identity as a Relational Analyst (Rachman, 2012), and to establish his understanding of the neglected area of trauma disorder (Rachman, 2014), can be seen as Ferenczi's motivations, and, not to supplant Freud as the head of psychoanalysis. Ferenczi's intent was to help psychoanalysis to understand that there was a new classification of patients, those whose psychopathology originates in actual childhood trauma. He wanted this issue to be a part of psychoanalysis by establishing it as a separate diagnostic category from neurosis, which he outlined in the Confusion of Tongues paper. What is more, analyzing trauma disorder necessitates considering changes in the traditional psychoanalytic method, which he developed with the help of his analysand and collaborator, Elizabeth Severn, into Trauma Analysis (Rachman, 2018).

We need to also understand how important it was to Ferenczi to find his own identity as a psychoanalyst based on his own ideas and clinical experiences. By the time Freud and Ferenczi were moving away from each other, professionally and personally in the late 1920s to early 1930s, Ferenczi had been working with difficult trauma-originating cases for about 20 years. He could not disavow his significant work, which was very different from Freud's theory and clinical functioning. The Confusion of Tongues paper and Trauma Analysis with Elizabeth Severn was *Ferenczi's Emancipation Proclamation.* He separated from Freud and found his own direction and purpose.

Chapter 14

A Catholic priest's audacious proposal: "the church should ordain women to be priests to reduce child abuse"

I have had a personal relationship with a Catholic priest for decades where we have exchanged ideas about the relationship between Judaism and Catholicism, homosexuality in the priesthood, and pedophilia and the priesthood. We have met for dinner regularly over our friendship. During the writing of this book, Father Charles (a pseudonym), who I address as Charlie, met for our regular dinner meeting and we had a groundbreaking discussion. The news of the Harvey Weinstein sexual scandal was in the headlines (see Chapter 23), which eventually led to our discussing the child sexual scandal in the Catholic Church. We had previously talked about the topic of priests and pedophilia many times. Usually, Charlie was very conservative in his discussions. What I would like to highlight in this discussion is the transformation in his thinking and feeling about the church and the pedophilia crisis.

It is important to describe the journey of a conservation member of the church has taken to understand sexual abuse by priests because it is a journey that the church could consider. Charlie's change occurred as he moved beyond religious orthodoxy and became educated to other forms of intellectual understanding. As I will describe it, he began a journey in expanding his awareness to include the contributions of psychology and psychoanalysis. This kind of journey should be considered by the Catholic Church. Understanding the sexual scandal involving priests, in the United States, Europe, and other parts of the world, sexually molesting children and youth, and finding solutions to this enormous human problem cannot only come from the church. In the same way, investigation and remedies of this

DOI: 10.4324/9780429298431-14

issue must come from outside the church. The church must become psychologically minded to deal effectively with the issue of pedophilia among priests. Father Charles' remarkable recommendation about women priests, which some liberal members of the church endorse, needs to be examined. While it may seem like an important advance for the church, we need to ask whether it effectively deals with the issue of pedophilia among priests.

When the news of Harvey Weinstein's horrendous abuse of young women actresses during a 3-decade period had become known in the fall of 2017 (Farrow, 2017; Kantor & Twohey, 2017), we had scheduled one of our regular dinner meetings. Our conversation naturally turned to the sexual abuse crisis in the church. In the past, Charlie had defended priests who were accused of sexual abuse because he felt they were innocent and being unjustly removed from the priesthood. He said he knew such men and their careers and lives were ruined. On this particular evening, Charlie took a completely new direction on the topic of the church and the sexual abuse scandal. He seemed to be indicating he had a new attitude about the church's behavior in the sexual scandal. Being careful not to offend my friend, I asked him this question:

> What in your opinion could the Catholic Church do to better relate to the sexual abuse of priests?

Without hesitating, my friend felt he had a permanent solution to this complicated, age-old problem in the church. Then he raised his voice and affirmed the answer:

> There is only one thing to do, make women priests! That's the solution.

I was incredulous by this statement. It was a remarkable change that this traditionally trained Catholic cleric was offering. His was a solution that the most liberal, non-religious members of our society have proposed. Personally, I never thought Charlie would ever propose that women would be ordained as priests. The fact that he did readily suggest this remedy indicated that we may be entering a watershed moment in our society. In one of the world's most male dominated hierarchies, the Catholic Church, where power is not easily shared with other men, it is astonishing to hear a male voice being raised to give equal power to women. I was not yet finished mining my friend's thinking to solve the child abuse problem in the church. I now asked him why he thought women priests would positively contribute to the child abuse problem. He answered again without hesitation. I wondered if he realized how far he had come in his thinking and whether he really meant to say the following:

> Women generally do not sexually abuse children. Men do! Women are different. They are focused. Get things done. Do their work. They can control their sexual impulses, keep satisfactions within the family.

This was amazing, I said to myself. How did this "good little Catholic boy," as a relative had called him as a child, as well as his mother's desire for him to become a priest, become a part of the liberal, dissident voices in his church?

A priest turns toward psychoanalysis

The proclamation announced at one of our recent dinner meetings championing the ordination of women as the remedy to the church's problem with pedophilia became a major focus in our relationship. Over the next year or so, we unpacked his journey from the thinking of a Catholic conservative to an intellectual liberal and in opposition to the traditions of the church's conservative thinking. Our contact became a kind of *mutual encounter*, where we confessed and analyzed our backgrounds, religious beliefs, education, personal feelings, and thoughts about pedophilia and the clergy.

My friend never found in his priesthood the satisfaction for which he yearned. He revealed he was always looking for human contact (emotional/physical/interpersonal) to repair the parental deprivation of childhood. In the years of adolescence and young adulthood while preparing for the priesthood, he repressed these feelings of deprivation channeling his impulses into his dedication to study, obedience, love of the church and God. But "there was always an ache that never went away." This deficit increasingly became more of an ache as he entered mid-adulthood. He began to feel his priesthood was never to be fulfilling enough. This is when he decided to study psychology as a way to understand his aches and longings. Having earned two doctorates in religious studies, he hoped the next level of study would help him to solve his human problems.

First, came the graduate study of psychology, where this priest earned a doctorate in clinical psychology. Studying clinical psychology was a gift for him. He felt something was opening up inside of him, in a way that elevated his spirit. Examining human behavior became a hallmark in his thinking and feeling. He knew his relationship to his parents had caused great pain, which he had buried underneath his studies and devotion to being a priest. In his study of humans, a burden was being lifted from his shoulders. The intellectual and emotional landscape in which he now resided threw a light on the nature and psychology of the intrapsychic and interpersonal interaction between himself and others. He now went to school with individuals who did not turn toward religion and the church, but turned inward, or toward each other to find answers.

In what he first found as a new sense of personal vitality, then became a source of confusion, irritability and a circle of questioning. It was disturbing to him to explore his childhood relationships with his mother and father. Examining his relationship with his father came more easily. The father was a quiet, sensitive, distant individual who was completely subservient to his wife. The priest's mother was a cold, taskmaster who would not tolerate anything but success and excellence. He felt unloved, yearned for a loving caress and relationship with his mother. The only way to get what passed for love was to enroll in school, to obey your mother, and to dedicate yourself to your church. His elder brother was a rival for the meager emotional goods that were available in the family. Unpacking his emotional aches and pains was unsettling. The next step was clear, but a completely different enterprise from his family, education, or church experiences. This priest was amazed how he began to dive into being an analysand in a three-session a week analysis as part of his training to become a psychodynamic psychotherapist.

He jumped into the fray of opening himself up to be analyzed. "Tell me where you want me to go, I will go there!" he told his analyst. This became his therapeutic mantra, and he was sincere in its application. When he faulted, he would tell his analyst, "I'm having trouble doing this. Don't let me falter. Keep my nose to the grindstone." This was a highly motivated individual who matched his motivation with a dedication to working on and through his basic faults. He realized his mother's coldness and focus on excellence left him with yearnings for warmth and nurturance in human contact. Becoming a dedicated priest in a community of other priests did not satisfy this need. After all, his religious community consisted of men very much like himself. He needed a new kind of life. Living in a religious community was not a warm, empathic experience. In fact, it exacerbated the yearning for physical and emotional touch. He was dealing with repressed priests. Although they may have shared his need for emotionality and responsiveness, their dissociation was so severe they were very distant from satisfying and expressing it.

As he explained to me, the church had institutionalized an antidote to the yearning for emotionality. When I asked him to describe the so-called Catholic-solution for the human need for contact beyond religious or spiritual fulfillment, he described the regular use of alcohol to dull the human need for fulfillment. There were two duly scheduled *therapeutic sessions with alcohol.* Prior to dinner, the cocktail hour was open to all residents of the rectory. He described this experience to me repeatedly. So, one day I asked him if I could see the cocktail hour for myself. He graciously invited me to cocktails and dinner one evening at the rectory where he resided, which I gratefully accepted.

My friend first escorted me to the pre-dinner cocktail hour. The event was held in a men's club room. Just off this room my friend showed me what from the outside looked like a large closet. When opened up, it contained floor to ceiling shelves, completely stored with every conceivable type of alcoholic beverage imaginable. I was in shock when I saw this. The only other time I had ever seen so much alcohol in one space was in a very large hotel bar where people congregated to drink and socialize. My friend had one cocktail and I had a diet-soda before dinner. There were many priests who were lounging with a glass full of scotch, rye, or bourbon. Looking at some of them and their brief interchanges, it was clear they were inebriated. My friend said this was not unusual. The residence had a group of priests who were serious alcoholics. Some of the more serious alcoholics would continue drinking, forget dinner and then retire to their rooms.

This Catholic Priest Cocktail Hour, as I am labeling it, and as I saw it in action, is intended to calm, quiet, and suppress the clergy's emotional needs for contact, intimacy, affection, and sexuality. It is the Catholic version of a sexual and affection sedative for the clergy. In essence the church is saying, "we would rather have you drink alcohol to calm down your impulses than to express them."

My friend, the emotionally needy catholic priest, did enjoy a cocktail before dinner, or wine with dinner, and even an after-dinner drink, but, he never used alcohol to suppress his natural desires. He promised himself he would never become "a loveless drunkard priest who be farmed out to an old age home for alcoholic priests."

A priest examined himself

In his psychological studies for his doctorate, he became acquainted with Erik Erikson's Eight Stages of Man (E. Erikson, 1950; J. Erikson, 1958). After he read this material for the first time, he believed it described his psychology during his earlier development, but, especially, at the present time of his life. He decided to ask his professor for a consultation. Their talk produced important results. First, the professor of clinical psychology helped him understand that he was probably entering a severe mid-life crisis, identified as Erikson's Sixth Stage of Development, Intimacy vs. Isolation. This developmental phase usually occurs in adulthood, roughly between 21 and 39 years old. His life as a priest and his childhood of emotional deprivation delayed his psychological development. Now, in his 50s, he faced Stage 6 with a carnivorous sense of emptiness. He longed for emotional and interpersonally meaningful relationships with male peers and affectionate contact with a woman.

A second result of the consultation with the priest's psychology professor changed his life. A series of conversations revealed that this human being who happened to be a priest was confused, depressed, and serious about wanting to understand himself. It became clear he needed and was ready to confront his unexamined life. The psychologist asked the priest if he was willing to engage with him about the next step in his determination to deal with his mid-life crisis.

The next step was a meaningful period of therapeutic contact, some form of psychotherapy or psychoanalysis. "Well, which one should I do," the priest quickly responded. The psychologist felt he was talking to someone who wanted "to dive deep into his inner space," so he recommended psychoanalysis. Not unexpectedly, the priest blurted out:

Let's do it! I have to do it! I should have done it a long time ago.

The next series of consultations were going to be more difficult. The psychologist felt they needed to talk about the gender of the analyst to whom he was going to refer the priest. He asked the priest to spend some time talking to me about psychoanalysis. In our next dinner meeting, it was necessary to tackle the task about choosing an analyst in terms of gender, the person's frame of reference, style of relating and personality. The priest had shared with me, the professor's ideas about his mid-life crisis and the childhood parental traumas. With great care, I assimilated the information and formulated a series of issues to discuss with my friend. We went over the issue of his mid-life crisis first. I told him I knew a group of Relational analysts who were familiar with Erikson's developmental theory and were acquainted with analyzing a wide variety of analysands. At first, I suggested the priest should start with seeing a male analyst, with whom that he easily established a working relationship. After working out his childhood traumas, he then could decide to switch to a female analyst to work through his maternal deprivation and need for affection and responsiveness with a woman. As soon as he heard me say he could switch from a male to a female analyst, electricity seemed to rush into his brain, as he shouted out in mid-sentence:

I can see a female analyst from the start. *I do not need to be coddled.* I can see a woman analyst from the start and, I will.

Respecting my friend's need to affirm his capacities to meet a challenge and excel, I referred him to a female colleague who was known for her kind, gentle, empathic approach. In her analytic attitude, she explored his childhood trauma and his adaptation to it. He had to deal with his basic fault issues of childhood and the emotional and social limitations of adulthood. The priests jumped into his analysis with such fervor, as he did with everything else, that his analyst suggested he slow down so they could take the necessary time to get to know each other. My friend was very pleased with his analyst. He felt she was very thoughtful and compassionate, and he was surprised how comfortable he felt in her presence. For the first time, he realized that *a woman could have a therapeutic presence*, someone who he could experience as being kind, empathic, affectionate, and help him be himself. Another key ingredient, that I believed would help my friend in his analysis was the emotional warmth his female analyst possessed. Her personal warmth as well as her capacity to discern his basic fault, as being his childhood trauma with what he now called a harsh, taskmaster, and ramrod of a mother. This clinical behavior helped him believe his analyst understood him. He accepted she would help him work through his intimacy and social isolation issues.

They worked together for 5 years, three times a week. His analyst felt he was a well-motivated, hardworking analysand, who desired to confront his emotional issues. She also greatly admired his considerable intellect and spirituality. During this analysis, the priest struggled greatly with the trauma of his maternal deprivation and the consequent yearning for an affectionate relationship with a woman. The years of uncovering involved confronting his hurt, reflection, and sense of being haunted by his negative, disturbing, and damaging experience with his mother. His father's minimal emotional presence also contributed to his emotional difficulties. The father's willingness to be eclipsed by his domineering wife, did not provide an assertive, positive role model for his son as a man engaged in a mutual interpersonal experience with a woman. The priest felt pity for his father as well as venomous anger and a never-ending yearning for a woman's affectionate touch.

There was a gradual, but, significant change in the priest's intrapsychic and interpersonal feeling and behavior toward women. As reported his interaction with his female analyst grew into a proactive, empathic relationship. He thanked me almost every time he saw me for sending him to, "an elegant, caring, and warm woman. I wish I could find a woman like that." There was an important period of analyzing the positive transference, which became and erotic transference. In her characteristic, gentle, empathic way, his female analyst helped him transfer his desire to have relationships with women to developing peer contact with his new community of psychologists, analysts, and mental health professionals. He began attending professional meetings and developed a series of friendships with women as well as with men. For the first time, he had regular interpersonal contact with a nonreligious community, a community focused on understanding themselves and others. There was another benefit in being-with-others in an open community. This priest no longer felt the weight of the authority of the church hierarchy on his shoulders. Rather, for the first time, he felt he was in a family of friends where he was not concerned about being examined, criticized, or controlled.

The yearning for touch was ever-present and a continuing ache. His analysis helped him formulate the derivation of this need, but it could not solve the issue of clerical celibacy in the Catholic Church. The vow of celibacy means an ordained priest cannot marry (with some exceptions among the Eastern Catholic Churches). The church also considers deliberate sexual thoughts, feelings, and behavior as sinful:

> People should cultivate chastity in the way that is suited to their state of life. Some profess virginity or consecrated celibacy which enables them to give themselves to God alone with an undivided heart in a remarkable manner. Others live in the way prescribed for all of the moral law, whether they are married or single. (Catechism of the Catholic Church, 1997, 2349)

Priests (and let us not forget nuns) do struggle with sexual expression as witness the following admissions:

> I'm 45 and I do have sexual longings. What do I do about it? I acknowledge them first of all. I don't pretend they're not there. I don't try and drive them away. I ask what my body is trying to tell me – my body is telling I'm a normal male. But there's a message from God as well. If we deny it we are denying something that God has given us. But to deny having this is to fool oneself, and that can be dangerous. (Zwar, 2012)

My priest friend certainly struggled with his sexual feelings, which he shared with me as well as his analyst. He wanted a secular approach to sexuality, having been burdened with the religious and vocational vows approach. I respected his privacy as well as his devotion to his vows and spiritual philosophy. I never inquired about his adaptation to his sexual desires, but, after several years in analysis, he openly shared them with me.

There are Catholic women, who remain singled, are very connected to the church, and have social friendships with priests. Usually, these relationships are based on friendship, affection, and social interaction. I have met some of these women, through my social engagements with my priest friend. In one instance, he invited a fellow priest whom I also knew to attend a talk at a university. The second priest was accompanied by an attractive, independently wealthy woman, in her 60s, who was a social companion to him. She would regularly keep in touch with him and invited him to attend functions. In talking to the two priests about this, they both said they have had such contacts throughout their clerical careers. Such contacts usually began in church and evolved into friendship by the women making the contacts to bring the relations into the social sphere. My priest friends suggested they were orthodox catholic believers whose piety interfered with their sexual expression, had a history of negative trauma with father, male authority or peers, and lead unexamined lives where sexual and social maturity have been developmentally arrested. Generally speaking, these relationships could be compared to the *walkers*, where rich socialite, heterosexual women, whether married or single, use homosexual men to escort them to social events.

Although the "woman companion" of my friend's fellow priest was not involved in any sexual contact, he being homosexual, there are woman companions to priests who are. Recent discussions have indicated that priestly vows of celibacy have undergone personal revision. Father Richard McBrien, professor of theology at Notre Dame University, believes the vows of celibacy and the Catholic Church's teaching on human sexuality have caused the worst crisis in the Catholic Church (McBrien, 2003). McBrien explained that the Eastern rite of the Catholic Church did not have a sexual abuse crisis because they allow clergy to marry. Sipe (2003) believes about 50% of priests practice celibacy. He adds these estimates: 30% of priests are involved in heterosexual relationships, 15% are involved in homosexual relations, and 6% are involved with children.

Toward the last phase of his analysis, my friend had two major issues with which to cope: how could he satisfy his need for affection and touch with a woman?; was it necessary to leave the church to work through and satisfy his basic fault trauma of maternal deprivation? Having taken a deep dive into psychoanalysis, the priest gained a meaningful understanding of his maternal childhood trauma. The insights did not provide fulfillment of his need for the long sought after affection and internal longings for the soft, sensual touch of a woman. His female analyst talked to him about his mother's deprivation causing his emotional need and the transference implications of his erotic transference to her. Actually, going over these materials made him so horny he had to make sure he crossed his legs tight enough that his analyst did not see his erection. At moments like this, he had no idea how he would solve the need for actual fulfillment of these needs. His opinion was he would never be happy without fulfillment. He also knew all those fantasies and dreams he now allowed himself to have helped him understand that love and sex preoccupied him.

In some way, he did not fully know yet, he was going to find fulfillment. But, he did know he really did not want to leave the church. His identity as a priest helped him form his life's purpose, ever since he entered the seminary at 17 years old. As much as he wanted fulfillment, he was not willing to pay the price of being a man without an identity. What is more, he did not want the identity as a former priest, who was now a husband. This unsatisfied priest was "a man of God." He was no longer a conventional believer, but he still was a believer in God, in the church, in his own way. Leaving the church for a woman was out of the question.

The solution appeared one day. A woman parishioner, who had been circling around him for a while, became an object of desire. He asked her to join him at a lecture on biblical archeology, and academic interest. She was a mature woman, conservative in looks and manner, who did arouse his libido. She had no need to dominate or assert her will. This was a blessing to someone who suffered from the remnants of a maternal taskmaster. Emotionally, he chose wisely, because the woman who became his partner turned out to be a warm, kindly, empathic human being. She resembled the priest's female analyst rather than his mother. The couple was cautious in their contacts, but, they gradually grew closer to each other and they fell in love. What is more, their sexual contact was as much a blessing as was their friendship. Two wounded souls healed their traumas by their faith in God and each other. She found in him the quiet, thoughtful, non-abusive man she so badly needed to quiet her history of physical, emotional, and sexual abuse with her father. They reached a compromise in living arrangements. He would remain in the rectory of his order during the week, attending to his work as a priest. On the weekends and holidays, they would share her apartment.

A softening in my friend's heart and mind became noticeable. He went from being "tough to tender." The tough-minded conservative, who worked hard and played hard, began to soften into a softer, more nuanced thinker. His basic emotional needs were being met and it was like, "his insides were softening." This may have explained his audacious comment to me that night at dinner when he said:

> There is only one thing to do, make women priests! That's the solution to cure the church's pedophilia crisis.

Women who sexually abuse children

My priest friend's idea of women priests as the answer to the Catholic Church's pedophilia crisis needs to be examined to see if it is a plausible idea. There is some beginning data on women who sexually abuse children, now that clinicians and researchers are paying attention to the reality that women are sexual abusers (Mallett, 2017; McLeod, 2015). It has been established that sexual abuse of children was the province of adult males, sexually abusing their daughters (Herman, 1981). When attention is paid to female sexual abusers, the following data have emerged:

1. A child sexual abuse study in Australia recently found that about 5% (or 96 of the 1,860 accused) in Catholic institutions were women.
2. Incidents of individual nuns being involved in sexual abuse of children are now being reported. Although rare, there has been some institutionalized sexual abuse of children by nuns (McCluskey & Hooper, 2000). Allegations of child sexual abuse

by the Sisters of Mercy in Ireland (some of them substantiated) have been made (McDonald, 2009). A 9-year investigation by Ireland's commission into child abuse, which drew on testimony of thousands of former inmates and officials from more than 250 church-run institutions found that molestations and rape were "endemic" in boys facilities. Girls supervised by orders of nuns, chiefly the Sisters of Mercy, also suffered from sexual abuse.

3. It seems ironic that presently, in the tipping point of raising our consciousness about men in authority sexually abusing women, that we can talk about our profession and society overlooking the issue of women who abuse (Mallett, 2017).

4. A study for the Home Office in the United Kingdom in 1998 indicated less than 5% of child sex offenses were committed by women (Richards, 2011). This is supported by data coming out of the Royal Commission that 5% of the alleged abusers associated with the Catholic Church were religious sisters—as well as research based on correctional services in Australia (Statopoulos, 2014).

5. In 2009, the BBC reported a large rise in the number of children calling the UK Charity Childline to report sexual abuse by a female. In 2005 and 2006, 2,142 children reported they had been sexually victimized by a female (Richardson, 2009).

Women offenders who abuse children

More offenders in prison are male than female. The percentage of incidents of sexual abuse by female perpetrators that come to the attention of the legal system is usually reported to be between 1% and 4% (Denov, 2003). Studies of sex misconduct in US schools with female offenders have shown mixed results with rates between 4% and 43% female offenders (Shakeshaft, 2004). A 2015 study looked at virtually every substantiated child sexual abuse reported to child protective services in the United States in 2010. It concluded more than 20% of child sexual abuse cases reviewed involved a primary female perpetrator (McLeod, 2015).

It is likely that the #MeToo movement has also influenced the reporting of the abuse by women of children. Instances of female teachers sexually abusing male students has been rare. Lately, a new platform has been established at FoxNews.com. In several months, the posting of teachers having sex with their young male students jumped from 20 stories to 98. Nearly 30% of the articles posted under FoxNews.com's "Sex Crimes" category between July and December were focused on female teachers. There is some contradictory statements made by Leilah Gilligan of the Center for Sex Offender Management and Professor Franca. Cortoni of the University of Montreal (Galinsky, 2018).

These latest data, as well as the other reported studies, indicate that women cannot be overlooked as sexual predators of children. But, it is clear from the relevant data that women are significantly less involved in the sexual abuse of children than men, whether they are clergy or incarcerated offenders.

There are some surprising data that concerns women and sexual assault. A survey found women state prisoners were more than three times as likely to experience sexual victimization perpetrated by women inmates (13.7%) than were men to be victimized by other male inmates (4.2%) (Friedersdorf, 2016).

My Catholic priest friend's suggestion to ordain women as priests seems relevant to curtailing the incident of child sexual abuse in Catholic religiose. His personal experience indicated that, as a child he felt emotionally abused by the most important woman in his life, his mother. But, his dedication to overcoming his childhood emotional trauma through the study of psychology and personal analysis, helped him to realized that peer relationships with women who were not abusers, but became, to him, nourishing figures. To transform his fundamental thinking and feeling of a woman from cold, distant, and unresponsive (the transferential perception from his continuing negative experience with his very difficult mother) to seeking out, or responding to, women who are kind, empathic, and willing to respond, this priest had to go beyond the world of the Catholic religious community.

Rise up brothers and sisters!: the Catholic laity finds their voice

On Sunday, August 26, 2018, Pope Francis visited Ireland, the first papal visitation in 39 years, to win back the Irish Catholics who turned away from the church since the revelation of abuse of children (boys and girls) by priests and nuns. Some Irish protested, in full sight of the Pope, by carrying placards decrying the church's coverup of the abuse and asking for action (Horowitz, 2018). The need for action voiced by the survivors of abuse was drowned out by a bombshell statement released by a member of the Catholic Church, the first of its kind on the sexual abuse scandal. Pope Francis asked for prayers and forgiveness in a profound series of statements:

> —In a special way we apologize for all the abuse committed by institutions run by male and female religious and other members of the church. And we ask for forgiveness for the crimes so many members were subjected to.
>
> Some members of the hierarchy didn't own up to these painful situations and kept silence. We ask for forgiveness.
>
> For all these times when it was said to many single mothers who tried to look for their children who had been estranged from them, or to the children who were looking for their mothers, that it was a mortal sin. It is the Fourth Commandment. We ask for forgiveness.
>
> None of us can fail to be moved by the stories of young people who suffered abuse, were robbed of their innocence, who were taken from their mothers, and left scarred by painful memories. This open wound challenges us to be firm and decisive in the pursuit of truth and justice. I beg the Lord's forgiveness for these sins and for the scandal and betrayal felt by so many others in God's family.
>
> (Barry & de Freytas, 2018, p. A8)

It is an emotional, moving moment to read these words by a Pope, who everyone views as a man of the people, an advocate of social justice, and someone who leads a simple life, decrying luxury. He is a good person trying to do good. But, something in his prayers asking for forgiveness is missing. The survivors of sexual abuse by the predatory priests of the church have repeatedly expressed what is missing in the Pope's prayers for forgiveness. They express in their spoken words, placards in Boston and Pennsylvania, rainbow-colored umbrellas unfurled in Ireland, their confusion, hurt, and anger. As the *Confusion of Tongues explains, survivors of childhood trauma hunger, as adults, for redemption.* They are tongue-tied; they cannot speak of their traumas, needing their abusers, or their authorities who allowed the abuse, to offer redemption. Catholic survivors face a serious dilemma. They are asking for redemption from people who make a deliberate attempt to remain silent. The Christian theme of redemption centers on God as the ultimate redeemer, saving the individual from sin, evil, and trouble. Redemption is an act of God's grace, by which he rescues and restores his people (Zavada, 2017). A biblical reference to redemption is

> In the same way we also, when were children, were enslaved to the elementary principles of the world. But when the fulness of time had come, God sent forth his Son, born of woman, born under the law, to redeem those who were under the law, so that we might receive adoption as sons. (Galatians 4:3-5 – Bryant, 1967)

Catholic survivors have naturally turned toward God's agent on earth, the Pope. But, the Pope has asked for forgiveness, but, this is not what survivors consider redemption. Survivors want action, not prayers. They need their abusers and the church to take responsibility for their being abused as children and having their life negatively altered. The church's inability to own their "evil deeds," to see the predatory priests as criminals, to punish Bishops and Cardinals for covering up the abuse, and, finally, not changing the philosophy and functioning of the church to prevent child sexual abuse, is what Catholic survivors of sexual abuse see as *the church losing their voice* in being able to confront the issue. As one survivor in the church's Pennsylvania diocese scandal said: "I have a hole in my soul." Are prayers going to repair that hole or are actions? A catholic survivor, Patricia McCormick, described the hole in her soul in a recent courageous self-disclosure of the sexual abuse she endured, which started when she was 12-years old and lasted through high school:

> He was wearing a long black cassock and stiff white clerical collar. I was in my school uniform and knee socks. With no warning he pulled me to him, crushing me in the blackness of his robe… I looked away, terrified…then he kissed me…his mouth open wide enough that his teeth dug into my lower lip. His tongue

probed for mine. I stood frozen, my arms at my sides. It was my first kiss. This ritual, where I would entertain Father Bradel in the living room…took place three or four times a year all throughout high school; it was as unchanging as the consecration of the host at mass. No one had to tell me it was my duty to give this strange comfort to our parish priest. (McCormick, 2018, p. SR3)

Patricia McCormick reflected on the psychodynamics of those dark moments of youth, realizing that although Father Bradel was not Godly, rather evil in his abuse of her, they shared: "…a deep, keening loneliness…" (McCormick, 2018, p. SR1). Years after the abuse was in the rear view mirror, Patricia McCormick wanted to report her experience with Father Bradel to church officials, but she was pushed aside. But, now she is getting redemption:

Now, thanks to a grand jury in Pennsylvania, there's a real list, – and it includes my report to the counselor… I'm grateful that the attorney general did what the diocese wouldn't. I'm still curious, though, as to whether I'm the only one Father Bradel preyed upon. I hope so. But I doubt it. (McCormick, 2018, p. SR3)

Chapter 15

The conspiracy within the Orthodox Jewish Community to protect sexual abusers

In the Ultra-Orthodox Jewish communities of New York, London, and Israel, there have been, in the recent years, rampant allegations of child molestation and rape, which some people believe suggest a sex abuse scandal similar to the Catholic Church. The alleged abusers are schoolteachers, rabbis, and family members—male authority figures. The victims, like those in the Catholic community, are mostly boys. Rabbi Nuchem Rosenberg has been a member of Brooklyn's Satmar Hasidim, a fundamental branch of Orthodox Judaism. Rabbi Rosenberg started blogging about sexual abuse in his community and opened a New York City hotline to receive sexual abuse complaints. He has posted appeals on YouTube, appeared on CNN, and given speeches across the United States, Canada, Israel, and Australia. He is considered the lone wolf whistleblower within the Ultra-Orthodox Jewish community. Rabbi Rosenberg believes about half of young males in Brooklyn's Hasidic community—the largest in the United States and one of the largest in the world—have been victims of sexual assault perpetrated by their elders. Advocates for Orthodox sexual abuse survivors believe the incidence may be higher. In fact, there is a belief that sexual abuse of boys by Jewish authorities within the Ultra-Orthodox community may be a rite of passage (Murdock, 2013).

The Orthodox community responses to sexual abuse accusations have often involved failure to report offenses to the police, intimidating witnesses, and shunning victims and those members who speak out against cases of abuse (Otterman & Rivera, 2012). Rabbi

DOI: 10.4324/9780429298431-15

160 The conspiracy to protect sexual abusers

Rosenberg's also designs and repairs *mikvahs* (ritual baths) in compliance with Torah Law. The mikvah is a ritual Jewish bath house used for purification. Devout Jews are required to cleanse themselves in the mikvah on a variety of occasions: women must visit following menstruation, and men have to make an appearance before the High Holidays, such as Rosh Hashanah and Yom Kippur. Many of the devout also purify themselves before and after the act of sex, and before the Sabbath. A *schvitz* (steam bath) is another Orthodox Jewish ceremonial bath house. These ceremonial baths are considered holy sites intended for purification of the body and soul. Given the holiness of the sites and their religious functions, Rabbi Rosenberg was a witness to a striking defilement of a young boy in such a holy site by an elderly Orthodox Jewish male:

> I opened a door that entered into a *schvitz* (an Orthodox Jewish ceremonial bath house)...and I see an old man, (about 68 years old), long white beard, a holy-looking man, sitting in the vapors. On his lap, facing away from him, is a boy, maybe seven years old. And the old man is having anal sex with this boy. This boy was speared on the man like an animal, like a pig, and the boy was saying nothing. But on his face—fear. The old man [looked at me] without any fear, as if this was common practice. He didn't stop. I was so angry, I confronted him. He removed the boy from his penis, and I took the boy aside. I told this man, 'It's a sin before God... What are you doing to the boy's soul? You're destroying this boy!' He had a sponge on a stick to clean his back, and he hit me across the face with it. 'How dare you interrupt me!' he said. I had heard of these things for a long time, but now I had seen. (Burns, 2018)

Rabbi Rosenberg has been ostracized from his Orthodox community. Caricatures of Rosenberg as a snake circulated among the sect. He has also been attached physically. In 2012, he was the victim of a bleach attack. The example of child sexual abuse he described is remarkable for several reasons. The abuser said he has the right to anally rape a seven-year-old boy. He told Rabbi Rosenberg: "How dare you interrupt me" and angrily hit the Rabbi. What is the mentality of a highly religious person that gives him the right to sexually abuse a child? Is this his privilege? A partial answer come from mores that have developed within the Ultra-Orthodox Jewish community. Members of the Ultra-Orthodox communities believe that a member who turns an abuser over to an authority outside their religious community is committing a transgression against fellow Jews and their community.

The concept of *mesirah*, a Hebrew word, which means "to turn over," refers to the action in which one Jew reports the conduct of another Jew to a non-Rabbinic authority, such as the police, which has become forbidden by Rabbinical law (Otterman & Rivera, 2012). Rather than reporting to police, Orthodox Jews may take a case of sexual abuse to the *shomrim*, a Hebrew concept, which is the plural of the word *shamar* and literally means to guard, watch, or preserve. Shomrim are local Jewish street patrol who keep the names of suspected child molesters on file, but do not share them with law enforcement or take other measures to end abuse, and sometimes try to discourage people from taking a case to the police (Pinto, 2011). In general, reports of abuse to religious authorities rarely result in punishment for the offender.

There have been reprisals within the Orthodox communities when someone is accused of sexual abuse. Victims, their families, and advocates for the sexual abused have been threatened with violence (Ketcham, 2013); fake police reports (Otterman & Rivera, 2012); loss of kosher licenses or other harm to business, and/or eviction; physical harassment, and coercion (Ketcham, 2013; Otterman & Rivera, 2012). The Orthodox community has developed reprisals against sexually abused children and their parents. Parents have been shunned by the community, with rabbis forbidding congregants to speak to them, and abused children have been barred from schools (Powell, 2013).

Changes in the Orthodox Jewish community regarding sexual abuse: arresting sexual abusers

The New York District Attorney's office has developed a new policy as it began to vigorously pursue convictions in sexual abuse cases in the Orthodox Jewish community. In the past, Charles J. Hynes, the former Kings County (Brooklyn) District Attorney from 1990 to 2013 in the New York City county in which the largest number of Ultra-Orthodox Jews live, was criticized for his alleged reluctance to prosecute sexual abuse against children in the Ultra-Orthodox communities. In an apparent change of policy, 118 cases of sexual abuse were pursued, and 25 sex offenders have received prison sentences. The longest sentence of 103 years was handed down to Nechemya Weberman, and unlicensed therapist who had abused a girl starting when she was 12 years old.

The prosecutors in District Attorney Hynes's office reported that they believe a change in some segments of the Orthodox community has developed. They believe more people are reporting sexual abuse and are willing to be part of the criminal justice system (Edelman, 2013).

Disobedience, the novel

The novel, *Disobedience*, by Naomi Alderman (Alderman, 2007), is a first-person narrative of a 30-year-old woman, non-practicing Orthodox Jew, who returns home when her father dies. She reconnects emotionally and physically with a woman with whom she fell in love with as a teenager. In the background of the Orthodox Jewish community of North London, the once lesbian couple resume their relationship. The Orthodox Jewish Community is presented as a strange and foreboding world, revealing its restrictions on human behavior, and representing it as having meaning (Peyton, 2006). It is a story, however, which attempts to shine a light into the impossibility of an Orthodox Jewish woman to have the freedom to be a believer and be in a lesbian relationship. Naomi Alderman wrote her way out of her Orthodox Jewish community in London and out of her being an observant Jew. This novel provides an alternative to being a captive of a male-dominated system of belief, where freedom means disobedience.

Tradition: a journal of Orthodox Jewish thought

There is an indication that the Orthodox community is now willing to examine and intellectually debate the issue of sexual abuse in the

Orthodox Jewish community. A journal published in 2017 by the Rabbinical Council of America, *Tradition: A journal of Orthodox Jewish thought*, has dedicated an issue to sexual abuse in the Orthodox Jewish community. The six essays in the 2017 volume were intended to raise awareness, to educate, to challenge, and to inspire Orthodox Jewish communities to adapt policies for preventing sexual abuse, and to adapt policies for addressing accusations. The unique issues in the Orthodox community are related to the sexual abuse crisis. These are *halakhah* questions, translated as, "the way to behave," which is derived from the collective body of Jewish religious laws, which include the written and oral Torah (Schiffman, 1991). The use of the *halakhah* tradition is very significant because it shifts dependence on the written tradition to adding the oral tradition of Rabbi's. This tradition relies on rabbinic interpretation, as to the pure, written words recorded in the Hebrew Bible. In turn, rabbinic interpretation in the Ultra-Orthodox community illustrates the conspiracy this religious group has had developed against confronting sexual abuse. This journal issue has also addressed the issue of *mesirah*, reporting fellow Jews to the civil authorities. Another aspect of the conspiracy in the Orthodox community, *lashon hara*, is the *halakhic* term for "evil tongue"—"ye shall not wrong one another" found in Leviticus 25:17 (Jenkins, 2013). The tradition developed refers to wronging a person with one's speech. Having an evil tongue is considered to be a very serious sin in the Jewish tradition. For example, in the Ultra-Orthodox section of Jerusalem, Israel, *lashon hara* signs are posted (see Figure 0.6., p. 54):

Please No Lashon Hara (see Figure 0.7, page 164)

This Hebrew term, "evil tongue," is the *halakhic* term for derogatory speech about another person. Such prohibitions refer to accusations of sexual abuse.

164 The conspiracy to protect sexual abusers

Figure 0.7 Lashon Hara: the consequence of hate speech. Public displays of prohibition against speaking evil about someone. Signs displayed in Israel. Collage by Arnold Wm. Rachman, March 1, 2021.

Sexual abuse accusations in the Conservative and Reform Jewish communities

Accusations of sexual abuse are beginning to surface in the Conservative and Reform Jewish communities. In September 2017, sexual abuse accusations were published about two longtime and much-admired former leaders of United Synagogue Youth (USY). One such individual is Jules Gutin, 67 years, who was an iconic and much beloved figure for adolescents over his decades-long administration as national director of USY. The other alleged sexual abuser is Robert Fisher, 70 years, a former charismatic and popular West Coast director of USY. A very different reaction emerged from these conservative Jewish leaders' accusations than is credited to the Orthodox community. Both of the accused did not deny their negative behavior. When Fisher was confronted with the accusations, he acknowledged his transgressions with boys. What is more, he apologized for his sexually inappropriate behavior. Guten said the administration was correct in removing him from his post. He also apologized for his actions (Rosenblatt, 2017).

Female Rabbis are now speaking out about what some people believe is a pervasive sexual harassment. Conservative and Reform Jewish communities have reacted quickly to address this problem in the following ways:

1. The Conservative community's Zeigler School of Rabbinic Studies in California will introduce a course to train female rabbis to handle sexual harassment
2. Jewish communal workers have created a closed Facebook page, *GamAni* (Me Too), to give support and a voice to sexual harassment in the Jewish world.
3. Fran Sepler, an authority on sexual harassment prevention had led a full day of training for 12 Jewish communal organizations in New York and New Jersey.
4. The Central Conference of American (Reform) Rabbis has formed a Task Force on the Experience of Women in the Rabbinate, which will deal with sexual harassment (Ain, 2017).

A ministerial exception, which is a legal doctrine in the United States, was originally developed to protect the freedom of religion by exempting religious institutions from anti-discrimination laws and protecting government from having to become entangled in internal religious affairs. In a US Supreme Court decision, the court ruled, for the first time, that the First Amendment requires a *ministerial exception* that allows employers to discriminate against their employees without any court review (Corbin, 2012). In essence, the court decision said: *you don't have the right to sue if you work for a religious employer* (Ain, 2017, p. 1). There are lawyers in the Reform movement who have said, they would be willing to take a case of sexual harassment against a female rabbi to trial.

Another legal issue in the Jewish community is the fact that Israel has been used as a safe haven for sex offenders from the United States. Sexual pedophiles are allowed to immigrate under Israel's Law of Return. Rabbi Yaakov Horowitz, founder and dean of a Yeshiva for boys in Monsey, NY, and founder and director of a program for at-risk teens, has been active in exposing the sexual offenders who flee the United States for Israel and has reported that a colleague has compiled a list of 34 names of sex offenders from the diaspora who have escaped to Israel. This alluding prosecution has been going on for at least 20 years.

Rabbi Horowitz and other activists have met Israeli lawmakers to convince them to establish a sex offender database. Being Jewish would therefore, remove the escape valve to Israel via the Law of Return. Mordechai Twersky, who was the lead petitioner in the case against Yeshiva University for allegedly covering up years of physical and sexual abuse, has made a strong statement about the Israel government:

> Every time a suspected or convicted pedophile is admitted to Israel, it is a failure of the Israel government...they have an obligation to make public the files of individuals accused of abuse in their former countries. (Chabin, 2018, p. 33)

Chapter 16

Sexual abuse in the Catholic Church in Australia

In December 2017, a Royal Commission investigating the sexual abuse in Australia found that this nation was involved in an epidemic dating back decades, with tens of thousands of children abused in religious organizations, including the Catholic Church (as well as abuse in schools and other institutions). The report was particularly critical of Catholic organizations. Criticisms of the church have centered on the nature and extent of the abuse, and on the history and contemporary management by church officials. The Royal Commission established that 4,444 claimants alleged incidents of child sexual abuse in 4,756 reported claims to Catholic Church authorities and at least 1,880 suspected abusers from 1980 to 2015. Most of those suspected of abuse were Catholic priests and religious brothers and 62% of the survivors who told the commission they were abused in religious institutions were abused in a Catholic facility (Williams, 2017). There has been a sense of alarm by Australians since a sex abuse scandal in Ballarat, the hometown of Cardinal George Pell, one of the highest-ranking Catholic prelates to face trial for charges of historic sexual offenses. In Ballarat, an investigation of a pedophile ring at local Catholic schools found that as many as 30 victims of sexual abuse had committed suicide. The charges brought against Cardinal Pell, a top advisor to Pope Francis, were that Pell's transgressions had covered up the widespread abuse of children by clergymen in Australia.

The Australian Bishops Conference and Catholic Religious Australia issued an extensive report in which church leaders expressed their concern over the abuse by priests and the church's

DOI: 10.4324/9780429298431-16

failure to confront the problem (Rojas, 2018). Interestingly, the Bishops recommended introducing voluntary celibacy for clergy believing that requiring celibacy contributes to priest child abuse. This recommendation touches on discussions in Chapter 12 about the need for the church to review their policies on adolescents being groomed for the priesthood before they are sexually mature and Chapter 13, which presents the audacious proposal that women should be ordained to be priests.

As responsive as the Australian Catholic Church was to the report of sexual abuse of children, they were unresponsive to the government's attempt to introduce a revolutionary idea to be able to detect priest's sexual transgressions with children. The Catholic leaders in Australia rejected a government proposal to force priests to report accusations heard during confession. As one would expect, the church said such a regulation would violate a sacred rite, would interfere with religious freedom, and does not really protect children. The church also took issue with a creative recommendation intended to protect children during the confession practice. The church also objected to the proposal that children practice confession in an open facility within the clear line of another adult. In rejecting the idea of priests reporting sexual abuse reports heard in the confessional and developing open space practice of confessionals for children indicates the Catholic Church's need to protect orthodox practice, even at the expense of human need. This is why sexual survivors feel they are not being heard.

Chapter 17

The Eleventh Commandment: thou shall not lie down with children

Scholars who work in the area of religion and psychology have pointed to the difficulty psychoanalysis and society has had in embracing the reality of sexual transgression:

> Given the prominence of the psychoanalytical tradition's claim that the etiology of psychological disorder lies in intrapsychic conflicts rather than externally caused traumas, the reality of childhood incestuous abuse was seriously minimized in our culture. (Beste, 2007, p. 38)

Inherent in the theme of the chapters of this book, is the idea that psychoanalysis and society have both neglected and, at times, deliberately suppressed data, clinical case studies, letters, which were related to sexual abuse, which remain unknown.

In researching the incidence of tales of sexual abuse in religious studies, I was able to discover a dramatic case of this is the Jewish Bible. I had never been taught this tale in all my Hebrew School studies as a student during my childhood and youth. This is the story of Amnon and the sexual abuse of his half-sister, Tamar. It is a clearly cited case of incest in the Jewish Bible found in Shumel/ Samuel, Chapter 13, between Amnon, the son of David, and Tamar, the daughter of David. It is an example, I believe, of how an important part of our culture and religious belief has neglected an important story of sexual abuse that can inform believers and non-believers of sexual transgression within the history of human

DOI: 10.4324/9780429298431-17

170 The Eleventh Commandment

beings and raise our consciousness to its existence. The story of Amnon and Tamar will be presented as it unfolds in the Bible in an abridged version, emphasizing a focus on the relationship between the participants in this iconic case of incest. It is an experience portrayed through the eyes of the abused, Tamar, providing an opportunity to gain an understanding of an important religious and moral mandate.

The story of Amnon and his sister Tamar: Sexual abuse in the Jewish Bible.

Verse 1   "And it came to pass...that Absalom, the son of David had a fair sister...Tamar; and Amnon the son of David loved her.

Verse 2   ...Amnon was distressed to the point of making him sick, on account of Tamar his sister, for she was a virgin; and it seemed difficult in Amnon's eyes to do anything unto her.

Verse 3   And Amnon had a friend,...Jonadab...[who] was a very sly man.

Verse 4   ...he said to him, 'Why are you becoming so thin'...Amnon said to him, 'I love Tamar, the sister of Absalom.'

Verse 5   ... Jonadab said to him: 'Lie down on your bed and feign sickness, and when your father comes to see you, say to him: 'Tamar come now...that I may eat from her hand.'

Verse 7   ...David sent home to Tamar saying, "Go now to your brother Amnon's house, and prepare the food for him." ...

Verse 10   ... Amnon said to Tamar, "Bring the food into the chamber that I may eat from your hand."...

Verse 11   ...She brought them near to him to eat, and he took hold of her and said to her, "Come lie with me, my sister."

Verse 12   ... she said to him, "No, my brother, do not force me, for it is not done so in Israel; do not do this wanton deed."

Verse 13   And I, where shall I lead my shame? ...[as for] you shall be like one of the profligate [degenerate] men in Israel. ...now I beg of you to speak to the king [David], for he will not withhold me from you."

Verse 14   But he would not heed her and he overpowered her and forced her, and lay with her.

The Eleventh Commandment 171

Verse 15 ...Amnon hated her with very great hatred, for greater was the hatred with which he hated her than the love with which he had loved her.... Amnon said to her, "Get up (and) go."

Verse 16 ...she said to him, "Do not do this wrong (which is) greater than the other one that you did to me, by sending me away." But he would not listen to her.

Verse 17 And he called his youth, his servant, and he said, "Send now this one away from me, outside, and lock the door after her!"

Verse 19 And Tamar put ashes on her head, and rent [teased] her garment of many colours that was on her. [Her garment was the kind the king's virgin daughter wore] ...[she] went her way, crying aloud as she went.

Verse 20 ...Absalom her brother said to her: 'Has Amnon your brother been with you? But now, my sister, remain silent; he is your brother; do not take this thing to heart' and Tamar stayed in solitude in her brother Absalom's house." (Stern, 2017, verses 1–20).

Commentaries on Samuel 1–13: Amnon's sexual transgressions with Tamar

In addition to the actual Biblical text, commentary on the Amnon/Tamar sexual transgression can add to our understanding of the behavior by Amnon, Tamar, Absalom, and King David, and the customs of the Israelites toward incest and sexual abuse. According to the Bible, God hates all types of wrong sex (Leviticus 18). Everyone knew that the sexual transgression of Amnon was wrong. According to the laws of Israel: A man should never rape a woman; A brother and sister should never have sex together; and unmarried people should not have sex. Tamar thought that Amnon should have married her after they had sexual contact. *In Exodus 22: 16–17, God's law says that a man who has sex with a woman should marry her* (Stern, 2017). Every man wanted to marry a woman who had not had sex with a man. Tamar knew that no man would want to marry her now that she was no longer a virgin. Amnon, therefore, would not marry Tamar. Amnon had ruined Tamar's future life. No one would

172   The Eleventh Commandment

marry her now. As cited, Tamar put ashes on her forehead as a sign of mourning, perhaps, for her virginity, or that she would be in mourning for her lost life as a bride. She had lost something precious in her spirit. She cried out loud, because life for her would never contain happiness.

Amnon's feelings toward Tamar seemed to change from love to hatred. Verse 15 of the Biblical story of their sexual transgression does not explain this change. His dramatic change in feelings suggests that he did not really love Tamar but was only interested in her as a vessel to fulfill his narcissistic need for sex with an attractive woman. In addition, being able to have Tamar sexually, even though Amnon took her by force, turned his half-sister into a prostitute, for which he developed loathing.

The son of David and brother of Tamar, Absalom, realized what his brother, Amnon, had done to his sister. Absalom comforted Tamar. He looked after her and he protected her in his home. Absalom developed a hatred for Amnon. He refused to speak to Amnon.

Verse 21 of the Biblical story of Amnon and Tamar says that David, the King, and father of Amnon and Absalom, was also very angry. But it does not say that David punished Amnon. Perhaps, the punishment was not forthcoming because he expected Amnon to become king after him. But a dramatic punishment of Amnon is described in the Jewish Bible. Verses 28–29, 32 and 39 are about the punishment:

Verse 28 "Then Absalom said to his servants, 'Watch Amnon. See when he has drunk too much wine. I shall say to you, kill Amnon! Then you must kill him. I have ordered you to do it, so do not be afraid. Be strong and brave.'

Verse 29 So Absalom's servants killed Amnon because Absalom had ordered them to...

Verse 32 But Jonadab, the son of David's brother Shimeah, said... only Amnon is dead. Amnon raped Tamar, Absalom's sister. Ever since that day, Absalom planned to do this.

Verse 39 David recovered after Amnon's death. Absalom had to run away after he killed Amnon... He went...to his grandfather Talmai...Absalom could never become king if he did not return to Israel. At the end of three years, David recovered from Amnon's death" (Stern, 2017 – Second Book of Samuel, Chapter 13, Verses 28–39).

In presenting a comprehensive presentation of the case of sexual transgression in II Samuel 13 in the Old Testament, between Amnon and Tamar, as well as commentaries on the after-effects on this significant event, I am suggesting that this event and its meaning in Jewish history defines a sexual abuse experience and the Jewish community's response to it, as well as the meaning of sexual transgression in human existence. As has happened in all other parts of society, religious groups have neglected or suppressed the classical Biblical example of sexual abuse of Amnon and Tamar. Religious communities in our society have failed to express a moral, ethical, and humanistic voice about the sexual abuse of children, youth, or adults. They have not always provided the standard for ethical and moral behavior for true believers. For a religious Jew, especially, members of the Ultra-Orthodox Jewish community, the story of Amnon and Tamar clearly presents the prohibition of God towards incest. It is a sin against God and man that such behavior presents for the abused, abuser, and their family and community. The tale in II Samuel 13 originally was a blueprint for observant Jews and Christians (who accepted the Old Testament and Judaic laws as relevant to Christianity) for their understanding as well as a mandate to confront sexual abuse in their midst and find an effective way to punish the abusers. Religious communities have failed to provide a moral and theological stance on sexual abuse.

Recently, however, an academician, not a religious leader, has offered a courageous, comprehensive, and illuminating statement on a theology of sexual abuse. Andrew J. Schmutzer, who is a Professor of the Old Testament at Moody Bible Institute in Chicago, provides a much-needed antidote to the lack of theological and moral leadership. His statement is as follows:

This study is one voice in a much-needed dialogue. The goals are to further educate Christian leaders by normalizing the crisis of sexual abuse, create an understanding that promotes healing for the abused, and foster biblical-theological reflection among biblical educators, pastors, and church leadership, by deepening our insight into foundational creation texts with an eye to sexual abuse. (Schmutzer, 2008, p. 786)

This integration of theology and a comprehensive understanding of sexual abuse is an attempt to: "bring a fuller biblical understanding of sexual abuse to various ministry contexts will go a long way to create agents of healing" (Schmutzer, 2008, p. 786). Schmutzer (2008) outlines what is necessary for the Christian Church (and I would add, the Jewish community and all other religious communities) to develop a theological/moral stance on sexual abuse:

1. "There is need for interdisciplinary research and dialogue...In both the church and theological education there is a desperate need for a more generous dialogue, one open to learning from other disciplines.
2. There is a need for a robust theology of personhood in general and the reality of embodiment in particular....Traditional views of sexual abuse as an external and isolated act of sin falls short of recognizing the embodied milieu between the abuser and the abused...
3. The need to support victims of sexual abuse is ignored to the peril of us all...The abused need safety and compassion... If the abused can risk speaking, the non-abused can risk expressing an empathetic voice.
4. There is a need for spiritual formation programs to address sexual abuse head on.... Theological healing means a moral sufficiency can come when God is drawn close to areas of deep pain, redeeming the suffering.
5. There is a need for some wounded within leadership. Ministering to the sexually traumatized requires a leadership style of vulnerable partnership rather than control. Such leaders draw the broken toward healing through an incarnational empathy (2 Cor. 1:3-11).
6. There is a need for honest preaching on sexual abuse....Churches should consider dedicating on Sunday a year to the full spectrum of abuse in their congregations—including sexual abuse....Between

the slumber of inattention and the silence of indifference, the problem of sexual abuse has gone woefully unaddressed....We shall build healing communities for our sexually broken out in the open light of acceptance where the warm comfort of wholeness and safety can overshadow the traditions of silence and 'victory'" (Schmutzer, 2008, pp. 806–812).

"The Eleventh Commandment: Thou Shall Not Lie Down with a Child": A collage, Rachman, 2015

In 2015, when I was writing a book on the incest trauma (Rachman, & Klett, 2015), I was so moved by the case studies of childhood sexual abuse I decided to create a collage expressing my feelings. I have previously constructed collages that served as covers for a book (Rachman, 1997, 2003). The collage that I created, which I intended to be the cover of *Analysis of the Incest Trauma*, I entitled, *The Eleventh Commandment: Thou Shall Not Lie Down with a Child*. The collage (see Figure 0.8) and its title were somewhat of a surprise for me. I usually collect material for the collage in advance, having some general idea of what theme I want to create. In this instance, I had collected materials over a 2-year period, not particularly paying attention to the specific nature of the materials. When I sat down to create the collage, what emerged was a picture that contained images of vulnerability, predatory behavior, and an undercurrent of religiosity. When it was finished, I decided to give it a title that reflected these elements. My feeling was that the religious community has blatantly neglected the sexual abuse of children youth, and adults. When I submitted this collage to the publisher, it was rejected because the editor said, "it was too disturbing." *I did not share that assessment, since it revealed the disturbing influence of sexual abuse by the religious community*. I was resentful and disappointed that this image was not used as the book's cover. There was also legal problems using the images contained in the collage. I decided to reconfigure the collage and developed a new figure which represents the addition of a new commandment which prohibits sexual abuse with a child.

176 The Eleventh Commandment

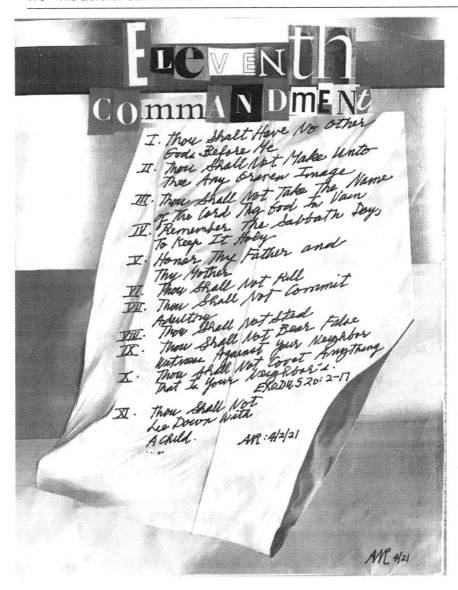

Figure 0.8 The Eleventh Commandment: Thou Shall Not Lie Down With A Child. Collage by Arnold Wm. Rachman April 22, 2021.

The Society of Tamar

The biblical tale of the sexual abuse of Amnon of his half-sister Tamar provides us with insight into the analysis of sexual trauma.

We can become aware of Tamar's experience as the victim, such as the debilitating loss of self, display of grief and mourning, crushing shame, degradation and prolonged social isolation with desolation. We also see the behavior of Amnon, the abuser, such as the manipulation, overpowering the will of the victim, using force and emotional seduction. Tamar was violated as Amnon violated her personal and social boundaries.

As has been discussed about the Christian community, there is a need for survivors within the Jewish community, supported by The Tamar Society leaders, to form an organization, such as, dedicated to helping the abused confront and recover from sexual abuse. As we listen to the voice of the abused, such as Tamar, we can also listen to the voice of the abused from the Christian community. Listening to the abused must become a fundamental dimension of the psychoanalytic and societal communities. Here is a contemporary voice of an abused by a Catholic. Let him help us understand what is needed to understand and help the abused within religious communities:

> When I was a child, I was sexually abused by a Catholic priest. *Trauma is the devil. It stays in the core of your being...I was prey, vulnerable to being groomed by the priest...The predator... tries to figure out what is missing by violating another – a child... People who were abused can heal, and the healing...must be woven into the fabric of today's broken church. The church should unleash the voices of...survivors.* (Horowitz, 2018, p. A27)

Chapter 18

The child sexual abuse scandal at Pennsylvania State University: Coach Joe Paterno, from idolatry to shame

Joe Paterno: a sports icon

Joe Paterno was an iconic figure in sports history. His 409-136 win-loss record made him college football's winningest NCAA Division 1 coach. His name is on the library he built at Pennsylvania State University; his legacy also involved his interest in intellectual and academic pursuits. He is admired for combining sports and academics to create the true student/athlete. He was known as "Joe Pa," a believed father figure at Penn State University campus by students, athletes, faculty, and the administration. He is quoted as saying:

> Success without honor is an unseasoned dish; it will satisfy your hunger, but it won't taste good. (Gobreÿ, 2012, p. 63)

Thirty-three of his players were selected in the first round of the National Football draft, 47 of them were also Academic All-Americans (Layden, 2012, p. 61). He was one of the important sports figures in American history.

Paterno was from Brooklyn, New York, from a second-generation Italian American family, who was expected to do big things. In high school, he played basketball and football and graduated second in his class. He attended the Ivy League school, Brown University, where he played football. His plans to attended Boston University Law School were changed when he accepted the quarterback coach at Penn State. He took the head coach position in 1964 (Anonymous, 2012, p. 29). The journey from idolatry to shame involves the child

DOI: 10.4324/9780429298431-18

The child sexual abuse scandal   179

sexual abuse scandal that was uncovered at Penn State University while Joe Paterno was the head football coach and one of his assistant coaches was Jerry Sandusky.

Jerry Sandusky: child predator

In the Autumn of 2011, the sexual abuse scandal unfolded when Jerry Sandusky, an assistant football coach at Penn State, was arrested and charged with abusing eight boys (although the number of victims had grown to 10). He had been an assistant football coach, in charge of defense, for 31 football seasons. There was mention he was a person who could become Penn State's head football coach. But, in 1999, Paterno told Sandusky he would not become the head coach. Sandusky reacted by suddenly announcing he would retire. He never returned to college football. Instead he began working with at-risk children at the Second Mile Charity, which he founded. He also volunteered at Central Mountain High School (Layden, 2012). Before formal legal action was announced against Sandusky for sexual abuse, there were two significant reported incidents. In 2002, a graduate assistant coach, Mike McQueary, witnessed Sandusky having sex with a 10-year-old boy in a Penn State shower (which will be discussed in detail in the next section). In 2009, a boy's mother at the Central Mountain High School made a troubling report to the school, that Sandusky had been sexually assaulting her son when he was 11 or 12 years old (Werthein & Epstein, 2011).

On November 4, 2011, Pennsylvania attorney Linda Kelly and State Police Commissioner Frank Noonan filed a grand jury report that detailed Sandusky's behavior as a sexual predator of young boys. Through his charity, The Second Mile, he gained access to young, vulnerable, socially at-risk boys and then sexually assaulted them. From 1994 to 2009, Sandusky sexually assaulted 10 boys (Werthein & Epstein, 2011). The grand jury report also included the aforementioned description of the witnessing of Sandusky having sex with a 10-year-old boy in a shower at a Penn State locker room. McQueary testified at Sandusky's trial in the following way:

> It was extremely sexual and that some kind of intercourse was going on…There's no question in my mind that I conveyed to them

that I saw Jerry in the showers, and that it was a severe sexual act, and that it was wrong and over the line. (Durantine, 2011, p. A1)

The grand jury report described Sandusky's use of his status, authority, and celebrity as a Penn State football coach to seduce his sexual victims by bringing them to football games, giving them gifts, cast them in instructional videos, introduced them to players and coaches, and taking one youngster to a bowl game. In addition to Sandusky, charges were brought against Penn State athletic director, Tim Curley, who was charged with perjury and failure to report Sandusky's 2002 sexual abuse charge. Penn State's senior vice-president in charge of campus police, Gary Schultz, was also charged.

Sandusky: a devil in a football coach's sweat suit

Sandusky's response to the sexual allegations was complete and utter denial. In a 4-hour interview over 2 days, in December 2011, about a month after he was indicted, Joe Becker, a reporter with *The New York Times*, outlined Sandusky's response. First, *Sandusky said he never sexually abused a child*. But it is clear from the predatory behavior that prosecutors uncovered in their investigation, that *Sandusky was a devil masquerading as a positive father to children*. As has been described, he used his contacts with children to seduce them, including giving them gifts. Prosecutors said he used such gifts to build trust and loyalty among boys he then repeatedly abused. Sandusky claimed his behavior was misunderstood:

> I had kid after kid...who might say I was a father figure. And they just twisted that all. (Becker, 2011, p. A1)

Sandusky's explanations for his predatory behavior border on denial or psychologically speaking, dissociation due to trauma. He sexually traumatizing children not only traumatized them, but him. His dissociated response was:

> It was...almost an extended family...precious times...just happened that way...I think a lot of the kids really reached out for that. (Becker, 2011, p. D3)

As for the gifts Sandusky gave to children, they were aspects of seduction, but he believed:

> I tried to reward them sometimes with a little money in hand, just so that they could see something. But more often than not, I tried to set up, maybe get them to save the money, and I put it directly into a savings account established for them. (Becker, 2011, p. D3)

A Sandusky victim speaks

Aaron Fisher, who was previously known as Sandusky *Victim No. 1*, has found his voice with help from his mother, Dawn Daniels, and psychologist Michael Gillim. In 2006, when Aaron was 12 years old, Jerry Sandusky began forcing him to have anal sex. At that time, he was 15 years old, he decided to stop being a victim. When he told Sandusky directly that he was physically abused by him, Sandusky answered, he was ungrateful for all the things he had done for him. Aaron told his mother he wanted to break contact with his abuser, and no longer take his calls. Sandusky began to stalk Aaron, coming to his school and telling the principal he needed to talk to Aaron. One day, Sandusky confronted Aaron on his home lawn. He told Sandusky he did not want to be with him. Sandusky sent him gifts. Aaron said Sandusky was like a clingy, jilted girlfriend. Finally, Aaron broke down, told his mother about Sandusky, and she called the school. Aaron and his mother were summoned to school, where he talked about Sandusky. His mother wanted the school to call the police, but they refused. This is the previously mentioned incident of sexual abuse allegation when a mother reported Sandusky's sexual abuse of her child.

His mother took Aaron to the County's Children and Youth Services office, where he met psychologist Gillim. Aaron developed serious psychopathology as a result of Sandusky's sexual abuse. He became depressed, fearful, and had panic attacks. He became preoccupied that Sandusky's fans would reach out and hurt him. In addition, he was considering suicide. Aaron has received psychological help and has developed a meaningful understanding of his trauma and is able to move forward in being angry at his abuser. He no longer feels like a victim. (Fisher, Gillim, & Daniels, 2012).

182 The child sexual abuse scandal

Paterno's silence about Sandusky's sexually abusive behavior: his downfall

Jerry Sandusky said he never spoke to Joe Paterno about the sexual accusations made against him:

> I never talked to him...that's all I can say, I mean, I don't know. (Becker, 2011, p. D3)

What is more, Paterno never once confronted Sandusky about allegations that he was molesting boys. Paterno never mentioned to Sandusky about the 1998 investigation by the Penn State campus police into a claim that Dawn Daniels that her son Aaron Fisher was molested by Sandusky. Nor did Paterno confront Sandusky about the report by Mike McQueary that Sandusky molested a child in the showers at Penn State (Burke, 2011, p. 6). McQueary did describe a meeting he had with Paterno the morning after he witnessed Sandusky molesting the boy in the shower at Penn State. He told Paterno what he had seen Sandusky doing to a naked boy. Paterno's response was:

> Well, I'm sorry you had to see that. It's terrible. I need to think and tell some people about what you saw, and I'll let you know what we'll do next. (Pellon, 2011, p. A1)

There were several reasons for Paterno being fired by Penn State. Paterno's failure to act more aggressively in following up the information given to him by Mike McQueary, an assistant football coach, that Sandusky had sexually molested a boy in a Penn State athletic facility; and he never spoke with law enforcement about Sandusky's transgressions. Furthermore, Paterno was criticized for not following through with Tim Curley, Penn State's athletic director, and Gary Schultz, senior vice president with whom he shared Sandusky's molestation accusations. It was unclear whether he ever sought to learn what Curley and Schultz had done with the information (Durantine, 2011).

John P. Surma, the chief executive of US Steel and the vice chairman of Penn State University's board of trustees, reacted quickly to the sex scandal. They decided to remove Graham Spencer as president because he failed to keep them informed of the nature and scope of the Pennsylvania attorney general's investigation of Sandusky as well as the investigation of University officials. The trustees then fired Paterno for what they consider sufficient reasons: the failure to do more when told about the suspected assault by Sandusky in 2002; his questioning of the board's authority in the days after Sandusky's arrest; their assessment of Paterno's inability to effectively continue coaching with continuing questions surrounding his program (Thamel & Viera, 2012).

When Paterno was fired on November 9, 2011, nine games into Penn State's football season he was broken by the scandal and its fallout. He did have regrets:

> This is a tragedy...It is one of the great sorrows of my life. With the benefit of hindsight, I wish I had done more. (Layden, 2012, p. 56)

Paterno also explained, in an interview published on January 15, 2012, that he was not able to meaningfully respond to the Sandusky sexual abuse:

> [I] didn't know exactly how to handle it [the McQueary sexual accusations toward Sandusky] and I was afraid to do something that might jeopardize what the university procedure was. So I backed away and turned it over to some other people, people I thought would have a little more expertise than I did. It didn't work out that way. (Layden, 2012, p. 61)

Nearly 6 months after Joe Paterno's death by cancer, his family sent an essay he wrote to former Penn State football players. The following statement is believed to be the only thing he wrote about the child sexual abuse scandal before he died:

> I feel compelled to say, in no uncertain terms, that this is not a football scandal...nothing alleged is an indictment of football or evidence that the spectacular collection of accomplishments and dedicated student athletes be in anyway tarnished...I have heard Penn State officials decrying the influence of football

and have heard such ignorant comments like Penn State will no longer be a "football factory" and we are going to "start" focusing in athletics...Penn State is not a football factory and it is ALREADY a great university...Our graduates have gone on to change the world – even graduates with football letterman sweaters. That is why recent comments are so... damaging [by] our own administration...It must stop. Forget my career in terms of my accomplishments and look at the last 40 years as I do: as the aggregate achievements of hundreds of young men working to become better people as they got an education and became better football players...Whatever failings that may have happened at Penn State...these actions had nothing to do with this last time or any of the hundreds of prior graduates... This is a great university with one of the best academic performing football programs in major college athletics. (Brennan, 2012, pp. 1–2).

Paterno, the book: an attempt to save his legacy

The book, *Paterno*, written by Joe Posnanski, a former reporter for Sports Illustrated, which he calls a remarkable story about a man who was capable of becoming great in many ways who chose football to help contribute to America. He believed he could help American youth, one college player at a time. He chronicled what was called "the grand experiment" that Paterno was very proud of, stressing academic and athletic achievement as a focus. Posnanski who wrote on Paterno's dark exit from football and did resolve, for himself, the dilemma of being fond of and respectful of Paterno's achievement. He believing that his story about Paterno what has not about a single incident in one football coach's life, but, about a remarkable life. Posnanski truly believes Paterno was motivated to do something important for America through football (Posnanski, 2012). This is the author's belief even though he did write a chapter on Jerry Sandusky, who he called evil, who was the child sexual predator whose transgressions brought down Paterno. Posnanski said realizing what happened to the children who were abused was:

so vile, so grotesque, that it is human nature to want everyone to pay, innocent children were hurt, scarred, and as a parent, this is something so horrible that I cannot even think of a penalty harsh enough. (Cohen, 2012)

Posnanski's final assessment of Paterno states the need to include Paterno's silence on the awareness of the child sexual abuse allegations about his friend and assistant coach, Jerry Sandusky:

But in many ways, it's still the same...It's still about his life – a life that changed dramatically at the end. (Cohen, 2012, p. D7)

Sandusky was sentenced for sexually abusing 10 boys

In June of 2012, Jerry Sandusky was convicted of sexually abusing 10 boys, all from disadvantaged homes. It became clear Sandusky used his relationship with the Penn State football program and his own charity for disadvantaged youths, the Second Mile, to identify potential victims, to establish a relationship with them so he could sexually exploit them. He gave a statement in his defense at the termination of his trial where he maintained his innocence, proclaiming:

I did not do these alleged disgusting acts. (Rohan, 2012, p. B14)

In sentencing Sandusky 30–60 years in prison for 45 counts of abuse, Judge John M. Cleland scornfully proclaimed:

I'm not going to sentence you to centuries. It makes no sense for a 68-year-old man. This sentence will put you in prison for the rest of your life...[This] is a story of betrayal. You abused the trust of those who trusted you. (Rohan, 2012, p. B14)

Two other serious consequences were instituted for Penn State as a result of the child sexual abuse scandal. The school's football program developed over four decades by Joe Paterno was severely sanctioned. The National Collegiate Athletic Association fined the school $60 million, limited the number of athletic scholarships, officially stripping it of victories since 1998 and banned it from participating in post season bowl games. The NCAA stopped short of instituting the so-called *death penalty*, which would have suspended the Penn State football program (Lowry, 2012). University officials said they money for the settlement did not come from tuition, taxpayers or donations, but from liability insurance, which will cover the settlements and defense claims brought against Penn State, its officers, employees, and trustees. Rodney A. Erickson, the president of Penn State, characterized the settlement:

> Another step forward in the healing process for those hurt by Sandusky... We cannot undo what has been done, but we can and insure it never happens again at Penn State. (Drape, 2013, p. B11)

Clifford Rieders, a lawyer who negotiated one of the settlements, said the average settlement was similar to those involving the Catholic Church. The lawyer for two of the abused, Jeff Anderson, speaking for them focused on how Penn State and athletic programs can prevent further abuse and recover:

> They wanted to see new training and protocols...They broke the silence and stood up to the man who overpowered them...there's some deep and open wounds that can't be closed or healed. They've gotten the voice back they didn't have as kids, but it isn't a celebration or victory. (Drape, 2013, p. B15)

The aftermath of the Penn State sexual abuse scandal

Graham Spancer, "I never saw anything."

There were a host of issues and actions which define the aftermath of the Penn State sexual abuse scandal. The significant issue of Joe Paterno, and administrators of the university, such as, Graham Spanier, failed to protect the community against a child predator. Jerry Sandusky, who harmed children for over a decade. Louis Freeh, the former Federal Bureau of Investigation director, was hired by Penn State to review the university's dealings with Sandusky and its response he sexually abused a boy in a Penn State shower room, which was reported by Michael McQueary, an assistant football coach at Penn State. On July 12, 2012, Freeh issued his account of what happened at the university. The account indicates that investigators conducted 430 interviews of significant members of the university and other individuals who had knowledge of the events as well as 3.5 million pieces of pertinent electronic data and documents were analyzed. This Freeh Report reached dramatic and far-reaching conclusions:

> The most saddening finding by the Special Investigative Counsel is the total and consistent disregard by the most senior leaders at Penn State for the safety and welfare of Sandusky's child victims... Spanier, Paterno, Schultz and Curley [the senior members of Penn State]...failed to protect against a child sexual predator harming children for over a decade. (Sokolove, 2014, p. 29)

In essence, *the Freeh report exclaimed that the Penn State community and culture of athletics was a corrupt culture. Members of the administration and athletics departments conspired to cover up child sexual abuse to protect the football program.* Although this conspiracy was carried out by the four people mentioned in the report, the Penn State University had culpability as well. Spanier, who was president of Penn State when Sandusky's crimes were revealed, has continued to not only distance himself from Sandusky's adjudication as a sexual predator of children, but, is incredulous that he has any culpability in the sexual scandal. Spanier is quoted as saying the following:

> What does this have to do with me? I never saw anything I never spoke to a kid, a witness, a parent, Sandusky, McQueary, parent. (Sokolove, 2014, p. 46)

The incredulity issue belongs to Spanier's remarkable distance from such a serious problem for children and our society. There is a plausible hypothesis to explain his reaction. It may be an indication of a dissociative reaction. Spanier is the product of severe physical and emotional trauma in his childhood, administered by his father. He was severely beaten by his father as a youth, and he has the scars on his face as proof of his trauma. The father also was a dictator in his interaction with his family. To his credit, Spanier worked his way out of his trauma using his intellect to become a professor and

188 The child sexual abuse scandal

university president (Sokolove, 2014). But, he does not seem to have integrated his childhood trauma into his personality, rather, he has dissociated his trauma of paternal abuse. His previously quoted reaction to the Freeh Report, where he separates himself completely from his university's child sexual abuse scandal may indicate this. Given his abuse history, Spanier psychologically indicates his journey from his father's abuse of him did not educate him to empathy for child victims of abuse by authorities. His journey from childhood trauma to adult achievement bypassed self-examination and psychological recovery from trauma. Spanier's continued distance from empathy with the victims of Sandusky's sexual abuse of boys, Paterno's decision to protect his legacy of an iconic football program rather than confront the sex abuse, and Sandusky's absolute denial as a sexual predator, indicate psychoanalysis and society must become active in confronting sexual abuse as well as work toward treatment and prevention. As strong as the denial and neglect of sexual abuse, that is how vigorous the confrontation with facing the issue and ameliorating it must be. We cannot let the silence of icons like Joe Paterno authorities such as Spanier to define our response to the sexual abuse of children. *Anyone in the earshot of information about sexual abuse must find their voice to speak about this predatory behavior. Not speaking out make one a collaborator in abuse.*

Penn State's football culture

Penn State University has a cultural atmosphere, as does other very successful football/ athletic focused universities. The head coaches become icon figures, perhaps, can even be elevated to God-like leaders of their communities. The communities in college towns function in relation to the football program. Saturday, the day of the college game, revolves around going to, or watching the game. There are universities, like Penn State, at which a sports team is so central to student life and the school's identity. What is more, Joe Paterno, its iconic football coach, casted a revered shadow over the campus, the town, known as Happy Valley, in Pennsylvania, and for some, in the United States of America. There was an entire course at Penn State devoted to Paterno. Students often line up for days outside the stadium to get game tickets, and encampment known as Paternoville

The child sexual abuse scandal 189

(Schiveber & Pérez-Peña, 2011, p. B16). This culture of football and Paterno worship, in the university and community, enveloped Penn State in an emotionally blind atmosphere where football overshowed real life and real human beings. Football became life for Paterno and the Penn State community. As a respected sportswriter, George Vecsey has said about the Penn State sex scandal:

> At Penn State, it was even worse than prostituting education for the sake of a football powerhouse. The entire old-boy system in that university managed to overlook the possibility that children's lives were being ruined, within the dangerous cocoon of King football. We need to look beyond the alleged abuses. We need to look at the system that encouraged people to look the other way. (Vecsey, 2011, p. B14)

Joe Paterno's silence and emotional blindness

Joe Paterno, who believed he was the moral center of the Penn State University football program and its greater community, did not respond in an immediate and assertive manner to the information that his friend and former assistant football coach, Jerry Sandusky, had sexually molested young boys. He did report the allegations to University officials, but, then seemed to wash his hands of the matter. Paterno's feelings were not activated, his life was not changed by the idea that someone he befriended and hired to work for him had transcended the boundaries of human behavior to harm and damage children. As Joe Posnanski wrote in his book, *Paterno* (Posnanski, 2012), the iconic Penn State coach was an intelligent, decent human being, who was dedicated to doing positive things for his university, his community, and his country. But, *he was emotionally blind to the sexual abuse of a child encapsulated in the power, control, and status of a football coach*. He could not have the reaction as did an 18-year-old incoming Penn State freshman when she heard of the child sexual abuse news:

> I was just really upset for the victims. That really got me, how the children – I'm an education major – had to suffer when they didn't have to because of Paterno. I loved him so much, just the fact that he didn't do more really hurt me. When someone like

Joe Paterno – who I really looked up – I originally thought he did all he could, but in the [Freeh] report it obviously wasn't true. It was just really hurtful to hear what actually happened. (Pennington & Rohan, 2012, p. B13)

This freshman student was able to move beyond football, something Joe Paterno was not able to do as this latest information has been uncovered. The following quotation is from a 2014 deposition released Tuesday morning, July 12, 2016:

"Is it accurate that Coach Paterno quickly said to you, *I don't want to hear about any of that kind of stuff, I have a football season to worry about?*" a lawyer for the insurer asked the accuser, according to the deposition. "Specifically, yes," the man replied. Mr. Paterno then walked away, the man said. (Tracy, 2016, pp. B9-B10)

Grantland Rice (November 1, 1880 – July 13, 1954) was an early 20th century American who was an influential and important figure in the development of sports journalism. Although Rice was the first play-by-play announcer carried live on radio for the baseball World Series game, he preferred writing to radio. He rose to fame when his column in the *New York Herald Tribune* referred to the University of Notre Dame's football backfield as the *Four Horsemen of the Apocalypse.* In 1930, he started a national column that would eventually appear in 100 newspapers.

His expressive and poetic writing helped raise sport and its players to heroic status. He often compared the challenges of sports to mythic stories and the greater human condition. Rice frequently delved into the greater social and personal meaning of sports. He is famous for defining the playing of sport as having the highest of ethical and moral standard. Winning at sport was not as important as how you played your sport. Winning by standards of fairness, morality, and ethics defiled the game (Rice, 1954). The expression and poetic words about sport and its players that Grantland Rice epitomized raised the area of sports and its participants, emphasizing a sense of elegance, excellence, and morality. This ethic of being emotionally and interpersonally connected to the game of sport is very different from the climate that developed at Penn

State. Winning football games blinded the coach, the administration, and the university to turning their gaze towards the sexual abuse of children. Grantland Rice's ethic exemplified the meaningful positive response to the game of life, which takes precedence over winning a game in a sport contest. Joe Paterno's positive idea was supposed to enhance the academic experience at Penn State as part of his Grand Experiment. It is time to implement the Grand Experiment by paying tribute to Paterno by implementing a model of a sports program that is vigilant about sexual abuse in the university community and will confront the issue while vigorously pursuing its remedy.

No university should become captive to its sports program as Penn State was to football. At Penn State, football was such an importance and Paterno was such a God-like figure that it emotionally blinded their community to allowing a child sexual predator, Jerry Sandusky, to roam free in their midst. The importance of football, or any sport, should never emotionally blind us become aware of, confronting, and actively removing sexual predators from our schools and playing fields.

Chapter 19

The worst example of sexual abuse in sports history: the case of Lawrence G. Nassar, MD

Rachael Denhollander exposes Dr. Nassar

As dramatic was the sexual abuse scandal at Penn State University and the downfall of their late iconic football coach, Joe Paterno, the subsequent sexual abuse scandal in American gymnastics was equally dramatic and devastating. Another courageous woman survivor, who found her voice, Rachael Denhollander, a former gymnast who became a lawyer and a coach, told *The Indianapolis Star* newspaper in 2016 that Dr. Lawrence G. Nassar had sexually abused her as a child. A floodgate of women came forth after Rachael Denhollander's allegations. Over 150 women gave statements in court in Nassar's trial about his sexual abuse of them. The former doctor for the American gymnastics team, Dr. Lawrence G. Nassar, was sentenced to 40–175 years in prison for multiple sex crimes. Over 155 people had delivered victim impact statements to the court, among which were ones by Olympic gold medalists.

Rachael Denhollander, the star witness against Nassar was called a "five-star general" for an army of abuse survivors, said the presiding trial judge, Rosemarie Aquilina. The judge also said, "You are the bravest person I've ever had in my courtroom" (Macur, 2018, p. B10). Judge Aquilina's admiration for Rachael Denhollander came from her courageous move to bring Dr. Nassar's sexual abuse into the open as well as her emotional honesty in detailing her own abuse:

> He penetrated me, he groped me, he fondled me…And then he whispered questions about how it felt. He engaged in degrading

DOI: 10.4324/9780429298431-19

and humiliating sex acts without my consent or permission. (Macur, 2018, p. B10)

What is more, this survivor of sexual abuse also specified the damage sexual abuse can cause a human being. She told how her disturbing experience with Dr. Nassar as a teenager caused her, as an adult, to mistrust doctors. As she delivered her three children, she said:

A fear...hung over each birth...[Dr. Nassar] cast a horrific shadow over what should have been an occasion of pure joy. (Macur, 2018, p. 10)

The voices of the abused by Dr. Nassar

The chorus of sexual abuse survivors raised their voices against Dr. Nassar, gaining empowerment and taking back their physical and emotional sense of self. Here are some of these statements:

I thought that training for the Olympics would be the hardest thing that I would ever have to do. But, in fact, the hardest thing I would ever have to do is process that I am a victim of Larry Nassar. — Jordan Wieber, gymnast and Olympic Medalist

I was attacked on social media....People didn't believe me...They called me a liar, a whore, and even accused me of making all of this up just to get attention. — Jamie Dantzscher, gymnast and Olympic Medalist

My vagina was sore during my competition because of this man. How disgusting is that to even say out loud? — Amy Labadie, gymnast

Larry is the most dangerous type of abuser. One who is capable of manipulating his victims through coldly calculated grooming methodologies, presenting the most wholesome and caring external persona as a deliberate means to ensure a steady stream of young children to assault. — Rachael Denhollander, gymnast

Let this sentence strike fear in anyone who thinks it is OK to hurt another person. Abusers, your time is up. The survivors are here, standing tall, and we are not going anywhere. — Aly Raisman, gymnast and six-time Olympic Medalist (Louttit & Correa, 2018, p. A19)

Aly Raisman, the Olympian, recovers from Dr. Nassar's abuse

There is an amplification of the predatory sexual behavior of Dr. Nassar, as Aly Raisman, the Six-Time Olympic Medalist and captain of the 2016 US Women's Olympic gymnastics team, has written a book describing her physical and emotional experiences with him. At the age of 15, Aly Raisman sensed there was something wrong with her treatment sessions with Dr. Nassar. He did not wear gloves during his examinations and treatments. During his treatments, she would tense up, her hands balling up into fists. His hands would work their way under her clothing. Treatment sessions with him always made her tense and uncomfortable. As she was being abused by Dr. Nassar, she would survive the disturbance by convincing herself that his behavior was part of the healing process for her injuries. The irony was the treatments never helped her. It was only years later, when sexual abuse allegations began to arise that she began to realize that she had been molested. She realized that she had been brainwashed, having been told he was the top person in his field and he also presented himself as the athlete's savior. Aly and her fellow athletes began sharing their experiences with Dr. Nassar and realized the way he touched these females was not normal and harmful (Raisman, 2017).

Dr. Nassar convinced the athletes he worked with he was giving treatment, not abuse. This is the classical psychodynamic of a Confusion of Tongues Trauma. The abuser seduces the child, youth, or adult, by promising them that his behavior toward them is affectionate, caring, helpful. The individual wants and needs what the abuser offers. But the offer satisfies the abuser's narcissistic need for sexual satisfaction. It has nothing to do with satisfying the need of the individual. In fact, the abuser's behavior, as Aly Raisman described, was harmful, not helpful. Aly Raisman, as her colleagues were, functioned in a state of dissociation, which is the psychological consequence of the Confusion of Tongues experience. The individual splits off her feelings, thoughts, and experiences during the trauma, so she can psychologically survive, maintain self-cohesion, and go on with life. They who were abused by Dr. Nassar had their emotional lives damaged and their functioning arrested. Finding their voices has helped them recover from their Confusion of Tongues Trauma.

Chapter 20

Two sports champions and emotional heroes: R.A. Dickey and Kayla Harrison, find their voices about their sexual abuse

In this chapter, the stories of two courageous athletic champions, R.A. Dickey and Kayla Harrison, will be told to illustrate how two courageous athletes, who had childhood sexual abuse, struggled with the psychopathology that ensued from the damaging experiences with an abuser, whether they were a coach, babysitter, and stranger. They suffered with the anger, loss of self, dissociation, suicidal thoughts and attempts, and dysfunction, which nearly lost them their careers, relationship, and emotional equilibrium. It is also a story of how a person's significant relationships, with a parent, or friend, can help a survivor find their voice, share their abusive experience, identify the abuser, and begin the process of change. What is more, both R.A. Dickey and Kayla Harrison turned to psychotherapy to examine their sexual traumas and recover from them. These athletes have pioneered and become champions, both in their respective sports and in the area of sexual abuse studies by chronicling their experiences in the books they have written to help survivors find their voices. It is very rare for athletes to self-disclose their personal vulnerabilities, especially, a history of self-abuse. Such disclosure runs counter to the identity of power, control, status that defines an athlete's sense of self. These two champions demonstrate an axiom, which I believe is underappreciated. True emotional, intellectual, and interpersonal strength develops from emotional openness, honesty, and self-disclosure. In their narratives, which we shall examine in the next sections of this chapter, they provide an opportunity for survivors to use their experiences as a model for finding their voice, maintaining the motivation to break through to their trauma and turn toward psychotherapy and psychoanalysis to recover from their sexual abuse trauma.

DOI: 10.4324/9780429298431-20

R.A. Dickey

Robert Allen Dickey (born October 29, 1974) is an American former professional baseball pitcher. His Major League Baseball debut occurred on April 22, 2001, for the Texas Rangers, and his last Major League Baseball appearance was on September 26, 2017, for the Atlanta Braves baseball team. In between, he played for the Seattle Mariners, Minnesota Twins, New York Mets, and Toronto Blue Jays baseball teams. His baseball career highlights involved being an All-Star in 2012; National League Cy Young Award winner for a pitcher in 2012; Gold Glove Award in 2013, for fielding by a pitcher; and National League strikeout leader in 2012.

R.A. Dickey attended Montgomery Bell Academy in Nashville, Tennessee. Then, he played baseball at the University of Tennessee. He was also an excellent student where he majored in English literature, with a 3.35 Grade Point Average (out of 4) and was named Academic All-American. He was also named Academic All-Southeast Conference College Player (Lapointe, 2010). Dickey was drafted by the Texas Rangers in the first round (18th overall) of the 1996 Major League Baseball draft. Being drafted in the top 20 baseball prospects usually points to an exciting young baseball talent who has the potential for a successful career. But Dickey ran into difficulties that hampered his success for many years. In his 10-year tenure with the Texas Rangers, his first team, he was found to have a physical issue, for example, a missing ulnar collateral ligament in his right elbow joint. His ability to pitch was limited, and he was demoted to baseball's minor league. The next years, 2007–2009, where he played for three baseball teams, his functioning was mediocre.

A turning point in his baseball career developed in his pitching style. Dickey realized that he possessed a pitch, called a knuckleball, which could help him to extend his career. A knuckleball is a baseball pitch thrown to minimize the spin of the ball in flight, causing an erratic unpredictable motion (Neyer, 2012). The initial trial with the knuckleball was not successful. Finally, his baseball woes disappeared when he signed with the New York Mets, for which he played for the 2010, 2011, and 2012 seasons. The tenure with the Mets became the highlight of his career, with the following achievements: his performance in 2012 was considered some of the most dominant of the past 50 years; he set a new Mets franchise of scoreless innings pitched; he was named to the National League All-Star team; he was honored by being named Pitcher of the Month, he set new career bests in games started, wins, complete games, shutouts, innings pitched, strikeouts, and earned run average. Consequently, he won the National League Cy Young Pitching Award, becoming the third Met pitcher to win this award (Craig, 2012). Dickey also had an international career as a member of the 1996 United States Olympic Baseball team.

R.A. Dickey's personal life demonstrates intellectual interests and public service. He is married with four children, who struggled with maintaining his family connection during his struggles with sexual trauma. He helps to operate the Ocala, Florida-based Honoring the Father Ministries, which provides medical supplies, powdered milk, and baseball equipment to the impoverished in Latin America (Vecsey, 2010). Dickey is an avid reader. He said if he would not have become an athlete, he would have become an English professor (Kepner, 2010). Dickey climbed Mt. Kilimanjaro, fulfilling a boyhood dream after reading Hemingway's *The Snows of Kilimanjaro*. His climb raised awareness of the issue of human trafficking in India (Miller, 2011). It is now time to turn to Dickey's sexual trauma, which he reported in his book (Dickey and Coffey, 2012).

R.A. Dickey's sexual abuse experiences were described as being two incidents when he was a child. The first occurred from a 13-year-old girl babysitter when he was a child. His mother who was an alcoholic left him with a babysitter while she drank. This sexual abuser told him to take off his clothes as she pressed down on top of him. He was terrified and trembling with feeling what had just happened was wicked. But he had no understanding of what had happened to him. He faced this terror four or five more times that summer, drifting into a private place of fear, shame, and dissociation. Years later, as he was playing with a ball, throwing it off the roof of a relative's garage, a 17-year-old male came along, physically overwhelmed and molested him.

Dickey became connected to Christianity, attending teen fellowship meetings, studying scripture and reciting prayers. When the youngsters with whom he associated started to talk about sex he would walk away. He did not let anyone get physically or emotionally close so his sexual trauma could be detected. Neither his friends nor his family was aware of his wound. Dickey lost himself in Star Wars movies and Luke Skywalker. When he was 11, he left his mother and went to live with his father, who was nearby. Later when he was 17, he went to the edge of his existence, sleeping at friends' houses, in the back of his car, or houses that were for rent. His one sense of power, control, and status came from playing baseball in high school, where he became the state's high school player of the year. He won a scholarship to play baseball at the University of Tennessee. As has been described he was an outstanding player in high school and college, being drafted high on graduation by the Texas Rangers professional baseball team, but, he struggled during his early years as a major league pitcher due to physical and emotional issues. His baseball difficulties contributed to his trauma struggles causing his marriage to fall apart. He lost his house and developed thoughts of suicide. He did try to drown himself but was saved by his baseball teammates. He knew he was damaged and when his pain reached a crescendo, he went to see Stephen James, a therapist in Nashville, Tennessee. Dickey and James developed a robust clinical interaction where his childhood traumas were able to be retrieved and worked through. His recovery has been described in his baseball achievements in the latter part of his career, his reunion with his family, his intellectual interests, and his social activism and charitable work (Dickey and Coffey, 2012).

Kayla Harrison

Kayla Harrison was born into a judo family. She took up the sport at the age of six, having been introduced to the sport by her mother, Jeannie, who was a black belt. Kayla began training under coach Daniel Doyle and won two national championships by the age of 15. It was during her childhood that her coach, Doyle, began sexually abusing her. After an emotionally disturbing period, which lingered into adolescence, she finally could no longer maintain the emotional disturbance, which was shredding her insides, telling a fellow athlete about the abuse. Doyle was convicted and sentenced to a 10-year prison term. Kayla moved from her home in Ohio to Boston to train with a new coach, Jimmy Pedro.

Kayla won the Junior World Championship in 2008, and the following year placed second, becoming the first American to compete in two Junior World Championship finals. She won a gold medal in the

78 kg category at the World Judo Championships in 2010, the first American to do so since 1999 (when her coach Jimmy Pedro did so). At the 2011 World Judo Championship in Paris, she was placed third taking the bronze medal. On August 2, 2012, she won the Olympic title in the 78 kg category to become the first American to win an Olympic gold medal in judo. She earned a second Olympic gold medal in the same weight class in 2016 in Rio, Brazil (Perrotta, 2016). On August 31, 2016, the United States Judo Association promoted Kayla to ro-kudan (Sixth-Degree Black Belt) making her the youngest person in the United States ever to be awarded this rank. In October 2016, she signed with the World Series of Fighting. She signed as a commentator and fighter. In two seasons in the woman's 145 pounds division, she has won five fights. Kayla Harrison was a pioneering American athlete and a two-time gold medalist Olympic champion, who harbored such emotional turmoil that she was driven to the edge of her existence. We now turn to her sexual abuse trauma with her first coach, Daniel Doyle (Harrison, Kaplan & Aguirre, 2018).

Kayla Harrison's sexual abuse began when she was 9 years old, as her judo coach, Daniel Doyle, began a process of grooming her for abuse. Doyle ingratiated himself to her family being invited to family picnics, barbecues, and sleepovers. Yes, sleepovers. Kayla's parents invited a sexual predator of children to sleep over in their house. It is true that in the period of Kayla's childhood, society had not yet entered the #MeToo movement era. Then, coaches were not seen as a predator, but as priests were, authorities and icons who were in charge of developing children's character and helping them become good citizens. During these dark sleepovers, her coach would wait until Kayla's parents went to sleep and then massage her back, while telling her not to tell anyone. His grooming her for sexual contact would be their secret. She reported that these kinds of experiences struck fear in her as she could not resist the person she desperately needed to please. Daniel Doyle also groomed Kayla's parents. He ingratiated himself to them and became a family member by vacationing with the family, babysitting their children, and built an addition to their house.

Doyle developed the idea that Kayla could become an Olympian. Kayla's perfectionism, which she poured into judo as a way to find affirmation and love, intertwined with Doyle's obsessiveness. She would give him more than the high standard he demanded of her.

She thought she had to earn love. But her sexual experiences with her coach developed into a freezing of her feelings, which became dissociated, buried deep in her body and mind. Her trauma buried and dissociated, she excelled at her sport. At 13 she won the triple crown, all three junior national tournaments. She began to defeat women in her judo matches. The anger dissociated from her sexual abuse was projected into her sport as she became a ruthless, ferocious attacker.

Kayla, as did R.A. Dickey, buried herself in fiction. Her choice was the Harry Potter book series. She read all the books and saw the movies over and over again. She drifted into the world of magic, hoping the intrapsychic wound would disappear. In the world of Harry Potter, she could become a wizard or a witch. In adolescence, the delusion of magic did not penetrate the harsh reality of continuing sexual abuse, which occurred every day at judo practice. Her psychology began to move in a serious delusionary direction. She believed her coach would marry her, as if, his abusive behavior was an indication of love, suffering from a Confusion of Tongues trauma (Rachman & Klett, 2015). She confused his sexual contact as love, as sexual survivors are wont to do. She also convinced herself she needed him to be the Olympian. She accepted the reality of her abuser. But, she began to examine her delusion. She was emotionally connected to a man twice her age who was verbally and sexually abusive, and then told her she would be an Olympian judo athlete, during the same day.

Her frustration, shame, anguish, and anger finally broke through: she began screaming at her mother. She contacted the police when her stepfather tried to restrain her; she wrote in her journal she hated her mother and her life. What is more, she quit high school and began taking courses online. Her friends vanished. She began to have suicidal thoughts. A breaking point came when she was 16 years old during a senior national tournament. She had argued with her coach before her match and he stayed home. She broke down during the match, feeling she could not go on without her coach/seducer. Forcing herself to perform, she won the match. Her mother helped her.

Another breakthrough came when Kayla told her mother about her coach, Daniel Doyle's sexual abuse of her. First, Kayla told her mother about the abuse when her mother asked her why she was crying during her judo competition. Then, when she left the match with a male teammate who had become her best friend, he forced her to tell him what was behind her emotional vulnerability. She realized it was time to expose her trauma, as she was on the verge of quitting judo or committing suicide. Kayla told him she had been having sex with her coach for years. Her best friend told her that she must tell this to her mother, which she conceded to do after an emotional struggle. On hearing of her daughter's abuse, Kayla's mother went to Doyle's house and smashed all the windows of his car and in his house. After releasing her anger, the mother helped her daughter get psychiatric help.

With the help of her new coach, Jimmy Pedro, Kayla was accepted at a psychiatric ward for teenage girls, with a diagnosis of severe post-traumatic stress disorder. She needed therapy and she needed judo, so she got permission to do intensive therapy all day. She moved into a house with her judo teammates. Her new coach urged her to funnel her emotions, especially her anger, into judo. Her psychologist urged her to identify and release her feelings. She went through an emotional nightmare: she had panic attacks; somatic memories of her former coach's cologne; haunted by his screaming at her. Her teammates found her in a nature reserve deep in snow, after she had leaped out of a window in the team house. Her new coach, Jimmy Pedro, got tough with her, by urging her to release her emotional problems into her judo competition, while telling her that he would protect her from anyone who caused her any additional difficulty. He also counseled her to move on from her abusive experience with her former coach, Daniel Doyle, and begin to define herself in her own terms.

In 2008, Daniel Doyle pleaded guilty and received a plea-bargain. Kayla Harrison testified at his sentencing hearing telling the court-room the sexual abuse she suffered at his hands. The judge handed out the longest sentence allowed on the plea-bargain agreement, which was a 10-year sentence.

The Penn State sexual abuse scandal (see Chapter 17) was influential in piercing her dissociative defenses. She was emotionally moved to hear and see another coach, Jerry Sandusky, abusing another child. A national newspaper reporter interviewed Kayla to do a feature story. She responded by being self-disclosing and telling her abuse story. Her book would follow (Harrison et al., 2018).

Chapter 21

Sexual abuse of children in our schools: St. George's, elite boarding school in Rhode Island

St. George's is an elite boarding school in Rhode Island. It is one of the Saint Grottlesex schools, including Groton, Middlesex, St. Paul's, and St. Marks. They were founded in the 1800s as bastions of the White Anglo-Saxon establishment to educate the sons of the scions of capitalism in the Gilded Age of America. The sons who have graduated from St. George's were from the Vanderbilts, Bushes, Biddles, Astors, and Auchinclosses. These American boarding or prep schools were patterned after the English public schools of Eton and Harrow. St. George's has always stood apart from the other elite New England prep schools because of its magnificent setting on Aquid Neck Island, on a peninsula directly across from Newport, Rhode Island. The campus has been known as *St. Gorgeous*. The reputation that the school developed was that it was the home of sons of the very wealthy who were not too bright (Wallace, 2016).

St. George's was intended to be the depository of the moral, spiritual, and intellectual WASP values. From its founding until 2016, it seemed to the public that these values were being protected and elite families felt safe to send their sons and, later, daughters, to St. George's. But in December of 2016, an article in the *Boston Globe* newspaper reported on a sexual abuse scandal at St. George's occurring for decades with at least 40 alleged victims and a dozen staff and student perpetrators (English, 2016).

Howard "Woody" White: Associate Chaplain

Howard White, Associate Chaplain, was one of a series of staff members at St. George's who sexually abused a student. In 1974, parents of a

DOI: 10.4324/9780429298431-21

student reported to the school that their son had been raped by Chaplain White. The headmaster at that time, Anthony Zane, fired White, but, did not seem to understand the implications of the parents coming forward and reporting sexual abuse of a youth at his school. Zane did not report the chaplain to law enforcement authorities or to a family services department. He also gave him an additional month's salary and paid for his moving expenses. The headmaster did not investigate the chaplain's sexual behavior or the idea that the reported sex allegations might indicate that sexual abuse might be an issue to investigate at St. George's. This enabling attitude toward sexual predators would later characterize St. George's response to the unfolding of the existence of extensive school abuse of students by faculty, as well as by some students. The chaplain left St. George's, but, because he was not identified as a sexual predator, he went on to become a dean and chaplain at Chatham Hall in Virginia and rector at a church in North Carolina, where there were allegations of molestation of a teenage girl (Wallace, 2016).

Alphonse "Al" Gibbs: athletic trainer

Alphonse "Al" Gibbs was a 67-year-old athletic trainer who targeted girls for sexual abuse at St. George's. Three such girls were Kim Hardy Erskine, Joan "Bege" Reynolds, and Katie Wales. Hardy was a sophomore basketball player who reported Gibbs would come to practice sessions and kiss the female basketball players on the lips. He also gave Reynolds a gold necklace. Reynolds was a 13-year-old freshman when Gibbs told her to undress, get in the whirlpool, and then put his hands on her legs to the level of her vagina, while smothering her with kisses. He also took naked pictures of her while she was under a heat lamp. Wales was a three-sport athlete who went to see Gibbs for a knee injury. He would show her how to dry off after a shower. He would lift her breasts and dry off her genital area with the explanation he was demonstrating how to properly clean your body. Wales felt that he was considered medical personnel who was an expert. But, a part of her knew better. Gibbs showed the naked photos to boys in the school where they complemented her on her breasts. She became one of the girls that reported Gibbs to Headmaster Zane. Gibbs was fired by Zane after he interviewed a number of girls. At least 20 girls were abused by Gibbs over 7 years at St. George's. Once again, St. George's was exposed as an elite educational institution where sex abuse of youth was known but never was exposed by the faculty or administration. The headmaster announced at a school assembly that Gibbs left St. George's because of health reasons. He also was described as very competent.

Franklin Coleman: music teacher

Franklin Coleman was a charismatic music teacher, who was a rare African-American teacher and a leader of the school's music programs. There were two groups of students who were his acolytes. The Kulture Vultures was a club that met in Coleman's apartment in a dormitory to have snacks and listen to classical or jazz music. Then, there was the Colemanites, an exclusive group who would receive invitations to a small party. The boys wore black tie. As part of these special groups that surrounded Coleman, he chose his sexual victims. Hawkins Cramer was the prototype of Coleman's favorite prey, blond, with a good voice and vulnerable from father loss. He would give Hawkins gifts, long embraces, and take trips, which turned into sexual abuse experiences. Coleman would reserve a single bedroom, which allowed him to undress his prey, sleep with him, and massage his genitals. When Cramer told him he did not want his sexuality, Coleman had the audacity to respond to this boy by saying he was trying to help him to relax. Another student who was abused by Coleman, who is known as *Ethan* (not his real name), came forward with abuse allegations. He was a member of the Colemanites who was groomed for sexual abuse by Coleman giving him treats, writing love notes, showing him gay porn, giving him massages, and touching his penis. Finally, in 1988, Ethan told his experience of abuse to a St. George's school counselor, who, in turn, reported the abuse to the new Headmaster, the Reverend George Andrews. Coleman was fired immediately. At least a half dozen alumni have reported that they were targeted by Coleman. There were indications that Coleman's sexual contact with boys of St. George's was a secret that everyone knew about. There was bathroom graffiti referring to *Franklin's Organ* and someone sitting on *Franklin's Tower*. A St. George's alumnus reported that everyone knew Coleman was a pervert (Wallace, 2016).

206 Sexual abuse of children in our schools

The case of Anne Scott

A detailed presentation will be made about Anne Scott, a student at St. George's abused by Al Gibbs, the athletic trainer, which became one of the most egregious examples of sexual abuse. This case exemplified the failure of an educational institution in our society to protect a child from a predator, remove him from his opportunity to abuse, and cooperate with the judicial system to punish him. St. George's began admitting girls as boarding students in the fall of 1972. Anthony Zane was the headmaster at that time. Anne Scott registered at St. George's in 1977, at a time when there was an imposing masculine culture, few female faculty, and no athletic facilities for girls. Scott had a wrenched back playing field hockey when she was 14 years old and went to Al Gibbs for treatment. She described this trainer's method of treatment. He would start with some semblance of a treatment addressing the injury and move toward the girl's body. Gibbs would explain he was the caretaker of her body. In a month of Scott being treated by Gibbs, he had raped her, which continued for two years. She called her parents and told them she wanted to leave St. George's but could not find her voice to talk about the abuse. The trauma was manifested by an eating disorder and social isolation.

Eric MacLeish, a lawyer and alumnus of St. George's, was very emotionally connected to Anne Scott's case. He wanted to develop an article about Gibbs and his abuse of Scott to appear in the *St. George's Bulletin*. At a party, he met a fellow lawyer who knew Anne Scott. She had left the United States and worked in India, Botswana, and the Palestinian territories, doing global health and development work. In helping people in difficult positions, she found emotional peace, and could symbolically remove herself from her trauma. After being away from the United States for 25 years, she decided to return. McLeish contacted her in December of 2013, when he was able to get her approval to join him in speaking to St. George's. MacLeish became an aggressive advocate for Anne Scott, asking the present Headmaster Eric Peterson to lift the gag order on Scott. What is more, he arranged for a meeting between the previous Headmaster, Scott, and himself. Anne Scott told her story of sexual abuse by the athletic trainer, All Gibbs, to Headmaster Eric Peterson. But, what is more important, Anne Scott found her voice and made several requests from St. George's:

1. The creation of a therapy assistance fund to help students who had been sexually abused.
2. A release from her 1989 gag order.
3. The removal of the name of the former headmaster during her time, Anthony Zane, from the girls' dormitory.

Peterson did apologize to Scott which she appreciated.

The promise of a stage of truth and reconciliation disintegrated when alumni defenders of St. George's tradition and reputation sided with the school's increasing adversary stance. As is often the case, institutions when faced with responding to sexual abuse issues, step away from the truth and defend themselves, criticize or attack the victims, and hire lawyers to mitigate any responsibility or reconciliation. MacLeish was attacked by school defenders as someone who was using the victims of sexual abuse, such as Anne Scott, to work through his own issues. Scott, in particular, felt the school reacted to the pain and trauma of sexual abuse survivors with a legal attitude rather than with empathy and reconciliation. Eric MacLeish, however, was determined to change the culture of St. George's. On December 14, the Boston Globe, due to MacLeish's campaign, published the story of Al Gibbs' sexual abuse story (English, 2016). Furthermore, MacLeish held a press conference to issue a rebuttal to St. George's sexual abuse report. A Facebook campaign produced a response from 1,000 people describing first-person accounts of abuse, confessions of survivor guilt, and expressions of solidarity with the victims. The St. George's Headmaster, Eric Peterson, has held steadfast defending the school and believing there has been significant change. Survivors want Peterson fired. He finally said he would leave in 2017 (Wallace, 2016).

Two results have been reached in the time after the St. George's sexual abuse scandal. The Rhode Island State Police investigation of sex abuse charges against faculty, administration, and students were not brought because of the statute of limitations, referring to the 1970s when sexual abuse was not a crime (Smith & Lavine, 2016). Two dozen

208   Sexual abuse of children in our schools

students from St. George's reached a financial settlement over accusations of sexual abuse. No specific terms were disclosed (Seelye, 2016). St. George's handling of their sexual abuse scandal involving the youth entrusted to them does not live up to the school's motto:

Sapientia Utriusque Vitae Lumen – Wisdom, the light of every life. (Wikipedia, 2019)

St. George's Culture as a party school and the tolerance of sexual abuse

St. George's had a reputation as a *party school*, a place where students could believe the school rules could fit on one side of a piece of paper. An alumnus clarified that students all knew they could go to the beach, smoke pot, drink, and have sex. The school was characterized as a heaven for alienated children of the rich who used St. George's to function as *in loco parentis*, in place of a parent. But, St. George's was not a nurturing place, with an administration who neglected and was unresponsive to the allegations of sexual abuse. Moreover, freshman students in the dormitory were in the care of seniors who ran the dorms. Alumni reported incidents of hazing abuse by seniors, including: a student sodomized with a broomstick in public; seniors make unwanted nighttime visits to boys trying to fondle them; a freshman boy was raped with a pencil by seniors. We can speculate, there developed over a considerable period of time, a tolerance for sexual abuse by students, and a neglect of sexual abuse by faculty at St. George's. We can say, St. George's developed a *sexual abuse climate*, which allowed youth to be harmed, and left abusers unpunished (Wallace, 2016).

It is very important to apply the same standard of truth and reconciliation to the functioning of an educational institution, such as St. George's, as I have discussed in reaction to the neglect of sexual abuse in psychoanalysis, religious institutions, the entertainment industry, and society. The headmaster of St. George's, as well as administration and faculty, created a *wall of silence* knowing that there was a climate of, and reality of, sexual abuse in their midst. It was clear from the reports of alumni that both boys and girls were sexually abused by faculty at St. George's. Decades after the abuse has happened, a St. George's counselor revealed to the school's investigator that in the 1980s he had informed Headmaster Anthony Zane, the headmaster at the time, about Franklin Coleman giving students backrubs. Zane did not believe the information and said he hoped the whole sexual abuse scandal would disappear. He also responded that he did not remember being told of Coleman's transgressions. Besides the silence about abuse by the headmaster, there was also something about the school's social attitude that contributed to the silence of and neglect about sexual abuse. There was a kind of homophobia and racial defensiveness, which surrounded Franklin Coleman, the African American musical leader. The community did neither want to seem negative about a homosexual faculty member, nor prejudiced toward an African American. In essence, the school's social climate contributed to the harmful behavior by the school's sexual predators. A female alumnus told her advisor about Coleman's sexual abuse of students. He, in turn, told her he had gone to the administration and they told him to *mind his own business* (Wallace, 2016).

In outlining the details of the behavior of the administration, faculty, and the students, a clear pattern emerged. This pattern involves several attitudes and behavior, which is characteristic of institutions in our society, which has not only neglected the incidence of sexual abuse in their midst, but also refused to respond to sexual abuse, once revealed, with a sense of empathy, truth, and reconciliation. St. George's School's climate, which developed over an extended period of time, allowed sexuality to occur between students and between faculty and students. There were rumors about this behavior of which the students and faculty were aware. And *institutional silence* encapsulated the school's campus. This silence to each other and the outer community is connected to several factors.

One of the primary factors that maintained the *sexual abuse silence* was protection of St. George's prestige and reputation. Protection of their reputation and prestige came before confronting the transgression and revealing the truth. We saw the same phenomena in: Chapter 7, *Todschweigen, Death by Silence*, when traditional psychoanalysis protected the Oedipal Complex Theory at the expense of Sándor Ferenczi's attempt to inform psychoanalysis of the significance of the incest trauma; in Chapter 11, *The Sensuous Psychiatrist*, when the field of psychiatry remained silent when Renatus Hartogs sexually abused patients, when they know of his abuse; Chapter 13, *The Catholic Church's Sexual Abuse Scandal*, where popes, bishops, cardinals, and church administrators ignored the sexual predatory behavior of priests; Chapter 15, *The Conspiracy within the Orthodox Jewish Community to Protect Sexual Abusers*, where the Orthodox community conspired to protect sexual abusers of children from facing the criminal justice system; Chapter 16, *Sexual Abuse in the Anglican Church*, where the Anglican clergy were allowed to be sexual abusers of children; Chapter 18, *The Child Sexual Abuse Scandal at Pennsylvania State University*, where their coach, Joe Paterno, who was a sports icon, seriously neglected to pursue the sexual abuse allegations against his former assistant, Jerry Sandusky. This coach allowed his dedication to his football program and Penn State University to emotionally blind him to pursuing a sexual predator in his midst; Chapter 19, *The Worst Example of Sexual Abuse in Sports History*, focused on the horrendous predatory behavior of Dr. Lawrence Nassar, who was allowed to sexually molest female athletes over a period of decades without any athletic agency or school administration overseeing his behavior so that he could be stopped from harming youth, removed from his position, and adjudicated him for his criminal behavior; Chapter 21 (the present discussion), *Sexual Abuse of Children in our Schools*; Chapters 22 to 27, which describes the damaging scandal that was exposed in Hollywood and the entertainment industry, which, for at least a half-century, developed a climate of sexual abuse of female actors and entertainers, which was an open secret. It took talented investigating reporters in the communication industry and courageous women in entertainment who found their voices and disclosed the details of their sexual traumas. With these testimonies of sexual abuse by men in power over women who feared them, a change in society has developed. The #MeToo movement has changed the emotional and political climate so that sexual survivors are now able to disclose their sexual traumas standing up to the men in power who abused them and institutions that protected the predators.

A teacher's letter, which provides a window into the abused and the mind of a predator

Jane Marion was 16 years old when she received a series of five letters, written in 1979 and 1980, sent by Frederic Lyman, her English teachers at the elite and prestigious boarding school, Phillips Academy, in Andover, Massachusetts. The letters began as if they were innocent, friendly greetings to a student. However, they became an invitation to a romance. When Marion resisted Lyman's advances, he became angry and threatened her. Teacher and student never became physical, but the letters illustrate the process of grooming a youth as a process of sexual seduction. Marion, as well as a fellow student, developed a fantasy about their handsome and, what they thought, was a romantic man. They were naive teenagers, which Lyman used to seduce them. Lyman wrote personal notes on her academic papers, asking her to play tennis or saying he would help her to break curfew. She was flattered and thought she was in love with him. But she was also frightened and pulled herself back. When she looked at the letters as an adult, she felt what he had encouraged in their extra-school relationship haunted her. She wished she could have told her 16-year-old self then to run away from her predatory teacher.

Lyman left Andover for Choate Rosemary Hall in Connecticut where he sexually abused two young women and was forced to leave. Lyman was given Marion's letters and released a statement through his lawyers:

> In re-reading these letters nearly 40 years after writing them, I see the ramblings of a lovesick young man...However my lapse in judgement was inexcusable. I breached the trust and overstepped the boundaries between student and teacher. Due to my own immaturity, I considered my students to be peers and friends, which was a mistake that I will regret for the rest of my life. I am deeply sorry for any pain or discomfort my actions may have caused. (Harris, 2017, p. A23)

It is refreshing to hear an apology from a sexual predator of youth. Hopefully, Frederic Lyman, who has since his sexual abuses at Phillips Academy, and then Choate Rosemary Hall in Connecticut, left teaching. He has examined his inner self and no longer is a person of harm. Unfortunately, his behavior during his tenure as a teacher was not examined by himself or confronted by the academic communities in which parents trusted would be safe from sexual trauma. It is hoped that bringing attention to the existence of sexual exploitation in our schools and their neglect of confronting it will create a new culture of *truth to power* and our children will be protected from sexual predators in our schools.

Chapter 22

Untying the confusion of tongues in Hollywood: the advent of the #MeToo movement, sexual survivors find their voice

The tipping point in confronting the sexual abuse of girls and women in the entertainment industry

As I was writing this book, a remarkable, unforeseen series of events unfolded, which changed the social climate of the United States toward the issue of sexual abuse, especially toward young girls and women. During the month of October 2017, Jodi Kantor and Megan Twohey, investigating reporters for The New York Times, and Ronan Farrow, a lawyer and independent investigator, were all working on an investigation of Harvey Weinstein's sexual transgressions. Both Kantor & Twohey and Farrow were able, for the first time, to document the sexual allegations against one of the most powerful authority figures in contemporary society (Kantor & Twohey, 2017; Farrow, 2017). Kantor & Twohey and Farrow won Pulitzer Prizes in Public Service for their work about Weinstein. There was, however, a controversy with Farrow's journey towards publishing his account of the Weinstein scandal. Farrow had first been working on his story for NBC News. The producer, Rich Hugh, said that executives at NBC had impeded Farrow's attempts to fully investigate the Weinstein story. The chairman of NBC News, Andrew Lack, indicated that NBC did not obstruct these investigations. But, Farrow decided to leave NBC News and published his Weinstein expose 2 months later, after joining The New Yorker. These are people in the media and entertainment network who suggested NBC cancelled an interview Farrow had wanted to do with a Weinstein accuser. They wondered why NBC let Farrow leave with what turned

DOI: 10.4324/9780429298431-22

out to be an award-winning story that rocked society's consciousness (Koblin, 2018.).

Before we discuss the investigations, which led to the women of Hollywood finding their voices about being sexually abused, we need to try to understand the loss of capacity of survivors to speak about their sexual traumas.

Psychodynamics of losing your voice to speak about trauma

Sándor Ferenczi's pioneering paper, *The Confusion of Tongues Between Adults and Children: The Language of tenderness and passion*, introduced the first theory of trauma due to childhood sexual abuse (Ferenczi, 1933). Contained in this theory is how a molested child is damaged by a parent or authority figure by remaining mute or silent after the sexual trauma. The individual, as Ferenczi first stated, becomes *tongue-tied* as a result of the emotional trauma (Rachman, 2019). The issues of power, control, and status between parent and child encourages a psychodynamic that leads the child to lose their capacity to speak about their trauma. They suffer in silence. In the prototypical sexual trauma, the parent abuses the child, convincing them their behavior is a form of affection and love. But, this is insincere and deceptive. This behavior is actually the narcissistic expression of parental need for sexuality. Such behavior has nothing to do with love or caring for the child's welfare. It is a form of rape; an intrusive, aggressive physical, and emotional blow to the child. The child experiences the sexual behavior of their parent as intensely disturbing. It violates the child's need to have the safety of their own erotic feelings about parents without any intrusive reality. Actual sexuality shatters the child's emotional need for safety and trust in a parental figure.

Parental authority overwhelms the child and he/she loses their own grasp of reality, relying on the parent's definition of love. The parent can also threaten withdrawal of love or punishment if the child gives voice to the assault. The child fears the loss of love and does not want to face retaliation. In the light of the emotional disturbance, the victim become dissociated from the thoughts and feelings of the abusive experience. The child becomes tongue-tied and can no longer speak of the trauma. This so-called *elective mutism* can occur for years or a lifetime. Some incest survivors never recover their memories and feelings about their childhood sexual trauma. Some are fortunate and recover these memories through analysis or therapy, or revisiting a traumatic event, or being part of a social experience, which encourages giving voice to trauma.

Ferenczi astutely recognized that the analytic encounter is a relational experience where the childhood trauma can be recreated in the interaction with the analyst. He developed the concept of *professional hypocrisy* (Ferenczi, 1933, p. 159). If the analyst behaves in an insincere or emotionally deceptive way, it creates a disturbance for the analysand, where the analyst is recreating the confusion and emotional disturbance of the original childhood trauma. The analysand experiences some form of disturbance, sensing there is an unsettling element in the relationship and blames themselves for it. If the analyst does not take responsibility for their contribution to the disturbance, the analysand feels injured and traumatized. The analyst, by his/her silence, suggests the analysand is at fault and needs to do something to correct their dysfunction. However, it is the analyst who needs to make a correction. He/she needs to take their responsibility for the emotional disturbance in the relationship, and admit they contributed to the disturbance. The analyst needs to give voice to his/her emotional contribution to the empathic failure in their interaction with the analysand. Emotional honesty, in the here-and-now of the analytic encounter, prevents the analysand from feeling they are returning to their childhood trauma, which was characterized by emotional dishonesty, hurtful silence, and a lack of recognition they were being harmed by their parental abuser. Under such circumstances, the analysand would be reexperiencing a Confusion of Tongues Trauma of childhood in the analytic relationship (Rachman & Klett, 2015).

Hollywood became tongue-tied about Harvey Weinstein's predatory sexual behavior

Meryl Streep, the academy award-winning actress and one of the most respected members of the entertainment industry, has recently said she knew about Harvey Weinstein's sexual abuse of women, but defended her silence by saying by saying:

> You think you know everything about everybody. So much gossip. You don't know anything...in terms of Harvey, I really didn't know. I didn't think he was having girlfriends. But when I read rumors about actresses, I thought that was a way of denigrating the actress and her ability to get the job. (Streep, 2018)

Streep is the kind of exemplar that her peers and the public would naturally turn to help explain and empathize with actresses being sexually abused. Although she empathized with her abused women colleagues, she remained silent about Weinstein's predatory behavior. Was she caught in her ambivalence about whether he was an evil person or someone who helped actresses, and seduced the entertainment community by his good deeds?:

> How evil, deeply evil and duplicitous, a person he was, yet such a champion of really great work...The disgraceful news about Harvey Weinstein has appalled those of us whose work he championed, and the good and worthy causes he supported. (Rothman, 2018)

As we shall see when we discuss the psychodynamics of Weinstein's sexual abuse behavior with actresses, he was a seducer of women. He not only seduced women, but also, seduced Hollywood. However, a confidant of Weinstein recently said:

> Look, anybody who tells you that we didn't know [certain] things about Harvey is full of shit...We knew he was a bully, we knew he had a bad temper, and we knew he was a philanderer. (Ciralsky, 2018, p. 158)

Sexual survivors report their reasons for maintaining silence about Weinstein's abuse

As we have seen in the discussion of Ferenczi's concept of the Confusion of Tongues, survivors become tongue-tied as a result of the psychodynamics, which are activated when an individual is sexually abused. In the Weinstein sexual abuse scandal, survivors who he abused reported their reasons for the silence, which enveloped each one, as well as the entire entertainment industry:

1. Women were frightened of retaliation. They felt Weinstein could ruin their careers and lives if he found out they disclosed his abusive behavior.
2. These women would be targeted by Weinstein's associates and employees who would confront and intimidate them.
3. Mia Sorvino and Rosanna Arquette told Ronan Farrow Weinstein had them removed from projects or dissuaded people from hiring them.
4. When Ambra Battilana Gutierrez went to the police to report Weinstein's sexual abuse of her, suddenly, negative items about her sexual history began appearing in the New York gossip pages. It was thought Weinstein's connections to certain executives in the newspaper industry was influential in producing this defamation of Gutierrez's character.

Collective trauma: Hollywood's silence about Harvey Weinstein's predatory sexual behavior

Collective trauma

It can be suggested that the deafening silence that surrounded Hollywood and the entertainment industry over Weinstein's sexual abuse of women, over decades, indicated a *Collective Confusion of Tongues Trauma*. The sexual abuse survivors shared the inability to speak of their trauma to confront Weinstein or to share their experiences with each other. Traumatic events can stimulate collective sentiment resulting in a shift in society's developing an attitude and behavior, which reinforces the sentiment (Lipdegraff, Silver & Holman, 2008).

Vicarious experiencing

Originally, the idea of vicarious traumatization was developed to describe a phenomenon that was observed in mental health professionals, such as, psychoanalysts, psychotherapists, and mental health professionals who worked regularly with traumatized individuals. The psychodynamic involved can be described as follows:

> A therapist in a therapeutic relationship with a traumatized individual is susceptible to experiencing transformation in their own personality functioning as a result of their emphatic engagement with the traumatized individuals. (McCann & Pearlman, 1990)

Individuals can also vicariously experience a range of feelings that can be observed in other people and in indirect experiences: one can feel embarrassed, or even, physically wince, when watching an individual on television; say or create a socially embarrassing moment; groups of Americans became sad, anxious, and depressed when watching and re-watching the 9/11 terrorist attacks on the United States; when people watched the replay of the Sandy Hook Elementary School killing of children they were brought to tears, as if they were there or one of their children were murdered. Recently, neuroscientists have paid attention to the understanding of the *social brain* and the sharing of trauma experiences (Derbyshire, Osborn & Brown, 2013; Fitzgibbon, Ward & Enticott, 2014).

The Hollywood community shared similar experiences of Weinstein as a sexual predator of women, as will be described in Chapter 23, *Harvey Weinstein: The Heir Apparent to Harry Cohn as Hollywood's Primal Sexual Predator.* In a series of cases, it becomes clear that his behavior causes a Confusion of Tongues Trauma in the women he assaulted. They all became tongue-tied, no one was able to give voice to their sexual trauma, which caused them harm. What is more, the entertainment industry provided the psychosocial climate to reinforce the silence conspiracy within the industry. Executives and employees alike conspired to remain silent about Weinstein's abhorrent behavior. He did not sexually abuse these individuals, but, emotionally traumatized them by his angry outbursts, threatening behavior, and mean-spirited dealings. They conspired to protect Weinstein, so their positions of status, power, and control would also be protected. Weinstein's conspirators also allowed his power, authority to rule their sense of self, as were the sexual survivors who were overwhelmed by him.

Of course, we need to acknowledge there may have been individuals who shared Weinstein's misogynistic and psychopathic attitudes. In these instances, we cannot talk of them as trauma victims, but, rather a community of abusers, who are out of touch with their malevolence.

The #MeToo movement

A remarkable event in our society emerged as a result of the Harvey Weinstein sexual scandal, as we shall see in the upcoming discussions of the history of sexual abuse in Hollywood and detailing the Weinstein scandal. Women survivors began to become untongue-tied, find their voice, and report their sexual abuse by Weinstein. On October 15, 2017, Alyssa Milano encouraged spreading the hashtag #MeToo as a campaign to encourage the realization of sexual abuse and harassment (Khomami, 2017; Petit, 2017; D'Zurella, 2017). Milano took a courageous step forward by going on social media, leading a movement for women to find their voice, and speak out about being sexually abused by predator men. She was inspired to bring this awareness in the wake of the Weinstein sex scandal (Chen, 2017). Milano was one of the actresses who Weinstein abused. She became an activist for sexually abused women in the wake of the scandal. Milano developed the hashtag with the recognition that Tarana Burke had first introduced it. Her emphasis was to create a platform where women could give voice to sexually abusive experiences with Weinstein (Chen, 2017).

Tarana Burke: founder of the Me Too movement

Tarana Burke is a civil rights advocate from a disadvantaged family in the Bronx, New York, who founded the Me Too movement in 2006. She began using the phrase *Me Too* to raise awareness of the prevalence of sexual abuse in society. The phrase, adding the hashtag – # before the phrase developed after Alyssa Milano used it on social media to respond to the Harvey Weinstein sex scandal. Burke was raped and sexually abused both as a child and teenager. With her mother's support, she recovered from her sexual

220 Untying the confusion of tongues

traumas. Her sexual trauma experiences inspired her to become involved in social activism work with disadvantaged young girls on the issues of economic and racial justice (Ohlheiser, 2017). After graduating from Auburn University, she became a social activist working with survivors of sexual violence. She has won *Time Person of the Year* award in 2017, *The Ridenhour Prize for Courage* in 2018, the *VOTY (Voices of the Year) Catalyst Award* in 2018, and in 2019, *Trailblazer Award.* Burke's campaign was geared through empathy among underprivileged women of color who have experienced sexual abuse (Guerra, 2017). Burke has said she was inspired to use her famous phrase, *Me Too*, in an interaction with a child abuse survivor. She wished she could have responded to a 13-year-old child who told her about her abuse. Afterwards, she wished she could have said to the sexually abused child, *me too* (Ohlheiser, 2017).

The #MeToo movement is now an international movement against sexual harassment and assault (Edwards, Dockterman & Sweetland, 2018). One of the survivors of sexual abuse, who helped move the #MeToo movement into prominent focus, Alyssa Milano, described the importance of giving survivors a platform to express their voices, realizing there is now a *community of voices* to tell the truth to powerful predators.

Alyssa Milano clarified her mission with the #MeToo campaign and how it helped women to find their voice:

> #MeToo, which I started tweeting in the wake of the Harvey Weinstein allegations, was an opportunity to take attention away from the predator and bring it back to the victims. We're so focused on these villains, these horrible people who do these horrible things, and that doesn't help their victims feel like they can come forward or heal. To give women a platform where they don't have to say how, when or where they were hurt if it's too painful—where all they have to do is stand in solidarity—enables us all to feel how enormous of an issue this kind of abuse is....I have been assaulted and sexually harassed more times than I can really recall...not because I work in Hollywood. Some were times when I was out at bars with friends or just riding in a cab. This is

not just a Hollywood problem....We tend to push down the things that hurt us so they don't come to define us, but those traumas end up becoming a bigger part us when we haven't healed. To be able to take your experiences out, dissect them and share your stories with others is a powerful thing....*But because we've been so silent—and silenced—about this issue, we don't realize there is a community out there that's ready to embrace and support us.* (Freeman, 2017)

Chapter 23

"The Casting Couch": Harry Cohn, the godfather of sexual abuse of female actors

Hollywood, located in the City of Angels, has been, as Marilyn Monroe has said, "an overcrowded brothel...[where she] spent a great deal of time on my knees" (Summers, 2007). Even before Monroe's time, in the so-called "Golden Age of Hollywood," in the 1930s–1950s, the *Casting Couch* was a reality. Producers, directors, and heads of film studios asked actresses to exchange sex for being placed in one of their films. Long before Harvey Weinstein's name erupted in October of 2017 as the primal sexual predator of Hollywood, Harry Cohn, the head of Columbia Pictures in the 1930s–1950s, used his fame, power, and audacity to force actor, Evelyn Keyes, who is remembered as Suellen O'Hara in the 1939 classic, *Gone with the Wind*, to have sex with him:

> Columbia Pictures boss Harry Cohn ordered the almond-eyed blonde...to his office, grabbed her between the legs, and whispered, "Save that for me."

> Evelyn froze. She left....that night, she got furious [and] invited actor Sterling Hayden to go dancing... Let the paparazzi tell Cohn she wasn't his toy—... The next morning, Cohn fired her. "You'll never be a bigger star than you are right now...I'll see to that."

> He did. You won't find Evelyn's name on the Hollywood Walk of Fame. [At] the Dolby Theatre, the site of today's Academy Awards, you'll find a winding tile walkway of inspirational

DOI: 10.4324/9780429298431-23

quotes called "The Road to Hollywood: How Some of Us Got Here." The installation is by a satirical, feminist artist named Erika Rothenberg. At the end is a concrete casting couch. (Nicholson, 2017)

Cohn assault on Keyes evaporated into the smoke factory that was Hollywood in the Golden Era. Imagine what would have happened if someone had exposed Cohn's barbaric behavior to the world, 70 years ago. Instead of reporting that Evelyn Keyes went dancing and Cohn fired her, newspapers and magazines would have reported Cohn sexually assaulted her. Could we have then begun a movement to protect sexual assault? We are still ambivalent about exposing men of power and punishing them for sexual abuse. After the allegations of sexual abuse by Weinstein became public, the installation of the Road to Hollywood was removed because: "...it had attracted increased public attention and it was threatened with damage" (Rutenberg, Abrams & Ryzik, 2017, p. A11). It would take the *voices of the abused* to rise up in unison to change this sexual abuse narrative.

Chapter 24

Harvey Weinstein: the heir apparent to Harry Cohn, Hollywood's sexual predator

Jodi Kantor and Megan Twohey: New York Times report on Harvey Weinstein's sexual abuse

Two events occurred in October 2017, which broke open the sexual scandal of Harvey Weinstein's long-standing sexual abuse of girls and women actors. First, Jodi Kantor and Megan Twohey, reporters for *The New York Times*, found undisclosed allegations against Harvey Weinstein. Their research included interviews with current and former employees and film industry workers, legal records, emails and internal documents from Miramax and the Weinstein Company (Kantor & Twohey, 2017). Their evidence helped to establish that Weinstein sexually harassed and abused girls and women for nearly 30 years. Lauren O'Connor, an assistant to Weinstein, had written a potent memo to executives at the Weinstein Company exclaiming that there was an environment of sexual harassment and misconduct by Weinstein. Ms. O'Connor was one of these women with whom Weinstein arranged a settlement after which she withdrew her complaint against him and thanked him for the career opportunity he had given her.

Viewing his life and functioning from the outside, Weinstein was seen as a liberal icon, an academy award producer, a champion of women, supporter of the Democratic party and winner of artistic and humanitarian awards. But, in private, he was the *Predator of the Entertainment Industry. The loudest silence in Hollywood was the open secret of Weinstein's sexual harassment and abuse of women.* Ashley Judd, one of his victims has said:

DOI: 10.4324/9780429298431-24

Women have been talking about Harvey amongst ourselves for a long time, and it's simply beyond time to have the conversation publicly. (Kantor & Twohey, 2017, p. A18)

Judd described what she called Weinstein's *coercive bargaining*, in an incident that occurred when she was an aspiring actor. She was initially surprised that their meeting advertised as a business meeting was arranged to take place in Weinstein's suite in Beverly Hills. Weinstein began his *coercive seduction* in a series of sexual activities, to which she said no. He was relentless in his predatory activity, as if, it was a natural act for him to ask for a massage, then a body rub and watch him shower. Weinstein always had a sexual alternative to Judd's turning him down. He acted in this relentless, predatory way, knowing that his status, power, and control and arrogance would defeat a young, vulnerable female actor searching for fame and fortune. Here is how Lauren O'Connor described this kind of experience from her subjective point of view:

I am a 28-year-old woman trying to make a living and a career. Harvey Weinstein is a 64-year-old, world famous man and this is his company. *The balance of power is me: 0, Harvey Weinstein: 10*. (Kantor & Twohey, 2017, p. A18)

The deafening silence that surrounded Weinstein's sexual abuse of women was enhanced by a series of factors. In the legal settlements he arranged with the abused women by enforcing a code of silence, stipulating in all contracts signed that no employee can criticize him or the company. The women who signed the legal documents in the Weinstein abuse cases agreed to financial settlements, ranging from $80,000 to $150,000. What is more, the negotiated legal documents had the abused women agree to clauses prohibiting them from speaking about the deals or the events that led to them.

The women who were interviewed by Kantor & Twohey (2017), also reported they did not report Weinstein's abhorrent behavior because there were no witnesses and they feared retaliation by him. Others said they felt embarrassed. However, there was a kind of underground network of sexually abused women established as the abused shared their emotional disturbances with co-workers.

At first, Weinstein issued an apology to the public for his alleged sexual misconduct. After retaining counsel, the apology was rescinded. In its place, a spokesperson for Weinstein issued the following statement denying all charges:

> Any allegations of non-consensual sex are unequivocally denied by Mr. Weinstein. Mr. Weinstein has further confirmed that there were never any acts of retaliation against any women for refusing his advances. Mr. Weinstein obviously can't speak to anonymous allegations, but with respect to any women who have made allegations on the record, Mr. Weinstein believes that all of these relationships were consensual. Mr. Weinstein has begun counseling, has listened to the community and is pursuing a better path. Mr. Weinstein is hoping that, if he makes enough progress, he will be given a second chance. (Farrow, 2017, Section 1)

Ronan Farrow and The New Yorker article: from aggressive overtures to sexual assault: Harvey Weinstein's accusers tell their stories

Ronan Farrow was originally researching the Harvey Weinstein sexual assault scandal for NBC News, about the same time as the reporters for *The New York Times*, Jodi Kantor and Megan Twohey, were doing their research (Kantor & Twohey, 2017). He had run into difficulty with NBC News. There were stories that NBC had obstructed Farrow's attempts at investigation by cancelling an interview with a Weinstein accuser in August of 2017. Since then, members in the entertainment and media industries have questioned whether there was any obstruction in Farrow's reporting by NBC executives. The implication was that NBC was terminating the Weinstein investigation, without any explanation. Farrow decided to leave the network and took his investigation to *The New Yorker Magazine*.

Shortly after he left NBC News, Farrow published his investigation of Harvey Weinstein in *The New Yorker Magazine* on October 23, 2017 (Farrow, 2017). Farrow believed that his attitude and personality contributed to his being able to have Weinstein's sexual accusers self-disclose their abuse experiences, as he described this quality:

Anytime one of those sources feels that I'm a person that they can trust and come to if they have a significant story, and anytime someone knows that I will work carefully and meticulously to interrogate those claims but also create a space where they feel safe in coming forward with them, those are things I'm deeply grateful for. That's what's made this run of reporting possible. (Zengerle, 2018, Section 1)

Farrow's investigation revealed over the course of a 10-month research that 13 women, from the 1990s to 2015, were sexually harassed or assaulted by Harvey Weinstein. Farrow's allegations corroborate and overlap with the Kantor & Twohey (2017) New York Times reporting as well as including more serious sexual allegations. Asia Argento, an Italian film actress and director, and Lucia Evans, told Farrow they were raped by Weinstein, forcibly performing or receiving oral sex or forcing vaginal sex. Four women said they received unwanted touching. Ambra Battilana Gutierrez, a Filipina-Italian model was groped by Weinstein, which was reported to the New York Police Department in 2015. Four women reported that Weinstein exposed himself or masturbated in front of them. Sixteen former and current executive and assistants at Weinstein's companies had witnessed or had knowledge of unwanted sexual activities. Employees had been used to help Weinstein carry out his sexual advances. Assistants would be used as members of a so-called "business meeting," then Weinstein would dismiss them, and he would be left alone with his intended victims.

Farrow detailed incidents of actual sexual abuse by the women he had interviewed. Lucia Stoller, now Lucia Evans, who was a college student in 2004, who wanted to be an actress, was approached by Weinstein at a club in New York, letting him have her number. A meeting was arranged, which turned out to be in a place with exercise equipment with Weinstein there alone. After a brief interchange, where he demeaned her, he took out his penis and pulled her head down onto it. He overpowered her attempts to resist. As had happened in other descriptions of such sexual assaults, she finally gave in. She felt horrible about giving up, realizing that conceding to Weinstein's assault was added to the number of women he was able to abuse. They kept silent and blamed themselves for the abuse. Weinstein felt the experience was unremarkable for him, but Evans developed severe signs of trauma, for example, she had an eating problem for years, was disgusted with herself, she ruined relationships, her schoolwork suffered, her friends thought she was going to commit suicide. When she later ran into Weinstein, she was horrified, chills went down her spine, and she reported having continual nightmares about him.

Asia Argento was an Italian actress who Weinstein assaulted on the French Riviera. On the usual pretense of attending a meeting in which she thought, that she was going to be there with others. She however was left alone with Weinstein. She agreed to give him a message, realizing she was foolish. Then, he pulled her skirt up, pulled her legs apart, and performed oral sex on her. She went as far as to feign liking the sex. In what became a Confusion of Tongues Trauma, Argento developed trauma symptoms. These symptoms involved years of suffering guilt, feeling like a victim, feeling responsible for the abuse, feeling damaged, and unable to have oral sex. What is more, she yielded to his further advances and grew close to him. The abuser physically and psychologically alters the victim's vitality and functioning where his will dominates the interaction. Argento became a captive of Weinstein.

Farrow made public for the first time, a sexual abuse allegation by an employee of the Weinstein Company, Emily Nestor, in December 2014. On the first day of her employment, she was told by two employees she was Weinstein's physical type. When he arrived to meet her, he began his seduction. He sent everyone out of the room and began to boast about his sexual liaisons, telling her she could be part of his London office, asking her to be his girlfriend. She said no to all his requests, reporting she said no at least a dozen times. *Weinstein did not believe no was no.* In a weird interchange, Weinstein said he never had to do what Cosby did to force sexual activity with women, which implied he did not have to drug women to have sex with them. This admission sounded that Weinstein was admitting being a sexual predator in the mold of Cosby. Nestor told the Human Resources division of the company about it and nothing was done. What is more, the complaint would be funneled back to Weinstein. Nestor felt traumatized and decided not to go into the entertainment industry because of the abuse by Weinstein (Farrow, 2017).

Rosanna Arquette, a well-known actress, intended to meet Weinstein at the Beverly Hills Hotel to pick up the script for a new film. When she arrived, she was told to go up to his room. He was wearing a bathrobe and told her he needed a massage. When she deflected his request, he pulled her hand to his penis, which she also rejected. Weinstein told her she was making a mistake rejecting him because an actress who had given him sexual favors had her career advanced by him. Arquette said she would never trade sex for a career opportunity. After she rejected Weinstein, her career suffered. She believed she lost a role because she rejected Weinstein. Arquette believe Weinstein would silence people, like herself, by retaliating against them. Weinstein and his associates went after the employees warning them not to cooperate with Farrow's New Yorker article (Farrow, 2017).

In a flash of news and magazine print in the Autumn of 2017, sexual survivors of the "Kings of the Casting Couch," from Darryl F. Zanuck, Harry Cohn, and Howard Hughes to Harvey Weinstein found their voice thanks to the aforementioned courageous investigative reporters Ronan Farrow of *The New Yorker* and Jodi Kantor and Megan Twohey of *The New York Times*. These reporters alleged in print, for all to see, the abuser and the abused. They presented evidence that Harvey Weinstein, the contemporary *King of the Casting Couch*, was the *primal Hollywood sexual predator*. For more than 30 years, Weinstein's sexual abuse of young girls and women actresses has been an *open secret*. Previous attempts to find evidence of his abusive behavior had failed. *The New York Times* reporters, Jodi Kantor and Megan Twohey, said the following:

> An investigation by *The New York Times* found previously undisclosed allegations against Mr. Weinstein stretching over nearly three decades, documented through interviews with current and former employees and film industry workers, as well as legal records, emails and internal documents from the businesses he has run, Miramax and the Weinstein Company. (Kantor & Twohey, 2017, p. A1)

During this 30-year period when Weinstein was confronted with allegations of sexual harassment and unwanted sexual contact, he arranged for, at least, eight settlements with women to keep the silence regarding his abusive behavior, as reported by two company officials. It is interesting that in October of 2017, there was a new climate forming in society where being silent about sexual abuse was changing. It seemed as if, when Farrow, and Kantor and Twohey began their investigations of Weinstein, members of his company were waiting to be asking about Weinstein so they could shatter the open secret of his decades of sexually abusing young girls and women. Previously, individuals remained silent for decades. Asia Argento, the Italian film actress and director, who alleged that Weinstein forcibly performed oral sex on her, was afraid to break the silence because she imaged Weinstein would destroy her personally and professionally (Farrow, 2017). It was not only through emotional intimidation that Weinstein maintained the silence about his illicit affairs, but also he enforced a code of silence:

> Employees of the Weinstein Company have contracts saying they will not criticize it or its leaders in a way that could harm its "business reputation" or "any employee's personal reputation" a recent document shows. And most of the women accepting payouts agreed to confidentiality clauses prohibiting them from speaking about the deals or events that led to them. (Kantor & Twohey, 2017, p. A18)

Chapter 25

Psychodynamics of sexual abuse in Hollywood: Uma Thurman and Mira Sorvino

Uma Thurman revealed her experience of sexual harassment by Harvey Weinstein in the week before Thanksgiving 2017, for the first time. This revelation brought the charges of sexual abuse towards Weinstein approaching 80 women, over the period of about 10–20 years. Thurman's reaction to Weinstein's abuse is one of the clearest statements of anger by a survivor that has been revealed. Thurman said that she held off revealing her emotional reaction to the sexual abuse because when she is angry she can say things she later regrets. She waited a week after she revealed the abuse and on Thanksgiving Day in an Instagram said:

> Happy Thanksgiving Everyone! (Except you Harvey, and all your wicked conspirators. I'm glad it's going slowly – you don't deserve a bullet) – stay tuned.

There was also a note of support.

> "I am grateful today, to be alive, for all those I love, and for all those who have the courage to stand up for others," she posted.

> "I said I was angry recently, and I have a few reasons, #MeToo, in case you couldn't tell by the look on my face."

> She said she's taking her time so she can "be fair, be exact." (Cullcane, 2017)

DOI: 10.4324/9780429298431-25

Thurman's response reveals the emotional damage that can be done to an individual by sexual abuse. Her Instagram message reveals an individual who has carried around anger for years, unable, until recently, to reconnect with it and finally give voice to it. This is why the #MeToo campaign is so important, first for women who have been abused, and, second, for psychoanalysis and society.

Uma Thurman, who was one of the actresses who Harvey Weinstein began molesting when she was a young woman, has recently been interviewed by Maureen Dowd, a Pulitzer Prize winner for distinguished commentary and an Op-Ed columnist for The New York Times. She has presented us with a meaningful window into the psychodynamics that coalesce to produce sexual abuse by a male authority to a young woman. It has taking Thurman 47 years to confront, understand, and give voice to what she called, "lambs walked into slaughter" (Dowd, 2018). There are several stages that can be discerned from Thurman's reflections on the psychological damage and meaning in her description of her subjective experience.

1. When she was a 16-year-old aspiring actress, she was molested by an actor 20 years old. She astutely realized that she was *compliant*:

   I tried to say no, I cried, I did everything I could do. He told me the door was locked but I ran over and tried the knob. When I got home, I remember I stood in front of the mirror and I looked at my hands and I was so mad at them for not being bloody or bruised...You become more compliant or less compliant, and I think I became less compliant

2. Thurman's personality issue of compliance became part of the psychodynamics of abuse with Weinstein. She entered into a *grooming experience* with Weinstein:

   He used to spend hours talking to me about material and complimenting my mind and validating me. It possibly made me overlook warning signs. This was my champion...He had a chokehold on the type of films and directors that were right for me

3   The psychodynamics that Thurman has now understood coalesces
    into sexual abuse. In a meeting that Weinstein and Thurman were
    supposed to talk about a script, the trauma solidified:

    Things went off-kilter...in his Paris hotel room. It went right over
    my head...when the bathrobe came out...I didn't feel threa-
    tened...I thought he was being super idiosyncratic, like this was
    your kooky eccentric uncle. (Dowd, 2018, p. 4)

Weinstein's grooming behavior toward Thurman, her dissociative
reaction, and her compliant personality kept her in a semi-conscious
dissociated state, in which she became emotionally blind to her
mentor's predatory behavior.

4.   The first sexual encounter or *attack* came next. In Weinstein's
    suite at the Savoy Hotel in London, all pretentions about his
    being a mentor gave way to his being a sexual predator:

    "He pushed me down. He tried to shove himself on me...You're
    like an animal wriggling away, like a lizard..." (Dowd, 2018, p. 4)

The next day, having come out of the closet as a sexual abuser, he
sent Thurman a "vulgar bunch of roses," (Dowd, 2018, p. 4) and
Weinstein's assistants started calling about film projects. Weinstein
was indicating to his victim that he was grateful for her compliance
in his sordid plan to use her for his sexual needs.

5.   Thurman began to break through the abuse cycle by confronting
    Weinstein:

    If you do what you did to me to other people you will lose your
    career, your reputation and your family, I promise you. (Dowd,
    2018, p. 4)

Weinstein reacted by threatening to derail her career, expressing the
power and dominance of a male superior over a subordinate young
female in the entertainment industry. What is more, Weinstein neu-
tralized his predatory behavior by saying he was flirtatious with

Thurman, but, suggesting it was a part of what he took to be a mutual desire for sex. The predator not only seduces the victim but seduces his audience with the deception that he is not a predator, but a partner of his victim. Thurman began to view Weinstein as the enemy and was no longer positively connected to Weinstein. But, he continued with his campaign to prove their sexual contact was mutual by sending out pictures of him and Thurman as if they were close friends.

6. The emotional difficulties between Thurman and Weinstein interfered with her relationship with Quentin Tarantino. Thurman described a disturbing and dangerous scene from a movie in which she was directed by Tarantino. He bullied her in performing a scene in a car ride, which she considered dangerous. The car did crash, leaving Thurman feeling she may never walk again. Afterwards, Miramax, Weinstein's company, did not show any concern about the film's dangerous stunt or Thurman's concerns for her safety. After years of a lawsuit and fighting with Miramax and Tarantino, she was able to retrieve the footage of her car crash and turn it over to the police.

Thurman felt that Tarantino and Miramax (Weinstein) conspired in violence against a woman, treating her as if she were an object to be used for sensation:

> When they turned on me after the accident…I went from being a creative contributor and performer to being a broken tool…with my permanently damaged neck and my screwed up knees. (Dowd, 2018, p. 5)

Thurman has gone through a psychological transformation, which she described in the Dowd interview. She described a compliant youngster in the presence of a dominant male authority who sexually abused her to become an angry woman who found her voice to stop the abuse and contribute to the welfare of other vulnerable women:

> Personally, it has taken me 47 years…I think that as little girls we are conditioned to believe that cruelty and love somehow have a connection and that is like the sort of era that we need to evolve out of. (Dowd, 2018, p. 5)

A survivor of Weinstein's sexual abuse finds her voice

Mira Sorvino, one of the other survivors of Weinstein's sexual abuse, the Academy Award winning actress and U.N. Goodwill Ambassador, described the psychodynamics of her abuse. Ferenczi described this abuse as the Confusion of Tongues experience (Ferenczi, 1933):

> I have lived in vague fear of Harvey Weinstein for over 20 years... At the time I don't think I even knew that what happened — [Weinstein] using business-related situations to try and press himself sexually on a young woman in his employ — qualified as sexual harassment. Coming forward...has been a real struggle... I could no longer remain silent...tried to confide in a female employee at...Miramax. I was suddenly radioactive for daring to bring it up...I had no idea that the abuse was so widespread [or]... so long-term for the victims... My desire to break away from the tyranny of intimidation made me shakily agree to put my name... in Ronan Farrow's story...wondering if being a whistleblower would mean being blacklisted. *But once I knew the story was going to print, an enormous peace washed over me — a sense that finally I had taken my personal power back.*
>
> *I am here to encourage a mass speaking-out. Victim-shaming must be quelled, and the real evildoers called out and punished to the fullest extent of the law.* (Sorvino, 2017, p. 33)

Mira Sorvino's description of her emotional struggles after being abused by Harvey Weinstein is a courageous self-report of the Confusion of Tongues psychodynamics that an individual suffers as a result of sexual abuse. Both her cognitive, intellectual and emotional functioning were negatively altered, all characteristic of abuse survivors (Rachman & Klett, 2015). In essence, Sorvino lost her memory and her voice. No wonder, Weinstein's 75 victims have remained silent for about 30 years. Besides being altered by his abhorrent behavior, he used his power to intimidate, threaten, and force helplessness. The reporters, Kantor, Twohey, and Farrow, became for the survivors, their *therapeutic voices*, telling their abuser, and the world, that it was true they were sexually abused, and Harvey

Weinstein was their abuser. They could come out of the shadows and feel the power of being a survivor rather than a victim.

Harvey Weinstein's legal attack against women he sexually abused

In the descriptions that have been outlined in the Case of Harvey Weinstein, a nefarious methodology can be seen, which was developed to defeat the women who brought allegations of sexual abuse against him. This methodology is used by the abuser to attack the victim instead of trying to tell the truth and initiate reconciliation. Using Weinstein's behavior, as well as the behavior of his lawyers and his employees, the following outline was derived to defeat his sexual victims:

1. The abuser gives a complete denial of charges of sexual abuse. The defendant denies the allegations and presents a lie that the sexual relationship was consensual.
2. There is almost never a truth and reconciliation response from the abuser. He does not pause, indicate that some self-examination will be forthcoming, and the predator will consider entering some program that contains therapeutic interactions.
3. The accused immediately turns to high-powered legal help to defend himself and disavow charges. The legal team evokes a particular strategy against the victim:

   a. The victim is discredited. Investigators, detectives, and employees are employed to uncover any negative behavior of the victim, which can be used to discredit the abused.
   b. The victim is blamed. Negative data are developed, which reflects negatively on the behavior and personality of the victim.
   c. Whenever possible, countersue the victim, so the victim is on defensive.

4. What almost never happens, is that the accused admits the transgressions, apologizes for the harm they caused, and makes it clear they will make reparations.

Chapter 26

Celebrity privilege and sexual abuse: the case of Roman Polanski

Celebrities have long benefited from the practice of privilege bestowed on them by fans, followers, and the public. The concept of privilege involves a sense of immunity from wrongdoing, even from crimes that are considered immoral and criminal. The public treat celebrities as demigods, allowing them to hold special privilege in society. Celebrities feel they are immune from the law and social mores. The entertainment industry, politicians, sports figures, and intellectuals and scholars are among the celebrities who have been granted immunity for their transgressions. In the area of child sexual abuse, there is a case that stands out regarding a celebrity who was accused of child molestation but, because he was a world-wide celebrity, did not face the judicial system's punishments that ordinary individuals have suffered. Roman Polanski, the Academy Award motion picture director has demonstrated that celebrity privilege can insulate a child sexual abuser from punishment. Polanski fled the United States to avoid incarceration for the rape of a 13-year-old girl. He has been a fugitive since 1976, enjoying the protection of the French government, which seems to have a protective attitude toward individuals who they consider to have made considerable contributions to society, whether it be artists, intellectuals, or entertainers. Perhaps, Camille Paglia, the feminist scholar, reflects this ethos:

> The artist as a person should certainly be subject to rebuke, censure or penalty for unacceptable actions in the social realm. But art, even when it addresses political issues, occupies an abstract realm in our society. (Paglia, 2017, p. A16)

DOI: 10.4324/9780429298431-26

Roman Polanski's rape of a 13-year-old girl

Roman R. Polanski is a Polish-French film director, producer, writer, and actor who has become as famous for his celebrated film career as he has for his sexual abuse of a child. After beginning his film career in Poland, he became a celebrated Academy Award-winning director for such films as Rosemary's Baby (1968), Chinatown (1974), and The Pianist (2002). He is considered one of the greatest directors of his time. There appears to be no controversy about Polanski's artistic ability or achievement. However, Polanski's personal life has been filled with tragedy. He survived the Krakow Ghetto and the Holocaust. His mother died at Auschwitz. His wife Sharon Tate was brutally murdered on August 8–9, 1969, by members of Charles Manson's cult (Leaming, 1981; Parker, 1994; Polanski, 1973).

In 1977, when Polanski was 44 years old, he was introduced to a 13-year-old girl, named Samantha Gailey (now Geimer). According to Geimer, he told her and her mother that he was taking photographs of young girls for the French men's magazine, *Vogue Hommes*. On March 10, 1977, he took her to his friend Jack Nicholson's house and gave her champagne and part of a quaalude pill. While drugged, Samantha got into a jacuzzi with him and he had sex with her. The Grand Jury testimony of Samantha at Polanski's trial in Los Angeles, California, in 1977 has many statements of Polanski's rape of her when she was 13 years old. What is more, it also contains many instances of Samantha's protests and her saying "no" and asking him to stop (Grand Jury Testimony, 1977). These protests in the testimony are as follows (Grand Jury Testimony, 1977):

1. "He places his mouth on my vagina; I was ready to cry" [She said]- "No, come on. Stop it" (p. 29).
2. "He started to have intercourse with me; he placed his penis in my vagina" [She said]- "No, stop" (p. 31).
3. "Then he lifted up my legs further and he went in through my anus. He put his penis in my butt."
4. "Then he started to have intercourse with me again and then he just stopped. (Do you know whether he had a climax?) Yes. Because I could kind of feel it and it was in my underwear...

It was on my butt and stuff. (When you say that, you believe that he climaxed in your anus?) Yes (p. 34).

A woman who was not identified who testified at this trial revealed her reaction to the abuse:

> I was sitting in the car and I was crying. (Grand Jury Testimony, p. 36)

Polanski was initially charged with rape by use of drugs, perversion, sodomy, lewd, and lascivious act on a child under 14, and furnishing a controlled substance (methaqualone) to a minor. These charges were dismissed under the terms of his plea bargain. He pleaded guilty to the lesser charge of engaging in unlawful sexual intercourse with a minor. Under the terms of the plea agreement, the court ordered Polanski to report to a state prison for a 90-day psychiatric evaluation, but granted a stay of 90 days to allow him to complete his current project. Under terms set by the court, he was permitted to travel abroad. Polanski returned to California and reported to Chino State Prison for the evaluation period, and was released after 42 days. The expectation was that Polanski would only get probation because he was an honored and respected celebrity. The judge, after conferring with the Los Angeles District Attorney, made a completely different recommendation. The judge told Polanski's attorneys he would send him to prison and order him deported. In response to the threat of imprisonment, Polanski fled the United States.

Polanski initially fled to London on February 1, 1978, where maintained residency. Shortly after he fled to France, where he held citizenship, avoiding the risk of extradition to the United States by Britain. France can refuse to extradite its own citizens. When the United States filed extradition papers for Polanski, France refused. The United States government could still request the arrest and extradition of Polanski from other countries should he visit them. Polanski has avoided visits to countries that could extradite him (Polanski, 1984). He has not returned to the United States for the fear of being arrested. On September 26, 2009, Polanski was arrested while trying to enter Switzerland, in relation to his outstanding 1978 United States arrest warrant. Polanski had hoped to attend the

240 Celebrity privilege and sexual abuse

Zurich Film Festival to receive a Lifetime Achievement award. The Swiss Justice Ministry put Polanski in provisional detention. Reed Weingarten, a well-known criminal defense lawyer, was hired by Polanski for his defense. Polanski's defense team argued that his crime does not qualify for extradition, because he was originally sentenced to less than a year in prison, or that he has already effectively served his sentence, during a 42-day psychiatric evaluation. (Cieply & Barnes, 2009; Cieply & Carvajal, 2009).

Samantha Geimer (Gailey): The 13-year old rape victim of Roman Polanski

Samantha Gailey, Polanski's rape victim when she was a 13-year-old, who now uses her married name, Geimer, has broken a 35-year silence about her experience by publishing her story (Geimer, 2013). She wrote the book with the help of her lawyer, Lawrence Silver, and a journalist, Judith Newman. When the book was written in 2013, Samantha Geimer was a 50-year-old woman, dividing her time between Hawaii and Nevada with her husband and three sons. Basically, Samantha has forgiven Polanski for his sexual abuse of her. In fact, she says in the book she wished she had never told anyone that Polanski had anally raped her. She felt she had been hounded by the media since the sexual assault and subsequent trial. Her phone rang off the hook and people hung out outside her house. In fact, Geimer believes she was twice victimized, first by Polanski, and again by the media.

After coming home from the assault, she knew what had happened to her was wrong. She blamed herself, as sexual survivors are wont to do. Her sister overheard her description of the assault on the phone. Then the sister told her mother, and she called the police, turning the event into a scandal. It changed her life. Her family was traumatized, including herself and her mother. Her mother was criticized for being complicit in allowing the abuse to take place. Her mother was vilified for handing her 13-year-old daughter over to a middle-aged pedophile. Geimer hated the world during the time of, and after, the trial, until she was able to recover from her trauma, marry, and have a family. Samantha did not defend herself or her mother's behavior, believing she was a victim of a sexual assault and her mother was encouraging her daughter to be a liberal person open to new experiences.

Samantha Geimer was not interested in punishing Polanski, that is, does not want him to go to jail. She feels it would not solve anything. Her attitude is to move on from the trauma. Polanski and Geimer did exchange notes in 2009. Polanski apologized for his transgression, taking responsibility for negatively influencing her life. Geimer did not want an apology but was grateful for it. Her mother, husband, and her sons reported they reduced their pain and anger.

Renate Langer, another Polanski sexual abuse survivor

Recently, another woman has given voice to her sexual abuse by Roman Polanski. Renate Langer, a 61-year-old German actress contacted the Swiss police to report that Polanski raped her when she was 15 years old. Ms. Langer now becomes the fourth woman to accuse him of sexual assault while they were teenagers. She approached the Swiss police because they eliminated the statute of limitations on child sex abuse cases. Ms. Langer has never told her family of the abuse because she was afraid her mother would become ill, and she felt ashamed, embarrassed, lost, and alone. She did not tell friends but confided in a boyfriend years later. Ms. Langer reported Polanski was introduced to her after she began working for a modeling agency in Munich in high school. She traveled to visit him in Gstaad, Switzerland, with her parents' permission because he had indicated an interest in casting her in a movie. She said he raped her in a bedroom of his home despite her trying to defend herself against him. Polanski then offered her a small part in a movie, which she accepted, promising her he would act professionally. But, once again, he raped her despite her throwing a bottle of wine and perfume at him. Ms. Langer said of Polanski's sexual assaults:

This had an influence on all of my life. (Haigney, 2017, p. C4)

Celebrity privilege seems embedded in an argument developed by Fox (2013). He believed Polanski was demonized in the case of the sexual abuse of Samantha Geimer (Gailey). Fox (2013) believed Polanski was not convicted of rape, did not jump bail to flee the

United States, and did not escape with no punishment. He said Samantha Geimer's family wanted to protect her from a trial agreeing to a plea bargain. Polanski did not admit to rape, but, to unlawful sexual intercourse with a minor. Furthermore, he stated that several charges against him were to be dismissed, including providing a controlled substance to a minor, lewd or lascivious acts on a child under 14, rape by use of drugs, perversion, and sodomy. Fox believes these charges, however, became society's view of Polanski as a rapist. Did Fox fail to read the transcript of the Polanski/Gailey (Geimer) trial—(see this chapter, where Samantha clearly described how she was raped) Is he blaming a 13-year-old sexual survivor for being given a drug or alcohol, and then forced to have sex? Although Samantha Geimer refused to talk to him for his article, she wrote to Fox with the following response:

> "...it was rape. Not only because I was underage; but also because I did not consent..." (Fox, 2013, p. 331).

Roman Polanski's most recent film project indicates that he disavows any responsibility and feels no guilt or regrets in his child sexual abuse case. He is now portraying himself as a victim. Polanski has been working on a film, originally entitled *D*, a political thriller based on the story of Captain Alfred Dreyfus. This captain was a Jewish official in the French Army who was tried for treason in 1894 and sent to Devil's Island. Polanski feels there is a parallel between Dreyfus and himself:

> The age-old spectacle of the witch hunt of a minority group, security paranoia, secret military tribunal of control intelligence agencies, governmental cover-ups and the press. (Itzkoff, 2012, p. C2)

The film *D* was not made, perhaps due to Polanski's legal problems emanating from his sexual abuse scandal. The film was first scheduled to be shot in Warsaw, Poland in 2014. But this production was postponed after Polanski moved to Poland for filming and the US Government filed extradition papers. The Polish government eventually rejected them, by which time new French Film tax credits had been introduced, allowing the film to be shot on location in Paris. Apparently, the film is now titled *J'accuse*. This new version of the film *D* is reported to be the true story of the French officer, George Picquart's struggle to expose the truth about the doctored evidence that got Alfred Dreyfus, one of the few Jewish members of the French Army's general staff, wrongly convicted of passing military secrets to the German Empire. *J'accuse* began production in the fall of 2018. Recently, it has been announced to compete at the 2019 Venice Film Festival.

In 2018, Polanski was expelled from the Academy of Motion Picture Arts and Sciences. The Academy changed its rules, apparently in response to the #MeToo Movement, now stating:

> [there was] no place in the Academy for people who abuse their status, power or influence in a manner that violates recognized standards of decency. (Anonymous, 2019, p. C3)

Polanski has picked his next film to be about the Dreyfus Affair to reinforce to the public, legal authorities, and the entertainment industry that he is a victim of judicial authorities, society's mores, and public condemnation. He feels he is being hounded after 40 years by the press and society for his sexual abuse of a 13-year-old girl. In essence, he is going to demonstrate through his art that he is a modern-day Captain Alfred Dreyfus, falsely accused of a crime, imprisoned and prohibited from traveling. Polanski feels scorned and tortured by public opinion. Once again, a child sexual predator does not focus his energy on truth and reconciliation.

Chapter 27

Celebrities and sexual assault: Woody Allen, Bill Cosby, and Matt Lauer

As a result of the Harvey Weinstein sex scandal and the resultant development of the #MeToo Movement, society has shifted toward supporting sexually abused women to report their abusive experiences. In the entertainment industry, women are finding the courage to disclose the harm that was done to them by sexual predators, as investigating reporters have unearthed data, which has exposed a host of celebrities in the entertainment industry that have been accused of sexual abuse. Three of these individuals, Woody Allen, the well-respected writer, director, and actor in motion pictures, Bill Cosby, the comedian and television star once known as *America's Dad*, and Matt Lauer, the former co-anchor of the Today Show on the National Broadcasting Corporation television network will be discussed.

Woody Allen and the pedophile question

On Super Bowl Sunday in February 2014, when America celebrates its love of sports, a sexually abused adult drew a dark cloud over the celebration. Dylan Farrow, Woody Allen's adopted daughter, was 28 years old when she wrote an open letter to *The New York Times* via Nicholas Kristof's Op-Ed Column accusing Woody Allen of childhood molestation (Kristof, 2014). Dylan told Kristof that she has been traumatized for more than two decades. She had been diagnosed with posttraumatic stress disorder. When she heard that Allen was given a Golden Globe life-time achievement award, she curled up in a ball on her bed and cried hysterically. She decided it

DOI: 10.4324/9780429298431-27

was time to tell her story, since everyone else had been weighing in on the issue of whether Allen was a pedophile. She turned to Kristof to reveal her abuse at Allen's hands because he is a friend of her mother, Mia Farrow, and her brother, Ronan Farrow (who was one of the three investigative reporters who broke open the Harvey Weinstein sexual abuse scandal).

Here is Dylan's statement of the sexual abuse in her own words:

> When I was seven years old, Woody Allen took me by the hand and led me into a dim, closet-like attic on the second floor of our house. He told me to lay on my stomach and play with my brother's electric train set. Then he sexually assaulted me. He talked to me while he did it, whispering that I was a good girl, that this was our secret, promising that we'd go to Paris and I'd be a star in his movies. I remember staring at that toy train, focusing on it as it traveled in its circle around the attic. To this day, I find it difficult to look at toy trains. (Kristof, 2014)

Dylan goes on to stipulate that Allen would take her away from her mother, siblings, and friends to be alone with him. She reported multiple events that suggest sexual seduction when they were together. She coped with these experiences by hiding under beds or locking herself in the bathroom. She could not escape from his assaults as he always found her. Dylan's mother, Mia Farrow's, friends said that Allen was obsessed with Dylan. He would arrive at six o'clock in the morning at Mia's apartment and sit on the end of Dylan's bed until she woke up. He insisted on tucking her in at night. He was reluctant to leave her alone at school. A friend commented that Allen would only focus on Dylan in a room full of people (Hoban, 1992).

Dylan also addressed the charge that her mother implanted the sexual abuse charges against Allen in her head as a result of coaching her to believe this as a result of the mother's hatred toward him. Dylan was angry about Allen saying her mother planted the idea of sexual abuse in her head. Her mother said she could recant her allegation of his abuse if she wanted to and no trouble would come to her. But, Dylan insisted she could not take back the abuse charge because it was true. She also went on to say:

246 Celebrities and sexual assault

But sexual abuse claims against the powerful stall more easily. There were experts willing to attack my credibility. *There were doctors willing to gaslight an abused child....*That he got away with what he did to me haunted me as I grew up. I was stricken with guilt that I had allowed him to be near other little girls. I was terrified of being touched by men. I developed an eating disorder. I began cutting myself....Each time I saw my abuser's face – on a poster, on a t-shirt, on television – I could only hide my panic until I found a place to be alone and fall apart....*But the survivors of sexual abuse who have reached out to me* – to support me and to share their fears of coming forward, of being called a liar, *of being told their memories aren't their memories* – *have given me a reason to not be silent,* if only so others know that they don't have to be silent either....Woody Allen is a living testament to the way our society fails the survivors of sexual assault and abuse. (Kristof, 2014)

Dylan Farrow published another statement about Woody Allen's alleged sexual abuse of her, this time focusing on the issue of the silence of actresses who worked with Allen about her accusations, which was hurtful to her. She mentioned Kate Winslet, Blake Lively, and Greta Gerwig, who were in Allen's films, praised him for his direction, but, would not make any statements about her sexual abuse. Clearly, she felt unsupported by their silence, which had characterized Hollywood's response of its sexual predators. What was especially painful for Dylan was her belief that Allen enlisted her brother, Moses, to take sides against her. Moses joined Allen in believing that Mia Farrow had brainwashed him to believe Allen was Dylan's abuser. She felt devastated by Moses's allegiance to Allen. She questioned Moses's knowledge of the abuse, since he was not a witness to it.

As silent were some of the women who worked with Allen, there was also open support for Dylan Farrow. In an open letter to Dylan, Mira Sorvino apologized for her previous silence about Allen's sexual abuse:

I confess that at the time I worked for Woody Allen I was a naive young actress. I swallowed the media's portrayal of your abuse allegations against your father as an outgrowth of a twisted custody battle between Mia Farrow and him, and did not look further into the situation, for which I am terribly sorry. For this I also owe an apology to Mia.

It is difficult to severe ties and denounce your heroes, your benefactors, whom you fondly admired and felt a debt of gratitude toward for your entire career's existence.

But this does not excuse my turning a blind eye to your story simply because I wanted desperately for it not to be so.

In December I called your brother Ronan, sharing about the aftermath of my and other women's coming forward about Harvey Weinstein. How it had been a sometimes empowering, sometimes bitter and heartbreaking experience, as more and more details came out of hidden damage this man had done me.... I told him I wanted to learn more about you and your situation.

I am so sorry, Dylan! I cannot begin to imagine how you have felt, all these years as you watched someone you called out as having hurt you as a child, a vulnerable little girl in his care, be lauded again and again, including by me and countless others in Hollywood who praised him and ignored you.... This kind of abuse cannot be allowed to continue. If this means tearing down all the old gods, so be it.... I will never work with him again.

I believe you!!!...You are a true hero, and I stand with you. (Sorvino, 2018).

Woody Allen responds to Dylan Farrow's open letter

In responding to Dylan Farrow's open letter accusing Allen of being her sexual abuser, he defended himself by pointing out the logical fallacies in his adopted daughter's accusation. He does deny he molested Dylan. Allen alleges Dylan believes she was molested because her mother, Mia Farrow, implanted this idea in her mind. Furthermore, the exclaims that his letter is the final word on the issue of his molestation of Dylan. He will no longer address the issue (Miller, 2014).

Robert B. Weide is an Oscar-nominated and Emmy-winning filmmaker, who produced and directed the two-part special, *Woody Allen: A Documentary*, wrote an extensive piece defending Allen. Weide cites several issues, which he believes were inconsistencies which are worth examining: (1) There was no medical evidence of anal or vaginal penetration. (2) The family's nanny, Monica Thompson, swore in a deposition that she was pressured by Mia Farrow to support the molestation charges. (3) The Yale-New Haven investigative team felt Dylan was an emotionally disturbed child, coached or influenced by her mother. After reviewing the case, he stated that he accepts that Dylan and Ronan Farrow believe the sexual abuse took place. He concluded that Dylan is the real victim (Weide, 2014).

I find it difficult not to listen to an individual who maintains over a period of several decades she has been abused by a parental figure. In my clinical experience of over 40 years working with survivors of childhood sexual abuse, I have been aware of false claims in the literature or the existence of therapists who have inappropriately coached individuals to falsely uncover memories of sexual abuse. Dylan Farrow Malone (her married name) claims, however, appear authentic to me. Dylan's continued attempts to call Allen an abuser are worth listening to. Why she cannot put these accusations to rest? It is possible she is driven by a characteristic emotional reaction of sexual survivors. Those who have been harmed want those who have harmed them to take responsibility for and apologize for their aggression toward them when they were a vulnerable child. They want their abuser to admit they harmed them and derailed their development as a human being. Finally, survivors want their abusers to take an oath to change so they will stop harming other children. Survivors desperately want to be believed, that they are telling the truth when they say they were abused. If they are not believed or are attacked for their accusations, their trauma intensifies, and they suffer a loss of self. This understanding has been in the literature of psychoanalysis since the 1930s when Sándor Ferenczi first proposed his Confusion of Tongues paradigm (Ferenczi, 1933; also see Chapter 5: Sándor Ferenczi's Confusion of Tongues Paradigm: Introduction of trauma theory and trauma analysis). The reason psychoanalysis has not been able to provide this understanding has been discussed, which is clearly related to a successful campaign to silence and discredit Ferenczi's ideas (Rachman, 1989, 1994a, 1994b, 1999a, 1999b, 2000, 2003, 2016a, 2016b, 2018; Rachman & Mattick, 2012). As has been discussed in these references, traditional analysis deliberately suppressed Ferenczi's idea of childhood sexual abuse is a significance dynamic in human behavior (see Chapter 7: Todschweigen, Death by Silence: Traditional Psychoanalysis's Punishment of Dissidents). When traditional psychoanalysis is willing to recognize Ferenczi's contributions to understanding human behavior from a relationship perspective in the interaction between human beings as well as in the minds of individuals, they will expand the boundaries of psychoanalysis contributing to society.

Case of Bill Cosby: from "America's Dad" to sexual predator

Bill Cosby, the comedian and actor, was known as "America's Dad," Cliff Huxtable, the revolutionary Black American father and husband he played on *The Bill Cosby Show*. Through his performance on this show, he changed the persona of the Black Man. He elevated a black man to an intelligent, positive, head of a family, with a sense of humor and decent moral values. Cliff Huxtable became a good father and husband just like the rest of the white men in society. This was no mean feat, since it occurred in a racist society, strongly prejudiced against African Americans. The family he presided over were also portrayed as a normal, lovable, happy group. The image of a black man and his family that Cosby helped to create gave African Americans a sense of belonging to the American mainstream, held him up as an ideal human being, and provided a sense of positive identity. When he was accused as a sexual predator these valuable contributions were put into question, providing Cosby with a dramatic fall from grace. As in the Harvey Weinstein case, a sexual predator was lurking in the shadows of our society, abusing girls and women without out awareness or any consequence for his abusive behavior. What is more, Cosby's two trials may point to an important change in our society's view of sexual abuse of girls and women. The verdict of guilty in the second trial was likely influenced by the advent of the #MeToo Movement (see Chapter 21, #MeToo Movement section).

The fall from grace of Bill Cosby happened as a result of two trials based on the accusation of Andrea Constand, who worked for the Temple University women's basketball team, Bill Cosby's alma mater. She said that in January of 2004, Cosby assaulted her at his home after giving her wine and three pills. After she contacted her hometown Toronto police, they decided not to charge Cosby because of insufficient evidence. In March of 2005, when Constand sued Cosby, a dozen women agreed to present testimony of similar behavior on his part. Several months later Cosby admitted in a legal disposition he gave quaalude pills to young women for sex. This legal suit was settled for over three million dollars. About 10 years passed, with the monetary settlement never made public. Then, suddenly a video of a comedian's routine, where he calls Cosby a rapist went viral prompting a group of women to come forward. It is now October of 2014, pre-dating the Harvey Weinstein sex scandal, and on the eve of the #MeToo Movement. A new judge, Kevin R. Steele, is elected in the Pennsylvania county where Cosby's criminal investigation was first performed. Cosby is arrested on charges of aggravated indecent assault, as Judge Steele had criticized the 2005 decision not to prosecute Cosby. His first trial ends in a mistrial after jurors remain deadlocked following six days of deliberations. A second trial is scheduled, with an important difference. Judge Steele allows the testimony of five women who have come forth with similar accusations to Andrea Constand that Bill Cosby assaulted them. On April 26, 2018, the second jury found Cosby guilty on three counts of assaulting Constand: (1) penetration with lack of consent; (2) penetration while unconscious; and (3) penetration after administering an intoxicant. Five months later, the judge sentenced Cosby to 3–10 years in prison for drugging and sexually assaulting Andrea Constand. He was led away in handcuffs after bail was denied (Bowley & Coscarelli, 2018).

Andrea Constand described Bill Cosby's sexual assault during her testimony, when she was 30 years old and he was 66, when she visited his home on his pretense of helping her with her career. He gave her pills that left her immobile and caused her to drift in and out of consciousness:

I was kind of jolted awake and felt Mr. Cosby on the couch beside me, behind me, and my vagina was being penetrated quite forcefully, and I felt my breast being touched. I was limp, and I could not fight him off. (Bowley & Hurdle, 2018, p. A18)

The five other witnesses told similar experiences of being deceived, given intoxicants, and raped. The guilty verdict in the Bill Cosby trail is seen as a watershed moment in the #MeToo Movement. This case was the first high-profile trial to occur in the aftermath of the #MeToo Movement and one that relied on the reports of female accusers. It is hoped that now that female survivors of sexual abuse will be given greater credibility by the police, judges, and jurors. The National Organization for Women believed the guilty verdict gave notice to sexual predators. Rose McGowan, one of the accusers in the Harvey Weinstein sexual abuse case sent a tweet to the judge, jury, and society for waking up. Gloria Allred, the lawyer for many of Cosby's accusers said: "women were finally believed" (Bowley & Hurdle, 2018, p. A18).

Deborah Tuerkheimer, a former assistant district attorney in New York City, and now, law professor at Northwestern University in Illinois, saw the conviction as a change in society. Andrea Constand, the main accuser in the sexual abuse case was believed. In the past, police officers, prosecutors, and jurors have acted with what she called *credibility discounting*. These agencies of the justice system tend to doubt when evaluating the credibility of an accuser. There have been instances where corroborated allegations of sexual assault did not result in prosecution or conviction (Tuerkheimer, 2018, p. A23). The #MeToo Movement and the Cosby guilty verdict helps society realize that we live among sexual predators, which are harming youth and women.

Andrea Constand's case highlights the dynamics of power, control, and status for women in society. Women survivors of sexual abuse have suffered skepticism of law enforcement, judges, lawyers, jurors, and the public about their sexual accusations toward authority figures. Remarkably, in the past, women who filed rape accusations had to undergo psychological screening, as if their allegations meant they were emotionally unstable.

252 Celebrities and sexual assault

A final note about this case. Ms. Constand's continued contact with Cosby after the abuse. The defense used this against her, as defense attorneys in sexual abuse cases regularly do. The unexplainable behavior can be seen as part of her Confusion of Tongues trauma. The sexual survivor is bound to the abuser through the sexual trauma, which can distort the experience as an act of affection. The survivor needs to work through this distorted bond through separation from the abuser and some form of therapeutic recover from trauma (See Chapter 5: Sándor Ferenczi's Confusion of Tongues Paradigm).

The sexual assault complaint against Matt Lauer

On November 30, 2017, *The New York Times* reported Matt Lauer, the long-time co-anchor of NBC's Today Show, was fired because of a complaint of sexual abuse by a Today Show producer. The women described her assault but would not let her name be used (Gabler, Rutenberg, Grynbaum & Abrams, 2017). The woman told The Times that Lauer had made inappropriate comments to her shortly after she started as the show's producer in the 1990s. the reported assault of the NBC employee was described as follows:

1. Matt Lauer asked the female producer, in her 40s to his office to discuss a so-called "work issue."
2. When she sat down to begin what she thought was to be a work issue, he locked the door shut from a button behind his desk.
3. Lauer asked her to unbutton her blouse, which she did.
4. He then stepped out from behind his desk, pulled down her pants, bent her over a chair, and raped her.
5. She passed out and woke up on the floor.
6. Lauer had an assistant take his sexual assault victim to a nurse.
7. The sexual assault was never mentioned by Lauer or his victim to anyone at the NBC television network (Gabler et al., 2017).

Lauer had begun a grooming process of seduction before he acted out his narcissistic sexual assault on the female producer. While traveling with Lauer for a story, she said, he asked her inappropriate questions over dinner, like whether she had ever cheated on her husband.

On the way to the airport, she said, Lauer sat uncomfortably close to her in the car, she recalled. When she moved away, he told her she was no fun.

The woman told The Times that Mr. Lauer never made an advance toward her again and never mentioned what occurred in his office. She said she did not report the episode to NBC at the time because she believed she should have done more to stop Mr. Lauer. She left the network about a year later. The episode in Lauer's office was reported to NBC News after the woman told her then supervisor, who still works at the network. The woman said an NBC human resources representative has since contacted her. The woman, who was in her early 40s at the time, told her then husband about the encounter, which The Times confirmed with him in a phone call. The couple was separated at the time, and later divorced. She also described it to a friend 5 years ago, which the friend confirmed to The Times (Gabler et al., 2017).

The sexual abuse Matt Lauer perpetrated against the female producer at NBC produced a strong emotional reaction from me because it reminded me of a clinical experience I have had years ago with similar narrative of harm to an individual. What struck me about Lauer's abuse of a woman in her 40s is that it reminded me of a report of an analysand's experience of childhood sexual abuse by his father. They both indicated the naked predatory nature of the abuse that an adult analysand reported of a horrific sexual experience when he was 9 years old. This individual also drew a picture of the episode that highlighted the emotional impact of the harm that was inflicted.

The drawing can be described as follows: In a locked barn on the family property, a 9-year-old boy is bent over and tied to a work table. The child's face is inches away from an operating circular saw. His father is anally raping his child. The analysand's father deliberately creating an experience of sexual abuse to satisfy his own narcissistic need without consideration of the harm he was doing. This analysand's experience is similar to Lauer's rape of his female employee. The child being assaulted by his father and the employee assaulted by Lauer both suffered from the Confusion of Tongues Trauma (Rachman & Klett, 2015), as they suffered severe anxiety, fear, confusion, which destabilized these individuals.

Belief in a loving relationship of a benevolent parental or authority figure is a primary attachment need for an individual. Without this need, the individual becomes unstable. Dissociation and inability to speak of the trauma can predominate. Psychoanalysis helped the analysand who was raped by his father to confront and explore his trauma, after having dissociated it for 30 years. The woman in the Lauer assault initially lost her voice, but with the help of the #MeToo Movement (the emotional support of women sexual assault survivors) enable her to find her voice and begin to recover from the Confusion of Tongues Trauma.

Silence and neglect of sexual abuse, which are the themes of this volume, was a prominent factor in the two cases I am discussing. In the sexual abuse of the of the 9-year-old child who was assaulted by his father, a complete silence descended on the survivor's family. The father, as the abuser, not only never spoke of the abuse that he inflicted on his son, but also never attended to the psychological damage he inflicted on his child by his sexual abuse. The father went on with his own and the family's life, as if nothing of any significance had happened. After he locked his only son in the garage in a physically threatening situation to sexually assault him, he remained silent. The father used dissociation to distance himself from the trauma to his son he had initiated. This entire family was severely traumatized by the father's sexual assault of his son, as the dramatic drawing was presented by the survivor, further depicting the family emotionally frozen on the other edges of the family living room. Consequently, this individual's emotional health was completely neglected for his entire life after his trauma, until he entered psychoanalysis. This is the double tragedy of the Confusion of Tongues Trauma, first, the individual is emotionally harmed by the sexual assault, then the damage is confounded by the neglect the individual suffers from his inability to speak of the trauma and the family's neglect of confronting the trauma.

In the case of the sexual assault of a female producer of the Today Show by Matt Lauer, neglect was remarkably present. As my description of the assault was depicted by the survivor, it detailed the sexual abuse of this adult woman as a brutal physical and emotional invasion of an individual by a sexual predator. There can be no other conclusion from the victim's description of the rape: she was bent over a chair; her pants were pulled down; she was raped; she passed out from the assault; she was left on the floor; and finally, Lauer's assistant was told to take his victim to a nurse. The father anally raping his bent over son and Lauer raping the bent over woman, show both predators treating these vulnerable human beings as objects for sexual exploitation. Then, when these predators' primitive impulses were satisfied, they tossed their prey aside and neglected their welfare. Lauer did not show any concern about his victim as she lay passed out at his feet on the floor of his office. He was not moved to see if she was conscious, help her up, and see if she needed immediate attention. Apparently, there was no follow-up to determine whether the victim was in any physical or emotional difficulty. He, like other sexual predators, satisfied his pathological narcissistic needs, then neglected his victim, just when the victim desperately needs help. The father of the male analysand who was abused by him as a child, similarly showed absolutely no concern for his son's well-being. Not only did he not concern himself about the harm he had afflicted on his son, but also he had no concern for his family's welfare. Everyone in the family was expected to cater to the father's desire to keep silent about the abuse and continue to feed his narcissism.

We need to provide more understanding about sexual predators to the analytic community and society. Of course, to focus on this topic, we would first need to become more cordial and interested in studying and sharing data about our clinical experience with trauma survivors. With all the material that has emerged about the prevalence of sexual abuse in our society, traditional psychoanalysis has not yet been willing to embrace sexual trauma as a significant psychodynamic.

Chapter 28

The Confusion of Tongues explanation for psychoanalysis' neglect of childhood sexual abuse

Psychoanalysis needs a psychodynamic explanation for its basic neglect of childhood sexual abuse as a meaningful factor in the development of psychopathology, developmental arrest, and its role in trauma disorders. Although there are those in our field who continue to accept Freud's change in thinking from his original Seduction Theory to the Oedipal Theory in explaining psychological disorder, I have always found this change of perspective puzzling. His seduction theory was a brilliant finding, as I have said, worthy of a Nobel Prize. His finding of childhood incest within the family as an originator of psychological disorder shattered the widely held notion of child sexual predators as strangers lurking in the back alleys. Freud's finding demonstrated that children were molested by their parents or those known to them. What is more, those molested children came from middle and upper class, respectable families. This finding meant he and his colleagues could be part of the community that molests little children, not in a dark alley, but in their own homes. I believe this factor can, in part, add to our understanding of why psychoanalysis has such a vitriolic response to Ferenczi's Confusion of Tongues paper.

There have been a host of explanations for Freud's so-called abandoning the incest trauma. Just to cite once such contemporary view, Florence Rush (1980) argues from a feminist perspective that there was what she called a *Freudian Coverup*. Freud intentionally ignored, she believed, evidence that his patients were victims of sexual abuse. The abandonment of the Seduction Theory illustrates Freud's lack of willingness to believe in women's accounts of abuse and

DOI: 10.4324/9780429298431-28

The Confusion of Tongues explanation 257

replace it with an account where men are not to blame. The Oedipal Theory amounted to a cover-up, that is to say, Freud's refusal to name the offender and to hid illegal or immoral sex practices. It was within this time that Victorian men were permitted to indulge in forbidden sex practices, provided they managed to keep their indiscretions hidden (Rush, 1980).

Oedipal Theory allowed psychoanalysis to focus on the unconscious rather than the reality of sexual abuse

Freud's infatuation with the Oedipal Theory allowed the realm of the unconscious and fantasy life to become prominent. This allowed a focus on the unconscious fantasy of the child, not the actual reality of a childhood sexual trauma. This has done an enormous injustice to those individuals who have been molested as children. Very simply, for a time psychoanalysis lead us to believe that incest survivors were not to be believed when they claimed to be incested in their families. What is more, they were told what they thought was a reality was a cover-up for their inability to reach their unconscious where resides the true experience. The real experience was an unconscious desire to have sexual contact with a parent, which nullifies the reality of what the survivors believed happened. Consequently, the individual's hold on reality was weakened and begins to question their version and what is true. I have been interested in why Freud left the Seduction Theory behind and so strongly embraced the Oedipal Theory. What is known to the individual in the unconscious, is embraced. What is not, is discarded as not being significant.

I have suggested in Chapter 3, *Freud's Neglect of His Childhood Sexual Trauma*, that, in Freud's own words, he disclosed he was a survivor of childhood sexual abuse by a nursemaid, Resi Wittek. But, since he wrote those letters to Wilhelm Fliess in 1897, detailing his sexual experiences with Ms. Wittek, there has been a deafening silence about Freud's sexual self-disclosures, as if they are not relevant to any discussion of the theory or clinical practice of childhood sexual molestation. In other words, a taboo has been instituted in traditional psychoanalysis in which there is to be no discussion of Freud's personal life, no matter how relevant the data may be to an understanding of his thinking or behavior. In the issue under present discussion, I find the fact that Freud was sexually abused as a child, by his own admission, is relevant to his abandonment of his Seduction Theory, and the neglect of his integrating a theoretical and clinical account of childhood sexual trauma in his later formulations. To my knowledge, Freud's formulations have not included a discussion on the implications to diagnosis, personality development or the clinical implications of analytic therapy regarding the experience of being sexually molested by a parent or authority figure as a child. The neglect to integrate a theoretical and clinical formulation for childhood sexual trauma, I believe, was a consequence that Freud did not integrate his own childhood sexual trauma with his nursemaid into his developing personality. After disclosing it to Fliess, not only did he not mention or discuss this experience in his writings, but also he developed negative and harsh reactions to Ferenczi, who included childhood sexual seduction in his theory.

I believe that Freud's vehement criticisms and condemnation of Ferenczi's work on Trauma Analysis in developing an alternative analytic theory, the Confusion of Tongues, and the clinical implications of the analysis of Elizabeth Severn, as a survivor of severe trauma, has something to do with his dissociated childhood sexual abuse (Rachman 1997b, 2002, 2015, 2018). On the surface Freud's denunciation of Ferenczi were related to his belief that his student was deviating so far from the established Oedipal Complex Theory as the cornerstone of psychoanalysis that his Trauma Analysis could not be considered psychoanalysis. Freud believed that Ferenczi had regressed personally and professionally in believing the Seduction Theory, which he considered obsolete and incorrect. What is more, Freud believed Ferenczi was allowing himself to be unduly influenced by his analysand, Elizabeth Severn, who he saw as an unstable and suspect individual (Rachman, 2018).

Freud believed that his iconic cases, which he wrote to establish the basic tenets of psychoanalysis, such as the Case of Dora/Ida Bauer and the Wolf Man/Sergie Pankejeff, were indications of Oedipal Conflict cases. But, re-analysis of these two cases have indicated that both Ida Bauer and Sergie Pankejeff had suffered childhood sexual molestation. Their sexual traumas can be considered to be a psychodynamic in the development of their emotional disorders. In the case of Ida Bauer, Freud neglected the data that Herr K., a middle-aged male, made sexual advances to the 14-year-old Ida Bauer (Rachman & Mattick, 2012). In the case of Sergie Pankejeff, Freud was not aware that this analysand was anally raped by a member of his household, which was later revealed by Ruth Mack Brunswick (Rachman, 2019e). As a consequence of these re-analyses of two of Freud's iconic cases, the issue of childhood sexual trauma was neglected. Freud was emotionally blind to the incidence of childhood sexual molestation in his clinical interaction because he dissociated his own childhood sexual trauma, thereby not making it emotionally available for clinical interaction or intellectually available for theoretical formulation.

Confusion of Tongues between Ferenczi, Freud, and the psychoanalytic community

Freud and Ferenczi's Confusion of Tongues

The Confusion of Tongues that developed between Freud and Ferenczi during the later years of their relationship as Ferenczi, the student, found his own path differed dramatically from his teacher, Freud. As has been mentioned, Freud believed that the true path in psychoanalysis that all should follow was established by his Oedipal Complex Theory. Ferenczi, from the earliest period of his psychiatric training as an intern in the psychiatric hospital in Budapest, was drawn to work with the more so-called difficult patients; for example, those who were outside of the traditional psychiatric and societal accepted categories (Rachman, 1997a). As Ferenczi became a psychoanalyst and an important part of the analytic community, he continued his interest in and skill with the nontraditional analysands. This desire and capacity to work with pre-oedipal cases, rather than solely with what Freud termed as neurotics, was an important difference between them. Freud was the theoretical genius, Ferenczi, the clinical genius. If they would have remained professionally close, they could have integrated their different interests and perspectives into an evolutionary analytic perspective. The controversy over the Confusion of Tongues and Trauma Analysis, unfortunately, permanently separated these giants of psychoanalysis. Freud wanted Ferenczi to be a dutiful son, loyal follower, and advocate for his perspective. Ferenczi was destined to follow his own journey. Ferenczi wanted Freud to be the loving and affirmative father he lost when he was an adolescent. He also wanted Freud to accept and integrate his Confusion of Tongues perspective into mainstream psychoanalysis. Ferenczi wanted love and acceptance from Freud, which he received until he followed his own intellectual, emotional, and clinical direction. Then Freud rejected and became angry with him. But, the most devastating experience was that Freud (along with Ernest Jones) organized a campaign against Ferenczi to silence him and remove his work from psychoanalysis.

Confusion of Tongues between Ferenczi and the psychoanalytic community: Todschweigen, Death by Silence

I have been explicit and vigorous in discussing the Todschweigen, Death by Silence campaign that was deliberately instituted in removing Ferenczi, Elizabeth Severn, and the Budapest School of Psychoanalysis from mainstream psychoanalysis (Rachman, 1999, 2018, 2019b, also see Chapter 7). This campaign, spearheaded by Freud's anger toward Ferenczi and implemented by Jones and other orthodox followers of Freud, was successful in removing Ferenczi's work from the analytic literature and from study in the traditional analytic institutes. Ferenczi wanted acceptance from his analytic colleagues. He wanted his Confusion of Tongues perspective to be valued enough by his analytic colleagues to have them make reference to it in their discussions, presentations, and writings. He did deserve such a positive response to his introduction of an alternate perspective for clinical psychoanalysis because his ideas were based on meaningful intellectual formulations, years of clinical experience with trauma cases, and the mutual interaction with a thoughtful and gifted analysand, Elizabeth Severn. But, *political assassination* triumphed over rational and scientific considerations. The analytic community joined Freud and Jones in punishing Ferenczi for displeasing Freud and developing a new perspective. They wanted him to be what Fromm called *a company man*, someone who maintained a strong allegiance to the master, Freud and the orthodox analytic perspective (Fromm, 1959). They did not want to lose their standing in the analytic community, encourage Freud's anger and rejection, and run the risk of not

The Confusion of Tongues explanation 261

receiving referrals from colleagues. Once again, Ferenczi wanted affection, acceptance, and affirmation, the necessary components to have a positive and meaningful relationship with colleagues. Everyone wants a self-enhancing connection to a community of colleagues. Ferenczi easily established this experience with his Hungarian colleagues as head of the Hungarian Psychoanalytic Society. But, once he entered his studies of Trauma Analysis, he was criticized and rejected by Freud, the father, as well as the orthodox community. Ferenczi's adjustment to the disapproval, rejection, and lack of acceptance was to withdraw from the traditional analytic community. He did not accept Freud's offer to be President of the International Psychoanalytic Association, rather, he found refuge in his Hungarian analytic community. In this group, he received the status, acceptance, and praise he deserved. But, it took almost a century for Ferenczi and the Budapest School to become a valued and significant part of the contemporary psychoanalysis (Rachman 2016).

Confusion of Tongues between Elizabeth Severn, Freud, and the analytic community

Elizabeth Severn, Ferenczi's controversial analysand and contributor to his Confusion of Tongues perspective and Trauma Analysis also suffered a Todschweigen campaign toward her personal and professional functioning (Rachman, 2018). Toward the last 5 years of Ferenczi's life, when he was analyzing Severn with his Trauma Analysis alternative perspective to Freudian Analysis, Freud had formed an opinion that Severn was a very disturbed individual who had influenced Ferenczi to leave traditional psychoanalysis. As has been mentioned, Freud was alien to actual trauma as a significant issue in the development of psychopathology and emotional disorder. Consequently, Freud did not appreciate Trauma Analysis. He did not have empathy for Severn's illness and so he labeled Severn as a suspect individual. He felt her behavior and clinical ideas were a function of unsophisticated, untrained, emotionally disturbed mystical thinking and functioning. What he never understood was that Ferenczi and Severn co-created and introduced a new theory, diagnostic category and method to analyze Trauma Disorder. *Rather than try to understand his once favorite son's pioneering work, he condemned it, as well as Severn, who inspired it.*

Once Severn left Budapest in February 1933, Ferenczi could no longer work due to his fatal illness of pernicious anemia. Any mention of Severn's analysis with Ferenczi disappeared from the psychoanalytic literature. Of course, the most prominent report of this analysis was found in Ferenczi's *Clinical Diary* (Ferenczi, 1988), which also disappeared from the literature until it was published first in French in 1985, then in English in 1988. Severn never became a part of the analytic community. She eventually practiced as a psychoanalyst in New York City, from the 1940s until her death in 1959. Her work went unnoticed until her legacy was discovered, and a book was published attempting to bring her legacy to the attention of the analytic community (Rachman, 2018).

The Todschweigen campaign against Severn, deprived the analytic community of a pioneering woman analyst who contributed to the development of an understanding of the role of trauma in personality development, development of psychopathology, and the expansion of the psychoanalytic treatment to non-oedipal disorders. Severn wanted to help psychoanalysis recognize the significance of trauma disorders but was neglected and condemned as a negative factor in Ferenczi's life and in her own personal and professional functioning.

Confusion of Tongues between the traditional analytic and Ferenczi communities

As a result of the Todschweigen campaign, which removed Ferenczi's theoretical and clinical ideas form mainstream psychoanalysis, a breach developed between the traditional and Ferenczi analytic communities. Although traditional analysis did its best to discourage attention to Ferenczi and the Budapest School's contributions to psychoanalysis, over the past 25 years, a group of analysts from North America, South America, Europe, and the Pacific Rim have been gathering together to share their interest in the significance of Ferenczi's ideas and discoveries. The International Sándor Ferenczi Network (Meszaros, 2019) has now been established, which sponsors international conferences, meetings, seminars, and discussions among global membership. In 2011, Ferenczi's former apartment/office was purchased, spearheaded by Carlo Bonomi, PhD, Florence, Italy, and Judit Mesazors of Budapest, Hungary. The former Ferenczi office now is the Ferenczi House/International Ferenczi Center. In addition in 2014, the Elizabeth Severn Section of the Freud Archive, the Library of Congress, Washington, DC, was established, celebrated by the paper presentation about Elizabeth Severn (Rachman, 2014). These events now represent the vigorous establishment of a Sándor Ferenczi psychoanalytic community.

The International Sándor Ferenczi Community, over the past 25 years has contributed to the rehabilitating of the image and reputation of Sándor Ferenczi, Elizabeth Severn, and enhancing the status of the Budapest School of Psychoanalysis. It has taken its rightful place in the analytic community representing a historically important alternative to analytic orthodoxy and a contemporarily relevant contribution within the Relational Psychoanalysis perspective. It has made a significant contribution to psychoanalytic thinking and clinical functioning in the areas of trauma studies, feminine and gender studies, mutual analytic functioning, countertransference analysis, the subjectivity of the analyst, noninterpretative measures, analyst self-disclosure, and the recognition of neglected psychoanalytic pioneers.

Chapter 29

My attempts to confront the Todschweigen, Death by Silence campaign against Sándor Ferenczi, Elizabeth Severn and the Budapest School of Psychoanalysis

Confronting the Todschweigen campaign

As I became aware of how powerful the Todschweigen campaign to silence Ferenczi became, I dedicated myself to actively contributing to both confronting the silence by giving voice to the damage done by removing his ideas and methods from mainstream psychoanalysis, and bringing attention to the positive contributions Ferenczi and the Budapest school had made to the evolution of psychoanalysis (Rachman, 2007, 2010). This involved generations of analysts being ignorant of these contributions? When analysts did know about Ferenczi, all they generally knew was negative (Rachman, 1997a, 1997b). In the first 25 years of my research on Ferenczi, I had never heard anyone, who approached me to discuss Ferenczi, ever tell me anything positive about his clinical functioning.

Since 1978, I have been presenting lectures at conferences in the United States, Europe, and South America. These presentations were invited addresses in Belo Horizonte and San Paulo, Brazil in New York, Budapest, Hungary, Madrid, Spain, Florence, Italy, Athens, Greece, and Tel Aviv, Israel. At the time I discovered Ferenczi in 1976 (Rachman, 1997a), I was involved in the encounter and marathon group movement believing Ferenczi's original introduction of the role of activity into psychoanalysis (Rachman, 1997a), was historically relevant to these newer developments in clinical practice (Rachman, 1978). A reaction to my connecting Ferenczi's active analysis with contemporary clinical innovations was made by a well-known group analyst who said: "You have a lot of

DOI: 10.4324/9780429298431-29

chutzpah (audacity), to link Ferenczi with the encounter and marathon group movement." On reflection, I believe his polite criticism was relevant. In this first paper on Ferenczi, I was enthusiastically trying to revive Ferenczi's relevancy for contemporary clinical practice. This first paper was a beginning towards my campaign to contribute to the Ferenczi Renaissance (Rachman, 1999b).

I began my campaign to confront the Todschweigen campaign to silence Ferenczi by becoming active in my analytic community where I trained as an analyst, publishing papers, giving presentations at national and international conferences, developing relationships with colleagues who considered Ferenczi a neglected, but significant figure in analytic history, while developing an attitude that I would become an advocate for Ferenczi's ideas and clinical work. I was determined to make a positive contribution to our field by resurrecting Ferenczi and the Budapest School of Psychoanalysis. This basically was a fantasy when I embarked on my journey in the latter part of the 1970s. I had no idea if my efforts to help make Ferenczi relevant in contemporary psychoanalysis would be accepted.

My campaign took an upward turn when I was asked to give a lecture on Ferenczi at my analytic institute in 1985 for the Friday Evening Lecture Series (Rachman, 1984). This was the first time that the Postgraduate Center for Mental Health Psychoanalytic Institute had ever sponsored a Ferenczi event. I was particularly honored about this initial invitation because the institute was heading by the late Lewis Wolberg, MD, who was an analysand of Clara Thompson who was analyzed by Ferenczi. Yet, Wolberg never introduced Ferenczi to the Postgraduate Center. The Todschweigen silence of Ferenczi was unfortunately also practiced at this institute. It is particularly unsettling because Wolberg was an innovative psychoanalyst promoting active techniques, so it was mysterious why he never talked about Ferenczi. What is more, he had his analytic training at the William Alanson White Institute, where Ferenczi was considered a theoretical and clinical founding father. I introduced Ferenczi as a unique, pioneering voice in psychoanalysis, who was suppressed by Freud and Jones because he was an unacceptable dissident. I also described that for the greater part of the 25-year relationship between Freud and Ferenczi, Freud valued Ferenczi as inheritor of his psychoanalytic heritage. To my amazement, my presentation was so enthusiastically received that the audience of mostly analytic candidates and young analysts asked me to give an additional lecture. It became clear to me from the younger group of analysts' positive response to the Ferenczi material, that there was a generation of analysts who were interested in the ideas and methods even though they were deliberately withheld from them because of political and emotional prejudice. The unanticipated positive response from my analytic community gave me the motivation to continue on with my campaign to bring Ferenczi back from the damage the Todschweigen experience had done to his reputation. The positive response was crucial because since I discovered Ferenczi in 1976 until these two lectures in 1984, I had been researching Ferenczi's work in a vacuum. I did not know any colleagues who were interested in this work and I never had contact with any teacher, supervisor, or senior analyst who ever mentioned Ferenczi. I was looking for affirmation from an authority, but it became clear that my colleagues were placing me in the position of the authority on Ferenczi. Under those circumstances I needed to accept that my research was fruitful, and I should continue to share it with colleagues.

In the next years, a group of students approached me to teach a Senior Seminar on Ferenczi's ideas and methods. Again, this was the first time at the Postgraduate Center Psychoanalytic Institute that any course was offered about Ferenczi. One day I shared my surprise about the neglect of Ferenczi's work with my analyst, Betty Feldman, during one of our analytic sessions. She told me that the founder and leader of our institute, Lewis Wolberg, MD, was an analysand of Clara Thompson, MD, who, in turn, was an analysand of Sándor Ferenczi. Betty also said that she was analyzed by Wolberg, which mad me a fifth-generation analysand of Ferenczi, that is, Ferenczi/Thompson/ Wolberg/Feldman/Rachman (Rachman, 1997a). Betty's revelation about Wolberg and herself, intensified my interest in the Todschweigen experience, which I believe existed at my training institute. Wolberg, as the Head of the Institute, was rarely available as a teacher. As an analyst or supervisor, he was only available to any independently rich individuals because his fees were at least three times the fees of the faculty. There was no reference to Ferenczi by him at any time he addressed trainees. There was, however, an experience he conducted that was in the tradition of Ferenczi, in that it was a clinical demonstration of creativity and boundary expansion. Wolberg gave a demonstration of supervision with a psychoanalyst who was immersed in an erotic transference with a female analysand. Their therapeutic impasse was characterized by her wanting to have his child, a desire that he could not analyze to change her desire. The analyst turned toward Wolberg, the most prominent and respected analyst at the Institute to help him break this therapeutic impasse. Wolberg turned the supervision session into one of his rare teaching experiences by holding the supervision in a one-way vision classroom. First, Wolberg aksed the analyst to describe the woman's emotional difficulties and how he intervened to help her. Wolberg reflected that the analyst had meaningfully used a variety of traditional and contemporary analytic interventions, which did not solve the erotic transference issue. Then, he made a very unusual clinical suggestion. He said that the analyst needed to actively intervene by offering the analysand a *symbolic child*. He suggested the analyst give the woman a pet animal, like a kitten or dog, to satisfy her intense need for a child from her analyst. Wolberg was suggesting that this analysand's unresolved emotional needs were from such an early development phase, traditional analytic intervention would not help reduce her internal need. This analysand, it was suggested, needed actual satisfaction (Rachman, 1997a). Wolberg's supervision was in the heritage of Sándor Ferenczi in his work with difficult cases (Rachman, 2003).

In the discussion section of this case between the audience of young and senior analysts, which was led by Wolberg, critical remarks were made about the dramatic recommendation by Wolberg. The impression I had was that most of the analysts would not carry out the recommendation. I was one of the few who thought Wolberg's nontraditional approach was a creative, emotionally courageous approach to a very difficult clinical situation. We never knew the outcome of Wolberg's recommendation since we heard the analyst moved to California. Generally speaking, the audience of analysts thought the presenting analyst was to be congratulated for his willingness to expose his work for examination to an analytic community. But, many wondered if doing so he felt he had lost their confidence as a clinician, which prompted him to start over in a new place.

The experience of Wolberg's supervision of a very difficult analytic case and his unusual recommendation reinforced the mystery and confusion over Ferenczi's disappearance from psychoanalysis for almost 90 years. Wolberg, a distinguished analyst, analyzed by a Ferenczi analysand, Clara Thompson, who helped to introduce Ferenczi influences alternative to Freud's perspectives, Interpersonal Psychoanalysis (Rachman, 2003), never mentioned Ferenczi's active, and empathic non-interpretative measures (Ferenczi, 1988; Rachman, 1997a). Either Wolberg believed his recommendation was his own creation and his narcissism prevented him from giving credit to a progenitor, or he did not want to mention Ferenczi's work because he did not want to be identified with a *maligned dissident*. Remaining silent contributed to a reinforcement of the Todschweigen Campaign. Wolberg's supervisory behavior was also surprising because he offered no theoretical rationale for his clinical intervention. Although I can mention that his intervention was in the spirit of Ferenczi's clinical experimentation, Wolberg completely neglected Ferenczi's idea of countertransference analysis to explore with the supervisee whether his subjective experience was contributing to the analysand's intense erotic transference. What is more, Wolberg said nothing about Ferenczi's theory of Confusion of Tongues, which focused on childhood trauma and sexual abuse. There was also no exploration of the analysand's childhood background and family pattern of disturbed interaction. This neglect did not allow for an understanding about childhood sexual trauma be as a psychodynamic in the analysand's development of an erotic transference (Rachman, 2003, 2018; Rachman & Klett, 2015).

It has been clear to me ever since I discovered Ferenczi's work that his innovations in thinking and functioning are related to Freud's original discoveries. Freud also approved of many of Ferenczi's innovations. More importantly, *Ferenczi had no intention of founding a new form of psychoanalysis to compete with Freud's perspective.*

Over the past 40 years, since discovering Ferenczi, I have published a series of articles and books about him and the Budapest School of Psychoanalysis (Rachman 1997a, 2003, 2016, 2018; Rachman & Klett, 2015). There has been a positive response to these attempts to aid in the development of the Ferenczi Renaissance. Some of these presentations at professional gatherings have been helpful in advancing an appreciation of Ferenczi and the Budapest School's ideas.

My attempts to confront the Todschweigen 269

In the 1990s, a weekend retreat was sponsored by the Postgraduate Center, under the leadership of Donna Jacobs, LCSW, then President of the Postgraduate Psychoanalytic Society. This retreat turned out to be an important opportunity to present Ferenczi's ideas to a wider audience of the Postgraduate Analytic Community as well as the greater analytic community. Over this weekend at the Red Lion Inn in Stockbridge, Massachusetts, a panel discussion with Adam Phillips, MS, Marc Wayne LCSW, and myself, discussed the perspectives of Freud, Ferenczi, and Kohut. This was, again, a first for the Postgraduate Center analytic community, in that, Ferenczi's ideas were being elevated to the same importance as Freud and Kohut. The participants received the presentations with meaningful interest and praise.

In the afternoon, a paper on Ferenczi's work was given by Etty Cohen, PhD, and was discussed by the late Hannah Kapit, PhD, a senior training analyst and well-respected member of the institute. To my amazement, Dr. Kapit unleashed a diatribe against Ferenczi, which no one was expecting, and I found offensive. She did not address any theoretical or clinical issue about Ferenczi's ideas or clinical functioning. Rather, she revisited the *personal/political assassination method*, that Ernest Jones had initiated about Ferenczi in his Freud biography (Jones, 1957). She began her criticism of Ferenczi by saying she grew up in Europe (Vienna, Austria), and was very familiar with Hungarians, like Ferenczi. Hungarians, she said, were characterized as being undesirable people who you could not trust and were prone to illegal acts. As I heard these damning words, I realized how alive the Todschweigen experience was in contemporary psychoanalysis. Then, I turned to a cherished colleague to share my outrage and gain support for confronting the offender. My colleague did not support or encourage me. Rather, she said the following:

> Arnold, I know how angry you are about what you just heard about Ferenczi. These words are coming from an older person, who is losing it (becoming senile). No one of us pay attention to these horrible words.

I answered her by saying:

> But what is being said is so horrible, so false, so damning, I can't sit here and let this poison fill the air in the room.
>
> Arnold, if you confront her, everyone will turn on you, because you are attacking a revered senior analyst who is in an emotionally vulnerable state. It will damage your reputation and your views on Ferenczi.

It was a very difficult moment for me to remain silent as Ferenczi was being personally assaulted. As I tried to assimilate my friend's wise words, it became clear she was right. Confronting this Ferenczi abuser would add to the Todschweigen experience. I remained silent. But, I made a pledge to myself, namely, if I were to be in the presence of a Todschweigen experience again, I would find a way to respond. Little did I realize that a remarkable Todschweigen experience was on the horizon. What occurred in the winter of 2018, indicated to me how intrenched is the Todschweigen experience in contemporary psychoanalysis and how much our field needs a dramatic change to truly integrate Ferenczi and the Budapest School of Psychoanalysis's contributions. I will report what I experienced in another shocking Todschweigen experience in the sections to follow.

A very important event occurred in 1991, when I was invited to present a paper at the second International Ferenczi Conference, at Mt. Sinai Medical Center in New York City. My dear friend Beatrice Beebe, PhD, recommended I present to the conference. Co-chairs, Lewis Aron, PhD, and Adrienne Harris, PhD, who graciously accepted my paper, *Ferenczi's Sexuality*. The paper presented Ferenczi's ideas and clinical works about sexuality. A very early clinical interaction, the Case of Rosa K., presented, perhaps for the first time in a case study, the clinical interaction with a transgender patient (Rachman, 1997a). In addition, I examined the controversial romantic experience of Ferenczi with Elma Pálos, who was his future wife's daughter, concluding, based on my research, *there was no sexual contact between Elma and Ferenczi*. Some of the criticism of Ferenczi was linked to the controversy that he had sexual contact with Elma Pálos, who he analyzed for a time, before he sent her to Freud. My research indicated that there was a romantic interest in Elma, but, no sexual contact. What is more, there were no data to indicate any sexual contact with any analysands. This defense of Ferenczi was published (Rachman, 1993). My presence at this important meeting introduced my work and myself to an international community of Ferenczi scholars, such as, the late Georgy Hidas, MD, André Hynal, and Judith Mészaros, PhD, all who became cherished colleagues and friends. They affirmed my Ferenczi research and publications. At the American Psychological Association, Psychoanalytic Psychology Section Spring Conference in Chicago, Illinois, in March 2012, I became part of a new methodology for paper presentations. You posted your accepted paper online for all participants to read before the conference. My paper focused on the contribution of Ferenczi's work to the evolution of contemporary psychoanalysis, which was previously published (Rachman, 2007). The presentation session then was intended to be an interaction between the author and the participants, and between the attendees. The session was fully subscribed and became an active, lively and intellectually stimulating discussion. Several of the participants were very praising of the session. One attendee who wrote me a letter after the conference felt the Ferenczi session was the best event of the conference. With the enthusiastic and positive response to this event, I was motivated to propose an ongoing Ferenczi Seminar to take place at the annual Psychoanalytic Psychology Spring Meeting. My proposal was turn down, as apparently the success of the Ferenczi session did not move the selection committee to approve adding Ferenczi to the training program.

When I read Claude Lorin's book, *Le Jeune Ferenczi: Premier Ecrits: 1899–1906* (Lorin, 1983), he detailed his discovery of a treasury of Ferenczi's earliest publications in the Hungarian medical journal, *Gyögyászat* (Medical Journal). Lorin found these publications, stored in a back room, in an out of the way Hungarian bookstore in Budapest, Hungary. Lorin's discovery stimulated me to develop an ongoing fantasy of, one day, my being able to unearth a lost legacy of Sándor Ferenczi. I had no idea if I would ever fulfill my fantasy. A significant time passed with nothing happening to fulfill my fantasy. A trip to Budapest searching old bookstores for lost treasures was unsuccessful.

Then, one day, in 2003, I received a phone call from the late Hannah Kapit, PhD, a colleague previously mentioned. She told me that a friend of hers had Elizabeth Severn's papers and wanted to know if I was interested in purchasing them. My moment of discovering an unknown legacy of Sándor Ferenczi had appeared out of nowhere. As I began to formulate a response to Hannah Kapit, I was silently screaming my delight. I told her I was very interested and pleased to tell her contact to call me immediately. In a day or so, Peter Lipskis, Margaret Severn's literary, called me with the offer to purchase Elizabeth Severn's papers, to which I gladly agreed. Lipskis told me Hannah Kapit had been one of Margaret Severn's best friends, who was the daughter of Elizabeth Severn. Elizabeth was Ferenczi's most controversial and publicized analysand. Through the same negative mechanism of Todschweigen, Death by Silence, she was removed from psychoanalytic history by Freud, Jones, and traditional analytic followers (Rachman, 2018). Before I obtained *The Elizabeth Severn Papers* (Rachman, 2016), I had no idea The Severn Papers existed, nor did I know anyone in the International Sándor Ferenczi Network who knew about these materials. Since the time of my acquisition until the present day, I feel proud to have unearthed and restored one of the previously unknown legacies of psychoanalysis. For several years, in consultation with Nellie Thompson, PhD, Archivist of the A.A. Brill Library, The New York Psychoanalytic Institute, NYC, I worked on sorting, preparing, cataloging, and repairing the various materials in The Severn Papers. These letters, books, photographs, articles, and personal materials were restored and prepared so they could be studied. The Severn Papers were originally stored at the Archives Section of the A.A. Brill Library thanks to the generosity of Nellie Thompson.

After a period of several years of research and preparing the Severn Papers for a book, they were donated to the Freud Archives, Library of Congress, with a stipulation that the Severn Papers are completely unrestricted. This stipulation was made so that scholars would have free access to this important discovery, realizing the controversy that had previously emerged in the Freud Archives when researchers reported materials were sequestered without availability for unlimited times (Masson, 1984).

Being able to uncover Elizabeth Severn's lost legacy to psychoanalysis added to my satisfaction of having been able to have resurrected Ferenczi's contributions to psychoanalysis. Once the Severn materials were made ready to be researched, I collected the

My attempts to confront the Todschweigen 273

knowledge revealed into book form (Rachman, 2018). As the writing of the book took form and was completed, there were significant presentations that were made to introduce the significance of Elizabeth Severn for psychoanalysis. The first such presentation was in Athens, Greece, at International Forum of Psychoanalysis in 2010, entitled, "An Invitro" Study of Intersubjectivity: The Analysis of Mrs. Elizabeth Severn With Dr. Sándor Ferenczi. Ferenczi's pioneering analysis of Severn was discussed as an example of the pioneering clinical interaction, which emphasized the subjectivities of the analyst and the analysand (Rachman, 2010). At the International Sándor Ferenczi Congress in 2012, held in Budapest, Hungary, with a theme of *Faces of Trauma*, I presented the paper, The Confusion of Tongues between Sándor Ferenczi and Elizabeth Severn. Its focus was a detailed description of the clinical interaction between Severn and Ferenczi emphasizing the uncovering and working through of Severn's multiple childhood traumas (Rachman, 2012). What is more, for the first time, a detailed account of the interaction between Severn and Ferenczi during their Trauma Analysis was gathered together from the material presented in Ferenczi's *Clinical Diary* (Ferenczi, 1988).

In collaboration with Jim Hutson, PhD, Chief, Manuscript Division, the Library of Congress, and, the former Chief, Scientific Manuscript Department, Leonard Bruno, PhD, I donated the Elizabeth Severn Papers to the Library of Congress. My petition to establish an Elizabeth Severn section of the Freud Archives was accepted. To celebrate the establishment of the Elizabeth Severn Section of the Library of Congress, I organized, with the help of Jim Hutson, an Elizabeth Severn Symposium, which was held at the Library of Congress on Friday, June 20, 2014. The symposium was composed of my presentation, "The 'Evil Genius' of Psychoanalysis: Dr. Sándor Ferenczi's Partner in the Pioneering Study of Trauma" (Rachman, 2014), with Lewis Aron, PhD, and Joseph Lichtenberg, MD, as the discussants. The talk presented, for the first time, the research findings from the Severn papers on Severn's family background, relationships with her husband, daughter, friends, and colleagues. This previously unknown data from Severn's life, as well as her unknown clinical work, was intended to help rehabilitate the view of her as a disturbed patient who was criticized and ignored by

Freud, as well as considered by the traditional analytic community as a disturbing personal and professional influence on Ferenczi.

Under the auspices of the Sándor Ferenczi Study Center, of the New School University, in New York City, led by the late Jeremy Safron, PhD, Lewis Aron, PhD, and Adrienne Harris, PhD, the Co-Founders of the Sándor Ferenczi Center, an Elizabeth Severn Symposium was also developed. I presented a paper, entitled, "Elizabeth Severn: From Self-Taught Therapist to Psychoanalyst and Sándor Ferenczi's Mutual Analytic Partner" at the New School for Social Research, New York City, on September 15, 2015 (Rachman, 2015). One of the highlights of the presentation was a series of images related to Severn's life, work and relationships presented for the first time, which were part of the Elizabeth Severn Papers. An attempt was made to show that Severn was a talented, motivated, and intellectually oriented self-taught therapist who contributed to Ferenczi's ideas and methods.

Further attempts to confront the Todschweigen campaign were carried out in two European analytic communities in Florence, Italy, and Dublin, Ireland. I am very grateful to Carlo Bonomi, PhD, Co-Founder of the Ferenczi House in Budapest, Hungary, and one of the organizers and first President of the International Sándor Ferenczi Network for his enthusiastic, thoughtful, and creative efforts to help confront the Todschweigen campaign by making Florence, Italy, one of the world's centers for Ferenczi studies. Recently, Bonomi organized the first Sándor Ferenczi Seminars in July 2017, in Florence, Italy. The purpose of the Ferenczi Seminars was to provide an educational opportunity on the spectrum of Ferenczi and the Budapest School of Psychoanalysis studies offered to students, analysts and interested scholars. For a week in the summer of 2017, five Ferenczi scholars presented a half-day seminar on the topic chosen in consultation with Carlo Bonomi. Among the seminar topics were Ferenczi's Concept of Identification With The Aggressor and Trauma Theory and Treatment. I took the opportunity to introduce my research on the life and work of Elizabeth Severn to members of the International Sándor Ferenczi community (Rachman, 2017). I presented a seminar entitled, Elizabeth Severn, the "Evil Genius" of Psychoanalysis, which focused on introducing Severn's life, work, and importance for contemporary psychoanalysis and the contribution she made to Ferenczi's Trauma Analysis and Relaxation Therapy. It became an important event in advancing the Ferenczi Renaissance since it was very well-received, and contacts were made with analytic candidates from Italy, Australia, Ireland, Portugal, Spain, and Brazil.

In addition to hosting the Ferenczi Seminars, Carlo Bonomi and the Italian Sándor Ferenczi Society in consort with the International Sándor Ferenczi Network also organized the International Sándor Ferenczi Conference in Florence Italy in May 2018. One of the largest audiences gathered for a Ferenczi Conference. The gathering took place in a 15th century grounds, which was originally a mental hospital and then became a Catholic church nunnery, and finally, in modern times, a conference site, with hotel facilities. Analysts gathered from Europe, Asia, South America, and the United States. This wide-ranging attendance and its significant numbers indicated that the Ferenczi Renaissance had taken root in a segment of the analytic community that appreciated Ferenczi and the Budapest School's relevance for contemporary psychoanalysis. I presented, one again, my research on Elizabeth Severn, which was an important opportunity to re-evaluate Severn's prior acquired negative reputation from the Todschweigen campaign launched from traditional psychoanalysis. The paper was entitled, "The Uncovering of a Lost Psychoanalytic Legacy: The Papers of Elizabeth Severn" (Rachman, 2018). It was well-received and audience members became acquainted with Elizabeth Severn through my work. I felt very satisfied that I had become helpful in rediscovering Ferenczi, and now, Elizabeth Severn.

An important attempt to contribute to reviving Ferenczi's importance for psychoanalysis was offered at a symposium at the Postgrad Psychoanalytic Institute in 2012. Then president of the Institute, Susanne Klett, PhD, helped to organize a full-day symposium entitled "From Freud's Seduction Hypothesis to Ferenczi's Confusion of Tongues Paradigm: Childhood Sexual Abuse and Trauma." Louise de Costa, PhD, was the symposium leader, and Elliot Adler, PhD, was the discussant. The symposium was a lively, scholarly, and interpersonally meaningful experience. One of the senior members of the Postgrad analytic community said: "This is one of the most scholarly and open discussions I have ever seen at one of our meetings." I felt that this event had made a positive impact on appreciating Sándor Ferenczi's contributions to the study and treatment of sexual trauma as well as understanding the psychodynamic in the development of trauma as a psychological disorder and value of the Trauma Analysis for treating trauma disorder.

Martin Bergmann and Arnold Wm. Rachman's confrontation: a contemporary Todschweigen experience

After 40 years researching, studying, and writing about Sándor Ferenczi, I was faced with a dramatic Todschweigen, Death by Silence, experience (Rachman, 1999) by Professor Martin Bergmann over his denunciation of Ferenczi (Rachman, 2018). This event occurred at a special event hosted by the Postgraduate Psychoanalytic Institute in November of 2013. A group of analysts at the Postgraduate Institute lead by Louise de Costa, PhD, and Elliot Adler, PhD, developed a narrative play from the published Freud/ Ferenczi correspondence (Barbant, Falzeder & Giamperi-Deusche, 1993, Volume I; Falzeder, Barbant & Giamperi-Deusche, 1996, Volume II, Volume III; Falzeder, Barbant & Giamperi-Deusche, 2000). With Louise de Costa and Elliot Adler being the leaders of the narrative group, which also included Arnold Wm. Rachman, PhD, and Issac Tylim, PhD, we researched the three volumes of the Freud/ Ferenczi correspondence and developed a history of their relationship focusing on dramatic moments in their interaction. The material was written as a narrative play. The narrative was enacted by Louise de Costa playing Ferenczi's wife, Gisella, Elliot Adler playing Freud, Issac Tylim playing Sándor Ferenczi, and Arnold Rachman being the narrator (de Costa et al, 2013).

I was excited and felt positive about the Freud/Ferenczi Correspondence narrative. It was seen as a special event and was very well-attended. Hopefully, the Freud/Ferenczi narrative would provide a new opportunity to try to reverse the Todschweigen campaign against Ferenczi. What is more, the organizers of the narrative invited me to be part of this experience because of my reputation of being an advocate of Sándor Ferenczi. I very much appreciated the opportunity to be a part of an important event to, hopefully, bring the Freudian and Ferenczi communities together. In a dramatic Todschweigen experience, that this Freud/Ferenczi Narrative provided, my fantasy of a new positive experience for the Ferenczi community turned out to be a delusion. The Narrative experience can be divided into five phases:

1. The Narrative was presented to about 100 people.
2. Invited discussion of the Narrative by Professor Martin Bergmann.
3. Arnold Wm. Rachman's challenge to Professor Bergmann regarding his Todschweigen-style remarks about Ferenczi.
4. The audience's silence to the Bergmann/Rachman confrontation.
5. Post-Narrative phase: discussion with some audience members; the letter from Arnold Wm. Rachman to engage Professor Martin Bergmann in a discussion about the Todschweigen experience.

Presentation of the Freud/Ferenczi Correspondence Narrative

The Narrative, which was about an hour in length, was very well-received by the audience as they clearly appreciated the performance by the players who were dressed in the style of the 1920s–1930s, using the style and mannerisms of their characters. The setting of the narrative suggested a 1920s–1930s European-style consultation room. The performers were clear, assertive, and articulate in their presentations. The audience was very attentive and positive during the performance and gave the performers a rousing applause when the Narrative ended.

Professor Martin Bergmann's invited remarks

Professor Martin Bergmann was introduced by Louise de Costa to give his remarks about the Narrative and the Freud/Ferenczi Correspondence. There was an air of positive anticipation toward Bergmann's remarks. He was a revered figure in the analytic community in New York City, where individuals in the audience were members of his supervision groups. His reputation was also known through his professional writings and presentations. He also appeared as Professor Louis Levy in Woody Allen's 1989 feature film,

Crimes and Misdemeanors. Bergmann began his remarks by saying the following:

> I found the Narrative about the Freud/Ferenczi Correspondence very enjoyable, and the people being part of the narrative did a fine job. But, you didn't invite me here tonight just to say good things. (Rachman, 2018, p. 65)

When I heard Bergmann begin his remarks with his emphasizing he was not invited to speak to say good things only, an ominous feeling came over me. In my heart of hearts, I knew from my past experiences with traditional Freudians, something negative was going to be said about Ferenczi. But, I did not expect Bergmann to eviscerate Ferenczi with his slanderous claims. I felt myself getting angry and after I knew I would have to respond to Bergmann's attack on Ferenczi. A pledge I had made to myself after the Todschweigen experience I reported in the previous section. After these initial remarks, Bergmann made what I considered to be a false and outrageous accusation about Ferenczi:

> What this correspondence shows is that Freud was a psychoanalyst, Ferenczi was not a psychoanalyst. Ferenczi was not a psychoanalyst because he let patients kiss him! (Rachman, 2018, p. 65)

His accusations were disturbing not only because it continued the Todschweigen campaign that began in the 1930s, but also I was surprised by it. He had previously made positive comments about Ferenczi's work in an earlier period of his scholarship. In my first book about Ferenczi (Rachman, 1997a), I cited Bergmann and Hartman's book (1976) as a contribution to the Ferenczi Renaissance, which helped re-discover Ferenczi as a significant figure in psychoanalysis. Six papers of Ferenczi were included in the Bergmann and Hartman book, more than any other analytic pioneer. Technical papers from Ferenczi's work from 1919 to 1930 were featured, which spans the significant portion of his clinical career including his controversial Relaxation Therapy. It was clear then, from the Bergmann and Hartman book, that in 1976, Ferenczi was considered by these authors as a significant figure in the history and the evolution of clinical psychoanalysis. I had not kept up with Bergmann's writing, but I assumed that his invitation to talk would provide a positive response to Ferenczi and not add to the Todschweigen campaign to silence and discredit Ferenczi. But, my opinion was short-lived. When Bergmann finished his denunciation of Ferenczi, I was determined to speak and engage him in a discussion about his accusation. I made sure I got the attention of the discussion leader and signaled I wanted to be the first person to discuss Bergmann's Todschweigen statements about Ferenczi. I said the following to Bergmann, which began a confrontation between us:

> Professor Bergmann, with all due respect, I *completely disagree* with your characterization of Sándor Ferenczi. I have researched this issue of the myth that Ferenczi had regular physical contact with his patients. The only analysand with whom he had such contact was with Clara Mabel Thompson. Thompson was the one who initiated kissing Ferenczi. He did not initiate the contact. What is more, Ferenczi did not have this contact with other analysands. Thompson bragged to the analytic community that she could kiss "Papa Ferenczi anytime she wanted." Ferenczi allowed Thompson to kiss him in order to create a reparative therapeutic experience for her childhood sexual trauma by her father. (Rachman, 2018, p. 65)

Bergman did not respond to my clarification of Ferenczi's empathic response for Thompson's need for a holding environment for her childhood traumas. Thompson's acting out in the transference helped bring the issue into the analytic situation (Rachman & Klett, 2015). My feeling was that Bergmann, in essence, ignored my attempts to engage him in a meaningful conversation about the historical truth of Ferenczi's ideas and functioning. I reached a point of frustration where I wanted to confront Bergmann about Freud's unorthodox clinical behavior:

> Professor Bergmann, speaking of deviating from psychoanalytic standards, what do you think of Freud's analyzing his daughter,

Anna, as an example of inappropriate analytic behavior? (Rachman, 2018, p. 65)

Bergmann, once again, disregarded my comment, and in a condescending and dismissive manner said the following:

People always bring this issue up to discredit Freud. (Rachman, 2018, p. 65)

With Bergmann's disrespectful response, I felt completely frustrated with being able to create a respectful and scholarly interchange with him and discontinued my debate.

The aftermath of Bergmann's Todschweigen campaign against Ferenczi

While I was initiating my debate with Bergmann, the audience was generally silent. It was difficult to understand the lack of response. I was initially upset that no one in an audience of about 100 individuals was able to voice any concern about Bergmann's denunciation of Ferenczi. I did have the thought that I became the enemy being seen as someone who attacked an aged, prominent, and revered psychoanalyst. Perhaps, I was seen as a mean-spirited, maverick who attacked a vulnerable 100-year-old man. After talking to some members of the audience after the event was finished, several of them, who were silent during the discussion, congratulated me on standing up to Bergmann. There was no one who was openly critical of me in this audience. However, some very negative criticism of me did emerge in discussions with some colleagues. I made contact with individuals who knew me and attended the Narrative to get feedback about my behavior with Bergmann, to check to see if I was inappropriate in any way. I did have some concern that I was seen as attacking an aged and revered figure. I said to these individuals, I was upset and angry regarding Bergmann's Todschweigen campaign against Ferenczi. I was also upset that I was uninformed that Bergmann had been invited to be a discussant after the performance of the Narrative. One colleague said, in no uncertain terms, that my behavior toward Bergmann during the discussion and my continued discontent indicated that: "you had a severe problem with anger." I do accept that I was angry during my debate with Bergmann. My confrontation with Bergmann, I believe, was respectful, scholarly, and informed. My continued anger after the narrative was based on the feeling that the colleague who diagnosed me with an anger disorder showed no empathic understanding of my dedication to stopping the Todschweigen campaign against Ferenczi, which I believe continues to be a harmful unspoken activity of traditional psychoanalysis. Diagnosing a dissident as having a psychological disorder has, unfortunately, been an institutionalized way to silence an analyst with whom up have disagreements. Fearing that I had offended Bergmann with my debate with him, I sent him a letter inviting him to enter into a dialogue with me about Ferenczi. My letter was sent on November 15, 2013. I did not receive a response from Bergmann before he died in January 2014.

Investigating Margin Bergmann's Todschweigen slander of Ferenczi's so-called "kissing technique"

Bergmann's false claim that, "Ferenczi was not a psychoanalyst because he let patients kiss him!" (Rachman, 2018, p. 65), has been a statement that has gone uncontested since the early 1930s, when Thompson spread rumors about Ferenczi's so-called acting out behavior with her. Thompson's behavior and Freud's negative reaction to Ferenczi's so-called non-analytic behavior deserves special attention because it is the foundation of traditional analysts claiming he was sexual with his analysands.

Ferenczi's trauma analysis with Clara Thompson

It is very important to investigate and present an alternative to Bergmann's false accusations that Ferenczi kissed his patients as part of his clinical method. This accusation has become the most standard slander of Ferenczi by traditional psychoanalysis. I will present a detailed discussion of the history of Freud's original attack on Ferenczi, suggesting he was sexually acting out with his patients. Bergmann's reference to Ferenczi kissing his patients was a rumor that was spread in the analytic community by Clara Thompson while

282 My attempts to confront the Todschweigen

she was in analysis with Ferenczi in the 1930s. Thompson stated the experience as follows in Ferenczi's *Clinical Diary*:

> I am allowed to kiss Papa Ferenczi, as I like. (Ferenczi, 1988, p. 2)

It is accurate that Thompson did kiss Ferenczi in a session. She initiated the kissing as an acting out of her erotic transference to Ferenczi. Thompson's behavior in her analytic sessions with Ferenczi was an issue which Ferenczi addressed in his *Clinical Diary*. In fact, his *Clinical Diary* began with Ferenczi's discussion of the difficulty Thompson was presenting for him. Ferenczi believed that Thompson kissing him was a misunderstanding of his empathic approach. She took it on herself to act out:

> See the case of Dm, (Thompson-f2, p. 3) a lady who, "complying" with my passivity, *had allowed herself to take more and more liberties and even kissed me.* (Ferenczi, 1988, p. 2)

It was not part of Ferenczi's method for any analysand to kiss him. Rather, it was Thompson's need for her to express her sexually tinged childhood relationship with her father, acting it out in the erotic transference to Ferenczi. It is questionable whether Thompson followed Ferenczi's analytic method of Trauma Analysis, since she did not seem to work through the issue of her childhood sexual abuse by her father, which was reported in the *Clinical Diary*. In the report of her analysis, the acting out in the erotic transference or the absence of any discussion of sexual trauma in her writings, all give some evidence to Thompson not integrating childhood sexual trauma into her thinking and personal knowledge. It is clear that Ferenczi did not initiate the kissing experience, but he did allow Thompson to express her erotic transference. He found the experience unpleasant:

> I first reacted to the unpleasantness that ensued with complete impassivity...But then the patient began to make herself ridiculous, ostentatiously...in her sexual conduct (for example at social gatherings, while dancing). (Ferenczi, 1988, p. 2)

My attempts to confront the Todschweigen 283

Ferenczi was practicing his pioneering technique of relaxation therapy (Ferenczi, 1930), where the analyst responds with empathic understanding to an analysand's need to express his/her unresolved childhood trauma into emotional expression, then into words to work through childhood trauma (Rachman, 1997a, 2003, 2018; Rachman & Klett, 2015). What is more, Ferenczi did not develop a "kissing technique" as part of his relaxation therapy to be used with trauma cases. After investigating Ferenczi's clinical behavior, there is no evidence to suggest he regularly acted out in an erotic manner with analysands (Rachman, 1993). Ferenczi was acutely aware of the transference implications of this complicated interaction he had co-created with Thompson:

> It became evident that here again was a case of repetition of the father-child situation. As a child, Dm. had been grossly abused sexually by her father. (Ferenczi, 1988, p. 3)

Freud had accepted the rumors of Ferenczi's so-called "acting out" in his new Trauma Analysis without checking with his friend. Freud wrote the now infamous *kissing letter* in which he denounced Ferenczi as developing a technique of kissing his analysands as a method for treating their traumas. What is more, he accused him of returning to:

> The inclination toward sexual games with patients…not alien to you in the pre-analytic times, so that one could put the new technique into context with the old misdemeanor. (Letter from Freud to Ferenczi, December 5, 1931. Falzeder et al., 2000, pp. 421–422)

Ferenczi was emotionally wounded by his mentor's severe criticism of his professional and personal functioning. This cited letter came at a time when these two giants of psychoanalysis were drifting apart over Ferenczi's search for independence from Freud (Rachman, 2018). As part of this continued attempt at emancipation, Ferenczi defined his new analytic method as being educated by his emotional capacity to work through earlier emotional issues, in his desire to become an analytically informed and well-functioning clinician:

"I consider your fear that I will turn into another Stekel unfounded. 'Youthful misdemeanors' when they have been overcome and analytically worked through, can even make one wiser and more careful than people who did not go through such trauma...Now, I believe I am capable of creating a mild passionless atmosphere... since I fear the dangers just as you do..." (Letter from Freud to Ferenczi, December 27, 1931. Falzeder et al., 2000, pp. 424–425).

Hopefully, my clarifications about Freud's accusation of Ferenczi's sexually acting out in the analysis with Thompson can gain a new perspective as a pioneering attempt in Trauma Analysis.

Heinz Kohut's neglect of Sándor Ferenczi

During the 1980s, I reviewed Heinz Kohut's contributions to the evolution of psychoanalysis with a particular interest in establishing his knowledge and appreciation of Ferenczi as his progenitor in the introduction of clinical empathy into psychoanalysis. In this attempt, I reviewed all of Kohut's published work until 1988, as well as discussions I had with Michael Basch, MD, and John Gedo, MD. My disappointment and resentment of Kohut's silence about the historic and pioneering contributions of Ferenczi's to the essential nature of clinical empathy was intense. I noted my disappointment, which was well-received by members of the American Academy of Psychoanalysis (Rachman, 1988, 1989). As an attempt to decipher Kohut's dramatic silence about Ferenczi, I wrote to some of the leading members of the Psychology of the Self Perspective. The late Michael Basch answered my request for understanding by urging me not to nurse discontent about Kohut. In his own way, he contributed to lifting the silence about Ferenczi's contributions to psychoanalysis and empathy with his own important statement, which attempted to integrate Ferenczi's contributions into the evolution of Psychoanalysis (Basch, 1984). Robert Stolorow (1976), now one of the most important thinkers in the Psychology of the Self Perspective, had earlier than Basch, made an important link between Self Psychology and a significant pioneering contributor to the study of empathy, the late Carl Rogers, PhD, when he outlined the parallels in client-centered therapy and Self Psychology.

My attempts to confront the Todschweigen   285

John Gedo's response to my request for Kohut's silence about Ferenczi's contributions on empathy, produced a dramatic response. He said that in his experience, as one of Kohut's earliest collaborators, he found him to discount the contributions of others in favor of his own formulations. Perhaps, Gedo was also voicing one of his own reasons for dissociating himself from Kohut. Kohut was not cordial to Gedo's attempts to contribute to his formulation of Self-Psychology. My attempts to contribute to a dialogue between the Ferenczi Analytic and the Self-Psychology communities has continued. Through a colleague, I became acquainted with the thinking of Ernest Wolf, one of Kohut's collaborators. He reported to me that Wolf was very receptive to and appreciated Ferenczi's work. The colleague shared a quote Wolf had told him to convey to me:

> Self Psychology developed in the spirit of Sándor Ferenczi (Ernest Wolf). (Raubolt, 1992)

There is a leader in the Self-Psychology perspective who has provided significant opportunities for receptivity and integration of other meaningful ideas. Joseph Lichtenberg, MD, Editor-in-Chief of *Psychoanalytic Inquiry* and Series Editor of *Psychoanalytic Inquiry Book Series*, through his journal and book series has encouraged a wide and enriched perspective to the Psychology of the Self Perspective by his encouragement and receptivity to integrating theory, research, and methodology from other relevant perspectives.

Clara Thompson, Elizabeth Severn, and Ferenczi's so-called kissing technique: a further note

As has been noted, Clara Thompson, an analysand of Ferenczi, was in analysis with him at the same time as Elizabeth Severn, spread rumors throughout the analytic community of Budapest and Vienna that she could kiss Ferenczi anytime she wanted. Here are the exact words reported by Ferenczi in his *Clinical Diary* about this issue:

> See the case of Dm, (Clara Thompson – Dupont, 1988, f3, p.3) a lady who, 'complying' with my passivity, had allowed herself to

take more and more liberty and *occasionally* kissed me...she remarked quite casually in the company of other patients...*I am allowed to kiss Papa Ferenczi as I like.* (Ferenczi, 1988, p. 2)

If one examines this quote in Ferenczi's *Clinical Diary*, it becomes clear that he began the *Diary* by describing the acting out of an erotic transference by Thompson, which was unanalyzed. The analysis of an erotic transference was not yet understood. Also, he was employing the Trauma Analysis method co-created with Elizabeth Severn, which created an empathic clinical attitude toward psychopathology, allowing the manifestations of childhood sexual trauma to naturally emerge. What is more, full emotional expression was encouraged. Ferenczi's thinking at the time of their analysis that Thompson was sexually abused by her father as a child. His idea was to create an erotic-free therapeutic relationship where the analysand could express and fully explore their childhood trauma in the safety of an analytic encounter. Ferenczi, it should be noted, allowed the active expression of Thompson's childhood trauma in the analytic encounter so that it could be fully analyzed. *Thompson initiated the kissing of Ferenczi. Ferenczi did not encourage her to kiss him.* Should have Ferenczi interpreted Thompson's acting out? At some meaningful point in the analysis, the answer is yes. Interpreting her behavior was not employed to create a holding environment for the childhood sexual experience. As Balint has indicated, Trauma Analysis was an experimental method, the first analytic technique to analyze trauma disorder. Psychoanalysis, in the 1930s, when this methodology was developed, had not, as yet, equally developed the analysis of an erotic-transference (Rachman, 2014). Our understanding of analyzing an erotic transference has progressed so that we now realize Thompson's kissing behavior was the expression of her childhood sexual trauma in the transference to Ferenczi. Welcoming this expression of a transference reaction, we now understand, can be used to retrieve the childhood trauma and begin its analysis (Rachman, Kennedy & Yard, 2005).

The rumor of Thompson and Ferenczi's sexual acting out, which reached Freud's ears in Vienna, was used to maintain and intensify the Todschweigen campaign against Ferenczi and Severn. Freud seemed to welcome this rumor, which likely intensified the other rumors that were circulating about Ferenczi's dissident and unorthodox analysis with Severn. Freud sent the infamous *Kissing Letter* (Letter from Freud to Ferenczi—December 5, 1931), to Ferenczi excoriating him for this so-called sexual behavior with analysands:

> *You have made no secret of the fact that you kissed your patients and let them kiss you,* I had also heard the same thing from my patients. (Falzeder et al., 2000, p. 241)

Freud is declaring that the analytic community knew that Ferenczi's new Relaxation Therapy and Trauma Analysis (Ferenczi, 1929, 1933, 1988), that he had developed, contained a technique of sexual interaction between the analyst and analysand. Freud did not contact Ferenczi before he sent the kissing letter to check with him whether the kissing of analysands was a regular part of Ferenczi's clinical method. He therefore, sent the kissing letter as a deliberate attempt to suppress and silence Ferenczi from using his Confusion of Tongues Theory to understand trauma disorder and Trauma Analysis. Furthermore, he said Ferenczi as a clinician was not adhering to the established standards of behavior for a psychoanalyst:

> Up to now in technique we have held fast…that erotic gratifications should be denied the patient…Now…what will be the consequences of making your technique public. (Falzeder et al., 2000, p. 422)

Freud, with Jones whispering into his ears, pushed the kissing rumor from what Ferenczi admitted was Thompson expressing the manifestations of her childhood trauma via the transference, into a new technique in his Trauma Analysis. As previously mentioned, Thompson forced the kissing on Ferenczi. He was annoyed with Thompson for misinterpreting his empathic approach. She may have thought Ferenczi was giving her approval to act out her childhood sexual trauma. Neither Thompson nor Freud understood that Ferenczi was *accepting her need and giving her psychological space to express these developmentally arrested feelings, not encouraging them.* By establishing such an empathic relationship, he was laying the foundation for these dissociated feeling to re-emerge. *What Freud, Jones, and the orthodox analytic community of the 1930s did not understand was that clinical empathy was the new methodology that Ferenczi was introducing into psychoanalysis, not sexual contact between analyst and analysand.* Freud goes on in the kissing letter to condemn Ferenczi for introducing and encouraging sexual contact between analyst and analysand as his ongoing technique, which will destroy psychoanalysis:

> Why stop with a kiss?...one will achieve still more if one adds 'pawing,' bolder ones will...take the further step of peeping and showing...soon we will have accepted into the technique of psychoanalysis the whole repertoire of 'demiviergerie' [seductions] and petting parties...and *Godfather Ferenczi looking at the busy scenery that he has created*, will possibly say to himself, perhaps, *I should have stopped in my technique of maternal tenderness before the kiss*...To the best of my recollection – *the inclination toward sexual games...with patients was not alien to you in the pre-analytic times* [Ferenczi's relationship with Elma Palos (see Rachman, 1993)], *so that one could put the new technique into context with the old misdemeanor.* The need for defiant self-assertion seems to me to more powerful in you than you recognize. (Falzeder et al., 2000, pp. 421–422)

I have discussed the emotional blow Ferenczi suffered from Freud's campaign to suppress and remove his Confusion of Tongues paper from psychoanalysis (Rachman, 2018, 2019b; also see Chapter 7). To this traumatic event, we must add the sentiments Freud expressed in the kissing letter where he declared that Ferenczi, a mature adult psychoanalyst with an international reputation as a successful clinician working with difficult cases, was being called by Freud, a sexually acting out adolescent. What is more, Freud accused Ferenczi as someone who has had a history of sexually acting out with patients before he became a psychoanalyst. It is important to address this false accusation because it has become a significant part of the Todschweigen campaign. Freud's Kissing Letter established the accusation as the truth spoken by the founder and leader of psychoanalysis. As I have indicated in the confrontation I had with professor Martin Bergmann on November 13, 2013, this accusation still remains alive and is believed to be the truth in contemporary psychoanalysis.

The late André Haynal, MD, a distinguished Ferenczi scholar, former Chairman and Professor of Psychiatry at the University of Geneva, Switzerland, and the Editorial Consultant for *The Correspondence of Sigmund Freud and Sándor Ferenczi*, has researched along with Ernst Falzeder, PhD, the personal and professional life of Ferenczi, including the implied sexual contact between Elma Pálos and Ferenczi mentioned by Freud in the kissing letter (Haynal & Falzeder, 1994). A triangle developed when Ferenczi first fell in love with Gizella Pálos and then with her daughter, Elma, who was in analysis with him for depression following the suicide of a friend. He became tormented by wanting to marry Elma. When this happened, he sent Elma to Freud to continue the analysis. First, Elma spent several months in analysis with Freud. Then Ferenczi explored the emotional difficulty between himself and Elma with Freud. Elma subsequently, returned to analysis with Ferenczi. The experience was further complicated by Freud taking a stand that Ferenczi should marry Gizella, the eldest of the two women, and not Elma, the woman with whom Ferenczi could have had a child. Ferenczi was angered by Freud's interference with his love life (Covello, 1984). This complicated triangulation was resolved when Ferenczi married Gizella (Haynal, 1993). Elma eventually married and moved to the United States.

In Haynal's description of the romance between Ferenczi and Elma, he mentioned that he: "became infatuated with Elma" (Haynal, 1993, p. 55). There was no mention by Haynal that there was any sexual contact between Elma and Ferenczi. I had also contacted Haynal on the issue of my researching the accusation that Ferenczi sexually acted out with his analysands. I asked him if he had any evidence that pointed to Ferenczi having sexual contact with Elma Pálos, or any other analysand. It was his opinion that Ferenczi did not have any sexual contact with an analysand (Haynal, 1992). In my own research on this issue that I reported in 1993, I incorporated Haynal's opinion and reached the following conclusion:

> On the basis of more than ten year's research on Ferenczi's clinical behavior, as revealed in his own work and described by

> his analysands, his colleagues, his friends, and other researchers, I have concluded that *there is no evidence that he engaged in any direct sexual behavior with patients or encouraged any analytic candidate, supervisee, or colleague to do so.* (Rachman, 1993, pp. 84–85)

This conclusion is consistent with previous examination of Ferenczi's "sexual behavior" as a clinician (Kaplan, 1975).

There is now additional research to reinforce the idea that Ferenczi did not clinically act out sexually with analysands. We now have new data on Ferenczi's clinical behavior over a period of years during his most experimental period when he was developing his Confusion of Tongues perspective and Trauma Analysis methodology. During the early 1930s, Ferenczi was involved in his "Grand Experiment" with analysands, such as, Elizabeth Severn and Clara Thompson, both of whom developed erotic transference to Ferenczi. Under such clinical circumstances, the clinical interaction would be ripe for sexual acting out. In my research on Elizabeth Severn, I had the availability of the Elizabeth Severn Papers (Rachman, 2016), which contained Severn's own words regarding the intimacies of her analysis with Ferenczi. Such documents are: the letters of Margaret Severn to her mother, Elizabeth Severn; Margaret Severn's autobiography *Spotlight*; Kurt Eissler's interview with Elizabeth Severn; out-of-print copies of Elizabeth Severn's three published books; and letters from Anna Freud, Karen Horney, and other colleagues and friends (Rachman, 2018). These materials were thoroughly examined for any data that reported clinical or extra-mural contact between Ferenczi and Severn. There are no data that any sexual contact occurred in any analytic session in the analysis between Ferenczi and Severn. There were instances of extra-mural contact between them as Ferenczi reported in his *Clinical Diary* (Ferenczi, 1988). There were instances, such as, when Ferenczi visited Severn's apartment to conduct sessions when she reported she could not get out of bed to visit him in his office. There are no data that indicate any sexual contact between Ferenczi and Severn under these circumstances. Also, Ferenczi's detailed discussion of his analysis with Severn in the *Clinical Diary* (Ferenczi, 1988) has no mention of any such contact. Severn's interview by Kurt Eissler in 1952, 19 years after she was terminated by Ferenczi, also have no data about sexual contact. This interview is particularly important because, in my opinion, Eissler was questioning Severn, in part, to discover any unorthodox clinical behavior between Severn and Ferenczi. Severn was very emotionally open with Eissler revealing data about Ferenczi's behavior and feelings as well as her own feelings about their relationship. Severn did not mention any inappropriate clinical behavior, including sexuality (Eissler, 1952; Rachman, 2018).

As I have previously suggested in this chapter, the kissing letter Freud sent to Ferenczi admonishing him about his non-analytic sexual acting with analysands, was stimulated by Clara Thompson's bragging to the analytic community that she could kiss Ferenczi anytime she wanted. I have also discussed that Thompson did kiss Ferenczi during their analytic sessions, to Ferenczi's annoyance, as an acting out of her erotic transference to Ferenczi as an expression of her childhood sexual trauma. Recently, I have turned to a colleague and friend, Ann D'Ercole, PhD, who is presently writing a biography of Clara Thompson (D'Ercole, 2019a), to use her diligent research to throw light on the kissing technique issue. I asked her if, in her research on Clara Thompson, she discovered any data about actual sexual contact between her and Ferenczi. Here is D'Ercole's response:

Arnold,

There is nothing in any reading to suggest that Ferenczi had sexual contact with Thompson. Rather, he allowed her to kiss him as an expression of affection. Was that "flirting" with sexuality?

The answer I think is yes only if the definition of sexuality includes any affectionate contact with another person. What if she hugged Ferenczi anytime she wanted, would that be sexual? (D'Ercole, 2019b).

Once again, *the kissing of Ferenczi by Thompson was not an approved technique developed by Ferenczi that he used with his analysands during the period he co-created Trauma Analysis with Elizabeth Severn* (Rachman, 2018).

Retraumatization of the analysand in the analytic situation: the analyst as an empathic responder

One of the important contributions Ferenczi's Confusion of Tongues perspective makes to understanding sexual trauma is that the analyst can retraumatize a sexually abused analysand by behaving in an analytic session that mirrors aspects of the original trauma(s) evoked by the abusive parent of childhood. Understanding this previously unexamined phenomena, Ferenczi described the importance of a relational, two-person experience in the clinical interaction when he described the *concept of professional hypocrisy*:

> We ask...[the patient]...to start with his associations and promise him faithfully that we will listen attentively to him, give our undivided interest to his well-being...In reality...it may happen that can only with difficulty tolerate certain external or internal features of the patient, or...we feel unpleasantly disturbed in some professional or personal affair by the analytic session....I cannot see any other way out than to make the source of the disturbance in us fully conscious and to discuss it with the patient, admitting it perhaps not only as a possibility but as a fact. (Ferenczi, 1933, p. 159)

Ferenczi in examining his own subjective experience, realized that he had thoughts and feelings about an analysand that were relevant to their analytic experience that he needed to convey, understand and analyze:

> Something had been left unsaid in the relation between physician and patient, something insincere, and its *frank discussion freed, so to speak, the tongue-tied patient*, the admission of the analyst's error produced confidence in his patient. (Ferenczi, 1933, p. 159)

When Ferenczi was able to self-disclose the negative feelings he had to Elizabeth Severn in their analysis (Rachman, 2018), it helped create an atmosphere of safety and empathy, which allowed the analysis of childhood traumas. The professional hypocrisy that Ferenczi discovered was the emotional dishonesty of the analyst by not taking responsibility for his contribution for the disturbance in the relationship, which led to a therapeutic impasse and retraumatization:

> *The restrained coolness*, the professional hypocrisy and – hidden behind it but never revealed – a dislike of the patient...*was not essentially different from that which in his childhood had led to the illness. When, in addition to the strain caused by this analytical situation, we imposed on the patient the further burden of reproducing the original trauma, we created a situation that was indeed unbearable.* Small wonder that our efforts produced no better results than the original trauma...the willingness on our part to admit our mistakes and the honest endeavor to avoid them in future, all these go to create in the patient a confidence in the analyst. *It is this confidence that establishes the contrast between the present and the unbearable traumatogenic past*, the contrast which is absolutely necessary for the patient in order to enable him to re-experience the past no longer as hallucinatory reproduction but as an objective memory. (Ferenczi, 1933, pp. 159–160)

This Confusion of Tongues perspective makes it clear that the analyst needs to become aware of and analyze his/her unrecognized feelings toward an analysand, which includes any positive, negative, or erotic feelings so as to prevent recreating the original childhood trauma in the analytic situation. Through a two-person perspective, the analyst examines his/her own subjective experience as it impinges on the subjective experience of the analysand. The analyst's conscious and unconscious functioning determines whether the analytic encounter will become a therapeutic, healing experience, or recreate the childhood traumas.

The idea of retraumatization of analysands demands that the analyst creates an erotic-free analytic encounter. The analyst becomes a traumatogenic agent if he/she acts out sexually or harbors unanalyzed sexual feelings toward an analysand. I have taken a long journey discussing Ferenczi's clinical behavior with analysands, particularly, Elizabeth Severn and Clara Thompson. I believe there was no sexual contact with these analysands. What is more, I have also presented a discussion of Ferenczi's major theoretical thinking, the Confusion of Tongues perspective, and the central issue of re-traumatization in the psychoanalytic situation. Of singular importance in Ferenczi's theory, is that the analyst must guard against contributing sexuality to the clinical interaction because it is totally counter to creating a therapeutic experience where the childhood sexual trauma is retrieved, analyzed, and worked through in an atmosphere of safety and empathy (Rachman, 2018).

To return to Professor Bergmann's accusation that Ferenczi should not be considered an analyst because he kissed his patients, the clinical and theoretical discussion I have presented establishes two important findings:

1. Ferenczi's clinical theory, namely, the Confusion of Tongues, clearly states that actual sexual contact between analyst and analysand is traumatogenic. The analyst's mandate is to create an erotic-free therapeutic atmosphere in the analytic encounter. His introduction of countertransference analysis was a clinical safeguard against the analyst acting out any sexual feelings. The idea is that the subjective feelings of the analyst must be identified, confronted, and analyzed. This clinical mandate by Ferenczi to analyze the analyst's subjectivity is a landmark paradigm shift for psychoanalysis. It is a belief absolutely contradictory to being sexually involved with an analysand. If Freud was not open to listening to Ferenczi when he presented it. At that meeting, which has been discussed (See Chapters 5 and 7), Freud was angry at Ferenczi because he was convinced his once favorite student was encouraging sexual contact with analysands in his Trauma Analysis. He did not understand that Ferenczi's method discouraged that kind of behavior. Sexual contact in an analytic encounter is inherently anti-therapeutic and traumatogenic.

2. The results of investigating Ferenczi, his analysands and colleagues, has not revealed that he had actual sexual contact with analysands. Clara Thompson's desire to spread a rumor of Ferenczi's implied erotic contact with her, is puzzling. According to Ann D'Ercole (2019c), Thompson did not like Elizabeth Severn, the analysand with who Ferenczi spent the most time and energy. Was she angry at Ferenczi for preferring Severn to her, indicated by the time, energy,

and emotional connection he shared to Severn? Thompson was also critical of Ferenczi for allowing Severn to be so influential in his thinking and functioning (D'Ercole, 2019c). Thompson's silence in the face of the sexual accusations against Ferenczi contributed to the Todschweigen campaign. Of course, Thompson could not defend Ferenczi because, I believe, she may have been in a dissociative state, not aware her kissing behavior was sexually tinged or her bragging about it would do harm to her analyst's reputation. Her potential dissociative state could be attributed to her childhood sexual trauma, which was reported in Ferenczi's *Clinical Diary* (Ferenczi, 1988). Recently, D'Ercole (2019a) has raised the question as to whether Thompson was a sexual abuse survivor. We will need to wait for the publication of her biography on Clara Thompson to see whether Thompson's complicated behavior was due to sexual trauma.

Chapter 30

Contemporary activities which contribute to an appreciation of Ferenczi and the Budapest School of Psychoanalysis

There are some recent attempts to reverse the Todschweigen campaign against Ferenczi. Five such projects will be described: The Irish Psycho-Analytic Association (IPAA) Conference in Dublin, Ireland, The Budapest School of Analysis on May, 2019; Harold Kooden, Ph.D., Michael Larivière's, PhD, book, *Rediscovering Sándor Ferenczi: A festschrift for Arnold Wm. Rachman, Ph.D.* Kooden and Larivière are contributing their appreciation of Arnold Wm. Rachman's attempts to return Sàndor Ferenczi's pioneering contributions to contemporary psychoanalysis (Kooden & Larivière 2019). The third contribution will be the proposal of a new book by Clara Mucci, PhD, an Italian psychoanalyst, Ferenczi scholar, and traumatologist, and myself, entitled, *Confusion of Tongues Theory of Trauma: A relational/neurobiological perspective* (Rachman & Mucci, 2019d). A colleague and friend, Paul Mattick, PhD, formerly chairman, the Department of Philosophy, Adelphi University, and Professor of Philosophy, and I are preparing a book entitled, *Freud's Confusion of Tongues: The case of Dora, Oedipal conflict or childhood sexual abuse* (Rachman & Mattick, 2019e) (see Figure 0.9). The fifth project, in an attempt to contribute to a return of Ferenczi and the Budapest School to significance in contemporary psychoanalysis involves new evidence about the Wolf Man. In preparing my book on Elizabeth Severn (Rachman, 2018), I ran across a notation in Jeffrey Masson's book, *The Assault on Truth*, which listed that Ruth Mack-Brunswick had writing a paper on the Wolf Man which threw new light on the analysis of the case. I have contacted Jim Hutson, Head, Manuscript Division, the Library of Congress, to obtain the Mack-Brunswick paper. This paper, as well as Mack-Brunswick's

DOI: 10.4324/9780429298431-30

Contemporary activities 297

notes on her analysis of the Wolf Man were sent to me. In the near future, I plan to write a book on these new, never published materials entitled, *Freud's Case of the Wolf Man: Sergei Pankejeff as a Survivor of Sexual Abuse* (Rachman, 2019f).

Figure 0.9 Freud"s Confusion of Tongues: book cover collage by Arnold Wm. Rachman, April 2, 2021.

The Irish Psycho-Analytic Association (IPAA) Conference May 10–11, 2019, Dublin, Ireland

At the 2017, Sándor Ferenczi Seminars in Florence, Italy, I met Fergal Brady, PhD, for the first time. The Ferenczi Seminars were initiated and organized by Carlo Bonomi, PhD, at the time, the President of the International Sándor Ferenczi Network. For the first time, courses were offered to the international community by recognized Ferenczi scholars. Fergal Brady, who studied Ferenczi's work at the University of Sheffield, England, attended the Ferenczi Seminars in May of 2017, in which I gave a seminar on Elizabeth Severn and the development of trauma studies and treatment. The Severn Seminar was the first attempt I had made to report of my research about Severn to a European audience. Fergal was very interested in the case material about Severn as he felt he had been doing clinical work with similar patients. He also asked if I could spend some of the seminar time with his presenting a clinical case for supervision. The case was, as Fergal suggested, a very difficult case of sexual trauma. I attempted to integrate the ideas of Ferenczi, Severn, and Balint in the understanding and analysis of his analysand's childhood trauma. Fergal appreciated our interaction and we became friends as well as colleagues. The following May 2018, at the International Sándor Ferenczi Conference in Florence, Italy, we discussed organizing a Ferenczi Conference in Ireland. Fergal contacted me in the fall of 2018, saying he was interested in organizing a Ferenczi Conference on behalf of the Irish Psycho-Analytic Association (IPAA), of which Fergal was the president.

Irish Psycho-Analytic Association

The IPAA was the first psychoanalytic organization to be organized in Ireland. During the 1920s, Jonathan Hanaghan was sent to Ireland in the 1920s by Ernest Jones to initiate psychoanalysis there. Jones said: "It will take a Celt to start up psychoanalysis in Ireland" (Brady, 2019).

Over the period of the fall and winter of 2018, the program for the conference was developed (see Figure 0.10). The organizer of the conference, Fergal Brady, realizing the Irish Psycho-Analytical had a rich history of the Freudian tradition, invited a colleague, Dr. Marcus Bowman, to present the paper entitled, "The Development and Consequences of Freud's Seduction Theory." Brady also invited Dr. Judith Mezaros, the president of the Sándor Ferenczi Society,

IPAA 2019 - Conference Agenda
11 May, Lexicon Theatre, Dun Laoghaire, Dublin

09.30 Registration

10.00 Welcome – Barbara Fitzgerald – IPAA Vice President

10.05 IPAA President's Address – A Budapest State of Mind – Fergal Brady

10.45 Dr Marcus Bowman – The Development and Consequences of Freud's Seduction Theory

11.10 Coffee Break

11.30 Dr Arnold Rachman – Dr Elizabeth Severn: The Evil Genius of Psychoanalysis

13.00 Lunch

14.00 IPAA@The Movies – A special documentary on Ferenczi made as part of the 'Major Figures of the 20th century series' – Introduced by Dr Judit Meszaros

15.00 Dr Judit Meszaros – Why Ferenczi Today?

15.25 Coffee & Animated Short: The Confusion of Tongues – Em Cooper (2018 Emmy Nominee).

15.40 Dr Arnold Rachman – The Confusion of Tongues : Revolutionary Paradigm Shift for Psychoanalysis

16.05 Panel Session – Chair: Ros Forlenza

16.20 Bringing Psychoanalysis to the NHS: The Balint Group – Christine Christie

17.00 Video presentation: Circumcision, Self-analysis and Countertransference by Robin Buick RHA.

17.45 Conference Close

#Ipaa19

27 Seatown Place, Dundalk, Co Louth
Website: www.psychoanalyst.ie
Email: ipaa1942@gmail.com
Phone: +353 42 933 1803
Mobile: +353 86 811 9473

Figure 0.10 Announcement. Irish Psych-Analytical Association Conference. May 11, 2019.

Budapest, Hungary, to represent the contemporary perspective of the Budapest School of Psychoanalysis. I presented two papers: Elizabeth Severn "as a person, clinician and collaborator of Sándor Ferenczi"; discussing the clinical issue of childhood sexual abuse in the analysis between Sándor Ferenczi and Elizabeth Severn; "The Confusion of Tongues: Sándor Ferenczi and the Budapest School of Psychoanalysis: Revolutionary Paradigm Shift for Psychoanalysis" (Rachman, 2019b,c), discussing the paradigm shift of Ferenczi's alternate theory, from the consideration of the Oedipal Theory to the advance of a new alternative of a Trauma Theory. Finally, Christine Christie was invited to conduct a Balint Group.

This conference was the best experience I have had. The participants were very enthusiastic, positive, and knowledgeable. They were very receptive to the ideas and clinical experiences of Ferenczi and the Budapest School of Psychoanalysis. It is important to mention, there was an important ingredient to this conference. These individuals showed wonderful warmth, friendliness, and appreciation. I also very much appreciated that my books were available for sale, which was arranged by Fergal Brady, and they sold out. I never felt so welcomed or appreciated at any conference I have attended. The conference was reported to have stimulated new interest in Ferenczi and the Budapest School of Psychoanalysis. In the next section of this chapter, Fergal Brady will describe his interest in Ferenczi and Budapest School and impact of the conference on the Irish Psychoanalytic Community.

Fergal Brady on Arnold, Ferenczi, Elizabeth Severn, and the Todschweigen

"Over the course of my training and experience in and of psycho-analysis I have been struck by the mystery surrounding the experience clients report when talking about their experiences of sexual abuse. At the University of Sheffield my research interest was in what I called the phylogenetic structure of child sexual abuse. there I came across the work of Sándor Ferenczi. I read the Confusion of Tongues and thought about it as a tour de force, I still do. I also came across, for the first time, the work of Jeffrey Masson and the controversy of Freud's abandonment, or otherwise, of his seduction theory. I never put much time or energy into studying that latter issue, feeling as I did that it was a moot or academic point and of no particular use to my client. I come to this whole thing very much from the point of view of a clinician rather than an academic."

It does, however, give us a window into a key part of the whole issue of the sexual abuse of children and of vulnerable adults. That is, a kind of shoot the messenger attitude that we see again and again and certainly hear of it from clients in our consulting rooms. It seems clear that Sandor Ferenczi was very much aware of this in his final years. He made meticulous notes in his clinical diary but kept them secretly, from Freud in particular. He wrote the paper, the Confusion of Tongues from his experience of listening to the stories his clients were telling him at that time. In particular, he enjoyed (if that is the right word) a fruitful and deep working relationship with Elizabeth Severn, from whom he learned so much about the effects of abusive relationships on the psyche. And he seems to have had an innate sense that his insights would not be welcomed by mainstream psychoanalysis and by Freud in particular.

There is a peculiar kind of paradox and indeed pathos in what seems like a kind and sincere man working with these, mainly woman clients and having to hide the truth of what he was uncovering because of his anticipation of a hostile response. How right he was.

Through the work of Michael Balint in particular and in a small school of scholars who formed a loose Budapest School. And over decades, the work of Ferenczi gradually became known to a wider audience. I suppose you could say that I was part of that wider audience: I too was bitten by the bug, filled with all kinds of intrigue and identifications even with this extraordinary man. I began to travel to learn more about him and his work.

My travels brought me to Florence and the Summer School of the International Sándor Ferenczi Network. I had attended a few International Ferenczi events and saw the 2017 Summer Course advertised. It was a series of presentations over 5 days by experts in the field including Arnold. The idea was that there would be time for workshops and attendees were encouraged to bring clinical vignettes which could be discussed. I suppose you could say that that set in train a sequence of events that brought us all here today.

I spent a bit of time preparing a clinical vignette which illustrated in a new way a controversy which is central to the Freud Ferenczi conflict or controversy. It is central, I believe to what I call a Budapest State of Mind, which is the title of my talk. And finally, it points to a way of working in the Ferenczian tradition of experimentation and innovation. My supervisor in Ireland, Ros Forlenza translated my paper into Italian.

My paper was about real trauma versus fantasy. I think every one of us who works with supervisors of sexual abuse has experience of sitting with a client wondering and trying to help figure out what is real and what is not. It is one of the things that attracted me to Ferenczi in the first place. Reading his clinical diary and trying to understand how he and she made sense of Elizabeth Severn's recollections of her childhood trauma. I wanted to know how he worked with that.

Arnold and I got talking one day over coffee. I was just this guy from Ireland with this story to tell and he was presenting at the Summer school the ongoing research he was doing into Ferenczi's work with Elizabeth Severn, having secured her papers. He was very interested in my work and very generous with his time; arranging a meeting with me where I could tell him about my work around sexual trauma and the role, I felt fantasy played.

Over the next couple of days, it became clear that there wasn't going to be time in the daily schedule to hear the clinical vignettes. And then Arnold made an extraordinarily generous gesture. He cut his presentation short and devoted 90 minutes of the time allotted to him to give me an opportunity to present my paper. It was, as I have said, a very generous thing to do. He introduced me with the minimum of fuss and did not want to be thanked really and treated it like the most normal thing to do. I have never met anyone quite like him.

It was during our second trip to Florence the following Spring that we first agreed to the idea of organizing a Conference in Dublin.

In my research I had concluded that there was ancient, phylogenetic knowledge deep in the unconscious around how to behave when confronted with the sexual abuse of children. In my view groups give away this knowledge of you read the way they behave. The family is the primary group in this regard. How often do we find the group closing ranks and denying the experience of the individual who comes forward to speak of their abuse? It is my contention that this is at play within the field of psychoanalysis in the way Sándor Ferenczi's work with Elizabeth Severn in particular was treated over any decades. It is through the research and determination of Arnold and others that this is now being brought to light.

For this reason, I believe Elizabeth Severn's story is as relevant today as it ever was. It was worth bringing alive again and worth bringing to a wider audience. Arnold and I had discussion on this subject and he warmly accepted my invitation to come to Dublin and address a Conference which we called *The Budapest School of Psychoanalysis: from Ferenczi to Balint and Beyond.* Arnold suggested that Judith Meszaros might like to contribute and she also accepted an invitation and spoke at our conference.

During this time, the clinical vignette that I had presented in Florence at the Summer School of 2017 had grown and, with support from Carlo Bonomi it had become a paper, an extract of a case history. It was published in 2019 under the title *An Extract of the analysis of the Monkey Puzzle Boy*. It too formed part of the 2019 Dublin Conference and from it came an Avant Garde video art presentation called *Circumcision, Self-analysis and Countertransference* which formed part of the conference program.

The conference was well-attended and was well-received critically. So much so that we organized a follow-up event the following Autumn in the same venue. The follow-up event allowed much more time for discussion as time was at a premium the first time around and there was a thirst for further discussion of the themes of the conference.

I had not come across the term Todschweigen until the publication of Arnold's book on Elizabeth was published in 2018. I am very familiar with the feel of a Todschweigen all the same. It fits with what I had been studying and dealing with in my practice for 15 years. The person who brings the message of the sexual abuse of children is regarded as a threat to the cohesion of the group and is succinctly ignored. In a comment from one of the respondents to my research, it is described as being "like the tide going out."

As part of my presentation at the Dublin conference, I wove the fairy story of Chicken Licken into my talk. I believe in the United States it is better known as Ready Penny. My point in including this story, which almost everybody at the conference had heard of, is that my interpretation of the fairy tale is the very point I believe we come across with sexual abuse and a Todschweigen. The collective, the group feels it cohesiveness under threat when an individual had an important story to tell. A story of their own real experience. A real experience, not an imagined one, not a fantasy. This seems important. Part of the Todschweigen is to cast doubt on the voracity of the story being told. That is how it begins, the backlash.

Before I finish, let us return for a list visit to our intrepid hero Chicken Licken to see how he is getting on. When we left, Turkey Lurkey had met the fowl rabble and joined them in their odyssey to find the king to tell him the sky was falling in.

Shortly afterwards they all met Foxy Loxy on the road. He was a sly old fox and he saw an opportunity.

"'I know where to find the king,' said Foxy Loxy. 'you had better all follow me.'

Foxy Loxy led then straight into his den, where his wife and their little foxes were waiting for their dinners. Then the foxes ate Chicken Licken, Henny Penny, Cocky Locky, Ducky Lucky, Drakey Lakey, Goosey Loosey and Turkey Lurkey for their dinners. So, Chicken Licken never found the king to tell him that he thought the sky was falling down."

It's a bit of a sad end for Chicken Licken, the intrepid hero of the tale. But, well we all enjoy chicken or coq au vin or duck, goose or: Turkey especially at Christmas or Thanksgiving, in that regard we are being asked, seduced, into identifying with the fox. We all eat farmyard fowl. And Chicken Licken, you see, well did become hysterical running around, causing a fuss, spreading hysteria among the other farm yard fowl.

"Don't do that," is the moral of this tale. Don't hold up your hand and shout out your pain. Shut up and put up. The king doesn't want to know. You are only upsetting the cohesion of the farmyard.

There's one other thing; in my reading of this. We need to wonder about the narrator, the storyteller. What is their motivation? The lie, you see, in my reading of this, in the first few lines.

"One day an acorn fell from a tree and hit Chicken Licken on the head. Chicken Licken thought that the sky was falling down. So, he ran off to tell the king."

Harold Kooden, Southgate, Ladybird, 1969.

It is a sinister tale. We tell it to children. It tells them not to be hysterical, not to be going running around telling everyone everything. And the sky is not falling down, it is an acorn, get over it.

What if the Chicken Licken in the modern retelling is a homeless person? An Immigrant.

What if the Chicken Licken is a child? Saying 'a grown up touched me.'"

Rediscovering Sándor Ferenczi: A festschrift for Arnold Wm. Rachman, PhD

To contribute to the continuing effort to educate the psychoanalytic community to the significance of Sándor Ferenczi's contributions to the evolution of psychoanalysis as well as its contemporary application, Michael Larivière has developed a new book, *Harold Kooden, Ph.D. and Michael Larivière, Ph.D.'s book: A festschrift for Arnold Wm. Rachman, Ph.D.* (Kooden & Larivière, Larivière, 2019c).

They have gathered together a number of psychoanalysts, students, and analysands who are familiar with Arnold Rachman's research and publications on Sándor Ferenczi, his teaching on empathy, clinical responsiveness, noninterpretative therapeutic measures; countertransference analysis, and Trauma Analysis, as well as clinical practice of Relational Analysis. By highlighting these contemporary developments based on Ferenczi's ideas and methods, they contributing to reversing the Todschweigen campaign against Ferenczi.

"Arnold's imagination was very early on captured by psychoanalysis. So much so that it became for him, in William James' words as recalled by Adam Phillips, something 'to be going on from'.

He believes psychoanalysis can make people feel alive in ways they prefer, that it can even help them actually get the lives they want. And one of the psychoanalysts, he believes offers the kind of psychoanalysis needed for this to have a chance of happening is Sándor Ferenczi. In his work of over 40 years, Arnold has sought to, as it were, recreate Ferenczi, reimagine him, fully invoke him, resurrect him, to offer life to what had become a shadow. He has strived to forge a style that is capable of evoking the shivering ambiguities of what is experienced by both parties in the course of an analysis, coupling the need to show empathy with the need to be true to what it is liken all its variety and fullness.

His first contributions involved examining the issues of theory and technique in analytic group therapy, first and foremost with adolescents. He was one of the first analytic group therapists to publish papers in America on the introduction of encounter and intensive group therapy, as well as noninterpretative measures in analytic group psychotherapy. He then went on to publish books, as well as numerous articles, on Ferenczi's contribution to psychoanalysis, demonstrating that it was he, Ferenczi, and not Kohut, who had first insisted on the importance of clinical empathy in analysis. He further re-evaluated Ferenczi's introduction of noninterpretative measures as meaningful in the analysis of trauma cases.

He also contributed toward calling back to attention, in America, the work of other important analysts, such as Michael Balint and, more recently, Elizabeth Severn (and, with them, The Budapest School of Psychoanalysis).

So it was only right, that we should pay tribute to Arnold with a book honouring both his academic and clinical career: a *Festschrift.*"

Confusion of Tongues Theory of Trauma: A Relational/ Neurobiological Perspective

Clara Mucci, PhD, and myself are proposing a new book, entitled, *Confusion of Tongues Theory of Trauma: A Relational/Neurobiological Perspective* (Rachman & Mucci, 2019). Clara Mucci is an Italian psychoanalyst, traumatologist, Ferenczi scholar, and theoretician of the borderline disorder and its treatment. We have come together over our joint interest in childhood trauma, Ferenczi, and the Confusion of Tongues paradigm. It has been nearly a century since Ferenczi presented his Confusion of Tongues paper at the 12th International Psychoanalytic Conference in Wiesbaden. Immediately, Freud, Jones and the orthodox analytic community attempted to silence this alternate theory, by denouncing Ferenczi personally and professionally. In a courageous move, Ferenczi presented this important paper over the objections of Freud and his followers. The paper was so seriously neglected by the analytic community that it was not published in English until 17 years after it was presented (Rachman 1997b). The Todschweigen campaign to silence the ideas in the Confusion of Tongues paper was so successful, that the ideas disappeared from the psychoanalysis, including the United States and Europe, for over 50 years. Consequently, psychoanalysis has neglected the Confusion of Tongues paradigm and its significance as an important statement about the sexual abuse of individuals for our society.

We believe that it is time to recognize that the Confusion of Tongues idea created a paradigm shift for psychoanalysis in the following way:

1. It identified the phenomenon of trauma disorder where individuals suffered from the effects of actual trauma in their abusive relationships with their patients.
2. In a trauma disorder, there are a series of psychodynamic developments which have specific effects on personality development (e.g., confusion, fragmentation, and dissociation).
3. A new methodology, noninterpretive measures were developed for the treatment of trauma disorder.
4. A new treatment regime, called Trauma Analysis, was introduced.
5. The nature of the therapeutic relationship was changed so that a two-person, mutually analytic interaction was established.

It is time to establish the Confusion of Tongues perspective as a meaningful set of ideas and methods which are significant contribution to psychoanalysis and society in the necessity to confront and treat childhood sexual abuse of children, youth, and adults.

Present relational trauma theory and neurobiology, we believe, have confirmed Ferenczi ideas. Early relational trauma as described by Allen Schore (1944) aids in our understanding of how a lack of parent/child attunement affects the child's social and cognitive brain. The introjection of a victim—persecutor dyad (both early relational and active maltreatment) are responsible for the dissociative structure (Liotti, 2014), characteristic of severe pathology. The Confusion of Tongues concept has also been expanded into a relational-based perspective (Mucci, 2017; Rachman, 1994, 2000, 2007, 2012, 2016, 2019a; Rachman & Klett, 2015).

Mucci (2017, 2018), has developed the concept of "embodied witnessing." The Analysis of Trauma incorporates the analyst as a witness to the analysand's trauma. Ferenczi said: the analyst was as: "a benevolent and helpful witness" (Ferenczi, 1988). Analysands need a witness to the abuse to help them accept the trauma and recover from it. The analyst functions as a container and an embodiment of the analysand's dissociated parts, the parts that cannot be recognized within themselves because of splitting between mind and body. This concept has been uniquely applied to a wide range of clinical situations (Mucci, 2017, 2018; Rachman & Klett, 2015; Rachman, 2016, 2018b). We pay tribute to Ferenczi's capacity to witness and empathize with an analysand's traumatic suffering as rendered by his statement: "My ability to glue her lacerated soul into a whole" (Ferenczi, 1988).

Van de Kolk (2014) stated unequivocally that the society and the scientific community continue to be in denial regarding the epidemic proportions of the delirious effects of sexual abuse of children by parental figures. Why does this continuous neglect occur? It is our opinion that professional and the lay public alike, cannot accept that sexual abuse occurs by people like themselves. Freud changed the prevalent notion that sexual abusers of children were criminals. He demonstrated that the sexual abusers of children were from middle class families. We still do not want to accept that Freud's discovery, and Ferenczi's validation of it, was accurate. It is people like ourselves who are abusing children and are responsible for their trauma disorders. We believe that psychoanalysis and society continue to neglect the issue of the sexual abuse of children, youth, and adults. We will examine this neglect from a historical, psychodynamic, and neurobiological point of view.

Freud's Confusion of Tongues: The Case of Dora, Oedipal Conflict of Childhood Sexual Abuse

My colleague Paul Mattick, and I believe that Freud's analysis of Dora, Ida Bauer, was based on his interpretation that she suffered from an Oedipal conflict disorder which was inaccurate (Rachman & Mattick, 2019c). According to our investigation, Freud neglected data, which indicated that sexual abuse and maternal trauma were significant psychodynamics in the development of Dora's psychopathology. Mr. K., a family friend, approached Dora as a teenager with sexual overtures. Freud described this material in the case history, but did not use it in the analysis of the psychodynamics of her psychological disorder. In other words, the sexual overture by Herr K. was not taken into account in his Oedipal interpretation. Another issue that was neglected indicated Dora suffered emotional deprivation from her mother, which could explain some of her symptomatology. Our conclusions were that Freud was so bound by a unitary explanation for human behavior in his Oedipal theory, that he could not respond to any other data. This may have been true in the issue of empathy. Freud's aggressive interpretations of Oedipal issues may have interfered with his being empathic to Dora's sexual abuse or maternal deprivation.

Freud's Case of the Wolf Man: Sergei Pankejeff as a Survivor of Sexual Abuse

One of the most dramatic examples, I believe, in psychoanalysis' neglect of the issue of childhood sexual trauma is contained in Freud's iconic Case of the Wolf Man (Freud, 1918). In his description of the Wolf Man's childhood history, Freud does note that there was childhood sexual contact with his older sister. However, this sexual interaction does not inform Freud's psychodynamic formulation of Sergie Pankejeff's serious emotional problems. Rather his explanation for his diagnosis and treatment of Pankejeff was focused on *the Dream of Wolves*. The data of childhood sexual activity was ignored. I wish to present in a proposed book (Rachman, 2019e), that Freud ignored evidence, that sexual abuse was a necessary and sufficient explanation for Pankejeff's emotional disorder. What is more, I have done research on Pankejeff's second analysis with Ruth Mack Brunswick. On the suggestion of Jeffrey Mousiaeff Masson, PhD, found in his book, *The Assault on Truth* (Masson, 1984), that Ruth Mack Brunswick had written an unpublished paper citing that Pankejeff was sexually abused by a family member. Mack Brunswick did not inform Freud of this fact, which emerged in her second analysis of the former Russian nobleman. I have found Mack Brunswick's unpublished paper as well as an extensive series of notes she developed during her analysis of Pankejeff, which will be combined with my re-evaluation of Freud's case of the Wolf Man (Rachman, 2019e).

Chapter 31

Truth and reconciliation: traditional psychoanalysis owes Ferenczi an apology for their Todschweigen campaign against him

An apology is considered, "an admission of error or discourtesy accompanied by an expression of regret" (Merriam-Webster Dictionary, 2009). I believe Traditional Psychoanalysis owes an apology to Sándor Ferenczi and the Ferenczi Psychoanalytic Community for the deliberate attempts to suppress and silence his ideas and methods from what has been considered mainstream psychoanalysis. As has been pointed out, this Todschweigen, Death by Silence, campaign (Rachman, 1999, 2018) was very successful because Ferenczi's importance for the evolution of psychoanalysis disappeared from our field (Rachman, 1997b, 2007). Consequently, generations of psychoanalysts were deprived of his contributions: subjective experience of the analyst; clinical empathy; trauma disorder and trauma analysis; the Confusion of Tongues perspective; non-interpretive measures; two-person psychology perspective; and the origins of relational analysis to name a few. These ideas could have provided psychoanalysis with an opportunity to expand its boundaries to integrate a new perspective, which could have been integrated into the mainstream. Ferenczi's ideas and methods were pioneering innovations for the analysis so-called, *difficult cases* (sever neurotic, narcissistic, borderline, and psychotic disorders). What is more, Ferenczi's clinical work with difficult cases like Elizabeth Severn (Rachman, 2018) uncovered that such cases may have had at its origins in childhood sexual, as well as physical and emotional, abuse. Ferenczi's important discovery could have embraced a new category, for psychoanalysis, trauma disorders, for its theory and treatment perspective. It was Ferenczi's wish that his Confusion of Tongues paradigm would stand, side-by-side, with Freud's Oedipal

DOI: 10.4324/9780429298431-31

theory. By considering Ferenczi's ideas as harmful to psychoanalysis, rather than prophetic, mainstream analytic functioning became restricted and closed the door to consideration of trauma disorders, childhood sexual abuse, and analysis of trauma (Rachman, 2018).

There was also an emotional price paid for the Todschweigen campaign. An institutionalized philosophy was created where tradition triumphed over dissent. Doctrine triumphed over creative thinking and experimental activity. Orthodoxy triumphed over liberalism. Conformity triumphed over freedom. Freud's shattering of society's thinking about human behavior through his discovery of child sexual abuse as an origin of psychological disorder was a brilliant discovery. It should not have been changed. Freud should have won a Nobel Prize. If, he felt it was an insufficient explanation, he could have added the Oedipal Complex Theory to expand it. But the Seduction Theory should not have been discarded, because Ferenczi's work verified it. Contemporary work with trauma survivors demonstrated it was prophetic (Mucci, 2017, 2018; Rachman & Klett, 2015). It brought childhood sexual abuse into the light for society to see that it was an important psychological and social problem. Traditional psychoanalysis has played an influential role in society's thinking. When Freud and his orthodox followers made the Oedipal Complex Theory the cornerstone of psychoanalysis, the incest trauma and childhood sexual abuse disappeared from consideration. The *deadly silence* from psychoanalysis about the molestation of children influenced a neglect of interest in clinical circles of psychoanalysis and psychotherapy, and in society's concern about sexual abuse. If you combine this factor of neglect by psychoanalysis and society toward sexual abuse and combine it with incest and sexual abuse survivors losing their voice to speak about their trauma, the silence about sexual abuse of children, youth, and adults is deafening. Survivors of sexual trauma are beginning to find their voice, such as the #MeToo Movement (see Chapter 21). Survivors are asking authorities who harmed them to apologize to heal their wounds. I believe Traditional Psychoanalysis should apologize for the harm they did to Ferenczi and the Budapest School of Psychoanalysis to the International Sándor Ferenczi Community. There are precedents in society for groups and institutions to apologize for behavior that caused harm.

New York Police Department apologized for the Stonewall raid

New York City's Police Commissioner, James P. O'Neill, apologized in a formal statement for the infamous 1969 raid on the Stonewall Inn in Greenwich Village:

> The actions and the laws were discriminatory and oppressive and for that I apologize. (Goodman, 2019, p. A21)

The police raid was on the Stonewall Inn, a gay bar on Christopher Street in Greenwich Village, sometime after midnight on June 28, 1969. During this time, there were state laws against cross-dressing and sodomy. The gay men gathered at the Inn began a protest in what became a turning point for the modern gay rights movement. The crowds clashed with police officers. Six days of protest ensued. As decades passed and discriminatory laws were changed, the New York City Police Department never apologized for their harassment of the gay men, and for anatomical inspections. The culture of the Police Department did not believe in apologies. When the Police Commissioner apologized it became a landmark moment. In a rare moment, a societal group apologized for the harm they had done to gay men. A member of the law enforcement community gave voice to a sentiment which echoes Ferenczi's idea about the analyst being emotionally honest when he/she made a mistake. Charles Wexler, executive director of the Police Executive Research Forum said the following about the police commissioner's apology:

> What you're seeing today is a recognition that if you're going to talk about community trust and accountability, *the most important thing to be is honest when you make a mistake.* (Goodman, 2019, p. A21)

Ferenczi believed that if an authority made a mistake by *withholding the emotional truth*, as an authority in a difficult interaction with an analysand, he/she can traumatize the individual. The individual experiences the interaction as abuse, needing recognition from the authority that he/she contributed to the abuse and can recognize and apologize that they did harm (Ferenczi, 1933). Why did a conservative institution like the New York Police Department decide to apologize to the gay community? Once again, Mr. Wexler said:

> People say we have to change the culture ... It's not just apologizing for what happened; it's saying this is what this department stands for. (Goodman, 2019, p. A1)

The police commissioner, Mr. O'Neill, who issued the apology, agreed with Wexler's statement saying:

> *It's the right thing to do. Pure and simple.* (Goodman, 2019, p. A1)

Asking for forgiveness: a Catholic Bishop's plea on behalf of sexual survivors

In a landmark gesture, the archbishop of Hartford, Leonard P. Blair offered a special *Mass of Reparations*. He said the following at this mass:

> On my knees as a bishop...I ask forgiveness of God, of the wider community and our own Catholic community...I ask it especially of all the victims of sexual abuse and their families. I ask it for all the church leadership has done or failed to do.

Archbishop Blair is unique among the Catholic clergy by asking for forgiveness of sexual survivors. Importantly, this is the kind of response survivors want from the church. Survivors want their church leaders to take responsibility for the crimes and harm done to them. They want more than the prayers of their church leaders. They want the church to apologize for the harm that was done to them by priests. In another important move, Archbishop Blair released the names of priests accused of sexual abuse going back to 1953, when the archdiocese was formed. He is taking action by this measure and trying to repair the damage. As Nick Ingala, the communications director for Voice of the Faithful has rightly stated:

> But the apologies will only go so far. Where is the responsibility?

The accountability? You can't say "I'm sorry" over and over and over again. (Rojas, 2019, p. A15)

Authorities must not only apologize for the harm they have done, but also need to change their harmful behavior, take responsibility for the harm done, and initiate functioning which will attempt to repair the damage.

American Psychological Association and the gay community

Issuing an apology to a community of people by a mental health organization has begun to happen as sexual social issues are having an impact throughout our society. The American Psychological Association had adopted a resolution in removing the stigma of mental illness that has been associated with homosexuality, which is contained in the following statement:

> Therefore be it further resolved that the American Psychological Association opposes portrayals of lesbian, gay, and bisexual youth and adult as mentally ill due to their sexual orientation and supports the dissemination of accurate information about sexual orientation, and mental health, and appropriate interventions in order to counteract bias that is based in ignorance or unfounded beliefs about sexual orientation. (Conger, 1975, p. 633)

In 1974, the Council of Representatives of the American Psychological Association took a vote on whether homosexuality was a mental illness. Calling for the vote were the statements by one of the first openly gay psychologist, Harold Kooden, PhD, who appeared before the Council. Not only did the Council affirm that homosexuality was not a mental illness, Dr. Kooden was later charged with heading a taskforce to study gay and lesbian psychologists (Kooden, 2019).

In 1973, the American Psychiatric Association formally adopted the position that homosexuality was not a mental illness. Pressure had been put on the APA from the National Gay Task Force using a position paper written by Charles Silverstein, PhD, in which he used prevalent psychological and psychoanalytic principles to support the position that the APA's rationale was more a reflection of social norms than scientific evidence. One piece of evidence was his discussion of *drapetomania*, a medical diagnosis given to slaves who had a compulsion to run away from their captivity.

American Psychoanalytic Association apologized to the LGBTQ community

There is a precedence for psychoanalysis to apologize to a community of people. The American Psychoanalytic Association has apologized to the LGBTQ Community at the organization's 109th Annual Meeting in San Diego in 2019 (Assuncão, 2019). In 1973, as mentioned, the American Psychiatric Association had issued a resolution stating that homosexuality was not a mental illness or sickness. That decision was strongly rejected by the psychoanalytic community. Jack Drescher, MD, a psychoanalyst and an LGBTQ scholar has said the psychoanalytic community has for decades continued writing about homosexuality as a mental disorder and refused training at their institutes for gay and lesbian health professionals (Drescher & Merlino, 2007). The President of the American Psychoanalytic Association, Lee Jaffe, MD, added a significant statement on behalf of the analytic establishment, which emphasized taking responsibility and apologizing for the discrimination against the LGBTQ community:

> Regrettably, much of our past understanding of homosexuality as an illness can be attributed to the American psychoanalytic establishment. While our efforts in advocating for sexual and gender diversity since are worthy of pride, it is long past time to recognize and apologize for our role in the discrimination and trauma caused by our profession and say "we are sorry." (Drescher, 2019)

Dr. Jaffe is saying his organization's negative, and some people's hateful behavior toward LGBTQ individuals, caused a trauma. The APsaA considering that they caused harm to a community of individuals is a landmark statement. As I have suggested, over and over again, the traditional analytic establishment has been harmful to the

Ferenczi analytic community by their negative and hateful behavior, over the past 90 years toward Sándor Ferenczi and the Budapest School of Psychoanalysis. Traditional psychoanalysis initiated and deliberately continued a campaign to silence his contributions and importance as an evolutionary figure of psychoanalysis.

Psychoanalysis can be seen as a traditional conservative institution who has functioned to maintain the discoveries of its founder, Sigmund Freud. As its leader, Freud encouraged loyalty and adherence to his thinking. He found an organization to maintain his legacy (Fromm, 1959). Freud's dominance of psychoanalysis as its founder, and through his intellect, personality, and institutionalizing his perspective, allowed the silencing of dissidents. Ferenczi was to be condemned as not being a true adherent of the psychoanalytic perspective. As Ferenczi scholars have indicated:

> For decades...Sándor Ferenczi was dismissed by mainstream psychoanalysts, disregarded because of his radical clinical experiments, because of his revival of interest in the etiological importance of external trauma, and because he was perceived as encouraging dangerous regressions in his patients and attempting to cure them with love. All these criticisms were reinforced with personal aspersions on his character and accusations that he had mentally deteriorated and even gone mad in his final years of his life at the height of his clinical experimentation and in the midst of disputes with Freud. (Aron & Harris, 2010, pp. 5–6)

As Aron and Harris have summarized, the Todschweigen campaign against Ferenczi, contributes to why mainstream psychoanalysis should consider issuing an official statement, which apologizes for the deliberate campaign to silence Ferenczi, "politically assassinate" him, remove him from psychoanalysis, and defame him as a person and clinician.

I propose that a proposal for an apology by the International Psychoanalytic Association to the International Sándor Ferenczi Network for the Todschweigen (Death by Silence) campaign to remove Sándor Ferenczi and the Budapest School of Psychoanalysis

The Todschweigen campaign, which began in the early 1930s and has stretched into contemporary psychoanalysis, as has been discussed in this publication. This campaign indicates that traditional psychoanalysis has damaged Sándor Ferenczi's reputation as a person and psychoanalyst. If the APsaA can apologize to the LGBTQ community, which deserved an apology, it can make the same kind of apology to the community that now represents Ferenczi, the International Sándor Ferenczi Network (https://www.sandorferenczi.org). I would like to offer the following statement as an apology from the APsaA to the ISFN:

> Psychoanalysis, as represented by the International Psychoanalytic Association, has in its past history, conspired to silence the work of Sándor Ferenczi and the Budapest School of Psychoanalysis. Rather than work towards integrating Ferenczi's pioneering contributions in theory and clinical methodology for the evolution of psychoanalysis, the founder and original leaders of psychoanalysis deliberately silenced his innovative ideas and methodology from mainstream psychoanalysis, demeaned him as a person and as a psychoanalyst, conspired to prevent the publication of his major theoretical contributions to psychoanalysis and understanding trauma in human behavior, discouraged the dissemination of Ferenczi as a role as a creative, experimental, innovative psychoanalyst, and removed his heritage from the traditional psychoanalytic journals and training institutes. There is a realization that this silence and neglect damaged Ferenczi's legacy as a significant figure in the history of psychoanalysis and an important contributor to the evolution of psychoanalysis as a science and contributor to the welfare of our society. For these errors of judgement, we are truly sorry.

References

Ain, S. (2017). Female Rabbis speak out about pervasive harassment. *The Jewish Week.* December 20, pp. 1, 24–25.

Alderman, N. (2007). *Disobedience.* New York: Simon & Schuster.

Alpert, J.L. (Ed.). (1995). *Sexual abuse recalled: Treating trauma in the era of the recovered memory debate.* Mahwah, NJ: Analytic Press.

Anonymous (2012). Joe Paterno: The beloved coach with a conflicted legacy. *The Week Magazine.* February 3, p. 29.

Anonymous (2019). Polanski film slated for Venice Festival. *The New York Times.* Arts, Briefly. July 27, p. C3.

Aron, L. and Harris, A. (1993). *The Legacy of Sándor Ferenczi.* Hillsdale, NJ: Analytic.

Aron, L. and Harris, A. (2010). Sándor Ferenczi: Discovery and rediscovery. *Psychoanalytic Perspectives,* 7:5–42.

Assuncão, M. (2019). Mental health professionals long-overdue apology to the LGBTQ community: We recognize "our error in the discrimination and trauma caused by our profession." *New York Daily News.* June 20.

Back, K.W. (1972). *Beyond words: The story of sensitivity training and the encounter movement.* New York: Basic Books.

Balint, A. and Balint, M. (1939). On transference and countertransference. *International Journal of Psycho-Analysis,* 20:223–230.

Balint, M. (1949) Sándor Ferenczi Number. Whole Issue. *International Journal of Psychoanalysis,* 20:223–230.

Balint, M. (1958). Letter to the editor. Sándor Ferenczi's last years. *International Journal of Psycho-Analysis,* 39:68.

Balint, M. (1968). *The basic fault: Therapeutic aspects of regression.* London: Tavistock.

Barbant, E., Falzeder, E. and Giamperi-Deusche, C. (Eds.). (1993). *The correspondence of Sigmund Freud and Sándor Ferenczi: Vol. I: 1908–1914.* Cambridge, MA: Harvard University Press.

320 References

Barry, E. and de Freytas-Tamura, K. (2018). A plea for forgiveness, a prayer with pilgrims and a penitent mass. *The New York Times*. August 27, p. A8.

Basch, M.F. (1984). The self-object theory of motivation and the history of psychoanalysis. In P.E. Stepansky and A. Goldberg (Eds.). *Kohut's legacy: Contributions to self psychology*. Hillsdale, NJ: Analytic Press, pp. 3–17.

Becker, J. (2011). Center of Penn State scandal, Sandusky tells his own story. *The New York Times*. December 3, pp. A1, D3.

Beebe, B. (2005). Mother-infant research informs mother-infant treatment. *Psychoanalytic Study of the Child*, 60:7–46.

Bergmann, M.S. and Hartman, F.R. (Eds.). (1976). *The evolution of psychoanalytic technique*. New York: Basic Books.

Berlin, F.S. (2014, December). Pedophilia and DSM-5: The importance of clearly defining the nature of a pedophilic disorder. *Journal of the American Academy of Psychiatry and the Law*, 42(4): 404–407.

Beste, J.E. (2007). *God and the victim: Traumatic intrusions on grace and freedom*. Oxford: Oxford University Press.

Bettleheim, B. (1990). *Freud's Vienna and other essays*. New York: Knopf.

Biswanger, L. (1958). The case of Ellen West. In R. May, E. Angel, and F. Ellenberger (Eds.). *Existence*. New York: Basic Books, pp. 237–361.

Blanchard, R., Barbaree, H.E., Bogaert, A.F., Dickey, R., Klassen, P., Kuban, M.E. and Zucker K.J. (2000). Fraternal birth order and sexual orientation in pedophiles. *Archives of Sexual Behavior*, 29:463–478.

Bollas, C. (1987). *The shadow of the object*. New York: Columbia University Press.

Bollas, C. (1992). *Being a character*. London: Routledge.

Bonomi, C. (1994). "Why have we ignored Freud the 'pediatrician'": The relevance of Freud's pediatric training for the origin of psychoanalysis. In A. Haynal and E. Falzeder (Eds.). *100 Years of psychoanalysis: Contributions to the history of psychoanalysis*. London: Karmac, pp. 55–99.

Bonomi, C. (1999). Flight into sanity: Jones's allegations of Ferenczi's mental deterioration reconsidered. *International Journal of Psychoanalysis*, 80: 507–542.

Borch-Jacobsen, M. (1991). *The Freudian subject*. Palo Alto, CA: Stanford University Press.

Boston Globe Investigative Staff (2003). *Betrayal: The crisis in the Catholic Church*. New York: Little Brown and Company.

Bowley, G. and Coscarelli, J. (2018). Once a model of fatherhood, now an inmate: Cosby gets 3 to ten years for sexual assault. *The New York Times.* September 26, pp. A1, A20.

Bowley, G. and Hurdle, J. (2018). Jury finds Cosby guilty in a sexual assault case seen as a turning point. *The New York Times.* April 27, pp. A1, A18.

Brabant, E., Falzeder, E. and Giampieri-Deutsch, P. (1993). *The correspondence of Sigmund Freud and Sándor Ferenczi, Volume 1: 1908–1914.* Cambridge, MA: Harvard University Press.

Brady, F. (2019). Irish Psycho-Analytic Association Website.

Brennan, M. (2012). Joe Paterno defended PSU football. *FightOnState.com.* [Word file to PSU football players.]

Breuer, J. and Freud, S. (1895/2000). *Studies on hysteria.* New York: Basic Books

Bryant, T.T. (Ed.). (1967). *The new compact Bible dictionary.* Grand Rapids, MI: Zondervan Publishing Co.

Burke, C. (2011). Joe never asked. *New York Post.* December 4, p. 6.

Burns, J. (2018). Not just Catholics, Rabbi exposes rampant child sex abuse by high-level Jewish clergy. *Thefreethoughtproject.com.*

Catechism of the Catholic Church (1997). *English translation (U.S.A., 2nd ed.).* United State Catholic Conference, Inc. Libreria Editrice Vaticana.

Chabin, M. (2018). Israeli court ruling could limit warnings against convicted abusers. *The Jewish Week.* March 30, pp. 31–33.

Chen, J. (2017). Alyssa Milano on her #MeToo campaign, Weinstein conversation. *Rolling Stone.* October 17.

Chester, P. (1972). *Women and madness.* New York: Doubleday.

Chey, W.D., Kurlander, J. and Eswaran, S. (2015). Irritable bowel syndrome: A clinical review. *Journal of the American Medical Association,* 9:949–958.

Cieply, M. and Barnes, B. (2009). Polanski arrested in Switzerland in 1970s sex case. *The New York Times.* September 28, pp. C1, C6.

Cieply, M. and Carvajal, D. (2009). Powerful player joins Polanski team. *The New York Times.* September 30, p. A21.

Cioffi, F. (1999). *Freud and the question of pseudoscience.* New York: Open Court.

Ciralsky, A. (2018). Nightmare on Greenwich Street. *Vanity Fair.* January 18.

Cohen, N. (2012). The coach, the biographer, and the final chapter. *The New York Times.* April 30, pp. D1, D6–D7.

Conger, J.J. (1975). Proceedings of the American Psychological Association, incorporated, for the year 1974: Minutes of the annual meeting of the council of representatives. *American Psychologist,* 30:6, 633.

Connor, T. (2003). Beaten woman fears killer's release. *Daily News*. January 3.

Corbin, C.M. (2012). The irony of Hosanna-Tabor Evangelical Lutheran Church and school V. EEDC. *Northwestern University School of Law Review*, 106:2, 951–970.

Covello, A. (1984). Lettres de Freud: du scenario de Jones au diagnostic sur Ferenczi. *Confrontation*, 12:63–78.

Craig, M. (2012). Mets' R.A. Dickey wins 20th game of season. *Newsday*. September 27.

Cullcane, S. (2017). Uma Thurman turns anger on Harvey Weinstein in Instagram post. *CNN Money*. November 24: 11:34 am ET – Uma Thurman Instagram.

D'Ercole, A. (2019a). *Clara Mabel Thompson, An American Psychoanalyst*. (In preparation).

D'Ercole, A. (2019b). Clara Thompson and Ferenczi. Email. Tuesday, June 14.

D'Ercole, A. (2019b). Thompson, Severn and Ferenczi. Email. April.

D'Zurilla, C. (2017). In saying #MeToo, Alyssa Milano pushes awareness campaign about sexual assault and harassment. *Los Angeles Times*. October 16.

Davies, J.M. and Frawley, M.G. (1994). *Treating the adult survivor of childhood sexual abuse*. New York: Basic Books.

de Costa, L., Adler, E., Tylim, I. and Rachman, A.W. (2013). A narrative play of the Freud/Ferenczi correspondence. *Presentation*. Postgraduate Psychoanalytic Institute. New York City.

Denov, M.D. (2003). The myth of innocence: Sexual scripts and the recognition of child sexual abuse by female perpetrators. *The Journal of Sex Research*, 3:303–314.

Derbyshire, S.W.G., Osborn, J. and Brown, S. (2013). Feeling the pain of others is associated with self-other confusion and prior pain experience. *Frontiers in Human Neuroscience*, 7:296.

DeYoung, M. (2010). *Madness: An history of mental illness and its treatment*. Jefferson, NC: McFarland & Company Inc.

Diagnostic and Statistical Manual, 5th ed. (2013). New York: American Psychiatric Publishing.

Dickey, R.A. and Coffey, W. (2012). *Wherever I wind up: My quest for truth, authenticity and the perfect knuckleball*. New York: Blue Rider Press.

Dowd, M. (2018). A goddess, a mogul, and a mad genius. *The New York Times*. Sunday Review. February 4, pp. SR1, 4–5.

Drape, J. (2013). Penn State to pay nearly $60 million to 26 abuse victims. *The New York Times*. October 29, pp. B11, B15.

References   323

Drescher, J. (2019). Stonewall's 50th anniversary and an overdue apology: How the mental health professions evolved on LGBTQ rights. *Psychology Today*. June 21 (https://apsa.org/content/news-apsaa-issues-overdue-apology-lgbtq-community).

Drescher, J. and Merlino, J.P. (Eds.). (2007). *American psychiatry and homosexuality: An oral history*. New York: Routledge.

Durantine, P. (2011). Penn State aide tells court what he saw. *The New York Times*. December 17, pp. A1, D4.

Edelman, S. (2013). Brooklyn DA releases names of 46 child sex-abusers who terrorized the Orthodox Jewish Community. *The New York Post*. July 21.

Edwards, S.Z., Dockterman, E. and Sweetland, H. (2018). Time person of the year: The silence breakers. *Time Magazine*. April 14.

Eissler, K. (1952). Interview with Dr. Elizabeth Severn, December 20, 1952. Container 121. Sigmund Freud Papers. Sigmund Freud Collection. *Manuscript Division*, Library of Congress, Washington, DC.

English, B. (2016a). "Profoundly disturbing" abuse documented at elite R.I. school. *The Boston Globe*. December 16.

English, B. (2016b). R.I. prep school cites more sex abuse victims. *The Boston Globe*. December 14, p. 1.

Erikson, E.H. (1950). *Childhood and society*. New York: W.W. Norton & Company.

Erikson, E.H. and Erikson, J.M. (1998). *The life cycle completed: Extended versions*. New York: W.W. Norton & Company.

Eros, F., Szekacs-Weisz, J. and Robinson, K. (2013). *Sándor Ferenczi and Ernest Jones: Letters, 1911–1933*. London: Karnac.

Falzeder, E., Barbant, E. and Giamperi-Deusche, C. (Eds.). (1996). *The correspondence of Sigmund Freud and Sándor Ferenczi: Vol. II: 1914–1919*. Cambridge, MA: Harvard University Press.

Falzeder, E., Barbant, E. and Giamperi-Deusche, C. (Eds.). (2000). *The correspondence of Sigmund Freud and Sándor Ferenczi: Vol. III: 1920–1933*. Cambridge, MA: Harvard University Press.

Falzeder, E. (2010). Sándor Ferenczi between orthodoxy and heterodoxy. *American Imago*, 66:4, 395–401.

Farrow, R. (2017). From aggressive overtures to sexual assault: Harvey Weinstein's accusers tell their stories. *The New Yorker*. October 23, Sections 1–10.

Fenton, R., Rosner, E. and Golding, B. (2017). Notorious child-killer still living in Harlem – and shows no remorse. *The New York Post*. November 1.

324 References

Ferenczi, S. (1909). Introjection and transference. In *Contributions to psycho-analysis*, Vol. I. London: Hogarth Press, pp. 35–93.

Ferenczi, S. (1928/1980). The elasticity of psychoanalytic technique. In M. Balint (Ed.). *Final contributions to the problems and methods of psychoanalysis, Vol. III.* New York: Bruner/Mazel, pp. 87–102.

Ferenczi, S. (1929/1980). The principle of relaxation and neocatharsis. In M. Balint (Ed.). *Final contributions to the problems and methods of psychoanalysis, Vol. III.* New York: Bruner/Mazel, pp. 108–125.

Ferenczi, S. (1930/1980). The principle of relaxation and neocatharsis. In M. Balint (Ed.). *Final contributions to the problems and methods of psychoanalysis, Vol. III.* New York: Bruner/Mazel, pp. 108–125.

Ferenczi, S. (1933/1980). The confusion of tongues between adults and children: The language of tenderness and passion. In M. Balint (Ed.). *Final contributions to the problems and methods of psychoanalysis, Vol. III.* New York: Bruner/Mazel, pp. 156–167.

Ferenczi, S. (1985). *Journal Clinique: Janvier-Octobre.* Paris: Payot.

Ferenczi, S. (1988). *The clinical diary of Sándor Ferenczi* (J. Dupont, Ed., M. Balint and N.Z. Jackson, Trans.). Cambridge, MA: Harvard University Press.

Ferenczi, S. and Rank, O. (1925). *The development of psychoanalysis.* New York: Nervous and Mental Disease Publishing Company.

Fisher, A., Gillim, M. and Daniels, D. (2012). *Silent no more: Victim 1's fight for justice against Jerry Sandusky.* New York: Penguin Random House.

Fitzgibbon, B.M., Ward, J. and Enticott, P.G. (2014). The neural underpinnings of vicarious experience. *Frontiers in Human Neuroscience*, 8:384.

Fortune, C. (1993). The case of "RN": Sándor Ferenczi's radical experiments in psychoanalysis. In L. Aron and A. Harris (Eds.). *The legacy of Sándor Ferenczi.* Hillsdale, NJ: Analytic Press.

Fortune, C. (1996). Mutual analysis: A logical outcome of Sándor Ferenczi's experiments in psychoanalysis. In P.I. Rudynsky, A. Bokay and P. Giamperi-Deutsch (Eds.). *Ferenczi's turn in psychoanalysis.* New York: New York Univiersity Press, pp. 170–186.

Fox, J. (2013). Roman's holiday. *Vanity Fair.* October, pp. 328–331, 370.

Frawley, M.F. and Davies, J.M. (1994). *Treating the adult survivors of childhood sexual abuse.* New York: Basic Books.

Freeman, L. (2017). Alyssa Milano: How we can help women come forward. *Time Magazine.* October 18.

Freud, A. (1933). Report of the twelfth international psychoanalytic congress. *International Journal of Psychoanalysis*, 1:4, 138.

Freud, A. (1936/1992). *Ego and the mechanisms of defense*. London: Karnac Books.

Freud, S. (1896). The aetiology of hysteria. *Standard Edition*, 3:189–221.

Freud, S. (1905a). The aetiology of hysteria. *Standard Edition*, 7:187–221.

Freud, S. (1905b/1901). Fragments of an analysis of a case of hysteria. *Standard Edition*, 7:1–122.

Freud, S. (1918). From the history of an infantile neurosis. Reprinted in M. Gardiner (Ed.). (1971). *The Wolf Man: The double story of Freud's most famous case*. New York: Basic Books, pp. 153–262.

Freud, S. (1919/1918). Lines of advance in psycho-analytic therapy. *Standard Edition*, 17:157–168.

Freud, S. (1926). The question of lay analysis. Conversations with an impartial person. *Standard Edition*. London: Hogarth, p. 20.

Freud, S. (1954). *The origins of psychoanalysis: Letters to Wilhelm Fliess, drafts and notes, 1887–1902*. New York: Basic Books.

Freund, K. and Kuban, M. (1993). Toward a testable developmental model of pedophilia: The development of erotic age preference. *Child Abuse and Neglect*, 17:315–324.

Freund, K. and Langevin, R. (1976). Bisexuality in homosexual pedophilia. *Archives of Sexual Behavior*, 5:5, 415–423.

Freund, K. and Wilson, R. (1992). The proportions of heterosexual and homosexual pedophiles among sex offenders against children: An exploratory study. *Journal of Sex & Marital Therapy*, 18:1, 34–43.

Freyd, J.J. (1996). *Betrayal trauma: The logic of forgetting child abuse*. Cambridge, MA: Harvard University Press.

Freyd, J.J. (2015). Proposal for a National Institute on Sexual Violence. *Journal of Trauma and Dissociation*, 16, 497–499.

Friedersdorf, C. (2016). The understudied female sexual predator. *The Atlantic*. November 28.

Fromm, E. (1959). *Sigmund Freud's mission*. New York: Harper and Row.

Fromm, E. (1963). *The dogma of Christ*. New York: Holt, Rinehart and Winston.

Gabbard, G.D. (2002). Boundary violations and the abuse of power: Commentaries on paper by Phillip Kuhn. *Studies in Gender and Sexuality*, 3:4, 379–388.

Gabler, E., Rutenberg, J., Grynbaum, M. and Abrams, A. (2017). Longtime face of *NBC's Today* is fired as complains multiply. *The New York Times*. November 30, pp. A1, A22.

Gado, M. (2003). *Biography of Hedda Nussbaum*. New York: Random House.

326 References

Galinsky, J. (2018). Fox website puts focus on women as abusers. *The New York Times*. March 18, p. B1.

Gay, P. (1984). *Freud: A life for our time*. New York: Norton.

Geimer, S. (2013). *The girl: A life in the shadow of Roman Polanski*. New York: Atria Books (Simon and Schuster).

Gillard, J. (2017). *Final report. Royal Commission of Australia*. Royal Commission into Institutional Responses to Child Sexual Abuse, December 15.

Goodman, J.D. (2019). How the police commissioner came to apologize for the Stonewall Raid. *The New York Times*. June 11, p. A21.

Grand Jury Testimony (1977). The County of Los Angeles State of California. The People of the State of California, Plaintiff vs. Roman Raymond Polanski, Defendant No. A-334,139. April 4.

Grosskurth, P. (1991). *The secret ring: Freud's inner circle and the politics of psychoanalysis*. New York: Addison-Wesley.

Guerra, C. (2017). Where the "Me Too" initiative really comes from? Tarana Burke, long before hashtags. *The Boston Globe*. October 17.

Haigney, S. (2017). Roman Polanski is accused of rape by a former actress. *The New York Times*. October 4, p. C4.

Hale, C.J. (2015). The Pope Francis statement that changed the church on LGBT issues. *Ideas Newsletter*. July 28

Hale, N.G. et al. (1971). *James Jackson Putnam and psychoanalysis: Letters between Putnam and Sigmund Freud, Ernest Jones, William James, Sandor Ferenczi, and Morton Prince, 1877–1917*. Cambridge, MA: Harvard University Press.

Harris, E.A. (2017). In a teacher's letters, an attempted seduction. *The New York Times*. May 26, pp. A1, A23.

Harrison, K., Kaplan, C. and Aguirre, B. (2018). *Fighting back: What an Olympic champion's story can teach us about recognizing and preventing child sexual abuse – And helping kids recover*. New York: The Guilford Press.

Hartogs, R. (1976). *Two assassinations. The Warren Report – A psychiatrist discusses what it really reveals about Oswald and Ruby*. New York City: Kensington Publishing Corp.

Havinghurst, R.J. and Neugarten, B.L. (1947). *Father of the man: How your child gets his personality*. New York: Houghton.

Haynal, A. (1992). Personal communication. Email – Elma Pálos and Sándor Ferenczi.

Haynal, A. (1993). Ferenczi and the origins of psychoanalytic technique. In L. Aron and A. Harris (Eds.). *The legacy of Sándor Ferenczi*. Hillsdale, NJ: The Analytic Press, pp. 53–74.

References 327

Haynal, A. (2002). *Disappearing and reviving: Sándor Ferenczi in the history of psychoanalyis.* London: Karnac.

Haynal, A. and Falzeder, E. (1994). *100 years of psychoanalysis.* London: Karnac.

Herman, J.L. (1981). *Father-daughter incest.* Cambridge, MA: Harvard University Press.

Herman, J.L. (1992). *Trauma and recovery.* New York: Basic Books.

Hoban, P. (1992). Everything you always wanted to know about Woody Allen (But were afraid to ask). *New York Magazine.* September 21, pp. 33–49.

Horowitz, J. (2018a). With Irish church in tatters, Pope voices regret for legacy of abuse. *The New York Times.* August 26, p. 11.

Horowitz, J. (2018b). Pope's accuser: Keeper of the faith or of grudges? *The New York Times.* August 29, pp. A1, A8.

Horowitz, J. and Dias, E. (2019). Francis invokes 'all-out battle' on sexual abuse: Calls to stop 'wolves'. *The New York Times.* February 25, pp. A1–A10.

Hunt, F. (2016). The history of the Chaise Lounge. *United Kingdom News.* July 14.

Itzkoff, D. (2012). Polanski to tackle a different long-running case. *The New York Times.* May 10, p. C2.

Jenkins, E.C. (2013). *The Hebrew Bible in English.* Stanford, CA: Stanford University Library. (Originally published in 1917). [JPS (1917) in PDF].

John Jay Report (2004). The nature and scope of sexual abuse of minors by Catholic Priests and Deacons in the United States. *John Jay College of Criminal Justice.* February 27. (Posted on the Internet).

Jones, E. (1911). The action of suggestion in psychotherapy. *Journal of Abnormal Psychology*, 5:217–254.

Jones, E. (1923). Cold illness and birth. In *Papers on psychoanalysis.* Boston, MA: Beacon Press, pp. 320–324.

Jones, E. (1953). *The life and work of Sigmund Freud, Vol I: The formative years and great discoveries.* New York: Basic Books.

Jones, E. (1955). *The Life and Work of Sigmund Freud. Vol II: Years of maturity, 1901–1919.* New York: Basic Books.

Jones, E. (1957). *The life and work of Sigmund Freud. Vol III: The last phase, 1919–1939.* New York: Basic Books.

Jones, E. (1959). *Free associations: Memories of a psychoanalyst.* London: Hogarth Press.

Kantor, J. and Twohey, M. (2017a). Harvey Weinstein paid off sexual harassment accusers for decades. *The New York Times.* October 17, pp. A1, A18.

References

Kantor, J. and Twohey, M. (2017b). Sexual misconduct claims trail a Hollywood Mogul: Oscar-winning producer has quietly settled at least 8 complaints in 3 decades. *The New York Times*. October 6, pp. A1, A18.

Kantrowitz, B., Wingert, P., King, P., Robbins, K. and Namuth, T. (1988). A tale of abuse. *Newsweek*. December 12, pp. 56–59.

Kaplan, A.G. (1975). Sex in psychotherapy: The myth of Sándor Ferenczi. *Contemporary Psychoanalysis*, 11, 175–187.

Kepner, T. (2010). Mets knuckleballer Dickey keeps his fingers crossed. *The New York Times*. July 8.

Ketchum, C. (2013). The child-rape assembly line. *Vice*. November 12.

Kerr, J. (1993). *A most dangerous mind*. New York: Random House.

Khomami, N. (2017). #MeToo: How a hashtag became a rallying cry against sexual harassment. *The Guardian*. October 20.

King, L. (2003). An interview with Hedda Nussbaum. *Larry King Live, Television Program*. June 16. *Transcript #061600 CN.V22*.

Koblin, J. (2018). *NBC News* boss says network did not obstruct reporting on Weinstein. *The New York Times*. Tuesday, September 4, p. B4.

Kohut, H. (1984). *How does psychoanalysis cure?* (A. Goldberg and P.E. Stepansky, Eds.). Chicago: University of Chicago Press.

Kooden, H. (2019). APA and gay psychologists. November 19.

Kristof, N. (2014). Dylan Farrow's story. Op-Ed Column. *The New York Times*. Sunday Review. February 1.

Krüll, M. (1986). *Freud and his father*. New York: Norton.

Kuhn, P. (2002). "Romancing with a wealth of detail": Narratives of Ernest Jones's 1906 trial for indecent assault. *Studies in Gender and Sexuality*, 3:4, 344–378.

Lapointe, J. (2010). Dickey, man of letters. Lets numbers do talking. *The New York Times*. August 15.

Larivière (Eds.), M. (2019). *Rediscovering Sándor Ferenczi: A festschrift for Arnold Wm. Rachman, Ph.D*. (In preparation).

Layden, T. (2012). Joe Paterno, 1926–2012. *Sports Illustrated*. January 30, pp. 56–62.

Leaming, B. (1981). *Polanski, the filmmaker as voyeur: A biography*. New York: Simon & Schuster.

Levinson, D.J., Darrow, C.N., Klein, E.B. and Levinson, M. (1978). *Seasons of a man's life*. New York: Random House.

Levinson, D.J. and Levinson, J.D. (1996). *Seasons of a woman's life*. New York: Alfred A. Knopf.

Liebeler, W.J. and Hartogs, R. (1964). Testimony of Dr. Renatus Hartogs.

Jfkassassination.net/riess/testimony/hartogs.htm. 7 East 86th Street, NY, 5:20 pm, April 16th.

Liotti, G. (2014). Disorganized attachment in the pathogenesis and psychotherapy of borderline personality. In A.N. Danquah and K. Berry (Eds.). *Attachment theory in adult mental health: A guide to clinical practice.* New York: Routledge, pp. 113–128.

Lipdegraff, J.A., Silver, R.C. and Holman, E.A. (2008). Searching for and finding meaning in collective trauma. *Journal of Personality and Social Psychology*, 95, 709–722.

Lipka, H.B. (2006). *Sexual transgression in the Hebrew Bible.* Sheffield: Sheffield Phoenix Press.

Little, M.L. (1990). *Psychotic anxieties and containment: A personal record of an analysis with Winnicott.* New Jersey: Jason Aronson.

Lorand, S. (1975). The founding of the Psychoanalytic Institute by the State University of New York Downstate Medical Center: An autobiographical history. *Psychoanalytic Review*, 64:4, 677–714.

Lorin, C. (1983). *Le Jeune Ferenczi: Premier Ecrits: 1899–1906.* Paris: Aubier-Montaigne.

Lothan, H.Z. (1992). *In defense of Schreber: Soul murder and psychiatry.* Hillsdale, NJ: The Analytic Press.

Louttit, M. and Correa, C. (2018). His accusers, their words. *The New York Times.* January 5, pp. A18–A19.

Lowry, R. (2012). Penn State's shame. *New York Post.* July 24, p. 23.

Macur, J. (2018). Front and center, one voice eventually raised an army. *The New York Times.* January 25, pp. B10, B14.

Makari, G.J. (2002). On "Romancing with a wealth of detail": Commentary on paper by Phillip Kuhn. *Studies in Gender and Sexuality*, 3:4, 389–394.

Mallett, X. (2017). Women also sexually abuse children, but their reasons often differ from men's. *The Conversation*, University of New England, February 19.

Maroda, K. (1992). *The power of countertransference.* New York: John Wiley & Sons.

Martin, J. (2000). The church and the homosexual priest. *America*, 183:14, 11–15.

Marvin, G. (2012). *Wolf.* London: Reaktion Books Ltd.

Masson, J.M. (1984). *The assault on truth.* New York: Farrar, Straus and Giroux.

May, R., Anger, E. and Ellenberg, F. (Eds.). (1958). *Existence.* New York: Basic Books.

330 References

McBrien, R. (2003). Foreword. In A.W. Sipe (Ed.). *Celibacy in crisis: A secret world revisited*. London: Routledge.

McCann, I.L. and Pearlman, L.A. (1990). Vicarious traumatization: A framework for understanding the psychological effects of working with victims. *Journal of Traumatic Stress*, 3:1, 131–149.

McCluskey, N. and Hooper, C.A. (2000). *Psychodynamic perspectives on abuse: The cost of fear*. London: Jessica Kingsley.

McCormick, P. (2018). What Father Bradel did to me. *The New York Times*. August 19, pp. SR1 & 3.

McDonald, H. (2009). Endemic rape and abuse of Irish children in Catholic care, inquiry finds. *The Guardian*. Wednesday, May 20.

McElivee, J.J. (2016). Francis: Christians must apologize to gay people for marginalizing them. *National Catholic Reporter*. June 26.

McGuire, W. (1974). *The correspondence between Sigmund Freud and C.G. Jung*. Princeton, NJ: Princeton University Press.

McLeod, D. (2015). Female offenders in child abuse cases: A national picture. *Journal of Child Sexual Abuse*, 24:1, 97–114.

Menaker, E. (1982). *Otto Rank: A rediscovered legacy*. New York: Columbia University Press.

Menaker, E. (1985). *Appointment in Vienna*. New York: St. Martin's Press.

Menaker, E. (1991). On Anna Freud: A discussion of personal analytic reactions in the early days of psychoanalysis. *Journal of the American Academy of Psychoanalysis*, 19:4, 606–611.

Menaker, E. (1995). *The freedom to inquire*. Northvale, NJ: Jason Aronson.

Menaker, E. (1996). Ann Freud's analysis by her father: The assault on the self. Eight Biennial Conference. New York University Postdoctoral Program, "Self Expression: Analysand and Analyst". February 3. New York City.

Merriam-Webster Collegiate Dictionary. Springfield, MA: Merriam-Webster Incorporated.

Mészáros, J. (2019). About Ferenczi: Sándor Ferenczi July, 7 1873 (Miskolc) – May 22, 1933 (Budapest). *International Sándor Ferenczi Network*.

Miller, B. (2011). Mets pitcher Dickey risking $4 million salary to climb Mount Kilimanjaro. *The Post Game*. November 11.

Miller, J. (2014). Woody Allen responds to Dylan Farrow's open letter. *Vanity Fair*. February 7.

Modell, (1991). A confusion of tongues or whose reality is it? *Psychoanalytic Quarterly*, 60:2, 227–244.

Mucci, C. (2017). Ferenczi's revolutionary therapeutic approach. *American Journal of Psychoanalysis*, 77:3, 239–254.

References 331

Mucci, C. (2018). *Borderline bodies: Affect regulation therapy for personality disorders*. New York: W.W. Norton.

Murdock, A. (2013). Whistle blower Rabbi exposes Ultra-Orthodox Jewish sex abuse. *FreeThoughtNation.com* (S/D 14). November 13.

Nemiroff, H., Schindler, R. and Schriber, A. (2000). An Interpersonal psychoanalytic approach to treating adult survivors of childhood sexual abuse. *Contemporary Psychoanalysis*, 36:4, 665–684.

The New York Times (1988). Metropolitan section. December 7.

Neyer, B. (2012). Will R.A. Dickey's angry knuckleball change the game? *Baseball Nation*. June 29.

Nicholson, A. (2017). Harvey Weinstein and the alternative history of Hollywood. *The Village Voice*. Film. October 16.

Ohlheiser, A. (2017). The woman behind "Me Too" knew the power of the phrase when she created it – 10 years ago. *Washington Post*. December.

Otterman, S. and Rivera, R. (2012). Ultra-orthodox shun their own for reporting child sexual abuse. *The New York Times*. May 9, p. A1.

Paglia, C. (2017). Email to S. Lyall, B. Izkoff. *The New York Times*. November 25, p. A16.

Parker, R. (1994). *Polanski*. London: Victor Gollancz Ltd.

Paskauskas, R.A. (1993). *The complete correspondence of Sigmund Freud and Ernest Jones, 1908–1939*. Cambridge, MA: Belknap Press/Harvard University Press.

Pellon, M. (2011). Penn State aide tells court what he saw. *The New York Times*. December 17, pp. A1, D4.

Pennington, B. and Rohan, T. (2012). Penn State inquiry's findings puncture the coach's image. *The New York Times*. July 13, pp. B11, B13.

Pérez-Peña, R. (2018). Behind the scandal and the claims that could sink a papacy. *The New York Times*. August 28, p. A9.

Perrotta, T. (2016). How an American took down judo. *Wall Street Journal*. July 20.

Petit, S. (2017). #MeToo: Sexual harassment and assault movement tweeted over 500,000 times as celebs share stories. *People Magazine*. October 16.

Peyton, S. (2006). Lesbian caught between religion and outside world. *San Francisco Chronicle*. September 10.

Pinker, S. (2011). *The better angels of our nature*. New York: Viking Books.

Pinto, N. (2011). The Shomrim: Gotham's crusaders. *The Village Voice*. September 7.

Polanski, R. (1973). *What?* New York: Third Press.

Polanski, R. (1984). *Roman by Polanski*. New York: William Morrow & Co.

332 References

Popock, H. (2006). *The Great King of Israel: An easy English Bible version and commentary on the Book of Samuel*. UK: Wycliffe Associates.

Posnanski, J. (2012). *Paterno*. New York: Simon & Schuster.

Powell, M. (2013). After sexual abuse case, a Hasidic accuser is shunned, then indicted. *The New York Times*. June 17.

Quinsey, V.L. and Chaplin, T.C. (1988). Penile responses of child molesters and normals to descriptions of encounters with children involving sex and violence. *Journal of Interpersonal Violence*, 3:3, 259–274.

Rachman, A.W. (1975). *Identity group psychotherapy with adolescents*. Springfield, IL: Charles C. Thomas.

Rachman, A.W. (1978). The first encounter session: Ferenczi's case of the female Croatian musician. *Presentation*. American Group Psychotherapy Association. New Orleans, LA.

Rachman, A.W. (1984). The relationship between Freud and Ferenczi: The meaning for the development of psychoanalysis. *Presentation Postgraduate*. Psychoanalytic Institute for Mental Health. New York City. March.

Rachman, A.W. (1988a). The rule of empathy: Sándor Ferenczi's pioneering contributions to the empathic method in psychoanalysis. *Journal American Academy of Psychoanalysis*, 16:1, 1–27.

Rachman, A.W. (1988b). Liberating the creative self through active combined therapy. In N. Slavinska-Holy (Ed.). *Borderline and narcissistic patients in therapy*. New York: International Universities Press, pp. 309–340.

Rachman, A.W. (1989a). Confusion of tongues: The Ferenczian metaphor for childhood seduction and emotion trauma. *Journal of the American Academy of Psychoanalysis*, 17:2, 192–205.

Rachman, A.W. (1989b). Ferenczi's contributions to the evolution of a self psychology framework in psychoanalysis. In D.W. Detrick and S.P. Detrick (Eds.). *Self psychology: Comparison and contrast*. Hillsdale, NJ: Analytic Press, pp. 81–100.

Rachman, A.W. (1991). An oedipally conflicted patient. In A. Wolf and L. Kutash (Eds.). *Psychopathology of the submerged personality*. Northvale, NJ: Jason Aronson, pp. 215–238.

Rachman, A.W. (1992). The confusion of tongues between Hedda Nussbaum and Joel Steinberg: Ferenczi's theory of victimization and abusive relationships. *Presentation*. International Psychohistorical Association. New York City. June 12.

Rachman, A.W. (1993a). The evil of childhood seduction. *Presentation*. American Academy of Psychoanalysis. New York City. December.

References   333

Rachman, A.W. (1993b). Ferenczi and sexuality. In L. Aron and A. Harris (Eds.). *The legacy of Sándor Ferenczi*. Hillsdale, NJ: The Analytic Press, pp. 81–100.

Rachman, A.W. (1994). The confusion of tongues theory: Ferenczi's legacy to psychoanalysis In A. Haynal and E. Falzeder (Eds.). *100 years of psychoanalysis*. London: Karnac, pp. 235–255.

Rachman, A.W. (1997a). *Sándor Ferenczi: The psychotherapist of tenderness and passion*. Northvale, NJ: Jason Aronson.

Rachman, A.W. (1997b). The suppression and censorship of Ferenczi's confusion of Tongues paper. In A.W. Rachman (Ed.). *Psychoanalysis' favorite son: The legacy of Sándor Ferenczi. Psychoanalytic inquiry*, 17:4. November.

Rachman, A.W. (1998). Ferenczi's "relaxation-principle" and the contemporary clinical practice of psychoanalysis. *American Journal of Psychoanalysis*, 58:1, 63–81.

Rachman, A.W. (1999a). Death by silence (Todschweigen): The traditional method of silencing the dissident of psychoanalysis. In R.M. Prince (Ed.). *The death of psychoanalysis: Murder, suicide, or rumor greatly exaggerated?* Northvale, NJ: Jason Aronson, pp. 153–163.

Rachman, A.W. (1999b). Ferenczi's rise and fall from analytic grace: The Ferenczi Renaissance revisited. *Group*, 23:4, 103–119.

Rachman, A.W. (2000a). Ferenczi's confusion of tongues theory and the analysis of the incest trauma. *Psychoanalytic Social Work*, 7:1, 27–53.

Rachman, A.W. (2000b). Issues of power, control and status: From Ferenczi to Foucault. *Journal of Eastern Group Psychotherapy*, 7:1, 121–144.

Rachman, A.W. (2002). Beyond neutrality: The clinical function of analyst self-disclosure in the psychoanalytic situation. In J. Reppen, M.A. Schulman, and J. Tucker (Eds). *Way beyond Freud: Postmodern psychoanalysis evaluated*. London: Open Gate.

Rachman, A.W. (2003a). Freud's analysis of his daughter Anna: Confusion of tongues. In A. Roland, B. Ulanov, and C. Barbre (Eds.). *Creative dissent: Psychoanalysis in evolution*. Westport, LT: Praeger, pp. 59–71.

Rachman, A.W. (2003b). *Psychotherapy of difficult cases: Flexibility and responsiveness in clinical practice*. Madison, CT: Psychosocial Press.

Rachman, A.W. (2007). Sándor Ferenczi's contributions to the evolution of psychoanalysis. *Psychoanalytic Psychology*, 24:1, 74–96.

Rachman, A.W. (2010a). The origins of a relational perspective in the ideas of Sándor Ferenczi and the Budapest School of Psychoanalysis. *Psychoanalytic Perspective*, 7:1, 43–60.

334 References

Rachman, A.W. (2010b). An "invitro" study of intersubjectivity: The analysis of Mrs. Elizabeth Severn with Dr. Sándor Ferenczi. *Presentation*. International Forum of Psychoanalysis. Athens, Greece.

Rachman, A.W. (2012a). The analysis of the incest trauma: From Freud's seduction hypothesis to Ferenczi's confusion of tongues theory of trauma. *Symposium*. The Institute of the Postgraduate Psychoanalytic Society. The Hungarian Society. New York City. Saturday, November 17.

Rachman, A.W. (2012b). The confusion of tongues between Sándor Ferenczi and Elizabeth Severn. *Plenary Presentation. The International Sándor Ferenczi Conference.* "Faces of Trauma". Budapest, Hungary. June 3.

Rachman, A.W. (2012c). From Freud's seduction hypothesis to Ferenczi's confusion of tongues paradigm: Childhood sexual abuse and trauma. *Presentation*. Hungarian House. New York City. November 17.

Rachman, A.W. (2012d). The relational dimension in psychoanalysis: From Ferenczi to Mitchell. *Presentation*. The Czech Psychoanalytic Society. Prague. The Czech Republic. Saturday, May 26.

Rachman, A.W. (2014a). Sándor Ferenczi's analysis with Elizabeth Severn: "Wild analysis" or pioneering treatment of the incest trauma. *Psychoanalytic Inquiry*, 34:2, March, pp. 145–168.

Rachman, A.W. (2014b). The "evil genius" of psychoanalysis: Elizabeth Severn, Dr. Sándor Ferenczi's partner in the pioneering study of trauma. *Presentation*. The Library of Congress. Washington, DC. June 2 (Webcast – www.loc.gov).

Rachman, A.W. (2015). Elizabeth Severn: From self-taught therapist to psychoanalyst and Sándor Ferenczi's mutual analytic partner. *Presentation*. The Sándor Ferenczi Center at the New School University. NYC. September 19.

Rachman, A.W. (2016a). Psychoanalysis neglect of the incest trauma: The confusion of tongues between psychoanalysis and society. In A.W. Rachman (Ed.). *The Budapest School of Psychoanalysis*. London: Routledge, pp. 164–181.

Rachman, A.W. (2016b). Confusion of tongues trauma in child abduction: Revising the Stockholm syndrome. In A.W. Rachman (Ed.). *The Budapest School of Psychoanalysis*. London: Routledge, pp. 182–208.

Rachman, A.W. (2016c). *The acquisition restoration and donation of the Elizabeth Severn papers: A lost legacy of psychoanalysis.* (Unpublished).

Rachman, A.W. (2016d). *The Budapest School of Psychoanalysis: The origin of a two-person psychology and empathic perspective.* London: Routledge.

Rachman, A.W. (2017). *Elizabeth Severn, the "evil genius" of psychoanalysis.* Sándor Ferenczi Seminars. Florence, Italy. July.

Rachman, A.W. (2018a). *Elizabeth Severn: The "evil genius" of psycho-analysis*. London: Routledge.

Rachman, A.W. (2018b). Todschweigen (death by silence): Removal of Elizabeth Severn's ideas and work from mainstream psychoanalysis. In A.W. Rachman (Ed.). *Elizabeth Severn: The "evil genius" of psycho-analysis*. London: Routledge, pp. 57–70.

Rachman, A.W. (2018c). The uncovering of a Lost Psychoanalytic Legacy: The papers of Elizabeth Severn. *Presentation*. The International Sándor Ferenczi Conference. Florence, Italy. May.

Rachman, A.W. (2019a). The confusion of tongues: Sándor Ferenczi and the Budapest School of Psychoanalysis: Revolutionary paradigm shift for psychoanalysis. *Presentation*. Irish Psychoanalytic Society. Dun Loaghiere, Ireland. May 10.

Rachman, A.W. (2019c). A contemporary view of Freud's case of the Wolf Man/Sergei Pankejeff: New evidence of sexual abuse. *Proposal*. International Psychoanalytic Association. July.

Rachman, A.W. (2019c). Elizabeth Severn as a person, clinician and colla-borator of Sándor Ferenczi. *Presentation*. The Irish Psychoanalytic Society. Dun Loaghiere, Ireland. May 11.

Rachman, A.W. (2019d). *Freud's case of the Wolf Man: Sergei Pankejeff as a survivor of sexual abuse*. (In preparation).

Rachman, A.W. (2019e). Todschweigen, death by silence by silence (Rachman and Menaker): Traditional psychoanalysis' punishment of dissidents. In A.W. Rachman (Ed.). *"What have we done to you, poor child?" (Freud, 1897): Psychoanalysis and society's neglect of child, youth and adult sexual abuse.*

Rachman, A.W., Kennedy, R. and Yard, M. (2005). Erotic transference and the relationship to childhood sexual seduction: Perversion in the psychoanalytic situation. *International Forum of Psychoanalysis*, 14:3/4, 183–187.

Rachman, A.W. and Klett, S. (2015). *Analysis of the incest trauma: Retrieval, recovery, renewal*. London: Karnac Books.

Rachman, A.W. and Mattick, P. (2009). *Freud's confusion of tongues with Dora: The need for empathy not interpretation*. (Unpublished manuscript).

Rachman, A.W. and Mattick, P. (2012). The confusion of tongues in the psychoanalytic relationship. *Psychoanalytic Social Work*, 19:1–2, 167–190.

Rachman, A.W. and Mattick, P. (2019). *Freud's confusion of tongues: The case of Dora, Oedipal conflict or childhood sexual abuse*. (In preparation).

Rachman, A.W. and Mucci, C. (2019). *Confusion of tongues theory of trauma: A relational/neurobiological perspective*. (In preparation).

Raisman, A. (2018). *Fierce: How competing for myself changed everything*. New York: Little, Brown.

Raubolt, R. (1992). *Ernest Wolf and Sándor Ferenczi*. Personal Communication.

Rice, G. (1954). *The tumult and the shouting, my life in sports*. New York: Barnes. www.newworldencyclopedia.org/p/index/php?title=grantland_rice&oldded=100.

Richards, K. (2011). *Misperceptions about child sex offenders: Trends in crime and criminal justice*. Canberra: Australian Institute of Criminology. No. 420. September.

Richardson, H. (2009). *Claims of sex abuse by women grow*. British Broadcasting Corporation News. Monday, November 9.

Ritchey, D. (2011). Biographical note. Guide to the papers of Renatus Hartogs (1909–1998). *AR25183*. Leo Black Institute for Jewish History. New York City.

Roazen, P. (1969). *Brother animal: The story of Freud and Tausk*. New York: New York University Press.

Roazen, P. (1975). *Freud and his followers*. New York: Alfred A Knopf.

Roazen, P. (1993). *Meeting Freud's family*. Amherst, MA: University of Massachusetts Press.

Rohan, T. (2012). Sandusky gets 30 to 60 years for sex abuse. *The New York Times*. October 10, pp. A1, B14.

Rojas, R. (2018). Catholic leaders in Australia hold onto confessional seal. *The New York Times*. September 7, p. A4.

Rojas, R. (2019). "I ask forgiveness of God": Archbishop's effort to heal a Church. *The New York Times*. March 11, p. A15.

Rosenblatt, G. (2017). Whom to believe? In search of a sexual abuse policy. *The Jewish Week*. September, pp. 1, 7.

Rothman, M. (2018). Meryl Streep talks about Harvey Weinstein, own harassment experiences. *ABC News*. January 3.

Roy vs. Hartogs (1976). *Case 85 Misc. 2 d 891 – Julie Roy, Respondent, v. Renatus Hartogs, Appellant*. Supreme Court, Appellate Term, First Department. January 30, 1976.

Rush, F. (1980). *The best kept secret: The sexual abuse of children*. New York: Prentice Hall.

Rutenberg, J., Abrams, R. and Ryzik, M. (2017). Weinstein's fall opens floodgates in Hollywood. *The New York Times*. October 17, p. A11.

Schiffman, L.H. (1991). *From text to tradition, a history of Judaism in Second Temple and Rabbinic times*. Hoboken, NJ: KTAV Publishing, Inc.

Schimek, J.G. (1987). Fact and fantasy in the seduction theory: A historical review. *Journal of the American Psychoanalytic Association*, 35:4, 937–965.

Schiveber, N. and Pérez-Peña, R. (2011). *The New York Times*. November 11, p. N16.

Schmutzer, A. (2008). A theology of sexual abuse: A reflection on creation and devastation. *Journal of the Evangelical Theological Society*, 51: 775–812.

Schore, A.N. (1944). *Affect regulation and the origin of the self: The neurobiology of emotional development*. Yahiveh, NJ: Erebaum.

Schwartz, H.L. (2000). *Dialogue with forgotten voices: Relational perspectives on child abuse, trauma and treatment of dissociative disorders*. New York: Basic Books.

Searles, H. (1986). *My work with borderline patients*. New York: Jason Aronson.

Seelye, K.Q. (2016). Ex-students of St. George's School reach pact on sex abuse accusations. *The New York Times*. August 3, p. A10.

Seto, M. (2008). *Pedophilia and sexual offending against children*. Washington, DC: American Psychological Association, p. VII.

Severn, E. (1913). *Psychotherapy: Its doctrine and practice*. London: Rider.

Severn, E. (1916). "Dictated in a subjective or trance state". Friday morning, January 14.

Severn, E. (1920). *The psychology of behavior*. New York: Dodd, Mead and Company.

Severn, E. (1933). *The discovery of the self: A study in psychological cure*. London: Rider & Co.

Shakeshaft, C. (2004). *Educator sexual misconduct: A synthesis of existing literature*. U.S. Department of Education, Office of the Under Secretary. Doc #2004-09.

Shengold, L. (1989). *Soul murder: Child abuse and deprivation*. New York: Fawcett Columbine.

Sklar, J. (2013) *Introduction: Sándor Ferenczi – Ernest Jones: Letters 1911–1933*. London: Karnac, pp. xxv–x/ix.

Sklar, J. (2017). Book review: Sándor Ferenczi – Ernest Jones: Letters 1911–1933. *The International Journal of Psychoanalysis*, 97:2, 538–544.

Smith, M.R. and Lavine, L. (2016). No criminal charges after St. George's school abuse investigation. *The Boston Globe*. June 2.

Sobieraj, W. (2012). Joe Paterno. *People Magazine*. February 6, p. 63.

Sokolove, M. (2014). Silence and punishment. *The New York Times*. July 20, pp. 24–29, 47–49.

Sorvino, M. (2017). The power of speaking out. *Time*. October 23, p. 33.

Sorvino, M. (2018). Mira Sorvino's open letter to Dylan Farrow. *Huffington Post*. January 10.

Staff. (2018). Excerpts from the grand jury report on child sex abuse in 6 Pennsylvania Roman Catholic Dioceses. *Lancaster Online*. LNP. August 19.

Stafford-Clark, D. (1965). *What Freud really said: An introduction to his life and thought*. New York: Schocken.

Statopoulos, M. (2014). The exception that proves the rule: Female sex offending and the gendered nature of sexual violence. *ACSSA Research Summary*. Melbourne Australian Center for the Study of Sexual Assault. Australian Institute of Family Studies.

Steinberg, L. (2014). *Age of opportunity: Lessons from the new science of adolescence*. New York: Houghton Mifflin Harcourt.

Stern, D. (2017). *Complete Jewish Bible*. Peabody, MA: Hendrickson Publishers, Verses 1–20.

Stern, D.H. (2017). *The Jewish Bible: A material history*. Seattle, WA: University of Washington Press, Book of Samuel II, Chapter 13–14, Verses 1–20.

Stolorow, R. (1976). Psychoanalytic reflections on client centered therapy in the light of modern concepts of narcissism. *Psychotherapy: Theory, Research and Practice*, 13: 26–29.

Streep, M. (2018). Meryl Streep and Tom Hanks talk about power and the #MeToo movement. *The New York Times*, January 3.

Street, H.G. (2008). Self psychology at work in trauma therapy. *Thesis, Dissertation and Projects #1266. Smith Scholar Works – Online*.

Stuard, E.C. (1993). In K. Saunders and P. Stanford (Eds.). *Catholics and sex*. London: Heinemann.

Summers, A. (2007). *Goddess: The secret lives of Marilyn Monroe*. London: Orion Publishing Group.

Thamel, P. and Viera, M. (2012). We just terminated Joe Paterno. *The New York Times*. January 19, pp. B15.

Tolpin, M. (1992). The chief motive force: "There must be others who confirm me". *Presentation*. American Psychoanalytic Association. Baltimore, MD.

Tracy, M. (2016). Deposition, 2014. Penn State scandal. *The New York Times*. July 12, pp. B9–B10.

Tuerkheimer, D. (2018). The jury finally believes the women. *The New York Times*. April 26, p. A23.

Van der Kolk, B. (2014). *The body keeps the score: Mind, brain and body in the transformation of trauma*. London: Penguin Books.

Van der Kolk, B.A., McFarlane, A.C. and Weisaeth, L. (Eds.). (1996). *Traumatic stress: The effects of overwhelming experience on mind, body and society*. New York: Guilford.

Vecsey, G. (2010). Dickey is at home in any house. *The New York Times*. September 14.

Vecsey, G. (2011). The dangerous cocoon of king football. *The New York Times*. November 8, p. B14.

Wallace, B. (2016). St. George's hidden dragon. *Vanity Fair*. August, pp. 117–121, 153–157.

Weide, R. (2014). The Woody Allen allegations: Not so fast. *The Daily Beast*. January 24.

Weiss, E. (1970). *Sigmund Freud as a consultant: Recollections of a pioneer in psychoanalysis*. New York: Intercontinental Medical Book Corp.

Wertheim, J. and Epstein, D. (2011). Special report: Scandal. Shame. A search for answers: This is Penn State. *Sports Illustrated*. November 21, pp. 41–53.

Whitaker, B. (1989). Nussbaum vindicated, relieved: Doctors say she feared jury didn't believe her. *Newsday*. January 31.

Whitfield, C.L., Selberg, J.L. and Fink, P.J. (2001). *Misinformation concerning child sexual abuse and adult survivors*. New York: Hawthorn Press.

Wikipedia (2019). *St. George's School*, Newport, Rhode Island.

Williams, J. (2017). Australia and Catholic Church 'failed' abused children, inquiry finds. *The New York Times*. December 14.

Williams, M.J. (2019). The Catholic Church must listen to victims. *The New York Times*. Op-Ed. February 22, p. A27.

Wilson, S. (1997). *Sigmund Freud*. London: Sutton Publishing, Ltd.

Wolff, L. (1988). *Child abuse in Freud's Vienna: Postcards from the end of the world*. New York: Atheneum.

Wolstein, B. (1989). Ferenczi, Freud and the origins of American interpersonal relations. *Contemporary Psychoanalysis*, 25:672–685.

Wolstein, B. (1993). Sándor Ferenczi and American interpersonal relations: Historical and personal reflections. In L. Aron and A. Harris (Eds.). *The legacy of Sándor Ferenczi*. Hillsdale, NJ: The Analytic Press, pp. 175–184.

Young-Bruehl, E. (1988). *Anna Freud: A biography*. New York: Summit Books.

Zavada, J. (2017). Redemption in Christianity. *Thought Co*. November 27. www.thoughtco.com/what-is-redemption-700693.

Zengerle, J. (2018). Ronan Farrow, truth teller. *Gentleman's Quarterly*. December 13, Section 1.

Zhang, W., Ross, J. and Davidson, R.T. (2004). Social anxiety disorder in callers to the anxiety disorder of America. *Depression and Anxiety*, 20:3, 101–106.

Zwar, D. (2012). Priests talk openly about their feelings on sex and celibacy. *Union of Catholic News*. November 30.

Index

A
abandonment trauma 26
Abrams, A. 252, 253
Abrams, R. 223
The acquisition restoration and donation of the Elizabeth Severn papers: A lost legacy of psychoanalysis (Rachman) 52, 59, 272–3, 290
Adler, Alfred 80
Adler, Elliot 275, 276
"The aetiology of hysteria" (Freud, 1896) 6
affectionate abuse 49
Aguirre, B. 200, 202
Ain, S. 165
Alderman, Naomi 163
Allen, Woody 244–8, 277
Alpert, J.L 50
American Academy of Psychoanalysis 284
American pragmatism 57
American Psychiatric Association (APA) 61; apology to gay community 315–6
American Psychoanalytic Association (APsaA) 318; apology to LGBTQ community 316–7, 318
American Psychological Association 271; apology to gay community 315
Analysis of the incest trauma: Retrieval, recovery, renewal (Rachman & Klett) 176
analyst's chair 61
analyst's room 61–2
analytic couch 61

analytic encounter 60–4; blank screen transference in 62; dimensional definition of 60–2; in third decade of psychoanalysis 62
analytic psychology 51
Andreas-Salomé, Lou 34
Anger, E. 51
anxiety 112
aphonia 15
apology to Sándor Ferenczi 311–8
Aquilina, Rosemarie 192
Argento, Asia 227, 228, 230
Aron, Lewis 56, 97, 270, 273, 274, 317
Arquette, Rosanna 217, 229
The assault on truth (Masson) 14, 18, 139, 296, 310
Assuncão, M. 316
Australian Catholic Church's sexual abuse cases 167–8
automata 104

B
Back, K.W 119
Balint, A. 62
Balint, Michael 19, 42, 55, 59, 62, 78, 96, 97, 286, 298, 301
Barbant, E. 276
Barnes, B. 240
Barry, E. 157
Basch, Michael F. 97, 284
Becker, Joe 180, 181
Beebe, Beatrice 63, 270
Bergmann, Martin S. 276–81, 289, 294
Berlin, F.S 132

342 Index

Beste, J.E 169
The best kept secret: The sexual abuse of children (Rush) 256
Bettleheim, B. 51
The Bill Cosby Show (tv series) 249
Binswanger, L. 51
Binswanger's case of Ellen West 51
bio/psychosocial stage of development 134–5
BishopAccountability.org 138
Blair, Leonard P. 314
Blanchard, R. 130
Blum, Harold 140
Bollas, C. 43
Bonaparte, Marie 19
Bonomi, Carlo 47, 48, 78, 263, 274, 275, 298, 303
Borch-Jacobsen, M. 20
Boston Globe 130, 203
Boston Globe Investigative Staff 132
Bowley, G. 250, 251
Bowman, Marcus 298
Brabant, E. 68, 70, 71
Brady, Fergal 298
Brennan, M. 184
Breuer, Josef 1, 8, 51
British Object Relations 51
British Psychoanalytic Society 51, 67, 68
Brown, S. 218
Bruno, Leonard 273
Brunswick, Ruth Mack 18, 19, 259, 309–10
Bryant, T.T 158
Budapest School of Psychoanalysis 37, 260, 263, 264, 265, 268, 296, 300, 301, 306, 312, 317, 318
Budapest State of Mind 302
Burke, C. 182
Burke, Tarana 219–20
Burns, J. 161

C

Cable News Network (CNN) 160
Carvajal, D. 240
casting couch 222–3, 229
Catholic Church's sexual scandals 129–36, 143–5, 210; apologies for 314–5; ordination of women as remedy for 145–6; similarities with Ultra-Orthodox Jewish communities 160
Catholic survivors 157–9

celebrity privilege's sexual abuse cases 237–43, 244–55
celibacy, vows of 151–3; as cause of crisis in Catholic Church 152–3
Chabin, M. 165
Chaplin, T.C 130
Charcot, Jean-Martin 8, 47
Chen, J. 219
Chester, P. 120
Chey, W.D 108
childhood incest trauma 58; confrontation and recovery from 106–18
childhood trauma recreated with analyst 215
child seduction 40–5
child sexual abuse 2–3; compared to Confusion of Tongues 47–8; by father 112–8, 253–4; group analyst's neglect of 122–7; obstacle in exploration of 4; parental neglect case of 106–18; phylogenetic structure of 300; prevalent in all classes 98
Chinatown (movie) 238
Christie, Christine 300
Cieply, M. 240
Cioffi, F. 20
Ciralsky, A. 216
Cleland, John M. 185
clergy child abuse 128–31
The clinical diary of Sándor Ferenczi (Ferenczi) 29, 35, 52, 57, 60, 78, 80, 96, 97, 262, 273, 282, 285–6, 290, 295
clinical empathy and trauma analysis 53, 62–3
Coffey, W. 198, 199
Cohen, Etty 269
Cohen, N. 185
Cohn, Harry 218, 222–3, 224, 229
Coleman, Franklin 205, 209
Confusion of Tongues 17, 18, 19, 20, 28, 35, 56, 80, 93, 96, 102, 141, 142, 157, 194–5, 201, 228, 248–9, 252, 253–4, 256, 268, 290, 311–2; condemnation of 77–9; explanations for censorship of 46–7; between Ferenczi and psychoanalytic community 260–1, 262–3; between Freud, Severn and analytic community 261–2; between Freud and Ferenczi 259–60; Freudian dynamic of child abuse compared to 47–8; Hedda Nussbaum as survivor of 103–5; paradigm shift for

psychoanalysis 307–8; pedophile priests speak language of 139; psychodynamics of 216–7, 235–6; reasons for negative reaction to 45–6; reexperiencing of trauma 215; retraumatization and 292–5
"The confusion of tongues between adults and children: The language of tenderness and passion" (Ferenczi) 40, 44, 45, 214
Confusion of Tongues dilemma 49
Confusion of Tongues Theory 41–5
Confusion of tongues theory of trauma: A rational/neurobiological perspective (Rachman & Mucci) 296, 306–8
Conger, J.J 315
Connor, T. 103
Conservative and Reform Jewish communities 164–6; sexual abuse in 164–6
Constand, Andrea 250, 251–2
Corbin, C.M 165
Correa, C. 194
The correspondence of Sigmund Freud and Sándor Ferenczi (ed. Haynal) 289
Cortoni, Franca 156
Cosby, Bill 228, 244, 249–52
Coscarelli, J. 250
countertransference analysis 56, 101
The County of Los Angeles State of California vs. Roman Raymond Polanski (1977, Grand Jury Testimony) 238–9
Craig, M. 198
Cramer, Hawkins 205
credibility discounting 251
Crimes and Misdemeanours (movie) 278
Cullcane, S. 231
Cupich, Blase 131
Curley, Tim 180, 182

D
Daniels, Dawn 181, 182
Dantzscher, Jamie 193
Darrow, C.N 134
Darwin, Charles 34
Davidson, R.T 108
Davies, J.M 50, 122, 126
Decker, Hanna 17
de Costa, Louise 275, 276
de Freytas-Tamura, K. 157
Denhollander, Rachael 192, 193
Denov, M.D 155

depression 15, 51, 112
Derbyshire, S.W.G 218
D'Ercole, Ann 291, 294, 295
Deutsch, Helene 31
devil parent 100–2
Diagnostic and Statistical Manual of Mental Disorders, 5th edition (DSM-5) 131–2, 133
Dias, E. 136, 137
Dickey, R.A 196–9, 202
The discovery of the self: A study in psychological cure (Severn) 57, 60
Disobedience (Alderman) 163
Dockterman, E. 220
Dowd, Maureen 232, 233, 234
Doyle, Anne Barrett 138
Doyle, Daniel 200–1, 202
Drape, J. 186
Drescher, Jack 316
Dreyfus, Alfred 242, 243
Dupont, Judith 285
Durantine, P. 180, 182
dyspnea 15
D'Zurilla, C. 219

E
Edelman, S. 163
Edwards, S.Z 220
Edwards Street School for Mentally Defective Children 83
The Ego and the Mechanisms of Defense (A. Freud) 44
Eissler, Kurt 31, 57, 58–9, 79, 290, 291
Eitingon, Max 8, 35, 56, 69
"The Eleventh Commandment: Thou Shall Not Lie Down with a Child" (collage, Rachman) 176–7
Ellenberg, F. 52
embodied witnessing 308
English, B. 203, 207
entertainment industry's sexual abuse of women 213–21, 224–30; collective confusion of tongues trauma 217–8; psychodynamics of sexual abuse 231–6; vicarious traumatization 217–9
Enticott, P.G 218
Epstein, D. 179
Erickson, Rodney A. 186
Erikson, Erik H. 73, 134, 135, 136, 148
Erikson, Joan M. 134, 135, 136, 148
Erikson's stages of psychological development 135–6, 148–9

344 Index

"Ernest Jones Revisited: A Symposium"
  (*Studies in Gender and Sexuality*) 66
Eros, F. 67, 69, 71, 72
erotic transference 17
Erskine, Kim Hardy 204
Esterson, A. 20
Eswaran, S. 108
Evans, (*nee* Stoller) Lucia 227, 228
evil narrative (to Catholic
  Church) 132–3
evil predator 69, 100, 102
evil tongue (Hebrew term) 163
The evolution of psychoanalytic technique
  (Bergmann & Hartman) 278
extra-parental relationships 34–5

F
False Memory Institute 116
false memory syndrome 20, 115–6
Falzeder, E. 68, 70, 71, 78, 276, 283, 284,
  287, 288, 289
Farrow, Dylan 244–8
Farrow, Mia 245, 246, 247, 248
Farrow, Moses 246
Farrow, Ronan 144, 213, 217, 226–8,
  229, 230, 235, 245, 248
the father of interpretation 5
Federal Bureau of Investigation (FBI)
  128, 186
Feldman, Betty 266
female hysteria 61
female offenders as abusers of
  children 155–6
female sexual abusers of children 154–6
feminist perspective 256–7
Ferenczi, Giselle 79
Ferenczi, Sándor 5, 9, 18, 19, 20, 21, 28,
  29, 33, 35, 37, 38, 39, 40, 41, 44, 45, 46,
  50, 52–60, 65, 66, 67, 68, 69, 70–80, 87,
  88, 89, 90, 91, 93, 94, 95, 96, 97, 101,
  103, 112, 139, 140, 141, 142, 210, 215,
  216, 235, 248–9, 256, 258, 264–6, 268,
  281–2, 292–5, 308, 313–4, 317
Ferenczi/Freud letters 71, 77, 276–7,
  283–4, 287–9, 291
Ferenczi/Freud psychoanalysis 71
Ferenczi House/International Ferenczi
  Center 263
Ferenczi/Jones letters 66–9, 71–2
Ferenczi/Jones psychoanalysis 70–4
Ferenczi Psychoanalytic community 311
Ferenczi Renaissance 78, 265, 275

Ferenczi's case of R.N. (Elizabeth
  Severn) 52–60
Ferenczi's case of Rosa K. 270
Ferenczi's Confusion of Tongues idea 8
Ferenczi/Severn analysis 52–3, 75–6;
  importance of 52–3
*Fierce: How competing for myself
  changed everything* (Raisman) 194
51st International Psychoanalytical
  Association (IPA) Congress, London
  (2019) 140
*Fighting back: What an Olympic
  champion's story can teach us about
  recognizing and preventing child sexual
  abuse* (Harrison, Kaplan &
  Aguiie) 202
Fink, P.J 115
Fisher, Aaron 181, 182
Fisher, Robert 164
Fitzgibbon, B.M 218
Fliess, Wilhelm 1, 2, 4, 6, 7, 22, 48, 257
Forlenza, Ros 302
Fortune, Christopher 52
Four Winds Hospital, Westchester, New
  York 104–5
Fox, J. 241–2
Francis, Pope 129, 130, 131, 136, 137,
  138, 156, 167
Frawley, M.F 50
Frawley, M.G 122, 126
Freeh, Louis 186–7
Freeman, Dorothy 83, 84, 85, 86
Freeman, L. 221
Freud, Amelia (nee Nathanson) 24, 25
Freud, Anna 8, 13, 19, 20, 25, 44–5, 46,
  57, 68, 81, 95, 290
Freud, Dora and Vienna 1900
  (Decker) 17
Freud, Sigmund 1, 2, 4, 5, 6, 15, 16, 17,
  18, 22, 317; abandonment of
  Seduction Hypothesis 7, 8, 18, 47, 256,
  301; analysis of daughter Anna 20, 22,
  30–40, 44–5, 57, 81, 95; child abuse in
  Vienna at turn of century 47–8;
  childhood sexual trauma 20, 22, 23–9,
  257–8; child sexual abuse as origin of
  psychological disorders 10, 19;
  development of Oedipal theory 47,
  257–8; Ernest Jones and 66–94, 97;
  negative reaction to Confusion of
  Tongues paper 45–6; neglect of incest
  trauma 7, 14, 20; self-analysis 7, 9,
  11, 26

Freud and his Followers (Roazen) 30
Freud Archives 8, 31, 58, 79, 272;
 Elizabeth Severn section 263, 273
Freud/Fliess letters 1, 2, 4–6, 7, 12, 13–4,
 19, 22, 23–9, 257
Freud House, Maresfield Gardens 20
Freudian coverup 256–7
Freud/Jones letters 70, 91
Freud's case of Anna O (Berta
 Pappenheim) 51
Freud's case of Dora (Ida Bauer) 14–8,
 20, 35, 48–9, 51, 98, 258–9, 309
Freud's case of Dr. Daniel Schreber 75
Freud's case of the Wolf Man (Sergei
 Pankejeff) 18, 19, 20, 49, 50, 51, 98,
 139–42, 258–9, 296–7, 309–10
*Freud's case of the Wolf Man: Sergei
 Pankejeff as a survivor of sexual abuse*
 (Rachman) 297
*Freud's confusion of tongues: The case of
 Dora, Oedipal conflict or childhood
 sexual abuse* (Rachman &
 Mattick) 296
*Freud's Confusion of Tongues with Dora:
 A relational perspective* (Rachman &
 Mattick) 14
Freud's correction 12–3
Freud's Great Case Studies 51–2
Freud's infatuation with Oedipal Theory
 47, 257–8
Freud's Schreber case 49
Freund, K. 130, 133
Freyd, Jennifer 116
Freyd, Pamela 116
Freyd, Peter 116
Friedersdorf, C. 156
Fromm, Eric 19, 20, 37, 40, 73, 75, 77,
 79, 260, 317

G
Gabbard, Glen D. 70, 82, 87, 88, 90, 91
Gabler, E. 252, 253
Gado, M. 104
Galinsky, J. 156
Gardner, Muriel 18, 19
gastrointestinal (GI) symptoms 114, 118
Gautama Siddhartha Buddha 63–4
Gay 96
Gedo, John 284, 285
Geimer, (*nee* Gailey) Samantha 238–9,
 240–1, 242
Gender and Sexuality 82
Gerwig, Greta 246

Giampieri-Deusche, C. 276
Giampieri-Deutsch, P. 68, 70, 71
Gibbs, Alphonse "Al" 204–5, 206
Gilligan, Leilah 156
Gillim, Michael 181
Gilman, S.L 61
*The girl: A life in the shadow of Roman
 Polanski* (Geimer) 240
Glickhorn, R. 24
Goethe 14
Goldberg 104
Gone with the Wind (movie) 222
Goodman, J.D 313, 314
*The Grand Jury Report on Child Sex
 Abuse in Pennsylvania's Roman
 Catholic Dioceses* (Street) 128,
 132, 133
Great Case Studies in
 psychoanalysis 51–64
Grosskurth, P. 75
Grynbaum, M. 252, 253
Guerra, C. 220
Gutierrez, Ambra Battilana 217
Gutin, Jules 164
Gyögyászat medical journal 271

H
Haigney, S. 241
Hale, C.J 70, 131
Hall, Amelia 83
Hanaghan, Jonathan 298
Harrigan, Fanny 83, 85
Harris, Adrienne 56, 97, 270, 274, 317
Harris, E.A 211
Harrison, Kayla 196, 199–202
Hartman, F.R 278
Hartogs, Renatus (René) 119–21, 210
Hasidic community, Brooklyn, New
 York 160
Havinghurst, R.J 134
Hayden, Sterling 222
Haynal, André 78, 289
Hemingway, Ernest 198
Herman, J.L 154
Hidas, Georgy 271
Hoban, P. 245
Holman, E.A 217
the Holocaust 112, 238
homosexual currents in the Vatican
 129–30
homosexuality; pedophilia compared to
 130; Pope Francis's thoughts and
 actions about 131–2

346 Index

Hooper, C.A 155
Horney, Karen 290
Horowitz, J. 129, 132, 136, 137, 157, 177
Horowitz, Rabbi Yaakov 165, 166
housewife psychosis 15
Hugh, Rich 213
Hughes, Howard 229
Hungarian Psychoanalytic Society 261
Hunt, F. 61
Hurdle, J. 251
Hutson, Jim 273, 296
Hynal, André 271
Hynes, Charles J. 162–3
hysteria, sexual impulse role in 1

I
identification with the aggressor
   (IWA) 44
identity crisis 135
incest survivors 5; case of
   discouragement of childhood
   trauma 122–7
incest trauma 8, 20, 45, 46, 96, 176, 210;
   Freud's abandonment of 256–7;
   neglect of 22; reconciliation stage of
   working through 114
The Indianapolis Star 192
infantile sexuality theory 7
Ingala, Nick 314–5
International Ferenczi Conference 270
International Forum of Psychoanalysis
   (Athens, 2010) 273
The International Journal of Psycho-
   Analysis 93, 96
International PsychoAnalytical
   Association (IPA) 44, 261
International Sándor Ferenczi
   Community 80, 262, 312
International Sándor Ferenczi
   Conference (Florence, 2018) 275, 298
International Sándor Ferenczi Congress
   (Budapest, 2012) 273
International Sándor Ferenczi Network
   (ISFN) 298, 300, 318
interpersonal psychoanalysis 97, 122,
   125, 268
The Interpretation of Dreams (Freud) 7,
   9, 14, 15, 23, 25
Irish Psycho-Analytical Association
   (IPAA) 298–9
Irish Psycho-Analytical Association
   (IPAA) Conference (2019) 296, 297

irritable bowel syndrome (IBS) 108–9,
   110, 112
Itzkoff, D. 242

J
J'accuse (movie) 242–3
Jacobs, Donna 269
Jaffe, Lee 316
Jenkins, E.C 163
Le Jeune Ferenczi: Premier Ecrits:
   1899–1906 (Lorin) 271
John Jay Report, 2004 132
Jokl, Robert 30
Jones, Ernest 8, 22, 35, 56, 65, 66, 67, 68,
   69–94, 95, 140, 260, 265, 269, 272,
   287, 298
Judd, Ashley 224–5
Jung, Carl Gustav 46, 51, 56, 65, 66,
   80, 95
Jung/Freud letters 65–6
Jung's case of Sabina Spielrein 51

K
Kahn, Loe 66, 71
Kantor, Jodi 144, 213, 224, 225, 226,
   227, 229, 230, 235
Kantrowitz, B. 99, 100, 104
Kapit, Hannah 269, 271–2
Kaplan, A.G 290
Kaplan, C. 200, 202
Kassowitz, Max 47
Kelly, Linda 179
Kennedy, John F. 120
Kennedy, R. 286
Kepner, T. 198
Kerr, John 51, 82, 84, 85, 86, 87, 88, 90,
   91, 92, 93
Ketcham, C. 162
Keyes, Evelyn 222, 223
Khomami, N. 219
King, H. 61, 104
King, L. 99, 105
King, P. 99, 100
King Oedipus legend 10–1
Klagsbrun, Samuel 104
Klein, E.B 134
Klein, Melanie 68
Klett, Susanne 73, 83, 89, 92, 100, 101,
   103, 127, 140, 176, 201, 215, 235, 253,
   268, 275, 279, 283, 308, 312
Koblin, J. 214
Kohut, Heinz 52, 62, 63, 269, 284–5, 306
Kohut's case of Miss F. 52

Kooden, Harold 315
Kris, Ernst 13, 19
Kristof, Nicholas 244, 245, 246
Krüll, Marianne 20, 24, 25, 27, 28
Kuban, M. 133
Kuhn, Phillip 66, 70, 81–2, 83, 84, 85, 86, 87, 88, 89, 90, 91, 93, 94
Kurlander, J. 108

L
Labadie, Amy 193
Langer, Renate 241–3
Langevin, R. 130
Lapointe, J. 197
Larivière, Michael 296
Lauer, Matt 244, 252–5
Lavine, L. 207
lay analysis 68–9
Layden, T. 178, 179, 183
Leaming, B. 238
lesbian, gay, bisexual and transgender (LGBT) 131
letter from a predator 211–2
Levinson, D.J 134, 136
Levinson, J.D 134, 136
Levy, Kata 31
Lewis, Betram 65
Lichtenberg, Joseph 273, 285
Liebeler, W.J 120
The life and work of Sigmund Freud (Jones) 75–6, 92–3, 269
Liotti, G. 308
Lipdegraff, J.A 217
Lipskis, Peter 272
Lisa Steinberg child abuse case 99–105
Little, Margaret 51
Little Red Riding Hood (Perrault) 139
Lively, Blake 246
Lorand, Sándor 65, 66, 96
Lorin, Claude 271
Lothan, H.S 49
Louttit, M. 194
Lowry, R. 186
Lyman, Frederic 211
Lysova, Maria 57

M
Mack-Brunswick, Ruth 296
MacLeish, Eric 206, 207
Macur, J. 192, 193
madness/psychosis 74–6
Maines, R.P 61
Makari, George J. 82, 87, 88, 90, 91

Mallett, X. 154
Manson, Charles 102, 238
Marion, Jane 211
Maroda, K. 56
Martin, Fr. James 130
Masson, Jeffrey Mousiaeff 1, 3, 6, 8, 13, 14, 18–21, 37, 44, 46, 47, 50, 56, 96, 139, 296, 300, 310
Mattick, Paul 14, 15, 20, 35, 42, 48, 249, 296, 309
May, R. 51
McBrien, Fr. Richard 152
McCann, I.L 218
McCluskey, N. 155
McCormick, Patricia 158–9
McDonald, H. 155
McElivee, J.J 131
McFarlane, A.C 50
McGowan, Rose 251
McGuire, W. 65
McLeod, D. 154, 155
McQueary, Mike 179, 182, 186, 187
Menaker, Esther 31, 34, 36–9
Merriam-Webster Dictionary 311
Mészáros, Judith 262, 271, 298, 303
#MeToo movement 136, 155, 200, 210, 219–21, 231, 232, 243, 244, 250, 251, 254, 312
Milano, Alyssa 219, 220–1
Miller, J. 112, 248
Modell, A.H 43
Monroe, Marilyn 222
mother-daughter relationship case of incest 106–18
Mucci, Clara 296, 306, 308, 312
Murdock, A. 160

N
Namuth, T. 99, 100
narcissism 35, 44, 214, 252
Nassar, Lawrence G. 192–4, 210
Nathan, Joyce 36
National Broadcasting Company (NBC) News 213, 226, 253
National Gay Task Force 315
The National Organization for Women 251
Nemiroff, H. 122, 126
Nestor, Emily 228
Neugarten, B.L 134
neurosis; origin of in child sexual seduction 6, 10; sexuality in origin of 1; talking cure for 51

348 Index

Newman, Judith 240
New School of Social Research, New York City 76
The New Yorker Magazine 226, 229
New York Herald Tribune 190
New York Psychoanalytic Institute 272
The New York Times 99, 180, 213, 224, 226, 227, 229, 232, 244, 252, 253
Neyer, B. 197
Noonan, Frank 179
Nussbaum, Hedda 99, 100, 102, 103–5

O
object relations 97, 140, 141
O'Connor, Lauren 224, 225
Oedipal Complex Theory of neurosis 60–1, 309, 311–2; as centre of psychoanalysis 73; Freud's infatuation with 257–8; Jones's attempt to protect Freud's 81
Oedipal Conflict 5, 15; case of Dora presented to demonstrate efficacy of 49; Confusion of Tongues as threat to 19; development of 23; functions of development of 47; as mandate to analyze Anna 32–3; original outline for 9–10; from personal insights 12; preferred to Seduction Hypothesis 9, 22; psychoanalysis shift to from Seduction Hypothesis 8–9; psychological disorders explanation changed by 12; universal shift in child's mind 12
Oedipus Rex (Sophocles) 10
Ohlheiser, A. 220
O'Neill, James P. 313
The Origins of Psychoanalysis (Freud) 19
Osborn, J. 218
Oswald, Lee Harvey 120
Otterman, S. 160, 162

P
Paglia, Camille 237
Pálos, Elma 270, 289
Pankejeff, Sergei 19, 50
Papiasvili, Eva 140, 141
parental/child sexuality in personality development 47
Parker, R. 238
Paskauskas, R.A 70, 91
Paterno (Posnanski) 184–5, 189
Paterno, Joe 178–9, 182, 183, 185, 186, 187, 191, 192, 210

Pearlman, L.A 218
pedophilia 81, 87, 89, 93; homosexuality compared to 130; as psychiatric disorder 131–2; Woody Allen case 244–9
Pedro, Jimmy 199
Pell, George 167
Pellon, M. 182
Penington, B. 190
Pennsylvania State University child abuse scandal 178–91, 192, 210; Freeh Report into 186–8
Pérez-Peña, R. 130, 189
Perrault, Charles 139
Perrotta, T. 200
Peterson, Eric 206, 207
Petit, S. 219
Peyton, S. 163
Phillips, Adam 269, 305
Piaget, Jean 34
The Pianist (movie) 238
Picquart, George 243
Pinker, S. 138
Pinto, N. 162
plagiarism 67
Polanski, Roman 237–43
Porter, R. 61
Posnanski, Joe 184, 185, 189
Postgraduate Center, Mental Health Psychoanalytic Institute 265, 266, 269, 275, 276
Powell, M. 162
predatory pedophilic priests 133–4; as ravenous wolves 136–9
Prince, Robert 36
professional hypocrisy 215
prototype sexual abuse experience 111–3
psychoanalysis 8; Confusion of Tongues paper returned child seduction to 40–5; development of 1; evolution of 264; Freud/Fliess correspondence as origins of 23–9; golden age of silence and interpretation in 62–3; as important new treatment 7; incest trauma in 8–9; introduction of empathy and activity into 5; Masson's contributions to 18–9; Oedipal Complex changed explanation for psychological disorders 12–3; Oedipal tragedy as basis for 11; origins of a relational perspective in 53; pioneering days of 57; political and symbolic personal assassination in 80;

Index   349

psychodynamic explanation for neglect of child abuse 256–63; shift from Seduction to Oedipal Complex in 9–10; techniques and theory from case studies perspective 51–64; trauma analysis introduced into 52; wolf as symbol of sexual abuse 139

Psychoanalytic Inquiry (ed. Lichtenberg) 285

Psychoanalytic Inquiry Book Series (ed. Lichtenberg) 285

psychodynamic explanations 2, 20, 22; for neglect of child abuse 256–63; sexual abuse and 232–6

psychological disorders; child sexual abuse as locus of 6; child sexual abuse as origin of 19; neglect of sexual trauma as etiology of 22; origin of 1

psychology of self-perspective 284

psychoneurotic *vs.* normal 10

The psychopathology of everyday life (Freud) 26

psychosexual stages of development 51

psychotherapy 8

Putman, James Jackson 70

Q

Quaker philosophy 57

Quinsey, V.L 130

R

Rachman, A.W 5, 7, 12, 14, 20, 22, 25, 28, 29, 35, 36, 42, 44, 45, 46, 47, 48, 50, 52, 54, 55, 56, 57, 63, 66, 70, 73, 75, 76, 77, 83, 88, 89, 90, 91, 92, 93, 95, 97, 100, 101, 103, 127, 137, 140, 141, 142, 176, 201, 214, 215, 235, 249, 253, 258, 259, 260, 261, 263, 264, 265, 266, 267, 268, 270, 271, 272, 273, 274, 276, 277, 278, 279, 280, 283, 286, 288, 290, 291, 292, 294, 300, 307, 308, 309, 310, 311, 312

Rado, Sandor 31

Raisman, Aly 194–5

Rank, Otto 37, 46, 53, 76, 80, 95, 96

Raubolt, R. 285

Rediscovering Sándor Ferenczi: A festchrift for Arnold Wm. Rachman, PhD (Larivière) 296, 305

relational analytic perspective 72–4, 97, 122, 125, 142, 263, 308; of Wolf Man (Sergei Pankejeff) 141

relaxation therapy 278, 283, 287

retraumatization 45, 292–5

Reynolds, Joan "Bege" 204

Rice, Grantland 190, 191

Richards, K. 155

Richardson, H. 155

Rickinan, John 72

Rivera, Geraldo 101, 102

Rivera, R. 160, 162

Riviere, Joan 35, 56, 77, 78, 80

"The Road to Hollywood: How Some of Us Got Here" (installation, Rothenberg) 223

Roazen, Paul 8, 19, 30, 31, 32, 37, 46, 72, 95, 97

Robbins, K. 99, 100, 104

Roentgen, Wilhelm 34

Rohan, T. 185, 190

Rojas, R. 168, 315

"'Romancing with a Wealth of Detail': Narratives of Ernest Jones's 1906 trial for Indecent Assault" (Kuhn) 66

Rosemary's Baby (movie) 238

Rosenberg, Rabbi Nuchem 160, 161

Rosenblatt, G. 165

Ross, J. 108

Rothenberg, Erika 223

Rousseau, G.S 61

Roy, Julie 120

Roy *vs.* Hartogs, 1964 120–1

Roznau Spa 24

Rush, Florence 256–7

Rutenberg, J. 223, 252, 253

Ryzik, M. 223

S

Safron, Jeremy 274

Sajner, J. 24

Sándor Ferenzci Society 300

Sandusky, Jerry 179–91, 202

Sandy Hook Elementary School massacre (2012) 218

Schiffman, L.H 163

Schimek, J.G 20

Schindler, A. 122

Schindler, R. 122

Schiveber, N. 189

Schmutzer, Andrew J. 174–5

Schore, Allen 308

Schultz, Gary 180, 182

Schwartz, H.L 122, 126

Scott, Anne 206–8

Searles, H. 43

Seduction Hypothesis 4, 5, 6;

350 Index

abandonment of 20, 22, 23, 27, 35–6, 47, 50, 81, 82, 256, 300, 312; development of trauma disorder and trauma analysis from 50; doubts about 7; Freud's abandonment of 13; as myth shattering 98; psychoanalysis shift to Oedipal Complex 8–9; self-analysis emotionally linked to 7
Seelye, K.Q 208
Selberg, J.L 115
self-analysis 1, 7, 9, 10, 26; Oedipal myth in own psyche 11–2
self-psychology 52, 62–3, 97, 122, 125, 284–5
September 11, 2001 (9/11) attacks 218
Seto, M. 132
severe borderline disorder 53
Severn, Elizabeth 20, 52–60, 66, 76, 78, 79, 80, 89, 94, 101, 142, 260, 272, 285, 290, 292–3, 298, 302, 303, 311
Severn, Margaret 57, 79, 272, 290
Severn/Eissler interview 58–9, 290–1
sexual abuse; in boarding schools 203–12; climate for 208–9; Kayla Harrison's experience 196, 199–202; Matt Lauer case 252–5; psychodynamic explanations for 232–6; R.A. Dickey's experience 196–9, 202; in religious studies 169–76; silence and neglect of 254; theological/moral stance required on 175; within Ultra-Orthodox Jewish communities 161–3; worst sports history example of 192–5
sexual abuse of patient by therapist case 120–1
sexual abuse survivors 100–1, 248–9
sexual seduction; Freud's denial of his own 46, 47; major defences for coping 44–5; parental unresponsiveness to 42; unreliability of children's memory of 41
sexual trauma 16, 45, 210
Shakeshaft, C. 155
Shapiro, Josh 128
Shengold, L. 50
Showalter, E. 61
Silver, Lawrence 240
Silver, R.C 217
Silverstein, Charles 315
Sipe, Richard 152
Sisters of Mercy, Ireland 155
Sklar, J. 67, 68, 72

Smith, M.R 207
The Snows of Kilimanjaro (Hemingway) 198
social brain 218–9
Society for Psychiatry and Neurology, Vienna 6
Sokolove, M. 187, 188
Sophocles 10
Sorvino, Mia 217, 231, 235–6, 246–7
Spanier, Graham 186, 187
Spencer, Graham 182
Spielrein, Sabina 51
spirituality 57
Spotlight: Letters to My Mother (M. Severn) 290
Stafford-Clark, D. 1
Statopoulos, M. 155
Steele, Kevin R. 250
Steinberg, Joel 99–102, 134
Steinberg, Lisa 99–100
Steinberg, Mitchell 99
St. George's Bulletin 206
St. George's School, Newport, Rhode Island sexual abuse cases 203–12; as party school 208–10
Stolorow, Robert 284
Stonewall Inn raid (1969) 313–4
Streep, Meryl 215, 216
Street, H.G 122, 126, 128
Stuard, Elizabeth 131
Studies in Gender and Sexuality journal 66
Studies on Hysteria (Freud) 14
Summers 222
Surma, John P. 182
Sweetland, H. 220

T
Tarantino, Quentin 234
Tate, Sharon 238
Thamel, P. 183
theology of sexual abuse 174–5
Thompson, Clara Mabel 78, 79, 265, 266, 268, 279, 281–4, 285–6, 290, 291, 293, 294
Thompson, Monica 248
Thompson, Nellie 272
Thurman, Uma 231–4
Today Show (NBC) 244, 252, 254
Todschweigen (death by silence) 20, 21, 31, 35, 65–6, 73, 75, 76, 78, 80, 81, 88, 89, 90, 92, 93, 94, 95–8, 139–40, 209–10, 260, 261, 262, 311–2, 317;

Index 351

confrontation of 264–77;
contemporary experience of 276–82;
stages in process of 95–7
"Todschweigen (death by silence):
Removal of Elizabeth Sever's ideas
and work from mainstream
psychoanalysis" (Rachman) 37
Tolpin, M. 34
tongue-tied from emotional trauma 214
Torah Law 161, 163
Tosatti, Marco 129
Tracy, M. 190
*Tradition: A journal of Orthodox Jewish
thought* (Rabbinical Council of
America) 163
trauma analysis 20, 72–4, 142, 249, 261,
282, 286, 287, 290; analyst as witness
in 308; definition of 55; Freud's
condemnation of 258; introduced into
psychoanalysis 52
Trauma Analysis and Confusion of
Tongue paradigm 46
trauma disorder 50, 52
trauma due to childhood sexual abuse
theory 214–5
trauma sharing 218–9
traumatogenic 63
trial of Ernest Jones for pedophilia,
1906 81–94
truth to power 212
Tuerkheimer, Deborah 251
12th International Psycho-Analytical
Association Congress, Wiesbaden
(1932) 40, 44, 45, 96, 307
Twersky, Mordechai 166
Twohey, Megan 144, 213, 224, 225, 226,
227, 229, 230, 235
Tylim, Issac 276

U

Ultra-Orthodox Jewish communities
160; child molestation and rape in
160–7; defilement of young boys in
holy sites 161; New York policy to
pursue sexual abuse cases 162–3;
protection of sexual abusers by 210;
reprisals when someone accused of
sexual abuse 162
unconscious 7; focus on rather than
reality 257
United Synagogue Youth (USY) 164

V

Van der Kolk, B.A 50, 308
Vecsey, George 189, 198
vicarious traumatization 217–9
Vienna Psychoanalytic Institute 36
Viennese Medical Society 6, 8
Viera, M. 183
Vigano, Carlo Maria 129, 130, 132
Vogue Hommes 238

W

Wales, Katie 204
Wallace, B. 203, 204, 205, 207, 208, 209
wall of silence 208–9
Ward, J. 218
Warren Commission 120
Wayne, Marc 269
Weberman, Nechemya 163
Weide, Robert B. 248
Weingarten, Reed 240
Weinstein, Harvey 106, 143, 144, 213,
215–9, 222, 224–30, 244, 249, 250
Weisaeth, L. 50
Weiss, Edoardo 32, 38
Werthein, J. 179
West, Ellen 51
Wexler, Charles 313, 314
*Wherever I wind up: My quest for truth,
authenticity and the perfect knuckleball*
(Dickey & Coffey) 198
Whitaker, B. 104
white, Anglo-Saxon, Protestant
(WASP) 203
White, Howard 203, 204
Whitefield, C.L 115
Wieber, Jordan 193
Wikipedia 208
William Alanson White Institute 265
Williams, J. 167
Wilson, R. 130
Wilson, S. 1
Wingert, P. 99, 100, 104
Winnicott, D.W 51
Winslet, Kate 246
Wittek, Resi 24, 25, 26, 27, 28, 81, 257
Wolberg, Lewis 265, 266, 267, 268
Wolf, Ernest 285
Wolfe, Tom 107
Wolff, L. 47, 49
Wolstein, B. 97
Woody Allen: A Documentary 248

Y

Yard, M. 286
Young-Bruehl, Elizabeth 30, 34, 67

Z

Zajic, Monica 24
Zane, Anthony 204, 206, 207, 209

Zanuck, Darryl F. 229
Zavada, J. 158
Zeitgeist (in Europe in late 19th century) 47, 62
Zengerle, J. 227
Zhang, W. 108

Printed in the United States
by Baker & Taylor Publisher Services